THE
SAUSAGE
COOKBOOK
BIBLE

THE
SAUSAGE
COOKBOOK
BIBLE

500 recipes for grinding, spicing, cooking, and enjoying the food that links the world

ELLEN BROWN

CIDER MILL PRESS

BOOK PUBLISHERS

The Beatles sang "we get by with a little help from our friends," and in my case "I get by with a lot of help from my wonderful family." This book is dedicated to Nancy and Walter Dubler, Ariela Dubler, Jesse Furman, David Krimm, Peter Bradley, Josh Dubler, and Lisa Cerami.

CONTENTS

INTRODUCTION

When I think about eating at a baseball game, one thing comes to mind: sausages. It could be anything from a hot dog topped with some sauerkraut or a bratwurst in a paper holder. When I think about breakfast, one thing comes to mind: sausage—the sound of sizzling of links or patties makes eating eggs or waffles all that more terrific. And when I think about Italian food, one thing comes to mind. You guessed it: sausage. Hot or sweet, whole in casings or crumbled into the meaty, cheesy layers of lasagna or topping a pizza loaded with sauce and mozzarella. Let's face it—I love sausage in all of its glorious, fabulous forms.

Sausages are part of many of my culinary memories—both from the number of cultures that create them to the times of day when I've enjoyed them.

Many times I have slowly walked past shops that line the narrow alleys of Venice or been hypnotically drawn to stalls in markets in Nice as I take in the dizzying array cylindrical foods of all diameters hanging from hooks and piled up on platters.

And then there are meals I've shared with friends as we tear off slices of pizza, trying to get them into our mouths before their garlicky pepperoni and fresh fennel and herb sausage toppings land on the plate below. But I guess that's why they invented forks.

There's no doubt that sausage is fun food. It's fun to eat, and as you'll discover, it's also really fun to make it yourself.

There's no question that you can find some really good sausages in almost every supermarket today, produced by manufacturers that use organic meats and no chemicals. But even with those "gourmet sausages" you can't have exactly the flavor you want or specify the ingredients.

That's where making it yourself comes in. You can choose the meat you want to grind, or you can buy some pre-ground meat and save yourself the time and trouble. You can season the meat with myriad herbs and spices. You can flavor the meat with wine or liquor. You can add nuts and fruits to add texture. You can add cheese to contrast dairy creaminess with hearty meatiness.

Sausage is a paradox. It's simple food, but it has a complex flavor because of all the additional ingredients added before it's cooked. As a simple food it has been around for more than two thousand years; there are references to sausages in Homer's "Odyssey." As a simple food, it also falls into the category of "comfort foods." There's nothing edgy about a sausage. It's about as straightforward a food as you'll find.

But it's a real hands-on process. And that's all part of the fun. You cube the meat, grind it, and knead the sausage mixture to blend its flavors to your personal taste and texture. You massage the meat into its casing, and twist it into links with your hands.

Although you can invest in some equipment and create professional-looking sausages, most of the recipes in this book can be cooked up as patties on the grill or in a skillet on the stove. I recommend making patties as a good first step, because some of the sausage making process may seem bit daunting and time-consuming at first. According to a quote often attributed to Otto von Bismarck, "To retain respect for sausages and laws, one must not watch them in the making." But the more you do it, the faster you'll become, and the sooner you can enjoy the fruits—or rather the meats—of your labor.

Today we all want to know that the food we eat is prepared under sanitary conditions and we want to be sure that only quality ingredients are used. That's just another reason to start making your own sausage.

So, from Cajun Shrimp Boudin to Sweet Italian Sausage, this is one grind you'll want to get into.

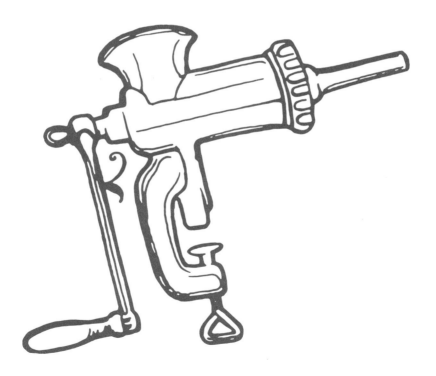

PART I:

MAKING YOUR OWN SAUSAGE

Making sausage is no more difficult than making meatloaf. Ground ingredients are seasoned, shaped, and cooked. That's it. In the first chapter, you'll learn the techniques necessary to make sausages either in casings or as patties, as well as how to cook them properly. In the chapters that follow are recipes for some of the world's classic sausages—from spicy Andouille Sausage of Cajun fame to delicate French Garlic Sausage to hearty Sweet Italian Sausage.

While sausage making has an illustrious past, it also is a contemporary food open to endless interpretations and improvisations. Included are my own innovative recipes for Lamb Sausage with Sun-Dried Tomatoes and Pine Nuts and Minnesota Boudin made with wild rice.

The sausage recipes are divided into chapters by the type of protein used as the main ingredient—pork, beef, lamb, veal, chicken and turkey, fish and seafood, and a few vegetarian options. The last chapter includes the plain and fancy cousins of sausages—homey scrapple from Pennsylvania and elegant country pork terrine from France.

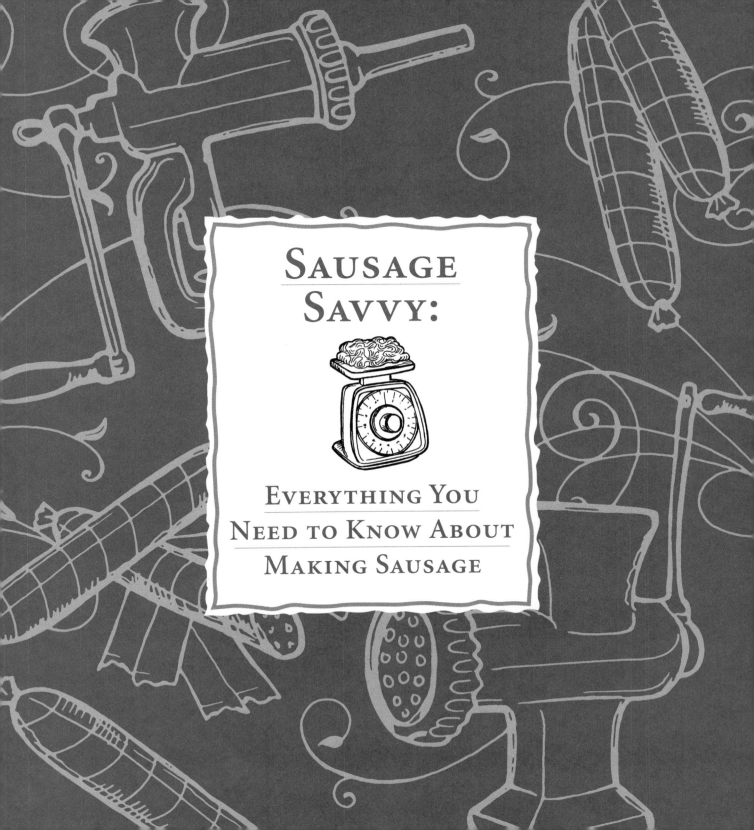

Sausage Savvy:

Everything You Need to Know About Making Sausage

Few culinary skills are involved when it comes to making sausage. There's no spinning a swan from molten sugar or folding layers of puff pastry. It takes some basic equipment, most of which you likely have and some of which you can improvise. It takes some ingredients—fresh ones you'll need to buy and dried herbs and spices you probably have in the pantry. And making sausage takes some time. Read this chapter through in its entirety to introduce yourself to the simple process of sausage making.

EQUIPMENT

You don't need much, and most items will already be on hand.

Kitchen scale. Absolutely necessary to make sure you have the correct amounts of meats and fat per recipe; sausage is not a food that should be "eye-balled" to determine your amount. The scale should be capable of weighing food up to five pounds.

Measuring cups and measuring spoons. An extra set of spoons means that one set can be used for liquid ingredients, the other for dry seasonings.

Good knives. These are essential for all cooking, including making sausage. Keep them sharp.

Kitchen twine. This used to be found in all kitchens, but a recent survey of my friends revealed that it no longer was, so buy some at a hardware or housewares store.

Instant-read thermometer. Along with good knives, this is essential. If you don't have one, here's a good excuse to buy one. Instant-read thermometers are how you determine if the sausages are cooked to a safe internal temperature.

Candy thermometer. Sometimes called a frying thermometer, it clips to the side of a pot. You'll use this to check the temperature of the water when poaching sausages. If you don't want to invest in one, keep popping your instant-read into the pot to keep the water at the correct temperature.

Kitchen funnel. You'll need this to flush out the casings. The nozzle should be narrow so as to not break the fragile casings.

Lots of kitchen towels or a roll of paper towels. Making sausage is messy, and you'll constantly be washing your hands during preparation.

WAYS TO GRIND THE MEAT

Even if you're planning on using pre-ground meat, a meat grinder is a good idea because it can also be used to stuff sausage casings. The food processor is a great grinding alterative. My food processor is so important in my kitchen that it has a reserved corner of the dishwasher; it's in there every time the dishwasher is run.

Sausage can be made in a food processor using the on-and-off pulse button, but it takes much longer than using a meat grinder because the ingredients are ground in small batches. A food processor is necessary for making seafood sausages. If you end up a serious sausage maker, chances are good you'll end up with a grinder. Make sure whatever grinder you buy has both a fine and coarse grinding plate; you'll need both for the recipes in this book.

Hand grinders. These are what Grandma used before there was such as thing as pre-ground beef in the market, and they can be purchased for very little money. They clamp on to a table or the edge of the counter, and your biceps get a good workout using them. Make sure the grinder is made from steel, not plastic; plastic is just not strong enough.

Mixer grinding attachments. If you have a sturdy stand mixer, such as those made by KitchenAid, a meat grinder attachment can be purchased. The cost is the same as a good hand grinder. I use one and recommend it without hesitation.

Electric grinders. Here's where you can spend some big bucks, so be sure you're going to make a lot of sausage before buying one.

Speed up the sausage making by making friends with a friendly butcher who will grind your meat and fat to your specifications. Butchers are sticklers for cleanliness and sanitation, so you know your meat won't be put through a grimy grinder.

HOW TO STUFF SAUSAGE

As I wrote in the introduction, there's no need to stuff casings to enjoy most of the recipes in this book. Unless the sausages are poached or baked slowly in the oven, the meat mixture can be formed into patties. But when a set form is desired, you need some device with which to stuff the sausage and some sort of casing into which it can be stuffed. As with meat grinders, there's a wide range of appliances that are united by the use of a long funnel, the stuffing horn.

Hand-held funnels. These are about 6 inches long, come in various widths, and correspond to the size of sausage casings. Most funnels are made from plastic, and they're very inexpensive. They're fine for a small amount of sausage of two pounds or less, and if you place one through the opening at the end of a pastry bag it works very well.

Mixer stuffing attachments. If you have the meat grinding attachment for a stand mixer, for about ten dollars you can get the sausage stuffing attachment, and the problem is solved.

Hand stuffing machines. These come as both push machines with a lever that pushes the mixture into the casings and crank models that push the meat in with a plunger as the crank is turned.

THE CASE FOR CASINGS

Historically, sausages were the first "fast food." They were hand-holdable, and the packaging was edible too. Keeping that in mind, it's not surprising that the intestines of pigs, cows, and sheep became part of the equation and are still the best casings.

My first choice is medium-size hog casings, followed by thin sheep casings. If you're only going to buy one, make it hog casings; if you fill them with less meat mixture you can make sausages as thin as those formed in a sheep casing. One pound of sausage mixture fills about two feet of hog casings and about four feet of sheep casings. While my local supermarket carries hog casings, I realize that's not the case everywhere. Look at the Resources on page 491 to order casings. Collagen casings are also available. They're natural because they're made from the connective tissue of animals. Collagen is the tissue that turns meltingly tender when meat is braised and it turns into gelatin. Collagen casings don't stretch like natural casings, making them difficult to work with.

So you open up your package of casings, and what do you find? A bunch of yucky-looking strands about the width of linguine. They're gritty because they're packed in coarse salt. Sausage casings can be kept refrigerated in that state up to six months; the salt acts as a preservative.

Here's how to prepare casings so they're ready for stuffing:

1. Gently pull strands off the hank. Depending on the brand you buy, they may either be tied together in the center with a plastic twist tie or just a mass of strands in a plastic bag.

2. Rinse the exteriors well under cold running water. This is the first step to riding them of excess salt and making them pliable.

3. Put the casings in a bowl, cover with lukewarm water, and soak for 20 minutes. The meat for almost all sausage recipes chills for 30 minutes prior to grinding it, so this soaking doesn't slow down the process.

4. Rinse them inside with cold water. If you think that those plastic bags in the produce section of the supermarket are hard to get open, they're a snap compared with a length of sausage casing! Start by cutting off a snip from one of the ends, and have a kitchen funnel handy. Pull apart the newly cut top of the casing, and insert the tip of the funnel. Pull about 3 inches of casing onto the funnel. Make sure your sink is empty, because this next part is similar to filling up water  balloons; you want to slowly run cold water through the funnel to rinse the salt out of the interior of the casing, straighten the casing, and make it wider. While doing this, the casing will be flying all over the sink. You'll soon get the hang of it. Then remove the casing from the funnel.

5. **Put the casings in a bowl, cover with lukewarm water and 1 tablespoon distilled white vinegar, and soak until you need them.** The vinegar both softens the casings, and makes them more transparent so they look nicer on the finished sausages. You can soak them this way for up to 30 minutes.

STEP-BY-STEP TO PERFECT SAUSAGE

Each chapter in Part I of this book suggests the appropriate cuts of meat to use for each category of sausages. Once your shopping is done, you're ready to begin making sausages.

1. Cut the meat. Cut the meat with a sharp knife into 1-inch cubes; that size works for all meat grinders and a food processor.

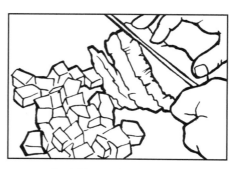

Meat should be cut into 1-inch cubes to make grinding easier.

2. Season: when and how. There are two schools of thought on when the best time is to season meat, and I use both of them. Once the meat is cut, either transfer it to a mixing bowl and add dry seasonings, salt, and pepper, or add those seasonings after the meat is ground and you're blending it. I pre-season meat if the

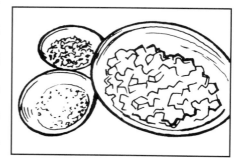

Meat can be seasoned before chilling.

recipe specifies a large number of herbs and spices, and after for only a few. The reason is that seasoning prior to chilling is an additional step. You toss everything together in a mixing bowl, and then transfer the seasoned cubes to a baking sheet.

3. Chill the meat. Arrange the meat cubes on a sheet of plastic wrap on a baking sheet, and place the cubes in the freezer for 30 minutes. Do not eliminate this step. Whether using a meat grinder or a food processor, cold meat is easier to grind.

4. Chill the mixing bowl. While the meat cubes chill, put the mixing bowl that will hold the ground meat into the freezer. A cold bowl keeps the meat cold while blending and stuffing.

5. Keep going. For many of these recipes vegetables are sautéed in oil or butter while the meat is chilling. Read the recipe from beginning to end, and see if there's something you should be doing rather than watching the clock.

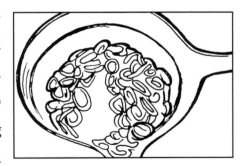

While the meat chills is the time to sauté any additional ingredients.

6. Grind the meat. If using a meat grinder, read the recipe carefully to see if it specifies a coarse or a fine blade. Then grind the meat, pressing the meat down into the grinder mechanism with the plunger given for that purpose. NEVER PUT YOUR HANDS INTO A MEAT GRINDER. If using a food processor, add only ½ to ¾ cup of meat cubes at a time, and chop them using the on-and-off pulse button. In either case, the ground meat will go into the chilled bowl.

7. Mix it together. Add all other ingredients to the meat, and knead the mixture with your hands until everything is well distributed. I keep a bowl of hot water with a tablespoon or two of white vinegar next to me along with a kitchen towel so that if I need to rinse my hands to fetch an ingredient or answer the phone it's handy.

The sausage mixture should be kneaded with your hands to blend it totally.

8. Taste for seasoning. Here is one rule of sausage making that should NEVER be broken: You don't taste raw sausage mixture. For all meat mixtures, fry one tablespoon portion in a small frying pan;

for seafood mixtures I cook the test sample in a microwave because all of those formulations are poached. Once you've cooked a bit, taste it. Then adjust the seasoning as needed. My recipes are written for a minimum of salt; if you want more, then add it. If you're turning your sausage into patties, skip to Step 12.

9. Arrange the casing. The first step is to bunch up the casing on the funnel of whatever device you're using to stuff the sausages. Pull one strand out of the water, and rinse it again under cold water, and pat it dry with a towel. If necessary, cut another bit off one end to be able to open it fully. The trick to easing the casing over the sausage horn is to do it slowly and carefully. Use one hand to keep the casing straight and feed it to the other hand that eases it over the stuffing horn.

The casing must be eased gently onto the stuffing horn.

10. Stuff the sausage. With the casing on the stuffing horn, pull the end of the casing about 3 inches down. Feed enough forcemeat into the horn so that it starts to enter the casing. Then tie a knot in the casing. You have to regulate the flow of forcemeat as it enters the casing to determine how tightly packed the sausage is. Hold the casing on the stuffing horn with your thumb and forefinger. Increasing or decreasing finger pressure on the casing will determine how tightly

Hold onto the casing so that the sausage fills evenly.

and consistently the sausage is packed. Keep filling the casing, holding on to the horn so that the casing fills evenly; you want it full but not bursting. Once all the forcemeat is inserted into the casing, take a minute to even out the width of the sausage. Then tie a knot in the casing at the other end leaving about 3 inches of casing unstuffed.

11. Link the sausage. At this point you have one long link of sausage. Each recipe gives a specific length for the links; they vary from 4 to 6 inches with the majority linked at 5 inches. Until you become accustomed to judging lengths, put a ruler on the counter in front of you. Measure off the length of your link, and then twist the link three or four times. Continue in the same manner down the whole coil. The extra casing at the end of your coil is to compensate for the amount of casing used in twisting. Chances are there will be almost no empty casing by the time you finish. If the links are going to be poached, use some kitchen twine and tie off each link with a knot. If not, cut apart the links.

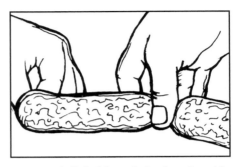

Sausage is linked by twisting lengths with your fingers.

12. Let the sausage "rest." Just as roasted meats need time to allow their juices to be reabsorbed, sausages benefit from time to allow the flavors to blend. For bulk sausage, if you can wait even 30 minutes before cooking, they'll taste even better. For links, refrigerate them overnight to allow the casings to dry; this will result in crisper casings when the sausages cook. Arrange the links on a wire cooling rack placed over a baking sheet, and refrigerate the sausages. This resting period is not as important for sausages that are poached or oven-baked as it is for links cooked with high-heat methods like grilling and broiling.

TROUBLESHOOTING

Here are some problems frequently encountered during this process, and what to do if…

The meat grinder stops working. If using the fine blade of a meat grinder, it can get clogged from time to time. Unscrew the cap holding the blade in place, use a metal skewer or toothpick to clean out the clogs, wash the plate well with hot water, and replace it onto the meat grinder.

The casing breaks. And this will happen. Sometimes it's because there was a small tear in the actual casing, and many times you'll find this out when flushing the casings with water. If that's the case, just cut it at that point. If it happens when you're midway through making a coil, stop stuffing immediately, and empty about 3 inches of filled coil. Tie off the coil, and begin again with the portion of casing remaining on the sausage horn. Casing is very inexpensive, so if I'm near the end of one when a rip occurs, I'm just as likely to throw out what's left and begin with a new casing.

There are air bubbles in links. A common problem, especially at the beginning of a coil. Just take a straight pin or a metal skewer, and bust the bubble.

The casing isn't filling evenly. It's difficult to fill evenly at the beginning, before enough casing is filled so that the sausage coils onto the counter. Build a platform with an overturned pot with a plate on top of it to hold the sausage and place it right under the stuffing horn to make filling easier.

HOW TO COOK SAUSAGE

Most sausages are raw once filled in casings or shaped in patties, and they need thorough cooking before you can enjoy them. Each recipe is annotated with the temperature the sausage should be; most are cooked to 160°F, while poultry sausages, like poultry itself, must be cooked to 165°F.

Cooking in the bulk sausage category is a no-brainer, because it's either crumbled and browned in a pan or shaped into patties and cooked. I treat patties like burgers. Shape into about 1-inch thick, and make an indentation with your thumb on one side; this keeps them from creating a dome when cooking them.

Broil, grill, or pan-fry the patties over medium-high heat, beginning with the side with the indentation facing up, until the desired temperature is reached. When cooking patties of beef or lamb sausage, I cook them medium-rare (about 130°F) rather than well done. If there's egg in the sausage mixture it should be cooked to 160°F.

There are many ways to cook raw sausage links, and each has its fans. If cooking them over high heat, prick them first with a toothpick or skewer, like a baking potato, to avoid explosions. Here's a summary of ways to reach your goal of a wonderful sausage:

Fry over low heat. Place the sausages in a heavy skillet over low heat, and allow them to cook up to 20 minutes, uncovered, turning them gently with tongs only after one section has crisped.

Fry in two steps. Place the sausages and ½ cup water in a cold skillet. Cover the pan, bring the water to a boil over medium-high heat, then reduce the heat to low and simmer the sausages for 10 minutes, turning them occasionally. Then drain the liquid from the pan, and cook over medium-high heat, uncovered, for 5 minutes, or until browned, turning them gently with tongs.

Simmer and roast. Prick the sausages evenly all over, and simmer them covered with water for 5 to 10 minutes, depending on the diameter; the simmering begins the cooking process and also removes some of the fat. Then roast them in a 475°F oven for 5 to 10 minutes, or until browned and crisp. If using this method, the two operations should happen in rapid succession. Don't refrigerate partially cooked sausages.

Bake in a hot oven. Preheat the oven to 425°F, and prick the sausages. Bake them for 12 to 18 minutes, depending on thickness, turning them with tongs midway as the sides brown.

Broil in the oven broiler. Prick the sausages evenly on all sides, and broil them 4 to 6 inches from the broiler element for 5 to 7 minutes, or until cooked through and no longer pink, turning them with tongs to brown on all sides.

Grill on a charcoal or gas grill. I've seen recipes that suggest splitting the sausages open to grill them flat, and I'd love to press charges about sausage homicide! Do prick them, but then cook them whole, uncovered if using a charcoal grill, on a medium-hot grill for 10 to 15 minutes, or until cooked. Turn them gently with tongs and not with a meat fork or fat will drip into the fire causing flare-ups.

Hot smoke on a covered grill. Prepare a grill for indirect cooking, which means there's part of the grate not over either lit charcoal or a live gas flame. If using a charcoal grill, soak 2 cups of wood chips in water to cover for 20 minutes; if using a gas grill, create a tin-foil packet for the dry chips to enclose them, and poke holes in the packet. Place the chips or chip packet on the hot side of the grill, and then place the sausages on the cold side of the grill. Cook them for 20 to 30 minutes, turning them halfway through and rearranging them so those closest to the fire are on the periphery, or to the correct internal temperature.

Poach in simmering water. To poach sausages, bring a large pot of salted water to a boil over high heat. Add sausages, and maintain water at a bare simmer. Cook sausages for 20 to 25 minutes, or until firm. Remove one sausage to a plate with tongs and insert an instant-read thermometer. If the temperature is 160°F, sausages are done. If not, return to the pot and continue cooking. Remove sausages from the pan with tongs, and serve immediately or cool to room temperature, lightly covered with plastic wrap, and refrigerate.

> Smoking is a method used to preserve meat. Necessary before refrigeration existed, smoking is still done for flavor and aroma. Smoke consists of tiny droplets of natural chemicals such as phenols and ketones that condense on the food being smoked and make their way into the meat. These chemicals kill or stop the creation of bacteria, yeast, and mold. Using ingredients such as smoked Spanish paprika and chipotle chiles replicates this flavor.

BROWNING FULLY-COOKED SAUSAGES

Many sausages, like Boudin Blanc (page 118) and Andouille (page 62) are completely cooked by poaching or slow oven-baking during the production process. These sausages are all in casings because it's impossible to poach or bake a sausage in bulk form.

Although you can eat them right from the pan or reheat them, I brown them gently as a way to reheat them and give them some texture—a crisp casing and a soft filling.

Heat a few tablespoons of olive oil, butter, or a combination of the two in a skillet over medium heat. Then add the sausage links, and cook them, uncovered, turning them gently with tongs. By the time they're evenly brown, they'll be heated through to the center.

A NOTE ON CHEMICALS

One of the best reasons to make your own sausages is to keep them free from additives and preservatives. Because that's important to me, none of the recipes in this book are made with curing salts, nitrites, or nitrates. While the FDA and the USDA have judged sodium nitrite to be a "safe ingredient," I don't agree. That's why, rather than cold-smoking sausages, they're cooked for many hours in the oven at a low temperature.

SAFETY FIRST

The first—and most important—requirement for good cooking is knowing the basic rules of food safety, whether cooking sausage, roasting meat, or using eggs. Food safety begins with trips to the supermarket and ends once leftovers are refrigerated or frozen at the end of a meal.

While the following tips may seem like common sense, this food writer has heard horror stories about people who have been come very sick from food-borne illnesses.

If you have any questions about food safety, the U.S. Department of Agriculture is the place to go. The Food Safety Inspection Service was designed to help you. The website www.fsis.usda.gov provides a wealth of information in a very user-friendly format.

Shop safely. Most supermarkets are designed to funnel you into the produce section first. But that's not the best place to start. Begin your shopping with the shelf-stable items from the center, then go to produce, and end with the other refrigerated and frozen sections. Never buy meat or poultry in a package that is torn and leaking. Place all meats and poultry in the disposable plastic bags available in meat and produce departments. Check the "sell-by" and "use-by" dates, and never purchase food that exceeds them. The case is always stocked with the least fresh on top, so dig down a few layers to find packages with more days of life in them. For the trip home, keep an insulated cooler in the back of your car if it's hot outside or if the perishable items will be out of refrigeration for more than an hour. In hot weather, ask someone in the seafood departments to put the wrapped fish or shellfish in a separate bag with crushed ice.

Banish bacteria. While fruits and vegetables can contain some bacteria, it's far more likely that the culprits will grow on meat, poultry, and seafood. Store these foods on the bottom shelves of your refrigerator so their juices don't accidentally drip on other foods. And keep these foods refrigerated until just before you cook them. Bacteria multiply at room temperature. The so-called "danger zone" is between 40°F and 140°F. As food cooks, it's important for it to pass through this zone as quickly as possible.

Avoid cross-contamination. Cleanliness is not only next to godliness, it's also the key to food safety. Wash your hands frequently with soap and water while cooking. Never touch cooked food if you haven't washed your hands after handling raw food. This rule is especially important when making sausage because you're handling raw food a lot. The cooked-food-and-raw-food-shall-never-meet precept extends beyond the cook's hands. Clean cutting boards, knives, and kitchen counters often. Don't place cooked foods or raw foods that will remain uncooked (such as salad) on cutting boards that have been used to cut raw meat, poultry, or fish. Bacteria from raw animal proteins can contaminate the other foods.

A good way to prevent food-borne illness is by selecting the right cutting board. Wooden boards might be attractive, but you can never get them as clean as plastic boards that can be run through the dishwasher. Even with plastic boards, it's best to use one for only cooked food and foods such as vegetables that are not prone to contain bacteria, and another one devoted to raw meats, poultry, and fish.

HOW TO USE THIS BOOK

All of my recipes include the number of servings, which is usually given as a range. If the dish is part of a multi-course meal—or if your table will be occupied by eaters with small appetites—the yield can be "stretched" to feed more people. The recipes for sauces and stocks are given as yields of cups or quarts.

"Active time," the second annotation, is the amount of hands-on prep time needed in the kitchen when you're slicing and dicing.

Use these times as general guidelines; some people are faster in the kitchen than others.

The third annotation is "Start to finish," the amount of time needed from the moment you start collecting the ingredients to placing the sausages on the table. The actual cooking time, as well as any time for chilling, is included in this figure. The unattended time is when you can be reading a book or readying other components of the meal.

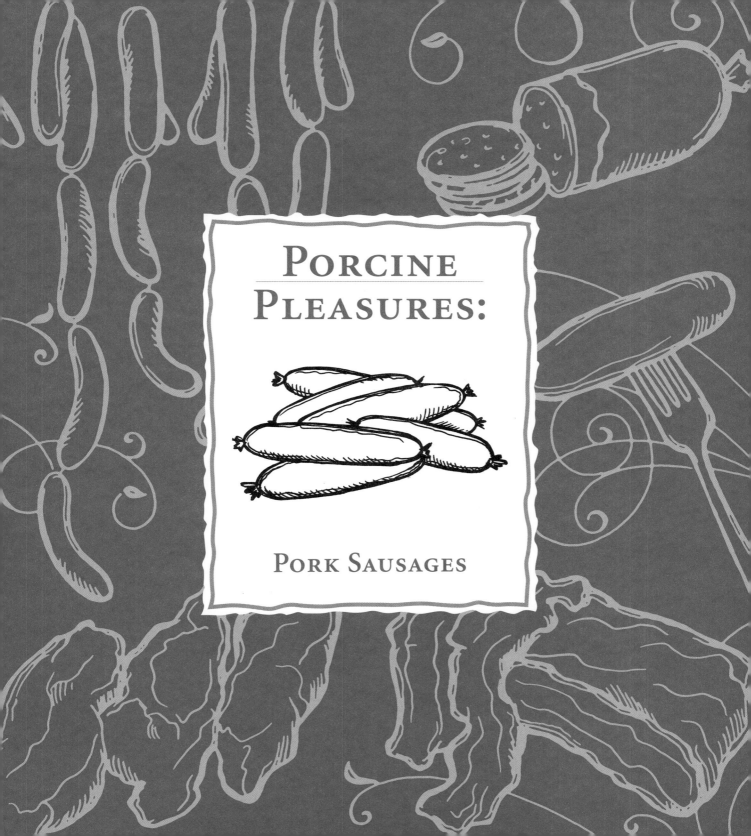

PORCINE PLEASURES:

PORK SAUSAGES

For many people, including me, the word *sausage* is synonymous with the word *pork*. Memories from my childhood are based on patties or links of breakfast sausage on the plate, and nubs of Italian sausage crumbled on top of a pizza or floating in a rich red sauce. While there were also semi-sausages, like kosher salami, that were made from beef, real sausage was made from pork.

Since pigs don't roam and graze on grasslands like cows and lambs, pork has very little internal connective tissue and is inherently tender. Pork is one of the few meats that are equally good roasted or braised in an aromatic liquid. Pork has layers of fat that encircle the meat rather than marbling it. For sausage making, the fattier cuts are the best, and you'll be happy to learn that they're relatively inexpensive, too.

The two best pork cuts for sausages are the butt and boneless country ribs. The loin and prized tenderloin are much too lean, so if using them, more pork fat needs to be added to retain moisture. Although you can find country ribs on the bone, it's time-consuming to bone them, and the ratio of meat to bone is so low that by the time you've cut off the meat it's just about the same cost as buying boneless meat. And those leftover pork bones, unfortunately, do not make a good stock for soups and general cooking as do beef and veal bones.

American Breakfast Sausage

Makes 2 pounds

**Active time:
1 hour, including
30 minutes to
chill meat**

**Start to finish:
2 hours**

Consider this recipe and its variations a template for building your own breakfast sausage. This sausage is mildly seasoned and contains the basic ingredients that I believe comprise breakfast sausage.

Thin sheep sausage casings
  (optional)
1½ pounds pork butt or boneless
  country ribs
½ pound pork fat
2 teaspoons dried sage
1½ teaspoons kosher salt
1 teaspoon freshly ground
  black pepper
½ teaspoon dried marjoram
¼ teaspoon freshly grated nutmeg
2 tablespoons vegetable oil
½ small onion, finely chopped
2 garlic cloves, minced

1. If using sausage casings, prepare them as directed on page 21.

2. Cut pork and pork fat into 1-inch cubes. Place cubes in a mixing bowl, and toss with sage, salt, pepper, marjoram, and nutmeg. Transfer cubes to a sheet of plastic wrap on a plate and freeze for 30 minutes, or until very firm. While meat chills, heat oil in a small skillet over medium-high heat. Add onion and garlic, and cook, stirring

VARIATIONS

Substitute 2 pounds boned chicken or turkey thigh meat, with skin attached, for pork and pork fat. Cook sausages to an internal temperature of 165°F.

Add 1 to 2 teaspoons crushed red pepper flakes.

Add 3 tablespoons chopped fresh parsley.

Add 1 to 2 teaspoons dry mustard powder.

Substitute ¼ cup pure maple syrup for water.

Substitute herbes de Provence for the sage and marjoram.

frequently, for 3 minutes, or until onion is translucent. Set aside.

3. Grind meat and fat through the coarse disk of a meat grinder, or in small batches in a food processor fitted with the steel blade, using the on-and-off pulse button. If using a food processor, do not process into a paste, but ingredients should be very finely chopped.

4. Combine ground meat, onion mixture, and ¼ cup ice water in a mixing bowl, and knead mixture until well blended. Fry 1 tablespoon of mixture in a small skillet over medium-high heat. Taste and adjust seasoning, if necessary.

5. Stuff mixture into casings as described on page 24, if using, and twist off into 4-inch links; prick air bubbles with a straight pin or skewer. If time permits, arrange links on a wire rack over a baking sheet and air-dry uncovered in the refrigerator for 1 day before cooking. Alternately, if keeping sausage in bulk, refrigerate mixture for at least 30 minutes to blend flavors.

6. Cook sausages as directed on page 31 to an internal temperature of 160°F when pierced with an instant-read thermometer or as directed in a specific recipe.

Note: Sausages can be refrigerated up to 2 days or frozen up to 2 months. Once cooked, they can be refrigerated up to 3 days.

Nutmeg, the seed of a tropical evergreen native to the Spice Islands, was the most popular spice with European aristocracy beginning in the fifteenth century. When the fruit of the tree is split, it reveals the inch-long nutmeg seed surrounded by a lacy membrane that is ground into mace, a spice similar in flavor.

British Bangers

Makes 2 pounds

Active time:
1 hour, including
30 minutes to
chill meat

Start to finish:
1½ hours

VARIATIONS

Substitute
cooked rice for
breadcrumbs.

Substitute
¾ pound veal for
¾ pound pork.

Mildly seasoned and almost as fine as a hot dog in texture, bangers are a beloved sausage in the British Isles. While they are most often poached, they can also be grilled.

Medium hog sausage casings
1½ pounds pork butt or boneless
    country ribs
½ pound pork fat
1 cup plain breadcrumbs
⅓ cup Chicken Stock (page 296) or
    purchased low-sodium stock
2 large egg yolks, beaten
1½ teaspoons kosher salt
1 teaspoon dried sage
¾ teaspoon ground mace
½ teaspoon ground ginger
½ teaspoon freshly ground
    white pepper
¼ teaspoon freshly grated nutmeg

1. Prepare sausage casings as directed on page 21.

2. Cut pork and pork fat into 1-inch cubes. Place cubes on a sheet of plastic wrap on a plate and freeze for 30 minutes, or until very firm. While meat chills, combine breadcrumbs, stock, and egg yolks in a small bowl, and mix well.

3. Grind meat and fat through the fine disk of a meat grinder, or in small batches in a food processor fitted with the steel blade using the on-and-off pulse button. If using a food processor, do not process into a paste, but ingredients should be very finely chopped.

4. Combine ground meat, breadcrumb mixture, salt, sage, mace, ginger, pepper, and nutmeg in a mixing bowl, and knead mixture until well blended. Then pass mixture through the fine disk of a meat grinder, or process until almost a paste in a food processor fitted with

the steel blade, using the on-and-off pulse button. Fry 1 tablespoon of mixture in a small skillet over medium-high heat. Taste and adjust seasoning, if necessary.

5. Stuff mixture into casings as described on page 24 and twist off into 5-inch links; prick air bubbles with a straight pin or skewer. If time permits, arrange links on a wire rack over a baking sheet and air-dry uncovered in the refrigerator for 1 day before cooking.

6. To poach sausages, bring a large pot of salted water to a boil over high heat. Add sausages, and maintain water at a bare simmer. Cook sausages for 20 to 25 minutes, or until firm. Remove one sausage to a plate with tongs and insert an instant-read thermometer. If the temperature is 160°F, sausages are done. If not, return to the pot and continue cooking. Remove sausages from the pan with tongs, and serve immediately or cool to room temperature, lightly covered with plastic wrap, and refrigerate. Sausages can also be grilled without poaching.

Note: Sausages can be refrigerated up to 2 days or frozen up to 2 months. Once cooked, they can be refrigerated up to 3 days.

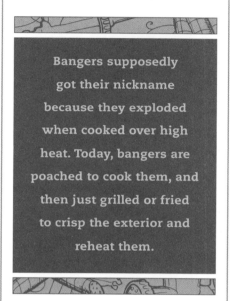

Bangers supposedly got their nickname because they exploded when cooked over high heat. Today, bangers are poached to cook them, and then just grilled or fried to crisp the exterior and reheat them.

Breakfast Sausage with Dried Fruit

Makes 2 pounds

Active time:
1 hour, including
30 minutes to
chill meat

Start to finish:
2 hours

I frequently serve breakfast sausages with fruit compote on the side, so I decided to develop a recipe in which the sweet fruity flavors are part of the sausage mixture itself. Kids seem to adore this sausage because it is slightly sweet.

Thin sheep sausage casings
   (optional)
1½ pounds pork butt or boneless
   country ribs
½ pound pork fat
¾ cup dried cranberries
½ cup orange marmalade
3 tablespoons sweet vermouth
   or cream sherry
1½ teaspoons kosher salt
½ teaspoon freshly ground
   black pepper
½ teaspoon ground ginger
¼ teaspoon ground allspice

1. If using sausage casings, prepare them as directed on page 21.

2. Cut pork and pork fat into 1-inch cubes. Place cubes on a sheet of plastic wrap on a plate and freeze for 30 minutes, or until very firm.

3. Grind meat, fat, dried cranberries, and orange marmalade through the coarse disk of a meat grinder, or in

VARIATIONS

Substitute dark or light chicken meat, with skin attached, for pork and pork fat. Cook sausages to an internal temperature of 165ºF.

Substitute chopped dried apricots for dried cranberries, and substitute apricot preserves for orange marmalade.

Substitute Grand Marnier, triple sec, or other orange-flavored liqueur for sweet vermouth.

Add 1 or 2 minced garlic cloves to sausage mixture.

small batches in a food processor fitted with the steel blade using the on-and-off pulse button. If using a food processor, do not process into a paste, but ingredients should be very finely chopped.

4. Combine meat mixture, vermouth, salt, pepper, ginger, and allspice in a mixing bowl, and knead mixture until well blended. Fry 1 tablespoon of mixture in a small skillet over medium-high heat. Taste and adjust seasoning, if necessary.

5. Stuff mixture into casings as described on page 24, if using, and twist off into 4-inch links; prick air bubbles with a straight pin or skewer. If time permits, arrange links on a wire rack over a baking sheet and air-dry uncovered in the refrigerator for 1 day before cooking. Alternately, if keeping sausage in bulk, refrigerate mixture for at least 30 minutes to blend flavors.

6. Cook sausages as directed on page 31 to an internal temperature of 160ºF when pierced with an instant-read thermometer or as directed in a specific recipe.

Note: Sausages can be refrigerated up to 2 days or frozen up to 2 months. Once cooked, they can be refrigerated up to 3 days.

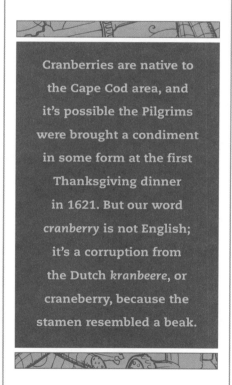

Cranberries are native to the Cape Cod area, and it's possible the Pilgrims were brought a condiment in some form at the first Thanksgiving dinner in 1621. But our word *cranberry* is not English; it's a corruption from the Dutch *kranbeere*, or craneberry, because the stamen resembled a beak.

Sweet Italian Sausage

Makes 2 pounds

Active time:
1 hour, including
30 minutes to
chill meat

Start to finish:
2 hours

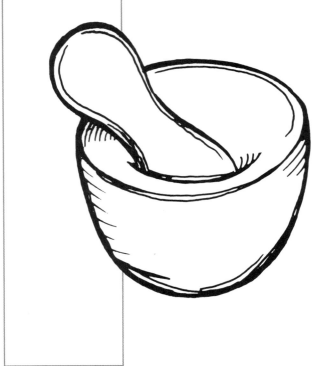

Here's my all-purpose sausage that I use when making some Italian dishes. It has all the requisite flavors—fennel, garlic, and herbs.

Medium hog sausage casings (optional)
1½ pounds pork butt or boneless country ribs
½ pound pork fat
2 tablespoons fennel seeds
3 tablespoons chopped fresh parsley
3 garlic cloves, minced
1½ teaspoons kosher salt
½ teaspoon freshly ground black pepper
¼ teaspoon crushed red pepper flakes
1 teaspoon Italian seasoning
¼ cup dry white wine

1. If using sausage casings, prepare them as directed on page 21.

2. Cut pork and pork fat into 1-inch cubes. Place cubes on a sheet of plastic wrap on a plate and freeze for 30 minutes, or until very firm. While meat chills, grind fennel seeds in a mortar and pestle or in a spice or clean coffee grinder. Set aside.

VARIATIONS

Substitute Sambuca or other anise-flavored liqueur for wine.

Substitute 2 pounds boned chicken or turkey thigh meat, with skin attached, for pork and pork fat. Cook sausages to an internal temperature of 165ºF.

Substitute 2 tablespoons chopped fresh oregano for the Italian seasoning.

Increase crushed red pepper flakes to 2 teaspoons for a spicier sausage.

3. Grind meat and fat through the coarse disk of a meat grinder, or in small batches in a food processor fitted with the steel blade using the on-and-off pulse button. If using a food processor, do not process into a paste, but ingredients should be very finely chopped.

4. Combine ground meat, ground fennel seed, parsley, garlic, salt, pepper, red pepper flakes, Italian seasoning, and wine in a mixing bowl, and knead mixture until well blended. Fry 1 tablespoon of mixture in a small skillet over medium-high heat. Taste and adjust seasoning, if necessary.

5. Stuff mixture into casings as described on page 24, if using, and twist off into 5-inch links; prick air bubbles with a straight pin or skewer. If time permits, arrange links on a wire rack over a baking sheet and air-dry uncovered in the refrigerator for 1 day before cooking. Alternately, if keeping sausage in bulk, refrigerate mixture for at least 30 minutes to blend flavors.

6. Cook sausages as directed on page 31 to an internal temperature of 160ºF when pierced with an instant-read thermometer or as directed in a specific recipe.

Note: Sausages can be refrigerated up to 2 days or frozen up to 2 months. Once cooked, they can be refrigerated up to 3 days.

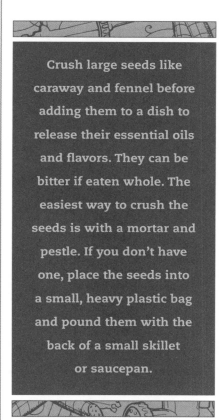

Crush large seeds like caraway and fennel before adding them to a dish to release their essential oils and flavors. They can be bitter if eaten whole. The easiest way to crush the seeds is with a mortar and pestle. If you don't have one, place the seeds into a small, heavy plastic bag and pound them with the back of a small skillet or saucepan.

Hot Italian Sausage

Makes 2 pounds

Active time:
1 hour, including
30 minutes to
chill meat

Start to finish:
2 hours

While some people add crushed red pepper flakes to sweet sausage to add some heat, I use a different recipe to make a more robust sausage. Warning: This is not a sausage for timid eaters, but you can tone down the heat by cutting back on the amount of red pepper.

Medium hog sausage casings
    (optional)
1½ pounds pork butt or boneless
    country ribs
½ pound pork fat
4 garlic cloves, minced
1½ teaspoons kosher salt
1 tablespoon paprika
1 tablespoon ground coriander
1½ teaspoons crushed red pepper
    flakes, or to taste
1 teaspoon Italian seasoning
¼ cup dry red wine

1. If using sausage casings, prepare them as directed on page 21.

2. Cut pork and pork fat into 1-inch cubes. Place cubes on a sheet of plastic wrap on a plate and freeze for 30 minutes, or until very firm.

3. Grind meat and fat through the coarse disk of a meat grinder, or in small batches in a food processor fitted with the steel blade using the on-and-off pulse button. If using a food processor, do not process into

VARIATIONS

*Substitute
2 pounds boned
chicken or turkey
thigh meat, with
skin attached, for
pork and pork fat.
Cook sausages
to an internal
temperature of
165°F.*

*Substitute 1 pound
veal shoulder
or boneless veal
breast for
1 pound pork.*

a paste, but ingredients should be very finely chopped.

4. Combine ground meat, garlic, salt, paprika, coriander, red pepper flakes, Italian seasoning, and wine in a mixing bowl, and knead mixture until well blended. Fry 1 tablespoon of mixture in a small skillet over medium-high heat. Taste and adjust seasoning, if necessary.

5. Stuff mixture into casings as described on page 24, if using, and twist off into 5-inch links; prick air bubbles with a straight pin or skewer. If time permits, arrange links on a wire rack over a baking sheet and air-dry uncovered in the refrigerator for 1 day before cooking. Alternately, if keeping sausage in bulk, refrigerate mixture for at least 30 minutes to blend flavors.

6. Cook sausages as directed on page 31 to an internal temperature of 160°F when pierced with an instant-read thermometer or as directed in a specific recipe.

Note: Sausages can be refrigerated up to 2 days or frozen up to 2 months. Once cooked, they can be refrigerated up to 3 days.

Paprika is a powder made by grinding aromatic sweet red pepper pods several times. The color can vary from deep red to bright orange, and the flavor ranges from mild to pungent and hot. Hungarian cuisine is characterized by paprika as a flavoring, and Hungarian paprika is considered the best product.

Porchetta-Style Sausage

Makes 2 pounds

Active time:
1 hour, including
30 minutes to
chill meat

Start to finish:
2 hours

VARIATIONS

Substitute
2 pounds boned
chicken or turkey
thigh meat, with
skin attached, for
pork and pork fat.
Cook sausages
to an internal
temperature of
165ºF.

Substitute 1½
pounds veal
shoulder or
boneless veal
breast for pork.

While traveling in Umbria a few years ago I became enamored with porchetta, a local delicacy of pork slowly roasted with rosemary and garlic. Here's a sausage version that also includes some aromatic lemon zest.

Medium hog sausage casings
    (optional)
1½ pounds pork butt or boneless
    country ribs
½ pound pork fat
¼ cup dry white wine
¼ cup chopped fresh rosemary
6 garlic cloves, minced
2 teaspoons grated lemon zest
1½ teaspoons kosher salt
½ teaspoon freshly ground
    black pepper

1. If using sausage casings, prepare them as directed on page 21.

2. Cut pork and pork fat into 1-inch cubes. Place cubes on a sheet of plastic wrap on a plate and freeze for 30 minutes, or until very firm.

3. Grind meat and fat through the fine disk of a meat grinder, or in small batches in a food processor fitted with the steel blade using the on-and-off pulse button. If using a food processor, do not process into a paste, but ingredients should be very finely chopped.

4. Combine ground meat, rosemary, wine, garlic, lemon zest, salt, and pepper in a mixing bowl, and knead mixture until well blended. Fry 1 tablespoon of mixture in a small skillet over medium-high heat. Taste and adjust seasoning, if necessary.

5. Stuff mixture into casings as described on page 24, if using, and

twist off into 5-inch links; prick air bubbles with a straight pin or skewer. Alternately, keep sausage in bulk. If time permits, refrigerate mixture for at least 30 minutes to blend flavors if being kept in bulk, or air-dry links refrigerated, uncovered, on a cooling rack placed over a baking sheet for 1 day before cooking.

6. Cook sausages as directed on page 31 to an internal temperature of 160°F when pierced with an instant-read thermometer or as directed in a specific recipe.

Note: Sausages can be refrigerated up to 2 days or frozen up to 2 months. Once cooked, they can be refrigerated up to 3 days.

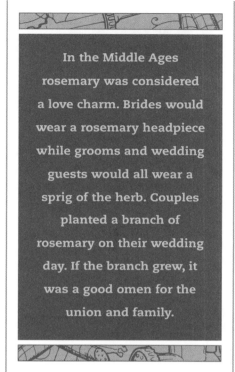

In the Middle Ages rosemary was considered a love charm. Brides would wear a rosemary headpiece while grooms and wedding guests would all wear a sprig of the herb. Couples planted a branch of rosemary on their wedding day. If the branch grew, it was a good omen for the union and family.

Luganega

Makes 2 pounds

Active time:
1 hour, including
30 minutes to
chill meat

Start to finish:
2 hours

VARIATIONS

*Substitute
2 pounds boned
chicken or turkey
thigh meat, with
skin attached, for
pork and pork fat.
Cook sausages
to an internal
temperature of
165°F.*

*Add ½ cup finely
chopped sun-
dried tomatoes to
meat mixture.*

Next to Sweet Italian Sausage (page 52), Luganega, which dates to the time the Romans lived in southern Italy, is my favorite when cooking Italian food. It contains some heady Parmesan along with spices. It's especially good in tomato sauces and risotto.

Medium hog sausage casings
   (optional)
1½ pounds pork butt or boneless
   country ribs
½ pound pork fat
½ cup freshly grated Parmesan
3 garlic cloves, minced
2 tablespoons chopped fresh parsley
1½ teaspoons kosher salt
½ teaspoon crushed red pepper
   flakes
1 teaspoon ground coriander
¼ teaspoon freshly grated nutmeg
¼ cup dry white wine

1. If using sausage casings, prepare them as directed on page 21.

2. Cut pork and pork fat into 1-inch cubes. Place cubes on a sheet of plastic wrap on a plate and freeze for 30 minutes, or until very firm.

3. Grind meat and fat through the fine disk of a meat grinder, or in small batches in a food processor fitted with the steel blade using the on-and-off pulse button. If using a

food processor, do not process into a paste, but ingredients should be very finely chopped.

4. Combine ground meat, Parmesan, garlic, parsley, salt, red pepper flakes, coriander, nutmeg, and wine in a mixing bowl, and knead mixture until well blended. Fry 1 tablespoon of mixture in a small skillet over medium-high heat. Taste and adjust seasoning, if necessary.

5. Stuff mixture into casings as described on page 24, if using, and twist off into 5-inch links; prick air bubbles with a straight pin or skewer. If time permits, arrange links on a wire rack over a baking sheet and air-dry uncovered in the refrigerator for 1 day before cooking. Alternately, if keeping sausage in bulk, refrigerate mixture for at least 30 minutes to blend flavors.

6. Cook sausages as directed on page 31 to an internal temperature of 160°F when pierced with an instant-read thermometer or as directed in a specific recipe.

Note: Sausages can be refrigerated up to 2 days or frozen up to 2 months. Once cooked, they can be refrigerated up to 3 days.

In recipes that list Parmesan cheese in the ingredients, what I'm referring to is Parmigianio-Reggiano, the hard Italian cheese that comes in a huge wheel. Buy a chunk and keep it well wrapped and refrigerated. It should be freshly grated just before using it to retain its unique flavors. Real Parmesan is *not* found pre-grated in cans. That stuff tastes like sawdust and should be avoided.

Sun-Dried Tomato and Olive Sausage

Makes 2 pounds

**Active time:
1 hour, including
30 minutes to
chill meat**

**Start to finish:
2 hours**

This sausage is a favorite in main course salads. The combination of succulent sun-dried tomatoes, heady Parmesan, and salty olives enlivens the palate.

*Medium hog sausage casings
   (optional)*
*1½ pounds pork butt or boneless
   country ribs*
½ pound pork fat
*½ cup sun-dried tomatoes packed
   in olive oil, drained with oil
   reserved, and finely chopped*
2 shallots, peeled and chopped
3 garlic cloves, peeled and minced
*⅓ cup chopped pitted oil-cured
   black olives*
¼ cup freshly grated Parmesan

2 tablespoons chopped fresh parsley
*1 tablespoon chopped fresh oregano
   or 1 teaspoon dried*
1½ teaspoons kosher salt
*½ teaspoon freshly ground
   black pepper*

1. If using sausage casings, prepare them as directed on page 21.

2. Cut pork and pork fat into 1-inch cubes. Place cubes on a sheet of plastic wrap on a plate and freeze for 30 minutes, or until very firm.

3. While meat chills, heat oil from tomatoes in a small skillet over medium-high heat. Add shallots and garlic, and cook, stirring frequently, for 3 minutes, or until shallots are translucent. Set aside.

3. Grind meat and fat through the coarse disk of a meat grinder, or in small batches in a food processor

VARIATIONS

*Substitute
2 pounds boned
chicken or turkey
thigh meat, with
skin attached,
for the pork
and pork fat.
Cook sausages
to an internal
temperature of
165°F.*

*Substitute
1 pound veal
shoulder or
boneless veal
breast for
1 pound pork.*

fitted with the steel blade using the on-and-off pulse button. If using a food processor, do not process into a paste, but ingredients should be very finely chopped.

4. Combine ground meat, shallot mixture, sun-dried tomatoes, olives, Parmesan, parsley, oregano, salt, and pepper in a mixing bowl, and knead mixture until well blended. Fry 1 tablespoon of mixture in a small skillet over medium-high heat. Taste and adjust seasoning, if necessary.

5. Stuff mixture into casings as described on page 24, if using, and twist off into 5-inch links; prick air bubbles with a straight pin or skewer. If time permits, arrange links on a wire rack over a baking sheet and air-dry uncovered in the refrigerator for 1 day before cooking. Alternately, if keeping sausage in bulk, refrigerate mixture for at least 30 minutes to blend flavors.

6. Cook sausages as directed on page 31 to an internal temperature of 160°F when pierced with an instant-read thermometer or as directed in a specific recipe.

Note: Sausages can be refrigerated up to 2 days or frozen up to 2 months. Once cooked, they can be refrigerated up to 3 days.

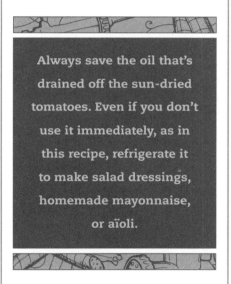

Always save the oil that's drained off the sun-dried tomatoes. Even if you don't use it immediately, as in this recipe, refrigerate it to make salad dressings, homemade mayonnaise, or aïoli.

Andouille Sausage

Makes 2 pounds

Active time:
1 hour, including
30 minutes to
chill meat

Start to finish:
5 hours

VARIATIONS

Omit the liquid smoke and hot smoke sausages as described on page 34.

Substitute 2 chipotle chiles in adobo sauce, finely chopped, for cayenne.

Andouille (pronounced *ahn-DEW-ee*) is a spicy, smoked Louisiana pork sausage used frequently in Cajun cooking. Here, the smoky flavor is from the ingredients, and it's very easy to make.

Medium hog sausage casings
1½ pounds pork butt or boneless
    country ribs
½ pound pork fat
3 garlic cloves, minced
2 tablespoons smoked Spanish
    paprika
1½ teaspoons kosher salt
1 teaspoon cayenne
½ teaspoon freshly ground
    black pepper
½ teaspoon thyme
Pinch of freshly ground nutmeg
¼ teaspoon liquid smoke

1. Prepare sausage casings as directed on page 21.

2. Cut pork and pork fat into 1-inch cubes. Place cubes in a mixing bowl, and toss with garlic, paprika, salt, cayenne, pepper, thyme, and nutmeg. Transfer cubes to a sheet of plastic wrap on a plate and freeze for 30 minutes, or until very firm.

3. Grind meat and fat through the coarse disk of a meat grinder, or in small batches in a food processor fitted with the steel blade using the on-and-off pulse button. If using a food processor, do not process into a paste, but ingredients should be very finely chopped.

4. Stir liquid smoke into ¼ cup ice water, and combine it with ground meat. Knead mixture until well blended. Fry 1 tablespoon of mixture in a small skillet over medium-high heat. Taste and adjust seasoning, if necessary.

5. Stuff mixture into casings as described on page 24 and twist off into 5-inch links; prick air bubbles with a straight pin or skewer. If time permits, arrange links on a wire rack over a baking sheet and air-dry uncovered in the refrigerator for 1 day before cooking.

6. Preheat the oven to 200°F, line a baking sheet with aluminum foil, and arrange sausages on a cooling rack on top of the baking sheet. Bake sausages for 4 to 5 hours, or to an internal temperature of 160°F

when pierced with an instant-read thermometer. Remove sausages from the pan with tongs, and serve immediately or cool to room temperature, lightly covered with plastic wrap, and refrigerate.

Note: Sausages can be refrigerated up to 2 days or frozen up to 2 months. Once cooked, they can be refrigerated up to 3 days.

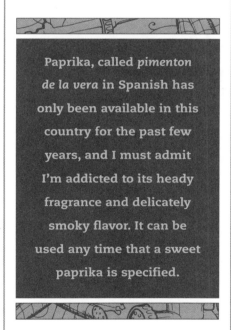

Paprika, called *pimenton de la vera* in Spanish has only been available in this country for the past few years, and I must admit I'm addicted to its heady fragrance and delicately smoky flavor. It can be used any time that a sweet paprika is specified.

Chaurice

Makes 2 pounds

Active time:
1 hour, including
30 minutes to
chill meat

Start to finish:
2 hours

Chaurice is another sausage used in much Creole and Cajun cooking. I prefer its fresh flavor to the smoky taste of andouille for dishes like red beans and rice.

Medium hog sausage casings
   (optional)
1½ pounds pork butt or boneless
   country ribs
½ pound pork fat
1 tablespoon chili powder
1½ teaspoons kosher salt
1 teaspoon sugar
1 teaspoon crushed red pepper
   flakes
½ teaspoon cayenne
½ teaspoon dried thyme
¼ teaspoon ground allspice
2 tablespoons olive oil
1 small onion, finely chopped
1 celery rib, finely chopped
3 garlic cloves, minced
¼ cup finely chopped fresh parsley

1. If using sausage casings, prepare them as directed on page 21.

2. Cut pork and pork fat into 1-inch cubes. Place cubes in a mixing bowl, and toss with chili powder, salt, sugar, red pepper flakes, cayenne, thyme, and allspice. Transfer cubes to a sheet of plastic wrap on

a plate and freeze for 30 minutes, or until very firm.

3. While meat chills, heat oil in a small skillet over medium-high heat. Add onion, garlic, and celery, and cook, stirring frequently, for 3 minutes, or until onion is translucent. Set aside.

4. Grind meat and fat through the coarse disk of a meat grinder, or in small batches in a food processor fitted with the steel blade using the on-and-off pulse button. If using a food processor, do not process into a paste, but ingredients should be very finely chopped.

5. Combine ground meat, onion mixture, parsley, and ¼ cup ice water in a mixing bowl, and knead mixture until well blended. Fry 1 tablespoon of mixture in a small skillet over medium-high heat. Taste and adjust seasoning, if necessary.

6. Stuff mixture into casings as described on page 24, if using, and twist off into 5-inch links; prick air bubbles with a straight pin or skewer. If time permits, arrange links on a wire rack over a baking sheet and air-dry uncovered in the refrigerator for 1 day before cooking. Alternately, if keeping sausage in bulk, refrigerate mixture for at least 30 minutes to blend flavors.

7. Cook sausages as directed on page 31 to an internal temperature of 160°F when pierced with an instant-read thermometer or as directed in a specific recipe.

Note: Sausages can be refrigerated up to 2 days or frozen up to 2 months. Once cooked, they can be refrigerated up to 3 days.

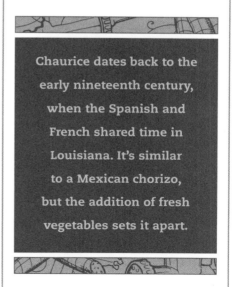

Chaurice dates back to the early nineteenth century, when the Spanish and French shared time in Louisiana. It's similar to a Mexican chorizo, but the addition of fresh vegetables sets it apart.

Fresh Mexican Chorizo

Makes 2 pounds

Active time:
1 hour, including
30 minutes to
chill meat

Start to finish:
2 hours

Making your own chorizo—with smoky chipotle chiles balanced by lots of aromatic fresh cilantro— is the basis for myriad Southwestern and authentically Mexican dishes. And it's really easy to make, too.

Medium hog sausage casings
   (optional)
1½ pounds pork butt or boneless
   country ribs
½ pound pork fat
2 tablespoons paprika
2 tablespoons chili powder
1 tablespoon ground cumin
1 teaspoon ground coriander
1½ teaspoons kosher salt
½ teaspoon freshly ground
   black pepper
½ teaspoon dried oregano
3 garlic cloves, minced
2 chipotle chiles in adobo sauce,
   finely chopped
¼ cup red wine vinegar
2 tablespoons dry red wine
½ cup chopped fresh cilantro

1. If using sausage casings, prepare them as directed on page 21.

2. Cut pork and pork fat into 1-inch cubes. Place cubes in a mixing bowl, and toss with paprika, chili powder, cumin, coriander, salt, pepper, and oregano. Transfer cubes to a sheet

VARIATIONS

Substitute 2 pounds boned chicken or turkey thigh meat, with skin attached, for pork and pork fat. Cook sausages to an internal temperature of 165°F.

Substitute 1 to 2 fresh jalapeño or serrano chiles for the chipotle chiles.

Substitute smoked Spanish paprika for the sweet paprika, and stir ¼ teaspoon liquid smoke into the vinegar before adding it to the meat mixture.

of plastic wrap on a plate and freeze for 30 minutes, or until very firm.

3. Grind meat and fat through the coarse disk of a meat grinder, or in small batches in a food processor fitted with the steel blade using the on-and-off pulse button. If using a food processor, do not process into a paste, but ingredients should be very finely chopped.

4. Combine ground meat, garlic, chiles, vinegar, and wine in a mixing bowl, and knead mixture until well blended. Add cilantro. Knead well again. Fry 1 tablespoon of mixture in a small skillet over medium-high heat. Taste and adjust seasoning, if necessary.

5. Stuff mixture into casings as described on page 24, if using, and twist off into 5-inch links; prick air bubbles with a straight pin or skewer. If time permits, arrange links on a wire rack over a baking sheet and air-dry uncovered in the refrigerator for 1 day before cooking. Alternately, if keeping sausage in bulk, refrigerate mixture for at least 30 minutes to blend flavors.

6. Cook sausages as directed on page 31 to an internal temperature of 160°F when pierced with an instant-read thermometer or as directed in a specific recipe.

Note: Sausages can be refrigerated up to 2 days or frozen up to 2 months. Once cooked, they can be refrigerated up to 3 days.

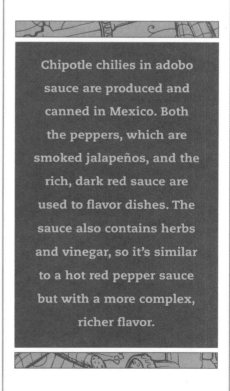

Chipotle chilies in adobo sauce are produced and canned in Mexico. Both the peppers, which are smoked jalapeños, and the rich, dark red sauce are used to flavor dishes. The sauce also contains herbs and vinegar, so it's similar to a hot red pepper sauce but with a more complex, richer flavor.

Linguiça

Makes 2 pounds

Active time:
1 hour, including
30 minutes to
chill meat

Start to finish:
2 hours

VARIATION

Substitute smoked Spanish paprika for the sweet paprika and stir ¼ teaspoon liquid smoke into the vinegar before adding it to the meat mixture.

While similar in flavor to both chorizo and chaurice, linguiça is Portuguese and more delicate in overall flavor. The combination of spices enlivened by sweet balsamic vinegar adds zesty flavors without too much spice.

Medium hog sausage casings
   (optional)
1½ pounds pork butt or boneless
   country ribs
½ pound pork fat
2 tablespoons paprika
2 teaspoons ground coriander
1½ teaspoons kosher salt
½ teaspoon freshly ground
   black pepper
½ teaspoon crushed red pepper
   flakes
½ teaspoon ground allspice
4 garlic cloves, minced
3 tablespoons balsamic vinegar

1. If using sausage casings, prepare them as directed on page 21.

2. Cut pork and pork fat into 1-inch cubes. Place cubes in a mixing bowl, and toss with paprika, coriander, salt, pepper, red pepper flakes, and allspice. Transfer cubes to a sheet of plastic wrap on a plate and freeze for 30 minutes, or until very firm.

3. Grind meat and fat through the coarse disk of a meat grinder, or in small batches in a food processor fitted with the steel blade using the on-and-off pulse button. If using a food processor, do not process into a paste, but ingredients should be very finely chopped.

4. Combine ground meat, garlic, and vinegar in a mixing bowl, and knead mixture until well blended. Fry 1 tablespoon of mixture in a small skillet over medium-high heat. Taste and adjust seasoning, if necessary.

5. Stuff mixture into casings as described on page 24, if using, and twist off into 5-inch links; prick air bubbles with a straight pin or skewer. If time permits, arrange links on a wire rack over a baking sheet and air-dry uncovered in the refrigerator for 1 day before cooking. Alternately, if keeping sausage in bulk, refrigerate mixture for at least 30 minutes to blend flavors.

6. Cook sausages as directed on page 31 to an internal temperature of 160°F when pierced with an instant-read thermometer or as directed in a specific recipe.

Note: Sausages can be refrigerated up to 2 days or frozen up to 2 months. Once cooked, they can be refrigerated up to 3 days.

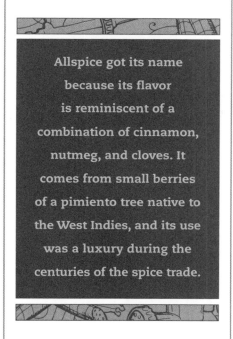

Allspice got its name because its flavor is reminiscent of a combination of cinnamon, nutmeg, and cloves. It comes from small berries of a pimiento tree native to the West Indies, and its use was a luxury during the centuries of the spice trade.

Fresh Kielbasa

Makes 2 pounds

Active time:
1 hour, including
30 minutes to
chill meat

Start to finish:
2 hours

*Substitute ½ to ¾
pound beef chuck
for ½ to ¾ pound
pork butt.*

*Substitute
2 pounds boned
chicken or turkey
thigh meat, with
skin attached, for
pork and pork fat.
Cook sausages
to an internal
temperature of
165ºF.*

Most Americans think of kielbasa as a cooked and smoked sausage; you'll find a recipe for that on page 126. It's difficult to find mildly seasoned fresh kielbasa, which is more similar to a subtle Italian sausage, like this one.

Medium hog sausage casings
    (optional)
1½ pounds pork butt or boneless
    country ribs
½ pound pork fat
1 tablespoon paprika
1½ teaspoons yellow mustard seeds
1½ teaspoons sugar
1½ teaspoons kosher salt
½ teaspoon freshly ground
    black pepper
½ teaspoon dried marjoram
½ teaspoon dried thyme
3 garlic cloves, minced
¼ cup dry white wine

1. If using sausage casings, prepare them as directed on page 21.

2. Cut pork and pork fat into 1-inch cubes. Place cubes in a mixing bowl, and toss with paprika, mustard seeds, sugar, salt, pepper, marjoram, and thyme. Transfer cubes to a sheet of plastic wrap on a plate and freeze for 30 minutes, or until very firm.

3. Grind meat and fat through the fine disk of a meat grinder, or in small batches in a food processor fitted with the steel blade using the on-and-off pulse button. If using a food processor, do not process into a paste, but ingredients should be very finely chopped.

4. Combine ground meat, garlic, and wine in a mixing bowl, and knead mixture until well blended. Fry 1 tablespoon of mixture in a small skillet over medium-high heat. Taste and adjust seasoning, if necessary.

5. Stuff mixture into casings as described on page 24, if using, and twist off into 5-inch links; prick air bubbles with a straight pin or skewer. If time permits, arrange links on a wire rack over a baking sheet and air-dry uncovered in the refrigerator for 1 day before cooking. Alternately, if keeping sausage in bulk, refrigerate mixture for at least 30 minutes to blend flavors.

6. Cook sausages as directed on page 31 to an internal temperature of 160°F when pierced with an instant-read thermometer or as directed in a specific recipe.

Note: Sausages can be refrigerated up to 2 days or frozen up to 2 months. Once cooked, they can be refrigerated up to 3 days.

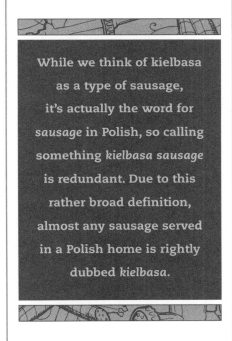

While we think of kielbasa as a type of sausage, it's actually the word for *sausage* in Polish, so calling something *kielbasa sausage* is redundant. Due to this rather broad definition, almost any sausage served in a Polish home is rightly dubbed *kielbasa*.

French Garlic Sausage

Makes 2 pounds

Active time:
1 hour, including
30 minutes to
chill meat

Start to finish:
5 hours

VARIATION

Substitute
2 pounds boned
chicken or turkey
thigh meat, with
skin attached, for
the pork and pork
fat. Cook sausages
to an internal
temperature of
165ºF.

Even with the growing popularity of sausage, it's still difficult to find this rich cooked sausage in American markets. Easy to make, it can be part of a classic Cassoulet (page 348), or just heated and enjoyed with some mustard.

Medium hog sausage casings
1½ pounds pork butt or boneless
    country ribs
½ pound pork fat
½ cup plain breadcrumbs
¼ cup heavy cream
2 tablespoons brandy
6 garlic cloves, minced
1½ teaspoons kosher salt
½ teaspoon freshly ground
    black pepper
½ teaspoon herbes de Provence
¼ teaspoon ground allspice

1. Prepare sausage casings as directed on page 21.

2. Cut pork and pork fat into 1-inch cubes. Place cubes on a sheet of plastic wrap on a plate and freeze for 30 minutes, or until very firm. While meats chill, combine bread-crumbs with cream and brandy in a small bowl.

3. Grind meat and fat through the fine disk of a meat grinder, or in small batches in a food processor

fitted with the steel blade using the on-and-off pulse button. If using a food processor, do not process into a paste, but ingredients should be very finely chopped.

4. Combine ground meat, breadcrumb mixture, garlic, salt, pepper, herbes de Provence, and allspice in a mixing bowl, and knead mixture until well blended. Fry 1 tablespoon of mixture in a small skillet over medium-high heat. Taste and adjust seasoning, if necessary.

5. Stuff mixture into casings as described on page 24 and twist off into 5-inch links; prick air bubbles with a straight pin or skewer. If time permits, arrange links on a wire rack over a baking sheet and air-dry uncovered in the refrigerator for 1 day before cooking.

6. Preheat the oven to 200°F, line a baking sheet with aluminum foil, and arrange sausages on a cooling rack on top of the baking sheet. Bake sausages for 4 to 5 hours, or to an internal temperature of 160°F when pierced with an instant-read thermometer. Remove sausages from the pan with tongs, and serve immediately or cool to room temperature, lightly covered with plastic wrap, and refrigerate.

Note: Sausages can be refrigerated up to 2 days or frozen up to 2 months. Once cooked, they can be refrigerated up to 3 days.

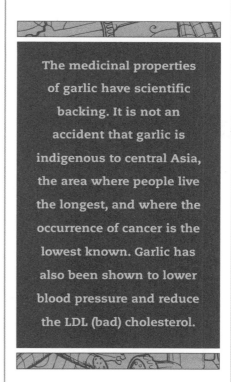

The medicinal properties of garlic have scientific backing. It is not an accident that garlic is indigenous to central Asia, the area where people live the longest, and where the occurrence of cancer is the lowest known. Garlic has also been shown to lower blood pressure and reduce the LDL (bad) cholesterol.

Sweet Chinese Sausage

Makes 2 pounds

**Active time:
1 hour, including
30 minutes to
chill meat**

**Start to finish:
4 hours**

VARIATIONS

*Substitute
2 pounds boned
chicken or turkey
thigh meat, with
skin attached, for
pork and pork fat.
Cook sausages
to an internal
temperature of
165ºF.*

*Add up to
1 tablespoon
Chinese chile
paste with
garlic for spicier
sausage.*

For many years I stopped in San Francisco's Chinatown on my way to the airport to buy Chinese sausages. I still recall the sight of those skinny links hanging in butcher shop windows. Aromatic and slightly sweet, stir-fry them with bok choy or broccoli.

Thin sheep sausage casings
*1½ pounds pork butt or boneless
    country ribs*
½ pound pork fat
2 garlic cloves, minced
1 tablespoon grated fresh ginger
2 tablespoons hoisin sauce
2 tablespoons soy sauce
2 tablespoons Scotch whiskey
1½ teaspoons five-spice powder
1 teaspoon grated orange zest
*½ teaspoon Chinese chile paste
    with garlic*

1. Prepare sausage casings as directed on page 21.

2. Cut pork and pork fat into 1-inch cubes. Place cubes on a sheet of plastic wrap on a plate and freeze for 30 minutes, or until very firm.

3. Grind meat and fat through the coarse disk of a meat grinder, or in small batches in a food processor fitted with the steel blade using the on-and-off pulse button. If using a food processor, do not process into

a paste, but ingredients should be very finely chopped.

4. Combine ground meat, garlic, ginger, hoisin sauce, soy sauce, Scotch, five-spice powder, orange zest, and chile paste in a mixing bowl, and knead mixture until well blended. Fry 1 tablespoon of mixture in a small skillet over medium-high heat. Taste and adjust seasoning, if necessary.

5. Stuff mixture into casings as described on page 24 and twist off into 6-inch links; prick air bubbles with a straight pin or skewer. If time permits, arrange links on a wire rack over a baking sheet and air-dry uncovered in the refrigerator for 1 day before cooking.

6. Preheat the oven to 200°F, line a baking sheet with aluminum foil, and arrange sausages on a cooling rack on top of the baking sheet. Bake sausages for 3 to 4 hours, or to an internal temperature of 160°F when pierced with an instant-read thermometer. Remove sausages from the pan with tongs, and serve immediately or cool to room temperature, lightly covered with plastic wrap, and refrigerate.

Note: Sausages can be refrigerated up to 2 days or frozen up to 2 months. Once cooked, they can be refrigerated up to 3 days.

Hoisin sauce, pronounced *hoy-ZAN*, is the ketchup of Chinese cooking. This thick sweet and spicy reddish-brown sauce is a mixture of soybeans, garlic, chilies, five-spice powder, and sugar. Like ketchup, it's used both as a condiment and as an ingredient.

Thai-Style Pork Sausage

Makes 2 pounds

**Active time:
1 hour, including
30 minutes to
chill meat**

**Start to finish:
2 hours**

VARIATION

*Substitute
2 pounds boned
chicken or turkey
thigh meat, with
skin attached, for
pork and pork fat.
Cook sausages
to an internal
temperature of
165ºF.*

Sausages are part of many Asian cuisines, but it's difficult to find them on this side of the Pacific. This one, made with tangy lemongrass, chiles, and cilantro, is great on the grill.

Medium hog sausage casings
   (optional)
1½ pounds pork butt or boneless
   country ribs
½ pound pork fat
2 tablespoons Asian sesame oil
4 shallots, diced
4 garlic cloves, minced
3 tablespoons fish sauce (nam pla)
3 tablespoons dry sherry
1 to 2 jalapeño or serrano chiles,
   finely chopped
¼ cup panko breadcrumbs
3 tablespoons chopped fresh cilantro
2 tablespoons finely chopped
   lemongrass
1 tablespoon sugar
1½ teaspoons kosher salt
½ teaspoon crushed red pepper
   flakes

1. If using sausage casings, prepare them as directed on page 21.

2. Cut pork and pork fat into 1-inch cubes. Place cubes on a sheet of plastic wrap on a plate and freeze for 30 minutes, or until very firm.

3. While meat chills, heat sesame oil in a small skillet over medium-high heat. Add shallot and garlic, and cook, stirring frequently, for 3 minutes, or until shallots are translucent. Set aside.

4. Grind meat and fat through the coarse disk of a meat grinder, or in small batches in a food processor fitted with the steel blade using the on-and-off pulse button. If using a food processor, do not process into a paste, but ingredients should be very finely chopped.

5. Combine ground meat, shallot mixture, fish sauce, sherry, chiles, breadcrumbs, cilantro, lemongrass, sugar, salt, and red pepper flakes in a mixing bowl, and knead mixture until well blended. Fry 1 tablespoon of mixture in a small skillet over medium-high heat. Taste and adjust seasoning, if necessary.

6. Stuff mixture into casings as described on page 24, if using, and twist off into 5-inch links; prick air bubbles with a straight pin or skewer. Alternately, keep sausage in bulk. If time permits, refrigerate mixture for at least 30 minutes to blend flavors if being kept in bulk, or air-dry links refrigerated, uncovered, on a cooling rack placed over a baking sheet for 1 day before cooking.

7. Cook sausages as directed on page 31 to an internal temperature of 160°F when pierced with an instant-read thermometer or as directed in a specific recipe.

Note: Sausages can be refrigerated up to 2 days or frozen up to 2 months. Once cooked, they can be refrigerated up to 3 days.

Lemongrass, technically an herb and used extensively in Thai and Vietnamese cooking, is characterized by a strong citrus flavor with a spicy finish similar to that of ginger. Fresh lemongrass is sold by the pale green stalk and looks like a fibrous, woody scallion. Cut the lower bulb 5-inches from the stalk, discarding the fibrous upper part. Trim off the outer layers as you would peel an onion; then bruise the stem to release its flavor. If you can't find lemongrass, substitute 1 teaspoon grated lemon zest plus 2 tablespoons lemon juice for each stalk of lemongrass specified in a recipe, along with a pinch of ginger powder.

MEATY MATTERS:

BEEF, LAMB, VEAL, AND GAME SAUSAGES

While pork may reign as the king of sausage meats, there are other noble contenders in this court— namely hearty beef, delicate veal, rich lamb, and flavorful game meats.

Boneless beef chuck roast and brisket are my two favorites for beef sausages. They both have a nice amount of fat and a rich flavor. When you're looking at beef in the case, seek deep red, moist meat generously marbled with white fat. Yellow fat is a tip-off to old age. Beef is purple after cutting but the meat quickly "blooms" to bright red on exposure to the air.

While cows have many parts from which to choose, lamb and veal have limited options. For both, the shoulder is the part of the animals that contain a good quantity of fat. Although lamb shanks also have lots of fat, they are almost impossible to bone, and they contain too much gristle for sausages that cook relatively quickly.

Breast of veal, if you can find one at your supermarket, is another contender for veal sausages. The breast is not difficult to bone, and the bones make superb stock.

While game meats such as bison and venison are usually very lean, there aren't that many cuts to choose from. Like pork, the fattier and the less expensive cuts of other meats, the better the sausage.

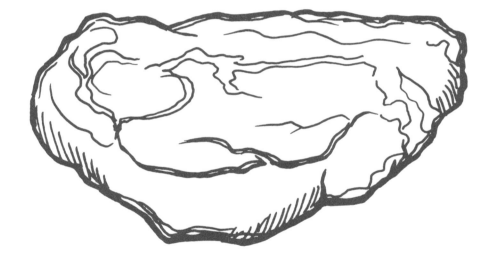

Smoky Beef Summer Sausage

Makes 2 pounds

**Active time:
1 hour, including
30 minutes to
chill meat**

**Start to finish:
5 hours**

VARIATIONS

Substitute tomato juice for water.

Omit liquid smoke and hot smoke sausage with soaked wood chips placed over coals as described on page 34 until sausage reaches 160ºF.

A bit of garlic and mustard seed characterize this sausage that is eaten cold, thus the reference to summer. Also, it is great paired with some old-fashioned baked beans.

Medium hog sausage casings
1¾ pounds boneless beef chuck
    or brisket
¼ pound beef fat
½ teaspoon liquid smoke
3 garlic cloves, minced
1 tablespoon mustard seeds
1½ teaspoons kosher salt
¾ teaspoon freshly ground
    black pepper

1. Prepare sausage casings as directed on page 21.

2. Cut beef and fat into 1-inch cubes. Place cubes on a sheet of plastic wrap on a plate and freeze for 30 minutes, or until very firm.

3. Grind beef and fat through the coarse disk of a meat grinder, or in small batches in a food processor fitted with the steel blade using the on-and-off pulse button. If using a food processor, do not process into a paste, but ingredients should be very finely chopped.

4. Stir liquid smoke into ½ cup ice water. Combine ground meat, water, garlic, mustard seeds, salt, and pepper in a mixing bowl, and knead mixture until well blended. Fry 1 tablespoon of mixture in a small skillet over medium-high heat. Taste and adjust seasoning, if necessary.

5. Stuff mixture into casings as described on page 24 and twist off into 5-inch links; prick air bubbles with a straight pin or skewer. If time permits, arrange links on a wire rack over a baking sheet and air-dry uncovered in the refrigerator for 1 day before cooking.

6. Preheat the oven to 200°F, line a baking sheet with aluminum foil, and arrange sausages on a cooling rack on top of the baking sheet. Bake sausages for 4 to 5 hours, or to an internal temperature of 160°F when pierced with an instant-read thermometer. Remove sausages from the pan with tongs, and serve immediately or cool to room temperature, lightly covered with plastic wrap, and refrigerate.

Note: Sausages can be refrigerated up to 2 days or frozen up to 2 months. Once cooked, they can be refrigerated up to 3 days.

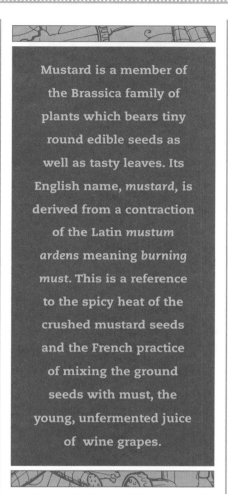

Mustard is a member of the Brassica family of plants which bears tiny round edible seeds as well as tasty leaves. Its English name, *mustard,* is derived from a contraction of the Latin *mustum ardens* meaning *burning must.* This is a reference to the spicy heat of the crushed mustard seeds and the French practice of mixing the ground seeds with must, the young, unfermented juice of wine grapes.

Swedish Beef and Potato Sausage

Makes 2 pounds

**Active time:
1 hour, including
30 minutes to
chill meat**

**Start to finish:
1½ hours**

VARIATION

*Substitute veal
shoulder or
boneless veal
breast for beef.*

While this sausage is authentically Swedish, it's also popular in Midwestern states where it arrived with Swedish immigrants in the late-nineteenth century. After poaching, all it needs is a sauce such as Sweet and Hot Mustard Sauce (page 472) or Homemade Ketchup (page 484).

Medium hog sausage casings
1¼ pounds boneless beef chuck
    or brisket
¼ pound beef fat
2 tablespoons vegetable oil
1 medium onion, chopped
2 garlic cloves, minced
½ pound baking potato, peeled
    and cut into 1-inch cubes

3 tablespoons nonfat dry milk
    powder
2½ teaspoons kosher salt
2 teaspoons caraway seed
½ teaspoon freshly ground
    black pepper
½ teaspoon dried thyme

1. Prepare sausage casings as directed on page 21.

2. Cut beef and fat into 1-inch cubes. Place cubes on a sheet of plastic wrap on a plate and freeze for 30 minutes, or until very firm.

3. While meat chills, heat oil in a small skillet over medium-high heat. Add onion and garlic, and cook, stirring frequently, for 3 minutes, or until onion is translucent. Set aside.

4. Grind beef, fat, and potato through the coarse disk of a meat grinder, or in small batches in a food processor fitted with the steel blade using the on-and-off pulse

button. If using a food processor, do not process into a paste, but ingredients should be very finely chopped.

5. Combine ground meat mixture, onion mixture, milk powder, salt, caraway seed, pepper, and thyme in a mixing bowl, and knead mixture until well blended. Fry 1 tablespoon of mixture in a small skillet over medium-high heat. Taste and adjust seasoning, if necessary.

6. Stuff mixture into casings as described on page 24 and twist off into 5-inch links; prick air bubbles with a straight pin or skewer. If time permits, arrange links on a wire rack over a baking sheet and air-dry uncovered in the refrigerator for 1 day before cooking.

7. To poach sausages, bring a large pot of salted water to a boil over high heat. Add sausages, and maintain water at a bare simmer. Cook sausages for 20 to 25 minutes, or until firm. Remove one sausage to a plate with tongs and insert an instant-read thermometer. If the temperature is 160°F, sausages are done. If not, return to the pot and continue cooking. Remove sausages from the pan with tongs, and serve immediately or cool to room temperature, lightly covered with plastic wrap, and refrigerate.

Note: Sausages can be refrigerated up to 2 days or frozen up to 2 months. Once cooked, they can be refrigerated up to 3 days.

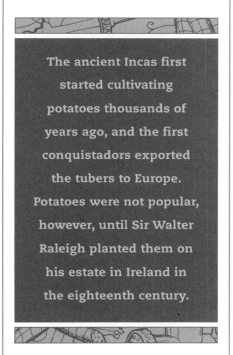

The ancient Incas first started cultivating potatoes thousands of years ago, and the first conquistadors exported the tubers to Europe. Potatoes were not popular, however, until Sir Walter Raleigh planted them on his estate in Ireland in the eighteenth century.

Peppery Mustard Beef Sausage

Makes 2 pounds

Active time:
1 hour, including 30 minutes to chill meat

Start to finish:
1½ hours

VARIATIONS

Substitute lamb and lamb fat for beef and beef fat.

Add 2 tablespoons nonpareil capers, rinsed and chopped.

A touch of heady red wine and some herbs flavor these hearty poached beef sausages that are similar in flavor to the classic French dish steak au poivre. Just put them out with additional Dijon mustard for dipping.

Medium hog sausage casings
1½ pounds boneless beef chuck
    or brisket
½ pound beef fat
½ cup dry red wine
¼ cup plain breadcrumbs
3 tablespoons grainy Dijon mustard
2 tablespoons chopped fresh parsley
2 shallots, finely chopped
2 garlic cloves, minced
2 tablespoons coarsely ground
    mixed peppercorns
1 tablespoon fresh thyme
    or 1 teaspoon dried
1½ teaspoons kosher salt

1. Prepare sausage casings as directed on page 21.

2. Cut beef and beef fat into 1-inch cubes. Place cubes on a sheet of plastic wrap on a plate and freeze for 30 minutes, or until very firm. While meat chills, combine wine and breadcrumbs in a small bowl, and stir well. Set aside.

3. Grind beef and fat through the coarse disk of a meat grinder, or in small batches in a food processor fitted with the steel blade using the on-and-off pulse button. If using a food processor, do not process into a paste, but ingredients should be very finely chopped.

4. Combine ground meat, wine mixture, mustard, parsley, shallots, garlic, pepper, thyme, and salt in a mixing bowl, and knead mixture until well blended. Fry 1 tablespoon of mixture in a small skillet over medium-high heat. Taste and adjust seasoning, if necessary.

5. Stuff mixture into casings as described on page 24 and twist off into 5-inch links; prick air bubbles with a straight pin or skewer. If time permits, arrange links on a wire rack over a baking sheet and air-dry uncovered in the refrigerator for 1 day before cooking.

6. To poach sausages, bring a large pot of salted water to a boil over high heat. Add sausages, and maintain water at a bare simmer. Cook sausages for 20 to 25 minutes, or until firm. Remove one sausage to a plate with tongs and insert an instant-read thermometer. If the temperature is 160°F, sausages are done. If not, return to the pot and continue cooking. Remove sausages from the pan with tongs, and serve immediately or cool to room temperature, lightly covered with plastic wrap, and refrigerate.

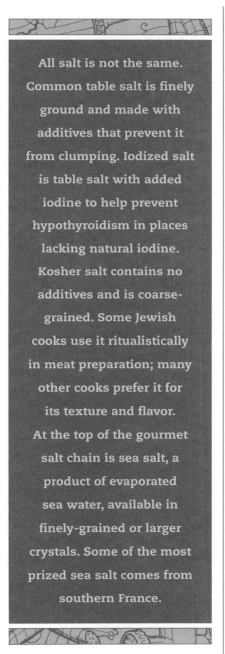

All salt is not the same. Common table salt is finely ground and made with additives that prevent it from clumping. Iodized salt is table salt with added iodine to help prevent hypothyroidism in places lacking natural iodine. Kosher salt contains no additives and is coarse-grained. Some Jewish cooks use it ritualistically in meat preparation; many other cooks prefer it for its texture and flavor. At the top of the gourmet salt chain is sea salt, a product of evaporated sea water, available in finely-grained or larger crystals. Some of the most prized sea salt comes from southern France.

Spicy Beef Sausage

Makes 2 pounds

Active time:
1 hour, including
30 minutes to
chill meat

Start to finish:
2 hours

VARIATION

Substitute lamb shoulder for beef.

While most sausages with chiles include pork, I decided to create a beef and chile version. They're delicious sautéed, too.

Medium hog sausage casings
    (optional)
1¾ pounds beef chuck or brisket
¼ pound beef fat
2 tablespoons paprika
1½ teaspoons kosher salt
1½ teaspoons freshly ground
    black pepper
1 teaspoon dried sage
½ teaspoon dried thyme
½ teaspoon ground allspice
½ cup dry red wine
4 garlic cloves, minced
1 jalapeño or serrano chile,
    seeds and ribs removed,
    and finely chopped

1. If using sausage casings, prepare them as directed on page 21.

2. Cut beef and beef fat into 1-inch cubes. Place cubes in a mixing bowl, and toss with paprika, salt, pepper, sage, thyme, and allspice. Transfer cubes to a sheet of plastic wrap on a plate and freeze for 30 minutes, or until very firm.

3. Grind beef and fat through the coarse disk of a meat grinder, or in small batches in a food processor fitted with the steel blade using the on-and-off pulse button. If using a food processor, do not process into a paste, but ingredients should be very finely chopped.

4. Combine ground meat, wine, garlic, and chile in a mixing bowl, and knead mixture until well blended. Fry 1 tablespoon of mixture in a small skillet over medium-high heat. Taste and adjust seasoning, if necessary.

5. Stuff mixture into casings as described on page 24, if using, and twist off into 5-inch links; prick air bubbles with a straight pin or skewer. If time permits, arrange links on a wire rack over a baking sheet and air-dry uncovered in the refrigerator for 1 day before cooking. Alternately, if keeping sausage in bulk, refrigerate mixture for at least 30 minutes to blend flavors.

6. Cook sausages as directed on page 31 to an internal temperature of 160°F when pierced with an instant-read thermometer or as directed in a specific recipe.

Note: Sausages can be refrigerated up to 2 days or frozen up to 2 months. Once cooked, they can be refrigerated up to 3 days.

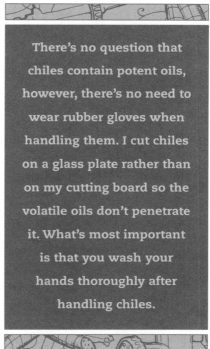

There's no question that chiles contain potent oils, however, there's no need to wear rubber gloves when handling them. I cut chiles on a glass plate rather than on my cutting board so the volatile oils don't penetrate it. What's most important is that you wash your hands thoroughly after handling chiles.

German-Style Beef Sausage

Makes 2 pounds

Active time:
1 hour, including
30 minutes to
chill meat

Start to finish:
1½ hours

VARIATION

Substitute veal shoulder or boneless veal breast for beef.

These beef sausages are similar to those that I ate at New York delis as a child. Finely textured, they include garlic, mustard, and spices. Serve them with some mustard and baked beans.

Medium hog sausage casings
1¾ pounds beef chuck or brisket
¼ pound beef fat
1½ teaspoons kosher salt
1 teaspoon sugar
½ teaspoon freshly ground
  black pepper
½ teaspoon ground coriander
½ teaspoon dry mustard powder
½ teaspoon celery seed
¼ teaspoon ground mace
½ small onion, diced
2 garlic cloves, pressed through
  a garlic press

1. Prepare sausage casings as directed on page 21.

2. Cut beef and beef fat into 1-inch cubes. Place cubes in a mixing bowl, and toss with salt, sugar, pepper, coriander, mustard powder, celery seed, and mace. Transfer cubes to a sheet of plastic wrap on a plate and freeze for 30 minutes, or until very firm.

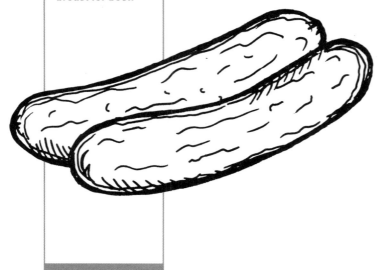

3. Grind beef, fat, and onion through the fine disk of a meat grinder, or in small batches in a food processor fitted with the steel blade using the on-and-off pulse button. If using a food processor, do not process into a paste, but ingredients should be very finely chopped.

4. Combine ground meat mixture, ¼ cup ice water, and garlic in a mixing bowl, and knead mixture until well blended. Fry 1 tablespoon of mixture in a small skillet over medium-high heat. Taste and adjust seasoning, if necessary.

5. Stuff mixture into casings as described on page 24 and twist off into 5-inch links; prick air bubbles with a straight pin or skewer. If time permits, arrange links on a wire rack over a baking sheet and air-dry uncovered in the refrigerator for 1 day before cooking.

6. To poach sausages, bring a large pot of salted water to a boil over high heat. Add sausages, and maintain water at a bare simmer. Cook sausages for 20 to 25 minutes, or until firm. Remove one sausage to a plate with tongs and insert an instant-read thermometer. If the temperature is 160°F, sausages are done. If not, return to the pot and continue cooking. Remove sausages from the pan with tongs, and serve immediately or cool to room temperature, lightly covered with plastic wrap, and refrigerate.

Note: Sausages can be refrigerated up to 2 days or frozen up to 2 months. Once cooked, they can be refrigerated up to 3 days.

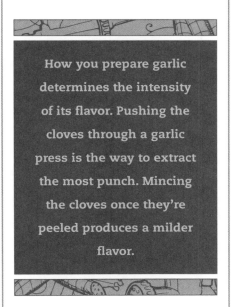

How you prepare garlic determines the intensity of its flavor. Pushing the cloves through a garlic press is the way to extract the most punch. Mincing the cloves once they're peeled produces a milder flavor.

Merguez

Makes 2 pounds

Active time:
1 hour, including
30 minutes to
chill meat

Start to finish:
2 hours

VARIATION

Substitute beef for lamb.

There's a lot going on in this classic North African sausage. With one bite you taste mint and parsley, and with the next you're relishing all those exotic spices. Merguez (pronounced *mir-GHEZ*) is great on its own or in any Moroccan or Middle Eastern recipe.

*Medium hog sausage casings
    (optional)*
1½ pounds boneless lamb shoulder
½ pound lamb fat or beef fat
1 tablespoon paprika
2 teaspoons kosher salt
1 teaspoon anise seed
1 teaspoon dried oregano
1 teaspoon ground cumin
1 teaspoon ground coriander

½ teaspoon cayenne
¼ teaspoon ground allspice
¼ teaspoon ground mace
3 tablespoons olive oil
1 medium onion, chopped
3 garlic cloves, minced
3 tablespoons tomato sauce
3 tablespoons chopped fresh parsley
1 tablespoon chopped fresh mint
1 teaspoon grated lemon zest
*1 tablespoon freshly squeezed
    lemon juice*

1. If using sausage casings, prepare them as directed on page 21.

2. Cut lamb and lamb fat into 1-inch cubes. Place cubes in a mixing bowl, and toss with paprika, salt, anise seed, oregano, cumin, coriander, cayenne, allspice, and mace. Transfer cubes to a sheet of plastic wrap on a plate and freeze for 30 minutes, or until very firm.

3. While meat chills, heat oil in a small skillet over medium-high heat. Add onion and garlic, and

cook, stirring frequently, for 3 minutes, or until onion is translucent. Set aside.

4. Grind lamb and lamb fat through the fine disk of a meat grinder, or in small batches in a food processor fitted with the steel blade using the on-and-off pulse button. If using a food processor, do not process into a paste, but ingredients should be very finely chopped.

5. Combine ground meat, onion mixture, tomato sauce, parsley, mint, lemon zest, lemon juice, and ¼ cup ice water in a mixing bowl, and knead mixture until well blended. Fry 1 tablespoon of mixture in a small skillet over medium-high heat. Taste and adjust seasoning, if necessary.

6. Stuff mixture into casings as described on page 24, if using, and twist off into 4-inch links; prick air bubbles with a straight pin or skewer. If time permits, arrange links on a wire rack over a baking sheet and air-dry uncovered in the refrigerator for 1 day before cooking. Alternately, if keeping

sausage in bulk, refrigerate mixture for at least 30 minutes to blend flavors.

7. Cook sausages as directed on page 31 to an internal temperature of 160°F when pierced with an instant-read thermometer or as directed in a specific recipe.

Note: Sausages can be refrigerated up to 2 days or frozen up to 2 months. Once cooked, they can be refrigerated up to 3 days.

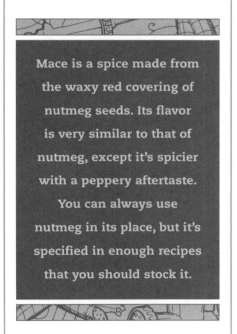

Mace is a spice made from the waxy red covering of nutmeg seeds. Its flavor is very similar to that of nutmeg, except it's spicier with a peppery aftertaste. You can always use nutmeg in its place, but it's specified in enough recipes that you should stock it.

Persian Lamb Sausage

Makes 2 pounds

Active time:
1 hour, including 30 minutes to chill meat

Start to finish:
2 hours

Persian cuisine is characterized by its combined use of lamb and dried fruit as in these hearty lamb sausages. Serve rice pilaf on the side.

Thin sheep sausage casings (optional)
1½ pounds boneless lamb shoulder
½ pound lamb fat or beef fat
2 tablespoons olive oil
½ small onion, chopped
2 garlic cloves, minced
¼ cup dry red wine
⅓ cup finely chopped dried apricots
1½ teaspoons kosher salt
½ teaspoon freshly ground
    black pepper
½ teaspoon turmeric
½ teaspoon ground ginger

1. If using sausage casings, prepare them as directed on page 21.

2. Cut lamb and lamb fat into 1-inch cubes. Place cubes on a sheet of plastic wrap on a plate and freeze for 30 minutes, or until very firm.

3. While meat chills, heat oil in a small skillet over medium-high heat. Add onion and garlic, and

VARIATIONS

Substitute beef and beef fat for lamb.

Substitute 2 pounds boned chicken or turkey thigh meat, with skin attached, for pork and pork fat. Cook sausages to an internal temperature of 165ºF.

Substitute chopped dried cranberries or dried currants for dried apricots.

Substitute up to 2 tablespoons curry powder for turmeric and ginger.

cook, stirring frequently, for 5 minutes, or until onion softens. Set aside.

4. Grind lamb and fat through the coarse disk of a meat grinder, or in small batches in a food processor fitted with the steel blade using the on-and-off pulse button. If using a food processor, do not process into a paste, but ingredients should be very finely chopped.

5. Combine ground meat, onion mixture, wine, dried apricots, salt, pepper, turmeric, and ginger in a mixing bowl, and knead mixture until well blended. Fry 1 tablespoon of mixture in a small skillet over medium-high heat. Taste and adjust seasoning, if necessary.

6. Stuff mixture into casings as described on page 24, if using, and twist off into 4-inch links; prick air bubbles with a straight pin or skewer. If time permits, arrange links on a wire rack over a baking sheet and air-dry uncovered in the refrigerator for 1 day before cooking. Alternately, if keeping sausage in bulk, refrigerate mix-

ture for at least 30 minutes to blend flavors.

7. Cook sausages as directed on page 31 to an internal temperature of 160ºF when pierced with an instant-read thermometer or as directed in a specific recipe.

Note: Sausages can be refrigerated up to 2 days or frozen up to 2 months. Once cooked, they can be refrigerated up to 3 days.

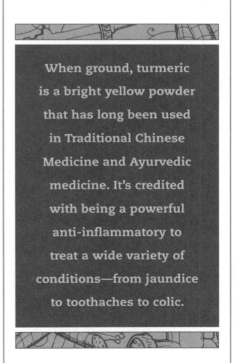

When ground, turmeric is a bright yellow powder that has long been used in Traditional Chinese Medicine and Ayurvedic medicine. It's credited with being a powerful anti-inflammatory to treat a wide variety of conditions—from jaundice to toothaches to colic.

Lamb Sausage with Sun-Dried Tomatoes and Pine Nuts

Makes 2 pounds

Active time:
1 hour, including
30 minutes to
chill meat

Start to finish:
2 hours

VARIATIONS

*Substitute
boneless
beef chuck and
beef fat for lamb.*

*Substitute
chopped blanched
almonds for
pine nuts.*

This sausage—crunchy from toasted pine nuts and flavored with herbs and sun-dried tomatoes—comes from both Middle Eastern and Greek traditions. Serve with stewed garbanzo beans.

Thin sheep sausage casings
    (optional)
1½ pounds boneless lamb shoulder
½ pound lamb fat or beef fat
1½ teaspoons kosher salt
1½ teaspoons ground cumin
1½ teaspoons ground coriander
½ teaspoon cayenne
½ cup pine nuts
¼ cup dry red wine
⅓ cup chopped sun-dried tomatoes
    packed in olive oil, drained
3 garlic cloves, minced
3 tablespoons chopped fresh parsley
1 tablespoon chopped fresh oregano
    or 1 teaspoon dried

1. If using sausage casings, prepare them as directed on page 21.

2. Cut lamb and lamb fat into 1-inch cubes. Place cubes in a mixing bowl, and toss with salt, cumin, coriander, and cayenne. Transfer cubes to a sheet of plastic wrap on a plate and freeze for 30 minutes, or until very firm. While meat chills, toast pine nuts in a small dry skillet over medium heat for 2 to 3 minutes, or until lightly browned. Set aside.

3. Grind lamb and fat through the coarse disk of a meat grinder, or in small batches in a food processor fitted with the steel blade using the on-and-off pulse button. If using a food processor, do not process into a paste, but ingredients should be very finely chopped.

4. Combine ground meat, pine nuts, wine, sun-dried tomatoes, garlic, parsley, and oregano in a mixing bowl, and knead mixture until well blended. Fry 1 tablespoon of mixture in a small skillet over medium-high heat. Taste and adjust seasoning, if necessary.

5. Stuff mixture into casings as described on page 24, if using, and twist off into 5-inch links; prick air bubbles with a straight pin or skewer. If time permits, arrange links on a wire rack over a baking sheet and air-dry uncovered in the refrigerator for 1 day before cooking. Alternately, if keeping sausage in bulk, refrigerate mixture for at least 30 minutes to blend flavors.

6. Cook sausages as directed on page 31 to an internal temperature of 160°F when pierced with an instant-read thermometer or as directed in a specific recipe.

Note: Sausages can be refrigerated up to 2 days or frozen up to 2 months. Once cooked, they can be refrigerated up to 3 days.

Smoky Lamb Sausage with Rosemary, Lemon, and Garlic

Makes 2 pounds

Active time:
1 hour, including
30 minutes to
chill meat

Start to finish:
2 hours

VARIATIONS

Substitute fresh oregano for rosemary.

Substitute beef and beef fat for lamb and lamb fat.

This sausage replicates the aroma and flavors of my favorite way to make lamb on the grill. I insert lots of rosemary, garlic, and lemon zest into a butterflied leg, and then smoke it on the grill. This sausage is my winter version.

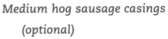

Medium hog sausage casings
   (optional)
1½ pounds boneless lamb shoulder
½ pound lamb fat or pork fat
¼ cup dry red wine
¼ teaspoon liquid smoke
3 tablespoons chopped fresh
   rosemary
4 garlic cloves, minced
2 teaspoons grated lemon zest
1½ teaspoons kosher salt
½ teaspoon freshly ground
   black pepper

1. If using sausage casings, prepare them as directed on page 21.

2. Cut lamb and fat into 1-inch cubes. Place cubes on a sheet of plastic wrap on a plate and freeze for 30 minutes, or until very firm. Combine wine and liquid smoke in a small cup, and stir well.

3. Grind lamb and fat through the coarse disk of a meat grinder, or in

small batches in a food processor fitted with the steel blade using the on-and-off pulse button. If using a food processor, do not process into a paste, but ingredients should be very finely chopped.

4. Combine ground meat, wine, rosemary, garlic, lemon zest, salt, and pepper in a mixing bowl, and knead mixture until well blended. Fry 1 tablespoon of mixture in a small skillet over medium-high heat. Taste and adjust seasoning, if necessary.

5. Stuff mixture into casings as described on page 24, if using, and twist off into 5-inch links; prick air bubbles with a straight pin or skewer. If time permits, arrange links on a wire rack over a baking sheet and air-dry uncovered in the refrigerator for 1 day before cooking. Alternately, if keeping sausage in bulk, refrigerate mixture for at least 30 minutes to blend flavors.

6. Cook sausages as directed on page 31 to an internal temperature of 160°F when pierced with an instant-read thermometer or as directed in a specific recipe.

Note: Sausages can be refrigerated up to 2 days or frozen up to 2 months. Once cooked, they can be refrigerated up to 3 days.

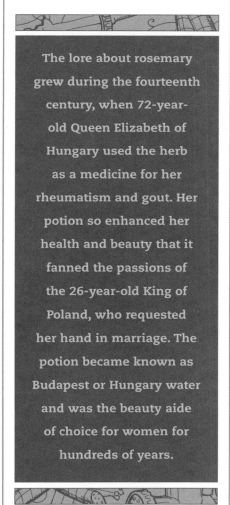

The lore about rosemary grew during the fourteenth century, when 72-year-old Queen Elizabeth of Hungary used the herb as a medicine for her rheumatism and gout. Her potion so enhanced her health and beauty that it fanned the passions of the 26-year-old King of Poland, who requested her hand in marriage. The potion became known as Budapest or Hungary water and was the beauty aide of choice for women for hundreds of years.

North African Lamb Sausage

Makes 2 pounds

Active time:
1 hour, including
30 minutes to
chill meat

Start to finish:
2 hours

VARIATION

*Substitute beef
chuck and beef
fat for lamb.*

I'm always looking for ways to cook with harissa, a fiery condiment common in North African cooking. These sausages are so flavorful that no sauce is necessary. Just a tossed salad is enough.

*Thin sheep sausage casings
   (optional)*
1½ pounds lamb shoulder
½ pound lamb fat or beef fat
¼ cup dry red wine
½ small onion, grated
2 tablespoons harissa
3 tablespoons chopped fresh cilantro
1 tablespoon chopped fresh mint
1½ teaspoons kosher salt
½ teaspoon dried oregano
*½ teaspoon freshly ground
   black pepper*

1. If using sausage casings, prepare them as directed on page 21.

2. Cut lamb and fat into 1-inch cubes. Place cubes on a sheet of plastic wrap on a plate and freeze for 30 minutes, or until very firm. While meat chills, combine wine and harissa in a small bowl, and stir well. Set aside.

3. Grind lamb and fat through the fine disk of a meat grinder, or in small batches in a food processor

fitted with the steel blade using the on-and-off pulse button. If using a food processor, do not process into a paste, but ingredients should be very finely chopped.

4. Combine ground meat, wine mixture, onion, cilantro, mint, salt, oregano, and pepper in a mixing bowl, and knead mixture until well blended. Fry 1 tablespoon of mixture in a small skillet over medium-high heat. Taste and adjust seasoning, if necessary.

5. Stuff mixture into casings as described on page 24, if using, and twist off into 4-inch links; prick air bubbles with a straight pin or skewer. If time permits, arrange links on a wire rack over a baking sheet and air-dry uncovered in the refrigerator for 1 day before cooking. Alternately, if keeping sausage in bulk, refrigerate mixture for at least 30 minutes to blend flavors.

6. Cook sausages as directed on page 31 to an internal temperature of 160°F when pierced with an instant-read thermometer or as directed in a specific recipe.

Note: Sausages can be refrigerated up to 2 days or frozen up to 2 months. Once cooked, they can be refrigerated up to 3 days.

Harissa, found in both tubes and small cans, is a hot North African paste. If you can't find it, here's a recipe: soak 10 to 12 dried red chiles in boiling water for 10 minutes. Drain peppers, and discard stems. Combine chiles, 3 peeled garlic cloves, 2 tablespoons olive oil, and 1 teaspoon each ground coriander, cumin, and caraway seeds in a food processor fitted with the steel blade or in a blender. Puree until smooth, and refrigerate, tightly covered, up to 1 week.

Italian Veal Sausage Marsala

Makes 2 pounds

Active time:
1 hour, including
30 minutes to
chill meat

Start to finish:
2 hours

Veal scallops and mushrooms cooked in a garlicky wine sauce flavored with Marsala is a perennial favorite in my house, so I developed a sausage with the same flavors. Serve these on penne or other pasta.

Medium hog sausage casings (optional)
1½ pounds veal shoulder or boneless veal breast
½ pound veal fat or beef fat
3 tablespoons unsalted butter
1 large shallot, chopped
3 garlic cloves, minced
¼ pound white mushrooms, wiped with a damp paper towel, and chopped
¾ cup dry Marsala wine
¼ cup chopped fresh parsley
1 tablespoon chopped fresh oregano or 1 teaspoon dried
1½ teaspoons kosher salt
½ teaspoon freshly ground black pepper

1. If using sausage casings, prepare them as directed on page 21.

2. Cut veal and fat into 1-inch cubes. Place cubes on a sheet of plastic wrap on a plate and freeze for 30 minutes, or until very firm.

3. While meat chills, heat butter in a medium skillet over medium-high heat. Add shallot, garlic, and mushrooms, and cook, stirring frequently, for 5 minutes, or until mushrooms soften and liquid evaporates. Set aside. Place Marsala in a small saucepan, and bring to a boil over high heat. Reduce the heat to medium, and cook until ¼ cup remains.

VARIATIONS

Substitute 2 pounds boned chicken or turkey thigh meat, with skin attached, for veal and beef fat. Cook sausages to an internal temperature of 165ºF.

Substitute fresh shiitake or Portabello mushrooms for white mushrooms.

Add ½ teaspoon crushed red pepper flakes for spicy sausage.

4. Grind veal and fat through the coarse disk of a meat grinder, or in small batches in a food processor fitted with the steel blade using the on-and-off pulse button. If using a food processor, do not process into a paste, but ingredients should be very finely chopped.

5. Combine ground meat, mushroom mixture, Marsala reduction, parsley, oregano, salt, and pepper in a mixing bowl, and knead mixture until well blended. Fry 1 tablespoon of mixture in a small skillet over medium-high heat. Taste and adjust seasoning, if necessary.

6. Stuff mixture into casings as described on page 24, if using, and twist off into 5-inch links; prick air bubbles with a straight pin or skewer. If time permits, arrange links on a wire rack over a baking sheet and air-dry uncovered in the refrigerator for 1 day before cooking. Alternately, if keeping sausage in bulk, refrigerate mixture for at least 30 minutes to blend flavors.

7. Cook sausages as directed on page 31 to an internal temperature of 160ºF when pierced with an instant-read thermometer or as directed in a specific recipe.

Note: Sausages can be refrigerated up to 2 days or frozen up to 2 months. Once cooked, they can be refrigerated up to 3 days.

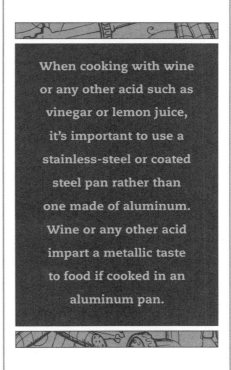

When cooking with wine or any other acid such as vinegar or lemon juice, it's important to use a stainless-steel or coated steel pan rather than one made of aluminum. Wine or any other acid impart a metallic taste to food if cooked in an aluminum pan.

Veal Sausage with Prosciutto, Sage, and Cheese

Makes 2 pounds

Active time:
1 hour, including
30 minutes to
chill meat

Start to finish:
2 hours

This has all the characteristic flavors of my favorite Italian veal dish—saltimbocca. It contains aromatic sage and salty prosciutto mellowed with creamy mozzarella.

Medium hog sausage casings

1½ pounds veal shoulder or boneless veal breast

½ pound veal fat or beef fat

2 garlic cloves, minced

½ cup finely chopped prosciutto

½ cup grated whole-milk mozzarella cheese

¼ cup dry vermouth or dry white wine

3 tablespoons freshly grated Parmesan

2 tablespoons chopped fresh sage

1 teaspoon kosher salt

½ teaspoon freshly ground black pepper

Pinch freshly grated nutmeg

1. Prepare sausage casings as directed on page 21.

2. Cut veal and fat into 1-inch cubes. Place cubes on a sheet of plastic wrap on a plate and freeze for 30 minutes, or until very firm.

3. Grind veal and fat through the fine disk of a meat grinder, or in small batches in a food processor fitted with the steel blade using the on-and-off pulse button. If using a food processor, do not process into a paste, but ingredients should be very finely chopped.

4. Combine ground meat, prosciutto, mozzarella, vermouth, Parmesan, sage, salt, pepper, and nutmeg in a mixing bowl, and knead mixture until well blended. Fry 1 tablespoon of mixture in a small skillet over medium-high heat. Taste and adjust seasoning, if necessary.

5. Stuff mixture into casings as described on page 24 and twist off into 4-inch links; prick air bubbles with a straight pin or skewer. If time permits, arrange links on a wire rack over a baking sheet and air-dry uncovered in the refrigerator for 1 day before cooking.

6. Cook sausages as directed on page 31 to an internal temperature of 160ºF when pierced with an instant-read thermometer or as directed in a specific recipe.

Note: Sausages can be refrigerated up to 2 days or frozen up to 2 months. Once cooked, they can be refrigerated up to 3 days.

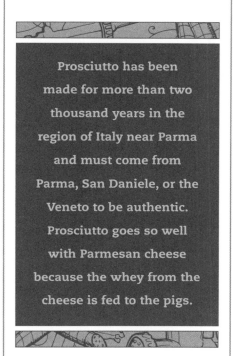

Prosciutto has been made for more than two thousand years in the region of Italy near Parma and must come from Parma, San Daniele, or the Veneto to be authentic. Prosciutto goes so well with Parmesan cheese because the whey from the cheese is fed to the pigs.

Veal Sausage Marengo

Makes 2 pounds

Active time:
1 hour, including
30 minutes to
chill meat

Start to finish:
2 hours

VARIATIONS

Substitute
2 pounds boned
chicken or turkey
thigh meat, with
skin attached, for
veal and beef fat.
Cook sausages
to an internal
temperature of
165ºF.

Substitute 1½
pounds pork butt
or boneless spare
ribs and ½ pound
pork fat for veal
and veal fat.

Aromatic orange zest joined with herbs, wine, tomato, and mushrooms invigorate the taste and texture of delicate veal. This sausage is an excellent way to top a salad.

Medium hog sausage casings
   (optional)
1½ pounds veal shoulder or
   boneless veal breast
½ pound veal fat or beef fat
3 tablespoons unsalted butter
1 large shallot, chopped
3 garlic cloves, minced
¼ pound white mushrooms, wiped
   with a damp paper towel
   and chopped
¼ cup dry vermouth or dry
   white wine
1 tablespoon tomato paste
2 tablespoons chopped fresh parsley
2 teaspoons grated orange zest

1½ teaspoons kosher salt
½ teaspoon freshly ground
   black pepper
½ teaspoon dried thyme
½ teaspoon dried tarragon

1. If using sausage casings, prepare them as directed on page 21.

2. Cut veal and fat into 1-inch cubes. Place cubes on a sheet of plastic wrap on a plate and freeze for 30 minutes, or until very firm.

3. While meat chills, heat butter in a medium skillet over medium-high heat. Add shallot, garlic, and mushrooms, and cook, stirring frequently, for 5 minutes, or until mushrooms soften and liquid evaporates. Set aside. Combine vermouth and tomato paste in a small cup, and stir to dissolve tomato paste.

4. Grind veal and fat through the coarse disk of a meat grinder, or in small batches in a food processor

fitted with the steel blade using the on-and-off pulse button. If using a food processor, do not process into a paste, but ingredients should be very finely chopped.

5. Combine ground meat, mushroom mixture, vermouth mixture, parsley, orange zest, salt, pepper, thyme, and tarragon in a mixing bowl, and knead mixture until well blended. Fry 1 tablespoon of mixture in a small skillet over medium-high heat. Taste and adjust seasoning, if necessary.

6. Stuff mixture into casings as described on page 24, if using, and twist off into 5-inch links; prick air bubbles with a straight pin or skewer. If time permits, arrange links on a wire rack over a baking sheet and air-dry uncovered in the refrigerator for 1 day before cooking. Alternately, if keeping sausage in bulk, refrigerate mixture for at least 30 minutes to blend flavors.

7. Cook sausages as directed on page 31 to an internal temperature of 160°F when pierced with an instant-read thermometer or as directed in a specific recipe.

Note: Sausages can be refrigerated up to 2 days or frozen up to 2 months. Once cooked, they can be refrigerated up to 3 days.

Veal Marengo, and its first cousin, Chicken Marengo, were supposedly created by Napoleon's chef after the 1800 Battle of Marengo in Northern Italy, during which the French defeated the advancing Austrian forces. This battle also plays a role in Puccini's opera *Tosca*, the action of which surrounds Napoleon's alleged defeat in Act I and real victory in Act II.

Dilled Veal Sausage

Makes 2 pounds

Active time:
1 hour, including
30 minutes to
chill meat

Start to finish:
2 hours

VARIATIONS

Substitute
2 pounds boned
chicken or turkey
thigh meat, with
skin attached, for
veal and beef fat.
Cook sausages
to an internal
temperature of
165ºF.

Substitute 1½
pounds pork butt
or boneless spare
ribs and ½ pound
pork fat for veal
and veal fat.

Veal and dill are frequently paired in Scandinavian cooking. These subtle poached sausages are ethereal topped with a simple cream sauce, served with steamed asparagus or green beans.

Medium hog sausage casings
1½ pounds veal shoulder or
    boneless veal breast
½ pound veal fat or beef fat
3 tablespoons unsalted butter
½ small onion, chopped
1 large egg
2 tablespoons whole milk
¼ cup plain breadcrumbs
¼ cup chopped fresh dill
1½ teaspoons kosher salt
½ teaspoon freshly ground
    black pepper

¼ teaspoon freshly grated nutmeg
Pinch ground allspice
Pinch ground ginger

1. Prepare sausage casings as directed on page 21.

2. Cut veal and fat into 1-inch cubes. Place cubes on a sheet of plastic wrap on a plate and freeze for 30 minutes, or until very firm.

3. While meat chills, heat butter in a small skillet over medium heat. Add onion, and cook, stirring frequently, for 3 to 5 minutes, or until onion softens. Set aside. Combine egg and milk in a small cup, and beat well. Stir in breadcrumbs, and set aside.

4. Grind veal and fat through the fine disk of a meat grinder, or in small batches in a food processor fitted with the steel blade using the on-and-off pulse button. If using a food processor, do not process into

a paste, but ingredients should be very finely chopped.

5. Combine ground meat, onion mixture, egg mixture, dill, salt, pepper, nutmeg, allspice, and ginger in a mixing bowl, and knead mixture until well blended. Fry 1 tablespoon of mixture in a small skillet over medium-high heat. Taste and adjust seasoning, if necessary.

6. Stuff mixture into casings as described on page 24 and twist off into 5-inch links; prick air bubbles with a straight pin or skewer. If time permits, arrange links on a wire rack over a baking sheet and air-dry uncovered in the refrigerator for 1 day before cooking.

7. To poach sausages, bring a large pot of salted water to a boil over high heat. Add sausages, and maintain water at a bare simmer. Cook sausages for 20 to 25 minutes, or until firm. Remove one sausage to a plate with tongs and insert an instant-read thermometer. If the temperature is 160°F, sausages are done. If not, return to the pot and continue cooking. Remove sausages from the pan with tongs, and serve immediately or cool to room temperature, lightly covered with plastic wrap, and refrigerate.

Note: Sausages can be refrigerated up to 2 days or frozen up to 2 months. Once cooked, they can be refrigerated up to 3 days.

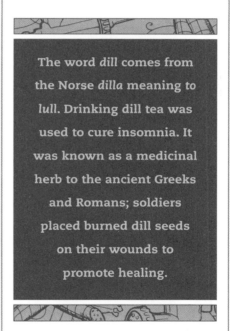

The word *dill* comes from the Norse *dilla* meaning *to lull*. Drinking dill tea was used to cure insomnia. It was known as a medicinal herb to the ancient Greeks and Romans; soldiers placed burned dill seeds on their wounds to promote healing.

Brandied Venison Sausage

Makes 2 pounds

Active time:
1 hour, including
30 minutes to
chill meat

Start to finish:
2 hours

VARIATIONS

Substitute beef for venison.

Substitute Grand Marnier or Sambuca for brandy.

The rich flavor of venison has made it a favorite game meat for centuries, and the spices and heady brandy in this recipe create a good foil for its inherent richness. Serve with Herbed Marinara Sauce (page 478) or Sherried Tomato Sauce (page 480).

Medium hog sausage casings
    (optional)
1½ pounds venison shoulder
½ pound beef fat
1 tablespoon fennel seeds
3 tablespoons brandy
1 large shallot, chopped
3 garlic cloves, minced
1 tablespoon paprika
1½ teaspoons kosher salt
¾ teaspoon freshly ground
    black pepper
½ teaspoon dried thyme
½ teaspoon dried sage
¼ teaspoon freshly grated nutmeg

1. If using sausage casings, prepare them as directed on page 21.

2. Cut venison and fat into 1-inch cubes. Place cubes on a sheet of plastic wrap on a plate and freeze for 30 minutes, or until very firm. While meat chills, grind fennel seeds in a mortar and pestle or in a spice or clean coffee grinder. Set aside.

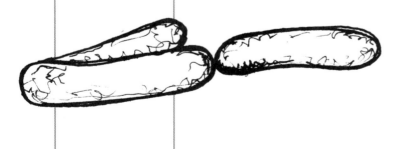

3. Grind venison and fat through the fine disk of a meat grinder, or in small batches in a food processor fitted with the steel blade using the on-and-off pulse button. If using a food processor, do not process into a paste, but ingredients should be very finely chopped.

4. Combine ground meat, fennel, brandy, shallot, garlic, paprika, salt, pepper, thyme, sage, and nutmeg in a mixing bowl, and knead mixture until well blended. Fry 1 tablespoon of mixture in a small skillet over medium-high heat. Taste and adjust seasoning, if necessary.

5. Stuff mixture into casings as described on page 24, if using, and twist off into 5-inch links; prick air bubbles with a straight pin or skewer. If time permits, arrange links on a wire rack over a baking sheet and air-dry uncovered in the refrigerator for 1 day before cooking. Alternately, if keeping sausage in bulk, refrigerate mixture for at least 30 minutes to blend flavors.

6. Cook sausages as directed on page 31 to an internal temperature of 160°F when pierced with an instant-read thermometer or as directed in a specific recipe.

Note: Sausages can be refrigerated up to 2 days or frozen up to 2 months. Once cooked, they can be refrigerated up to 3 days.

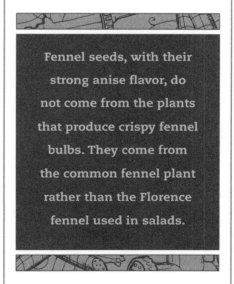

Fennel seeds, with their strong anise flavor, do not come from the plants that produce crispy fennel bulbs. They come from the common fennel plant rather than the Florence fennel used in salads.

Smoky Southwestern Bison Sausage

Makes 2 pounds

Active time:
1 hour, including
30 minutes to
chill meat

Start to finish:
5 hours

VARIATIONS

Substitute beef for bison.

Substitute 1 large jalapeño or serrano chile for chipotle chile; cook it with onion and garlic.

Bison has been showing up in supermarkets, and its rich flavor works well with the assertive seasonings of the Southwest. Serve these sausages with some Mexican rice.

Medium hog sausage casings
1½ pounds bison shoulder
½ pound beef fat
2 tablespoons olive oil
½ cup chopped red onion
3 garlic cloves, minced
½ cup beer
¼ teaspoon liquid smoke
¼ cup chopped fresh cilantro
1 chipotle chile in adobo sauce,
    finely chopped
2 tablespoons smoked Spanish
    paprika
2 tablespoons chili powder
2 teaspoons ground cumin
1½ teaspoons kosher salt
¼ teaspoon ground allspice
Pinch ground cinnamon

1. Prepare sausage casings as directed on page 21.

2. Cut bison and fat into 1-inch cubes. Place cubes on a sheet of plastic wrap on a plate and freeze for 30 minutes, or until very firm.

3. While meat chills, heat oil in a small skillet over medium-high heat. Add onion and garlic, and cook, stirring frequently, for 3 minutes, or until onion is translucent. Set aside. Combine beer and liquid smoke in a small cup, and set aside.

4. Grind bison and fat through the fine disk of a meat grinder, or in small batches in a food processor fitted with the steel blade using the

on-and-off pulse button. If using a food processor, do not process into a paste, but ingredients should be very finely chopped.

5. Combine ground meat, onion mixture, beer, cilantro, chipotle chile, paprika, chili powder, cumin, salt, allspice, and cinnamon in a mixing bowl, and knead mixture until well blended. Fry 1 tablespoon of mixture in a small skillet over medium-high heat. Taste and adjust seasoning, if necessary.

6. Stuff mixture into casings as described on page 24 and twist off into 4-inch links; prick air bubbles with a straight pin or skewer. If time permits, arrange links on a wire rack over a baking sheet and air-dry uncovered in the refrigerator for 1 day before cooking.

7. Preheat the oven to 200°F, line a baking sheet with aluminum foil, and arrange sausages on a cooling rack on top of the baking sheet. Bake sausages for 4 to 5 hours, or to an internal temperature of 160°F when pierced with an instant-read thermometer. Remove sausages from the pan with tongs, and serve immediately or cool to room temperature, lightly covered with plastic wrap, and refrigerate.

Note: Sausages can be refrigerated up to 2 days or frozen up to 2 months. Once cooked, they can be refrigerated up to 3 days.

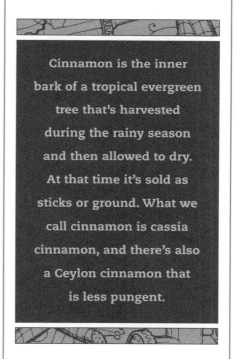

Cinnamon is the inner bark of a tropical evergreen tree that's harvested during the rainy season and then allowed to dry. At that time it's sold as sticks or ground. What we call cinnamon is cassia cinnamon, and there's also a Ceylon cinnamon that is less pungent.

DOUBLE YOUR PLEASURE:

SAUSAGES MADE WITH MORE THAN ONE MEAT

Most of the sausages in this book are made with one kind of meat and a related fat. It can be a red meat, a white meat, poultry, or even fish, but it's a singular flavor. In this chapter, they're all made from a combination of meats that complement one another to create the best flavor for the particular sausage.

Mixing meats for sausage is nothing new. Many supermarkets sell a pre-ground mixture of pork, beef, and veal called "meatloaf mix." In the case of these recipes, however, it should be called "sausage mix." Mixing beef and pork is quite common; the beef adds richness while the pork is more subtle and lends a delicacy to the mixture.

Most of these recipes are drawn from European cuisines; many German and other Eastern European sausages use more than one meat, as does the famed French *boudin blanc*. And, there are some American and Asian combos as well.

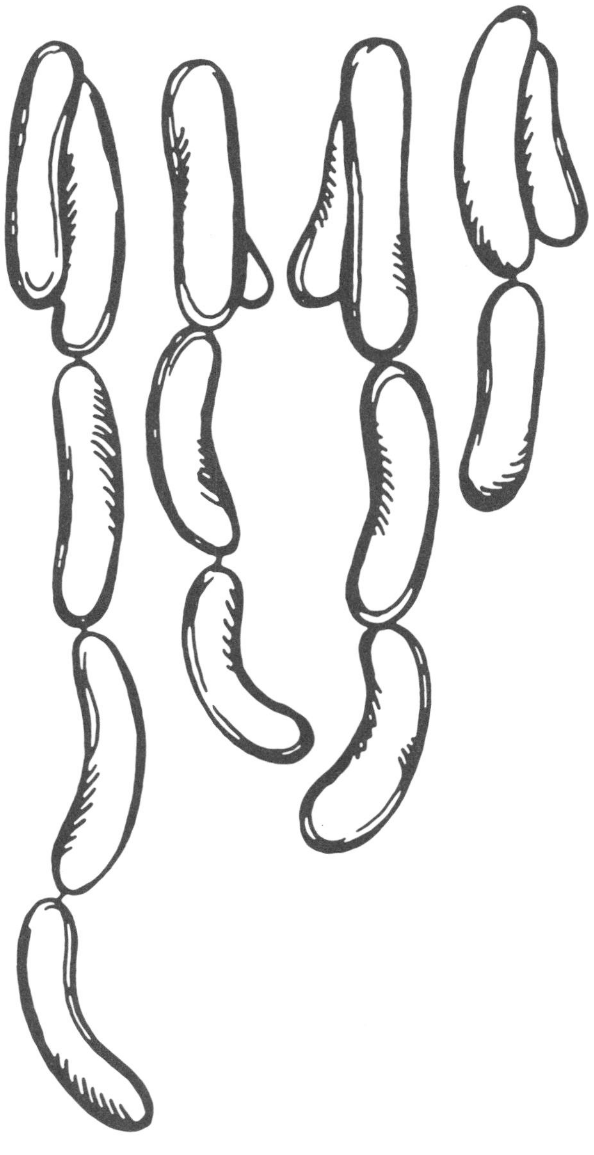

Boudin Blanc

Makes 2½ pounds

Active time:
1 hour, including
30 minutes to
chill meat

Start to finish:
1½ hours

I adore these subtly seasoned French sausages so much that I began making them years ago. They're light with a delicate texture, and all you need is a good mustard to call it a meal and you'll feel as if you're dining along in a Parisian brasserie.

Medium hog sausage casings
1 pound boneless chicken breast
    with skin attached
¾ pound pork butt or boneless
    country ribs
¼ pound pork fat
3 tablespoons unsalted butter
1 large onion, diced
2½ cups whole milk, divided
½ cup plain breadcrumbs
1 large egg
1 large egg white

½ cup heavy cream
1½ teaspoons kosher salt
¼ teaspoon freshly ground
    white pepper
¼ teaspoon freshly grated nutmeg
3 tablespoons olive oil

1. Prepare sausage casings as directed on page 21.

2. Cut chicken, pork, and pork fat 1-inch cubes. Place cubes on a sheet of plastic wrap on a plate and freeze for 30 minutes, or until very firm.

3. While meats chill, heat butter in a small skillet over medium heat. Add onion and cook onion, covered, over low heat, stirring occasionally, for 10 minutes, or until onion softens. Stir ½ cup milk and breadcrumbs together in a small bowl, and set aside.

4. Finely chop meats and fat in a food processor fitted with the steel blade, using on and off pulsing.

Add onion, egg, egg white, and cream to the food processor and puree until smooth. Scrape mixture into a mixing bowl.

5. Add salt, pepper, nutmeg, and breadcrumb mixture to the mixing bowl, and stir well. Fry 1 tablespoon of mixture in a small skillet over medium-high heat. Taste and adjust seasoning, if necessary.

6. Stuff mixture into casings *very loosely* as described on page 24, and twist off into 5-inch links; sausages will expand as they cook. Prick air bubbles with a straight pin or skewer. Tie links with kitchen twine. If time permits, arrange links on a wire rack over a baking sheet and air-dry uncovered in the refrigerator for 1 day before cooking.

7. To poach sausages, bring remaining 2 cups milk and 3 cups salted water to a boil over high heat. Add sausages, and maintain water at a bare simmer. Cook sausages for 20 to 25 minutes, or until firm. Remove one sausage to a plate with tongs and insert an instant-read thermometer. If the temperature is 165°F, sausages are done. If not, return to the pot and continue cooking. Remove sausages from the pan with tongs.

8. To serve immediately, heat oil in a large skillet over medium-high heat. Brown sausages on all sides. To serve later, cool sausages to room temperature, lightly covered with plastic wrap, and refrigerate. Brown them just prior to serving.

Note: Sausages can be refrigerated up to 2 days or frozen up to 2 months. Once cooked, they can be refrigerated up to 3 days.

The best place to store eggs is in their cardboard carton. The carton helps prevent moisture loss, and it shields the eggs from absorbing odors from other foods.

Bratwurst

Makes 2 pounds

- - - - - - - - - - - - - - - - - - -

**Active time:
1 hour, including
30 minutes to
chill meat**

- - - - - - - - - - - - - - - - - - -

**Start to finish:
1½ hours**

VARIATIONS

*Grill or broil
sausages as
directed on
page 33 instead
of poaching them.*

*Poach brats in
beer rather than
water. Bring 2
(12-ounce) canfuls
to a boil, and
simmer ½ small
onion in beer for
10 minutes. Then
add sausages and
cook as above.*

While "brats" arrived in the Midwest with the large wave of German immigrants in the nineteenth century, they're now as American as hot dogs. A touch of caraway is about the only spicing, so kids love them too.

Medium hog sausage casings
¾ *pound pork butt or boneless
    country ribs*
¾ *pound boneless veal shoulder
    or veal breast*
½ *pound pork fat*
1 *teaspoon caraway seeds*
1½ *teaspoons kosher salt*
½ *teaspoon freshly ground
    white pepper*
½ *teaspoon ground ginger*
½ *teaspoon dried thyme*
2 *tablespoons nonfat dry milk
    powder*

1. Prepare sausage casings as directed on page 21.

2. Cut pork, veal, and pork fat into 1-inch cubes. Place cubes in a mixing bowl, and toss with caraway seeds, salt, pepper, ginger, and thyme. Transfer cubes to a sheet of plastic wrap on a plate and freeze for 30 minutes, or until very firm.

3. Grind meats and fat through the fine disk of a meat grinder, or in small batches in a food processor fitted with the steel blade using the on-and-off pulse button. If using a food processor, do not process into a paste, but ingredients should be very finely chopped.

4. Combine ground meat and milk powder in a mixing bowl, and knead mixture until well blended. Fry 1 tablespoon of mixture in a small skillet over medium-high heat. Taste and adjust seasoning, if necessary.

5. Stuff mixture into casings as described on page 24 and twist off into 5-inch links; prick air bubbles with a straight pin or skewer. If time permits, arrange links on a wire rack over a baking sheet and air-dry uncovered in the refrigerator for 1 day before cooking.

6. To poach sausages, bring a large pot of salted water to a boil over high heat. Add sausages, and maintain water at a bare simmer. Cook sausages for 20 to 25 minutes, or until firm. Remove one sausage to a plate with tongs and insert an instant-read thermometer. If the temperature is 160°F, sausages are done. If not, return to the pot and continue cooking. Remove sausages from the pan with tongs, and serve immediately or cool to room temperature, lightly covered with plastic wrap, and refrigerate.

Note: Sausages can be refrigerated up to 2 days or frozen up to 2 months. Once cooked, they can be refrigerated up to 3 days.

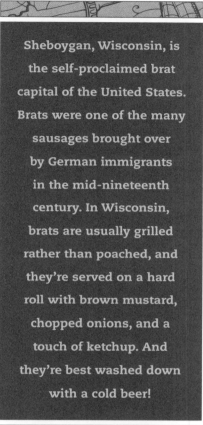

Sheboygan, Wisconsin, is the self-proclaimed brat capital of the United States. Brats were one of the many sausages brought over by German immigrants in the mid-nineteenth century. In Wisconsin, brats are usually grilled rather than poached, and they're served on a hard roll with brown mustard, chopped onions, and a touch of ketchup. And they're best washed down with a cold beer!

Bockwurst

Bockwurst is a mildly seasoned first cousin of bratwurst and made with leeks or onions. Serve with a bean salad or baked beans.

Makes 2 pounds

Active time:
1 hour, including 30 minutes to chill meat

Start to finish:
1½ hours

VARIATION

Substitute 2 pounds boned chicken or turkey thigh meat, with skin attached, for pork, veal, and pork fat. Cook sausages to an internal temperature of 165ºF.

Medium hog sausage casings
¾ pound pork butt or boneless
    country ribs
¾ pound boneless veal shoulder
    or breast
½ pound pork fat
2 tablespoons unsalted butter
1 large leek, white part only, finely
    chopped and rinsed
½ cup whole milk
1 large egg yolk
3 tablespoons chopped fresh parsley
2 tablespoons chopped fresh chives
1½ teaspoons kosher salt
½ teaspoon freshly ground
    white pepper
¼ teaspoon ground mace
¼ teaspoon ground ginger

1. Prepare sausage casings as directed on page 21.

2. Cut pork, veal, and pork fat into 1-inch cubes. Place cubes on a sheet of plastic wrap on a plate and freeze for 30 minutes, or until very firm.

3. While meats chill, heat butter in a small skillet over medium heat. Add leek, and cook over low heat, covered, stirring occasionally, for 10 minutes, or until soft. Set aside. Combine milk and egg yolk in a small mixing bowl, and whisk well.

4. Grind meats and fat through the fine disk of a meat grinder, or in small batches in a food processor fitted with the steel blade using the on-and-off pulse button. If using a food processor, do not process into a paste, but ingredients should be very finely chopped.

5. Combine ground meat, leeks, milk mixture, parsley, chives, salt,

pepper, mace, and ginger in a mixing bowl, and knead mixture until well blended. Fry 1 tablespoon of mixture in a small skillet over medium-high heat. Taste and adjust seasoning, if necessary.

6. Stuff mixture into casings as described on page 24 and twist off into 5-inch links; prick air bubbles with a straight pin or skewer. If time permits, arrange links on a wire rack over a baking sheet and air-dry uncovered in the refrigerator for 1 day before cooking.

7. To poach sausages, bring a large pot of salted water to a boil over high heat. Add sausages, and maintain water at a bare simmer. Cook sausages for 20 to 25 minutes, or until firm. Remove one sausage to a plate with tongs and insert an instant-read thermometer. If the temperature is 160°F, sausages are done. If not, return to the pot and continue cooking. Remove sausages from the pan with tongs, and serve immediately or cool to room temperature, lightly covered with plastic wrap, and refrigerate.

Note: Sausages can be refrigerated up to 2 days or frozen up to 2 months. Once cooked, they can be refrigerated up to 3 days.

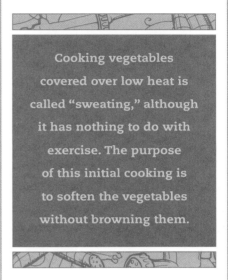

Cooking vegetables covered over low heat is called "sweating," although it has nothing to do with exercise. The purpose of this initial cooking is to soften the vegetables without browning them.

Hungarian Sausage

Makes 2 pounds

Active time:
1 hour, including
30 minutes to
chill meat

Start to finish:
1½ hours

VARIATION

*Substitute
2 pounds boned
chicken or turkey
thigh meat, with
skin attached,
for beef, pork,
and pork fat.
Cook sausages
to an internal
temperature
of 165ºF.*

These poached sausages are another Eastern European contribution. Use them in any baked bean dish, including Cassoulet (page 348).

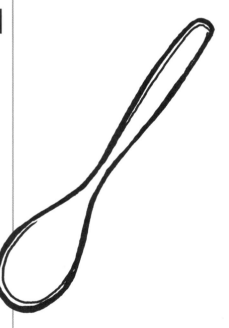

Thin sheep sausage casings
¾ pound beef chuck or brisket
½ pound pork butt or boneless
    country ribs
½ pound pork fat
¼ cup heavy cream
3 tablespoons nonfat dry milk
    powder
2 garlic cloves, minced
1 tablespoon paprika
1½ teaspoons kosher salt
1 teaspoon ground coriander
½ teaspoon freshly ground
    black pepper
¼ teaspoon freshly grated nutmeg

1. Prepare sausage casings as directed on page 21.

2. Cut beef, pork, and pork fat into 1-inch cubes. Place cubes on a sheet of plastic wrap on a plate and freeze for 30 minutes, or until very firm.

3. Grind meat and fat through the fine disk of a meat grinder, or in small batches in a food processor

fitted with the steel blade using the on-and-off pulse button. If using a food processor, do not process into a paste, but ingredients should be very finely chopped.

4. Combine ground meats, cream, milk powder, garlic, paprika, salt, coriander, pepper, and nutmeg in a mixing bowl, and knead mixture until well blended. Fry 1 tablespoon of mixture in a small skillet over medium-high heat. Taste and adjust seasoning, if necessary.

5. Stuff mixture into casings as described on page 24 and twist off into 4-inch links; prick air bubbles with a straight pin or skewer. If time permits, arrange links on a wire rack over a baking sheet and air-dry uncovered in the refrigerator for 1 day before cooking.

6. To poach sausages, bring a large pot of salted water to a boil over high heat. Add sausages, and maintain water at a bare simmer. Cook sausages for 20 to 25 minutes, or until firm. Remove one sausage to a plate with tongs and insert an instant-read thermometer. If the temperature is 160°F, sausages are done. If not, return to the pot and continue cooking. Remove sausages from the pan with tongs, and serve immediately or cool to room temperature, lightly covered with plastic wrap, and refrigerate.

Note: Sausages can be refrigerated up to 2 days or frozen up to 2 months. Once cooked, they can be refrigerated up to 3 days.

Sausages are sometimes made with dried milk powder, which keeps the sausages moist and flavorful. The powder rehydrates the meats' juices and keeps them in the sausages.

Smoked Kielbasa

Makes 2 pounds

Active time:
1 hour, including
30 minutes to
chill meat

Start to finish:
5 hours

VARIATIONS

Substitute
2 pounds boned
chicken or turkey
thigh meat, with
skin attached, for
pork and pork fat.
Cook sausages
to an internal
temperature
of 165ºF.

Omit liquid smoke,
and hot smoke
sausages as
described on
page 34.

The slightly garlicky-smoky flavor in these sausages is what most of us think as kielbasa. By slowly baking them in the oven they're easy to make.

Medium hog sausage casings
1 pound boneless beef chuck or
    beef brisket
½ pound pork butt or boneless
    country ribs
½ pound pork fat
2 tablespoons smoked Spanish
    paprika
2 tablespoons nonfat dry milk
    powder
1½ teaspoons yellow mustard seed
1½ teaspoons kosher salt
½ teaspoon freshly ground
    black pepper
½ teaspoon dried thyme
¼ teaspoon freshly grated nutmeg
¼ teaspoon liquid smoke
¼ cup beer
3 garlic cloves, minced

1. Prepare sausage casings as directed on page 21.

2. Cut beef, pork, and pork fat into 1-inch cubes. Place cubes in a mixing bowl, and toss with paprika, milk powder, mustard seed, salt, pepper, thyme, and nutmeg. Transfer cubes to a sheet of plastic wrap on a plate and freeze for 30 minutes, or until very firm. While meats chill, stir liquid smoke into beer. Set aside.

3. Grind meat and fat through the fine disk of a meat grinder, or in small batches in a food processor fitted with the steel blade using the on-and-off pulse button. If using a food processor, do not process into a paste, but ingredients should be very finely chopped.

4. Combine ground meat, beer mixture, and garlic in a mixing bowl, and knead mixture until well blended. Fry 1 tablespoon of mixture in a small skillet over medium-high heat. Taste and adjust seasoning, if necessary.

5. Stuff mixture into casings as described on page 24 and twist off into 5-inch links; prick air bubbles with a straight pin or skewer. If time permits, arrange links on a wire rack over a baking sheet and air-dry uncovered in the refrigerator for 1 day before cooking.

6. Preheat the oven to 200°F, line a baking sheet with aluminum foil, and arrange sausages on a cooling rack on top of the baking sheet. Bake sausages for 4 to 5 hours, or to an internal temperature of 160°F when pierced with an instant-read thermometer. Remove sausages from the pan with tongs, and serve immediately or cool to room temperature, lightly covered with plastic wrap, and refrigerate.

Note: Sausages can be refrigerated up to 2 days or frozen up to 2 months. Once cooked, they can be refrigerated up to 3 days.

The Roman Catholic rituals of feasting after fasting and eating no meat were introduced to Poland around 900 CE. Eating kielbasa at a feast, especially at Easter, has been part of the country's culinary culture for many centuries.

Smoky Mettwurst

Makes 2 pounds

Active time:
1 hour, including
30 minutes to
chill meat

Start to finish:
5 hours

Metts like Brats are interwoven into America's love of sausage and summers; in the Midwest they're sold at baseball games along with brats and hot dogs. These contain some mustard seed to provide a little kick.

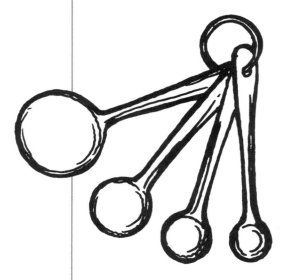

Medium hog sausage casings

1 pound beef chuck or brisket

½ pound pork butt or boneless
    country ribs

½ pound pork fat

½ teaspoon liquid smoke

¼ cup beer

3 garlic cloves, minced

1½ teaspoons kosher salt

1 teaspoon yellow mustard seed

½ teaspoon freshly ground
    black pepper

¼ teaspoon celery seed

¼ teaspoon freshly grated nutmeg

¼ teaspoon ground ginger

¼ teaspoon ground allspice

1. Prepare sausage casings as directed on page 21.

2. Cut beef, pork, and pork fat into 1-inch cubes. Place cubes on a sheet of plastic wrap on a plate and freeze for 30 minutes, or until very firm. While meats chill, stir liquid smoke into beer, and set aside.

VARIATIONS

*Substitute
2 pounds boned
chicken or turkey
thigh meat, with
skin attached,
for pork and pork
fat. Cook sausage
to an internal
temperature of
165ºF.*

*Omit liquid
smoke, and poach
sausages. Bring a
large pot of salted
water to a boil.
Add sausages,
and maintain
water at a bare
simmer. Cook
sausages for 20
to 25 minutes, or
until firm.*

3. Grind meat and fat through the fine disk of a meat grinder, or in small batches in a food processor fitted with the steel blade using the on-and-off pulse button. If using a food processor, do not process into a paste, but ingredients should be very finely chopped.

4. Combine ground meat, beer mixture, garlic, salt, mustard seed, pepper, celery seed, nutmeg, ginger, and allspice in a mixing bowl, and knead mixture until well blended. Fry 1 tablespoon of mixture in a small skillet over medium-high heat. Taste and adjust seasoning, if necessary.

5. Stuff mixture into casings as described on page 24 and twist off into 5-inch links; prick air bubbles with a straight pin or skewer. If time permits, arrange links on a wire rack over a baking sheet and air-dry uncovered in the refrigerator for 1 day before cooking.

6. Preheat the oven to 200ºF, line a baking sheet with aluminum foil, and arrange sausages on a cooling rack on top of the baking sheet.

Bake sausages for 4 to 5 hours, or to an internal temperature of 160ºF when pierced with an instant-read thermometer. Remove sausages from the pan with tongs, and serve immediately or cool to room temperature, lightly covered with plastic wrap, and refrigerate.

Note: Sausages can be refrigerated up to 2 days or frozen up to 2 months. Once cooked, they can be refrigerated up to 3 days.

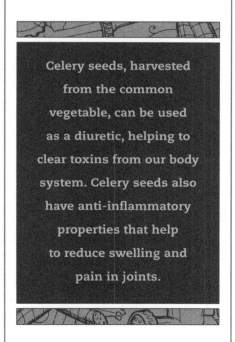

Celery seeds, harvested from the common vegetable, can be used as a diuretic, helping to clear toxins from our body system. Celery seeds also have anti-inflammatory properties that help to reduce swelling and pain in joints.

Minnesota Boudin

Makes 2 pounds

Active time:
1 hour, including
30 minutes to
chill meat

Start to finish:
1½ hours

VARIATIONS

Substitute
veal shoulder
or boneless
veal breast for
chicken.

Substitute dried
currants, chopped
dried apricots, or
raisins for dried
cranberries.

We usually think New Orleans, not Minnesota, when it comes to boudin, but adding wild rice to sausage is a Midwest-meets-South concept.

Medium hog sausage casings
1 pound boneless chicken or turkey
*   thigh with skin attached*
½ pound pork butt or boneless
*   country ribs*
½ pound pork fat
2 tablespoons vegetable oil
1 large shallot, chopped
2 garlic cloves, minced
1 cup cooked wild rice
⅓ cup chopped dried cranberries
2 tablespoons apple juice
*   concentrate*
1 tablespoon cider vinegar
1½ teaspoons kosher salt
½ teaspoon freshly ground
*   black pepper*
½ teaspoon dried sage
½ teaspoon dried thyme
¼ teaspoon ground allspice

1. Prepare sausage casings as directed on page 21.

2. Cut chicken, pork, and pork fat into 1-inch cubes. Place cubes on a sheet of plastic wrap on a plate and freeze for 30 minutes, or until very firm.

3. While meats chill, heat oil in a small skillet over medium-high heat. Add shallot and garlic, and cook, stirring frequently, for 3 minutes, or until shallot is translucent. Set aside.

4. Grind meats and fat through the coarse disk of a meat grinder, or in small batches in a food processor fitted with the steel blade using the on-and-off pulse button. If using a food processor, do not process into a paste, but ingredients should be very finely chopped.

5. Combine ground meats, shallot mixture, wild rice, dried cranberries, apple juice concentrate, vinegar, salt, pepper, sage, thyme, and allspice in a mixing bowl, and knead mixture until well blended. Fry 1 tablespoon of mixture in a small skillet over medium-high heat. Taste and adjust seasoning, if necessary.

6. Stuff mixture into casings as described on page 24 and twist off into 5-inch links; prick air bubbles with a straight pin or skewer. If time permits, arrange links on a wire rack over a baking sheet and air-dry uncovered in the refrigerator for 1 day before cooking.

7. To poach sausages, bring a large pot of salted water to a boil over high heat. Add sausages, and maintain water at a bare simmer. Cook sausages for 20 to 25 minutes, or until firm. Remove one sausage to a plate with tongs and insert an instant-read thermometer. If the temperature is 165°F, sausages are done. If not, return to the pot and continue cooking. Remove sausages from the pan with tongs, and serve immediately or cool to room temperature, lightly covered with plastic wrap, and refrigerate.

Note: Sausages can be refrigerated up to 2 days or frozen up to 2 months. Once cooked, they can be refrigerated up to 3 days.

Wild rice, native to the Chippewa Indian lands in the lake country of Minnesota, is America's only native species and is a distant cousin of Asian rice. It is really an aquatic grass, *Zizania aquatica*, and was named wild rice because of the visual similarity to familiar rice fields. It contains more protein than most rice and is processed by first fermenting it to develop the characteristic nutty flavor and then roasted until dark in color.

Cajun Boudin

Makes 2½ pounds

Active time:
1 hour, including
30 minutes to
chill meat

Start to finish:
1½ hours

VARIATIONS

Substitute 2 pounds boned chicken or turkey thigh meat, with skin attached, for pork, beef, and pork fat. Cook sausages to an internal temperature of 165ºF.

Omit fresh chiles for milder sausages.

Here's an authentic spicy Cajun sausage spicy and loaded with vegetables, too. In Louisiana these are eaten out of hand and used in cooking.

Medium hog sausage casings
1 pound pork butt or boneless
*   country ribs*
¾ pound beef chuck
¼ pound pork fat
3 tablespoons olive oil
1 medium onion, chopped
½ red bell pepper, seeds and ribs
*   removed, and chopped*
1 celery rib, chopped
1 to 3 jalapeño or serrano chiles,
*   seeds and ribs removed,*
*   and finely chopped*
3 garlic cloves, minced
2 cups cooked white rice
3 scallions, white parts and 3 inches
*   of green tops, chopped*
3 tablespoons chopped fresh parsley
2 tablespoons paprika
1½ teaspoons kosher salt
1 teaspoon dried oregano
1 teaspoon dried thyme
½ teaspoon cayenne

1. Prepare sausage casings as directed on page 21.

2. Cut pork, beef, and pork fat into 1-inch cubes. Place cubes on a sheet of plastic wrap on a plate and freeze for 30 minutes, or until very firm.

3. While meats chill, heat oil in a skillet over medium-high heat. Add onion, red bell pepper, celery, chiles, and garlic. Cook, stirring frequently, for 3 minutes, or until onion is translucent. Set aside.

4. Grind meat and fat through the fine disk of a meat grinder, or in small batches in a food processor fitted with the steel blade using the on-and-off pulse button. If using a

food processor, do not process into a paste, but ingredients should be very finely chopped.

5. Combine ground meat, vegetable mixture, rice, scallions, parsley, paprika, salt, oregano, thyme, and cayenne in a mixing bowl, and knead mixture until well blended. Fry 1 tablespoon of mixture in a small skillet over medium-high heat. Taste and adjust seasoning, if necessary.

6. Stuff mixture into casings as described on page 24 and twist off into 5-inch links; prick air bubbles with a straight pin or skewer. Tie links with kitchen twine. If time permits, arrange links on a wire rack over a baking sheet and air-dry uncovered in the refrigerator for 1 day before cooking.

7. To poach sausages, bring a large pot of salted water to a boil over high heat. Add sausages, and maintain water at a bare simmer. Cook sausages for 20 to 25 minutes, or until firm. Remove one sausage to a plate with tongs and insert an instant-read thermometer. If the temperature is 160°F, sausages are done. If not, return to the pot and continue cooking. Remove sausages from the pan with tongs, and serve immediately or cool to room temperature, lightly covered with plastic wrap, and refrigerate.

Note: Sausages can be refrigerated up to 2 days or frozen up to 2 months. Once cooked, they can be refrigerated up to 3 days.

Rice, an ancient and venerable grain, has been cultivated since at least 5000 BCE. Archaeological explorations in China have uncovered sealed pots of rice that are almost eight thousand years old. Today, rice is a staple food for half the world's population—particularly in China, India, Japan, and Southeast Asia as well as in Latin America.

Smoky Pork, Bacon, and Cheddar Sausage

Makes 2 pounds

Active time:
1 hour, including 30 minutes to chill meat

Start to finish:
2 hours

VARIATIONS

Substitute 2 pounds boned chicken or turkey thigh meat, with skin attached, for pork and pork fat. Cook sausages to an internal temperature of 165ºF.

Substitute Gruyère, Emmenthaler, or Gouda for cheddar.

Somehow I had to get bacon—one of my favorite foods—into this book. The crisp nuggets add texture as well as flavor, and the cheese adds a creamy feel.

Medium hog sausage casings
1¼ pounds pork butt or boneless country ribs
½ pound pork fat
¼ pound bacon, diced
4 scallions, white parts and 3 inches of green tops, chopped
1 cup grated smoked cheddar
1 teaspoon kosher salt
½ teaspoon freshly grated black pepper
¼ teaspoon freshly grated nutmeg

1. Prepare sausage casings as directed on page 21.

2. Cut pork and pork fat into 1-inch cubes. Place cubes on a sheet of plastic wrap on a plate and freeze for 30 minutes, or until very firm.

3. While meats chill, cook bacon in a heavy skillet over medium-high heat for 5 to 7 minutes, or until crisp. Remove bacon from the skillet with a slotted spoon, and set aside. Crumble bacon when cool enough to handle. Discard all but 3 tablespoons bacon grease from the skillet, and add scallions. Cook, stirring frequently, for 3 minutes, or until scallions are translucent.

4. Grind meat and fat through the coarse disk of a meat grinder, or in small batches in a food processor fitted with the steel blade using the on-and-off pulse button. If using a food processor, do not process into

a paste, but ingredients should be very finely chopped.

5. Combine ground meat, bacon, scallions, cheddar, salt, pepper, and nutmeg in a mixing bowl, and knead mixture until well blended. Fry 1 tablespoon of mixture in a small skillet over medium-high heat. Taste and adjust seasoning, if necessary.

6. Stuff mixture into casings as described on page 24 and twist off into 5-inch links; prick air bubbles with a straight pin or skewer. If time permits, arrange links on a wire rack over a baking sheet and air-dry uncovered in the refrigerator for 1 day before cooking.

7. Cook sausages as directed on page 31 to an internal temperature of 160°F when pierced with an instant-read thermometer or as directed in a specific recipe.

Note: Sausages can be refrigerated up to 2 days or frozen up to 2 months. Once cooked, they can be refrigerated up to 3 days.

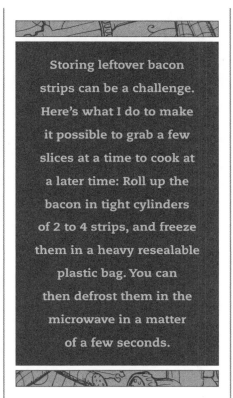

Storing leftover bacon strips can be a challenge. Here's what I do to make it possible to grab a few slices at a time to cook at a later time: Roll up the bacon in tight cylinders of 2 to 4 strips, and freeze them in a heavy resealable plastic bag. You can then defrost them in the microwave in a matter of a few seconds.

Gulf Coast Chicken and Shrimp Sausage

Makes 2 pounds

Active time:
1 hour, including
30 minutes to
chill meat

Start to finish:
2 hours

VARIATIONS

*Substitute
bay scallops
for shrimp.*

*Substitute pork
and pork fat
for chicken.*

*Add 1 or 2
jalapeño or
serrano chiles
to mixture for
spicy sausage.*

Inspired by Louisiana cooking, chicken and sweet shrimp pair very well. You also can shape this mixture into burgers and grill them.

*Medium hog sausage casings
  (optional)*
*1⅓ pounds boneless chicken breast
  meat with skin attached*
3 tablespoons unsalted butter
*4 scallions, white parts and 3 inches
  of green tops, chopped*
½ celery rib, chopped
*¼ red bell pepper, seeds and ribs
  removed, and chopped*
2 garlic cloves, minced
*⅔ pound raw shrimp, peeled and
  deveined*
¼ cup heavy cream
2 tablespoons chopped fresh parsley
1½ teaspoons kosher salt
*½ teaspoon freshly ground
  black pepper*
½ teaspoon dried thyme

1. If using sausage casings, prepare them as directed on page 21.

2. Cut chicken into 1-inch cubes. Place cubes on a sheet of plastic wrap on a plate and freeze for 30 minutes, or until very firm.

3. While meat chills, heat butter in a small skillet over medium-high heat. Add scallions, celery, red bell pepper, and garlic. Cook, stirring frequently, for 3 minutes, or until scallions are translucent. Set aside.

4. Grind chicken and shrimp through the coarse disk of a meat grinder, or in small batches in a food processor fitted with the steel blade using the on-and-off pulse button. If using a food processor,

do not process into a paste, but ingredients should be very finely chopped.

5. Combine ground meat, vegetable mixture, cream, parsley, salt, pepper, and thyme in a mixing bowl, and knead mixture until well blended. Fry 1 tablespoon of mixture in a small skillet over medium-high heat. Taste and adjust seasoning, if necessary.

6. Stuff mixture into casings as described on page 24, if using, and twist off into 4-inch links; prick air bubbles with a straight pin or skewer. If time permits, arrange links on a wire rack over a baking sheet and air-dry uncovered in the refrigerator for 1 day before cooking. Alternately, if keeping sausage in bulk, refrigerate mixture for at least 30 minutes to blend flavors.

7. Cook sausages as directed on page 31 to an internal temperature of 165°F when pierced with an instant-read thermometer or as directed in a specific recipe.

Note: Sausages can be refrigerated up to 2 days or frozen up to 2 months. Once cooked, they can be refrigerated up to 3 days.

To devein shrimp is to remove the black vein, actually the intestinal tract, from shrimp. To do this, hold the shrimp in one hand with the curved side up. Slice down the middle of the back with a paring knife, and pull out the black vein, if one is present. This can also be done with a specialized tool called a deveiner available where housewares are sold.

Loukanika

These spicy Greek sausages, made with a combination of pork and lamb, are scented with aromatic orange zest as well as spices. Grill them or use in traditional dishes like moussaka.

Makes 2 pounds

Active time:
1 hour, including 30 minutes to chill meat

Start to finish:
2 hours

VARIATIONS

Substitute beef chuck for lamb shoulder.

Substitute boneless chicken thighs, with skin attached, for pork. Cook sausages to an internal temperature of 165ºF.

Substitute brandy, preferably Greek Metaxa, for wine.

Thin lamb sausage casings
   (optional)
1 pound boneless lamb shoulder
½ pound pork butt or boneless
   country ribs
½ pound pork fat
2 teaspoons ground coriander
1 teaspoon ground cumin
1½ teaspoons kosher salt
1 teaspoon dried oregano
½ teaspoon dried thyme
½ teaspoon freshly ground
   black pepper
2 tablespoons olive oil
1 medium onion, chopped

4 garlic cloves, minced
¼ cup dry red wine
1 tablespoon grated orange zest

1. If using sausage casings, prepare them as directed on page 21.

2. Cut lamb, pork, and pork fat into 1-inch cubes. Place cubes in a mixing bowl, and toss with coriander, cumin, salt, oregano, thyme, and pepper. Transfer cubes to a sheet of plastic wrap on a plate and freeze for 30 minutes, or until very firm.

3. While meats chill, heat olive oil in a small skillet over medium-high heat. Add onion and garlic, and cook, stirring frequently, for 5 minutes, or until onion softens. Set aside.

4. Grind meats and fat through the coarse disk of a meat grinder, or in small batches in a food processor fitted with the steel blade using the

on-and-off pulse button. If using a food processor, do not process into a paste, but ingredients should be very finely chopped.

5. Combine ground meat, onion mixture, wine, and orange zest in a mixing bowl, and knead mixture until well blended. Fry 1 table-spoon of mixture in a small skillet over medium-high heat. Taste and adjust seasoning, if necessary.

6. Stuff mixture into casings as described on page 24, if using, and twist off into 5-inch links; prick air bubbles with a straight pin or skewer. If time permits, arrange links on a wire rack over a baking sheet and air-dry uncovered in the refrigerator for 1 day before cooking. Alternately, if keeping sausage in bulk, refrigerate mix-ture for at least 30 minutes to blend flavors.

7. Cook sausages as directed on page 31 to an internal tempera-ture of 160°F when pierced with an instant-read thermometer or as directed in a specific recipe.

Note: Sausages can be refriger-ated up to 2 days or frozen up to 2 months. Once cooked, they can be refrigerated up to 3 days.

Zest really does have something to do with zesty; it's the thin, colored outer portion of the citrus skin that contains all the aromatic oils. The white pith just beneath it is bitter, so take pains to separate the zest from the fruit without also taking any pith with it. Remove the zest using a special citrus zester, a vegetable peeler, or a paring knife. You can also grate it off using the fine holes of a box grater or a Microplane rasp.

Italian Cheese and Pepper Sausage

Makes 2 pounds

Active time:
1 hour, including 30 minutes to chill meat

Start to finish:
2 hours

VARIATIONS

Substitute Romano for Parmesan.

Add ½ to 1 teaspoon crushed red pepper flakes for spicy sausage.

Try these flavorful sausages, dotted with bits of sweet red pepper and lots of herbs, on hero sandwiches topped with Herbed Marinara Sauce (page 478) and some provolone cheese.

Medium hog sausage casings (optional)

1½ pounds boned chicken thigh meat with skin attached

¼ pound pork butt or boneless country ribs

¼ pound pork fat

2 tablespoons olive oil

1 small onion, finely chopped

½ red bell pepper, seeds and ribs removed, and finely chopped

3 garlic cloves, minced

⅓ cup freshly grated Parmesan

¼ cup dry white wine

2 tablespoons chopped fresh parsley

1 tablespoon chopped fresh oregano or 1 teaspoon dried

1½ teaspoons kosher salt

½ teaspoon freshly ground black pepper

1. If using sausage casings, prepare them as directed on page 21.

2. Cut chicken, pork, and pork fat into 1-inch cubes. Place cubes on

a sheet of plastic wrap on a plate and freeze for 30 minutes, or until very firm.

3. While meats chill, heat olive oil in a small skillet over medium-high heat. Add onion, red bell pepper, and garlic, and cook, stirring frequently, for 5 minutes, or until vegetables soften. Set aside.

4. Grind meats and fat through the coarse disk of a meat grinder, or in small batches in a food processor fitted with the steel blade using the on-and-off pulse button. If using a food processor, do not process into a paste, but ingredients should be very finely chopped.

5. Combine ground meat, vegetable mixture, Parmesan, wine, parsley, oregano, salt, and pepper in a mixing bowl, and knead mixture until well blended. Fry 1 tablespoon of mixture in a small skillet over medium-high heat. Taste and adjust seasoning, if necessary.

6. Stuff mixture into casings as described on page 24, if using, and twist off into 5-inch links; prick air bubbles with a straight pin or skewer. If time permits, arrange links on a wire rack over a baking sheet and air-dry uncovered in the refrigerator for 1 day before cooking. Alternately, if keeping sausage in bulk, refrigerate mixture for at least 30 minutes to blend flavors.

7. Cook sausages as directed on page 31 to an internal temperature of 165°F when pierced with an instant-read thermometer or as directed in a specific recipe.

Note: Sausages can be refrigerated up to 2 days or frozen up to 2 months. Once cooked, they can be refrigerated up to 3 days.

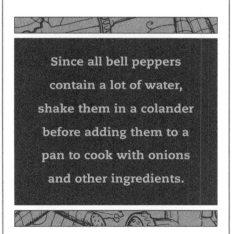

Since all bell peppers contain a lot of water, shake them in a colander before adding them to a pan to cook with onions and other ingredients.

Asian Pork and Shrimp Sausage

Makes 2 pounds

Active time:
1 hour, including
30 minutes to
chill meat

Start to finish:
2 hours

One of my favorite dim sum are steamed *shao mai*, dumplings made with a flavorful filling of pork and shrimp. A sausage made with the same combination sounded like a good idea to me, and it is.

Medium hog sausage casings
  (optional)
1¼ pounds pork butt or boneless
  country ribs
¼ pound pork fat
½ pound peeled and deveined
  shrimp
3 tablespoons Chinese plum wine
  or golden sherry
3 tablespoons Chinese oyster sauce
1 tablespoon grated fresh ginger
1 tablespoon Asian sesame oil
3 scallions, white parts and
  4 inches of green tops, chopped
2 garlic cloves, minced
½ teaspoon freshly ground
  black pepper

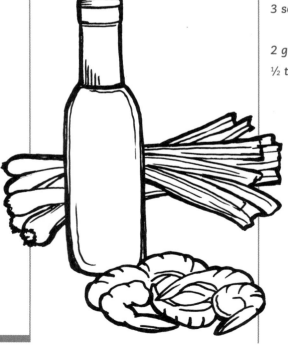

VARIATIONS

Substitute 1½ pounds boned chicken or turkey thigh meat, with skin attached, for pork and pork fat. Cook sausages to an internal temperature of 165°F.

Substitute up to 1 tablespoon Chinese chile paste with garlic for pepper.

Add ½ cup finely chopped water chestnuts to meat mixture.

1. If using sausage casings, prepare them as directed on page 21.

2. Cut pork and pork fat into 1-inch cubes. Place cubes on a sheet of plastic wrap on a plate and freeze for 30 minutes, or until very firm.

3. Grind pork, pork fat, and shrimp through the coarse disk of a meat grinder, or in small batches in a food processor fitted with the steel blade using the on-and-off pulse button. If using a food processor, do not process into a paste, but ingredients should be very finely chopped.

4. Combine ground meats, plum wine, oyster sauce, ginger, sesame oil, scallions, garlic, and pepper in a mixing bowl, and knead mixture until well blended. Fry 1 tablespoon of mixture in a small skillet over medium-high heat. Taste and adjust seasoning, if necessary.

5. Stuff mixture into casings as described on page 24, if using, and twist off into 5-inch links; prick air bubbles with a straight pin or skewer. If time permits, arrange links on a wire rack over a baking sheet and air-dry uncovered in the refrigerator for 1 day before cooking. Alternately, if keeping sausage in bulk, refrigerate mixture for at least 30 minutes to blend flavors.

6. Cook sausages as directed on page 31 to an internal temperature of 160°F when pierced with an instant-read thermometer or as directed in a specific recipe.

Note: Sausages can be refrigerated up to 2 days or frozen up to 2 months. Once cooked, they can be refrigerated up to 3 days.

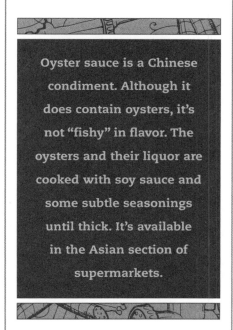

Oyster sauce is a Chinese condiment. Although it does contain oysters, it's not "fishy" in flavor. The oysters and their liquor are cooked with soy sauce and some subtle seasonings until thick. It's available in the Asian section of supermarkets.

Spicy Thai Sausage

Makes 2 pounds

Active time:
1 hour, including
30 minutes to
chill meat

Start to finish:
2 hours

VARIATIONS

Add 1 to 2 tablespoons finely chopped lemongrass to sausage mixture.

Substitute soy sauce for fish sauce and Chinese chile paste with garlic for red curry paste.

Substitute 1 additional pound chicken for pork and pork fat.

Sausages like these appear frequently in traditional Thai cuisine. The aromatic basil and cilantro, spicy chiles, and robust curry paste makes these a very special and spicy treat.

Medium hog sausage casings
    (optional)
1 pound boneless chicken breast
    meat with skin attached
½ pound pork butt or boneless
    country ribs
½ pound pork fat
2 tablespoons chopped fresh cilantro
2 tablespoons chopped fresh basil,
    preferably Thai basil
2 scallions, white parts and 4 inches
    of green tops, chopped
2 garlic cloves, minced
1 jalapeño or serrano chile, seeds
    and ribs removed, and finely
    chopped
3 tablespoons fish sauce (nam pla)
1 tablespoon red curry paste
½ teaspoon cayenne

1. If using sausage casings, prepare them as directed on page 21.

2. Cut chicken, pork, and pork fat into 1-inch cubes. Place cubes on a sheet of plastic wrap on a plate and freeze for 30 minutes, or until very firm.

3. Grind meat and fat through the fine disk of a meat grinder, or in small batches in a food processor fitted with the steel blade using the on-and-off pulse button. If using a food processor, do not process into a paste, but ingredients should be very finely chopped.

4. Combine ground meat, cilantro, basil, scallions, garlic, chile, fish sauce, curry paste, and cayenne in a mixing bowl, and knead mixture until well blended. Fry 1 tablespoon of mixture in a small skillet over medium-high heat. Taste and adjust seasoning, if necessary.

5. Stuff mixture into casings as described on page 24, if using, and twist off into 5-inch links; prick air bubbles with a straight pin or skewer. If time permits, arrange links on a wire rack over a baking sheet and air-dry uncovered in the refrigerator for 1 day before cooking. Alternately, if keeping sausage in bulk, refrigerate mixture for at least 30 minutes to blend flavors.

6. Cook sausages as directed on page 31 to an internal temperature of 165°F when pierced with an instant-read thermometer or as directed in a specific recipe.

Note: Sausages can be refrigerated up to 2 days or frozen up to 2 months. Once cooked, they can be refrigerated up to 3 days.

Fish sauce, also called *nam pla*, is a salty sauce with an extremely pungent odor made from fermented fish. It's used as a dipping sauce/condiment and seasoning ingredient throughout Southeast Asia. *Nam pla* is the Thai term; it's known as *nuoc nam* in Vietnam and *shottsuru* in Japan.

CLUCK AND GOBBLE:

CHICKEN AND
TURKEY SAUSAGES

Famed nineteenth-century French gastronome Jean Anthelme Brillat-Savarin once wrote that "poultry is for the cook what canvas is for the painter." Its inherently mild flavor takes to myriad methods of seasoning, and it is relatively quick to cook. And, as you'll discover when cooking the recipes in this chapter, it makes great sausages too. Some of these recipes use chicken, others turkey, but feel free to use the two interchangeably. Turkey gives sausages a slightly more robust flavor.

Look for packages of chicken that do not have an accumulation of liquid in the bottom, which can be a sign that the chicken has been frozen and defrosted. Chicken should be stored in the coldest part of the refrigerator (40°F or below), sealed as it comes from the market and used within 2 or 3 days.

If it should be necessary to keep it longer, freeze it. To defrost, place the frozen chicken it on a plate in the refrigerator or use the microwave, following manufacturer's instructions. To speed the thawing of uncooked chicken, place package in cold water, changing the water frequently.

Chicken should be rinsed under cold running water when it is removed from the wrapper, and have absolutely no aroma. If it has any off-smells, take it back to the supermarket if it's before the expiration date, or discard it if it's after that date or you took it out of the freezer.

Illness-causing bacteria such as salmonella can grow in high-protein, low-acid foods like poultry, so special handling should always be taken with raw chicken or turkey. To prevent transferring bacteria from one food to another, use warm water and soap to wash your hands, cooking utensils, and work surfaces before and after use.

The rules have changed for cooking poultry in the last year, and the revision means that you can avoid overcooked dry chicken and turkey. The minimum temperature is now 165°F for both white and dark meat. At that temperature there's no chance for microorganisms to survive, and the best way to test this is to use an instant-read meat thermometer. Insert it into the center of the sausage link.

Turkey, Apple, and Sage Sausage

Makes 2 pounds

Active time:
1 hour, including
30 minutes to
chill meat

Start to finish:
2 hours

Slightly sweet with fruity flavor, this is my favorite sausage to serve at breakfast when pancakes or waffles are on the menu.

Thin sheep sausage casings

2 pounds boneless chicken or turkey
    thigh meat with skin attached

2 tablespoons unsalted butter

1 large shallot, chopped

¼ cup frozen apple juice concentrate,
    thawed

½ cup finely chopped dried apple

2 tablespoons chopped fresh parsley

1½ teaspoons kosher salt

1 teaspoon dried sage

½ teaspoon freshly ground
    black pepper

¼ teaspoon ground allspice

1. Prepare sausage casings as directed on page 21.

2. Cut chicken into 1-inch cubes. Place cubes on a sheet of plastic wrap on a plate and freeze for 30 minutes, or until very firm.

3. While chicken chills, heat butter in a small skillet over medium-high heat. Add shallot and cook for 3 minutes, stirring occasionally, or until shallot is translucent. Add

VARIATIONS

Substitute 1½ pounds pork butt or boneless country ribs and ½ pound pork fat for chicken. Cook sausages to an internal temperature of 160ºF.

Add ½ to 1 teaspoon crushed red pepper flakes for spicy sausage.

Substitute chopped dried apricots, dried cranberries, or dried currants for dried apples.

apple juice concentrate and dried apple, and cook for 1 minute. Set aside.

4. Grind chicken through the coarse disk of a meat grinder, or in small batches in a food processor fitted with the steel blade using the on-and-off pulse button. If using a food processor, do not process into a paste, but ingredients should be very finely chopped.

5. Combine ground chicken, apple mixture, parsley, salt, sage, pepper, and allspice in a mixing bowl, and knead mixture until well blended. Fry 1 tablespoon of mixture in a small skillet over medium-high heat. Taste and adjust seasoning, if necessary.

6. Stuff mixture into casings as described on page 24 and twist off into 4-inch links; prick air bubbles with a straight pin or skewer. If time permits, arrange links on a wire rack over a baking sheet and air-dry uncovered in the refrigerator for 1 day before cooking.

7. Cook sausages as directed on page 31 to an internal temperature of 165ºF when pierced with an instant-read thermometer or as directed in a specific recipe.

Note: Sausages can be refrigerated up to 2 days or frozen up to 2 months. Once cooked, they can be refrigerated up to 3 days.

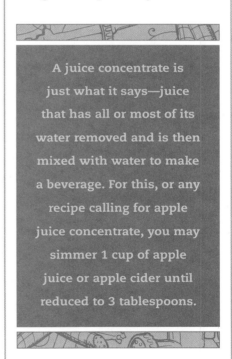

A juice concentrate is just what it says—juice that has all or most of its water removed and is then mixed with water to make a beverage. For this, or any recipe calling for apple juice concentrate, you may simmer 1 cup of apple juice or apple cider until reduced to 3 tablespoons.

Thanksgiving Turkey Sausage

Makes 2 pounds

Active time:
1 hour, including
30 minutes to
chill meat

Start to finish:
2 hours

VARIATIONS

Substitute walnuts or almonds for pecans.

Substitute rum or brandy for bourbon.

Substitute 1½ pounds pork butt and ½ pound pork fat for turkey. Cook sausages to an internal temperature of 160°F.

Enjoy this sausage with crunchy pecans, sweet dried cranberries, turkey, and traditional seasonings at the holiday or any time of the year. These can also be grilled.

Medium hog sausage casings (optional)
2 pounds boneless turkey or chicken thigh meat with skin attached
½ cup chopped pecans
2 tablespoons unsalted butter
½ small onion, chopped
1 garlic clove, minced
½ cup chopped dried cranberries
2 tablespoons apple juice concentrate
1 tablespoon bourbon
1½ teaspoons kosher salt
1 teaspoon dried sage
½ teaspoon freshly ground black pepper
Pinch ground cinnamon

1. If using sausage casings, prepare them as directed on page 21.

2. Cut turkey into 1-inch cubes. Place cubes on a sheet of plastic wrap on a plate and freeze for 30 minutes, or until very firm.

3. While turkey chills, preheat the oven to 350°F. Toast pecans for 5 to 7 minutes or until lightly browned. Set aside. Heat butter in a small skillet over medium-high heat. Add onion and garlic, and cook, stirring frequently, for 3 to 5 minutes, or until onion softens. Set aside.

4. Grind turkey through the coarse disk of a meat grinder, or in small batches in a food processor fitted with the steel blade using the on-and-off pulse button. If using a food processor, do not process into a paste, but ingredients should be very finely chopped.

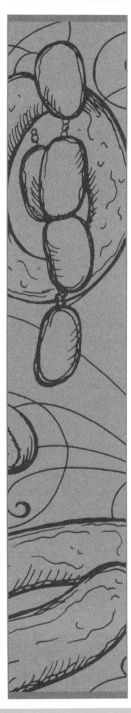

5. Combine turkey, pecans, onion mixture, cranberries, apple juice concentrate, bourbon, salt, sage, pepper, and cinnamon in a mixing bowl, and knead mixture until well blended. Fry 1 tablespoon of mixture in a small skillet over medium-high heat. Taste and adjust seasoning, if necessary.

6. Stuff mixture into casings as described on page 24, if using, and twist off into 5-inch links; prick air bubbles with a straight pin or skewer. If time permits, arrange links on a wire rack over a baking sheet and air-dry uncovered in the refrigerator for 1 day before cooking. Alternately, if keeping sausage in bulk, refrigerate mixture for at least 30 minutes to blend flavors.

7. Cook sausages as directed on page 31 to an internal temperature of 165°F when pierced with an instant-read thermometer or as directed in a specific recipe.

Note: Sausages can be refrigerated up to 2 days or frozen up to 2 months. Once cooked, they can be refrigerated up to 3 days.

Toasted nuts look more appealing and have a crisper texture and more pleasing flavor. Toasting releases the nuts' fragrant and aromatic oils.

Smoky Southwestern Turkey Sausage with Chiles

Makes 2 pounds

Active time:
1 hour, including
30 minutes to
chill meat

Start to finish:
5 hours

This sausage ignites your taste buds with robust flavors—including tequila. Try some in chili con carne in place of ground beef.

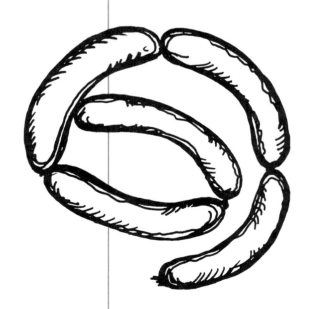

Medium hog sausage casings

2 pounds boneless turkey or chicken
    thigh meat with skin attached

¼ teaspoon liquid smoke

¼ cup tequila

3 tablespoons chopped fresh cilantro

2 tablespoons smoked Spanish
    paprika

3 garlic cloves, minced

1 or 2 chipotle chiles in adobo sauce,
    finely chopped

2 teaspoons ground cumin

1½ teaspoons kosher salt

3/4 teaspoon dried oregano

1. Prepare sausage casings as directed on page 21.

2. Cut turkey into 1-inch cubes. Place cubes on a sheet of plastic wrap on a plate and freeze for 30 minutes, or until very firm. Stir liquid smoke into tequila, and set aside.

Substitute 1½ pounds pork butt and ½ pound pork fat for turkey. Cook sausages to an internal temperature of 160°F.

Substitute 2 tablespoons diced mild green chiles, drained, for chipotle chiles.

Add ½ cup grated Monterey Jack or jalapeño Jack to sausage mixture.

3. Grind turkey through the coarse disk of a meat grinder, or in small batches in a food processor fitted with the steel blade using the on-and-off pulse button. If using a food processor, do not process into a paste, but ingredients should be very finely chopped.

4. Combine turkey, tequila mixture, cilantro, paprika, garlic, chiles, cumin, salt, and oregano in a mixing bowl, and knead mixture until well blended. Fry 1 tablespoon of mixture in a small skillet over medium-high heat. Taste and adjust seasoning, if necessary.

5. Stuff mixture into casings as described on page 24 and twist off into 5-inch links; prick air bubbles with a straight pin or skewer. If time permits, arrange links on a wire rack over a baking sheet and air-dry uncovered in the refrigerator for 1 day before cooking.

6. Preheat the oven to 200°F, line a baking sheet with aluminum foil, and arrange sausages on a cooling rack on top of the baking sheet. Bake sausages for 4 to 5 hours, or to an internal temperature of 165°F when pierced with an instant-read thermometer. Remove sausages from the pan with tongs, and serve immediately or cool to room temperature, lightly covered with plastic wrap, and refrigerate.

Note: Sausages can be refrigerated up to 2 days or frozen up to 2 months. Once cooked, they can be refrigerated up to 3 days.

It's a shame to waste herbs like parsley, cilantro, and dill, when all you need are a few tablespoons for a recipe. Trim off the stems, and then wrap small bundles in plastic wrap, and freeze them. When you need some, "chop" with the blunt side of a knife. The herbs chop easily when frozen, and this method produces far better flavor than dried herbs.

Herbed Turkey and White Wine Sausage

Makes 2 pounds

Active time:
1 hour, including
30 minutes to
chill meat

Start to finish:
2 hours

VARIATIONS

Substitute 1½ pounds pork butt and ½ pound pork fat for turkey. Cook sausages to an internal temperature of 160°F.

Substitute red wine for white wine.

Here's a subtle recipe to serve at elegant brunches and other celebrations. It's based on some classic French chicken dishes and goes very well on a salad.

Medium hog sausage casings
*   (optional)*
2 pounds boneless turkey or chicken
*   thigh meat with skin attached*
1 cup dry white wine
2 tablespoons olive oil
1 large shallot, chopped
2 garlic cloves, minced
3 tablespoons chopped fresh parsley
1 tablespoon chopped fresh
*   rosemary or 1 teaspoon dried*
1½ teaspoons kosher salt
1 teaspoon fresh thyme
*   or ½ teaspoon dried*
½ teaspoon freshly ground
*   white pepper*

1. If using sausage casings, prepare them as directed on page 21.

2. Cut turkey into 1-inch cubes. Place cubes on a sheet of plastic wrap on a plate and freeze for 30 minutes, or until very firm.

3. While turkey chills, boil wine in a small saucepan over high heat until reduced to ¼ cup. Set aside. Heat oil in a small skillet over medium-high heat. Add shallot and garlic, and cook, stirring frequently, for 3 minutes, or until shallot is translucent. Set aside.

4. Grind turkey through the fine disk of a meat grinder, or in small batches in a food processor fitted with the steel blade using the on-and-off pulse button. If using a food processor, do not process into a paste, but ingredients should be very finely chopped.

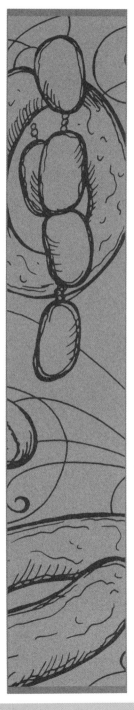

5. Combine turkey, wine reduction, shallot mixture, parsley, rosemary, salt, thyme, and pepper in a mixing bowl, and knead mixture until well blended. Fry 1 tablespoon of mixture in a small skillet over medium-high heat. Taste and adjust seasoning, if necessary.

6. Stuff mixture into casings as described on page 24, if using, and twist off into 5-inch links; prick air bubbles with a straight pin or skewer. If time permits, arrange links on a wire rack over a baking sheet and air-dry uncovered in the refrigerator for 1 day before cooking. Alternately, if keeping sausage in bulk, refrigerate mixture for at least 30 minutes to blend flavors.

7. Cook sausages as directed on page 31 to an internal temperature of 165°F when pierced with an instant-read thermometer or as directed in a specific recipe.

Note: Sausages can be refrigerated up to 2 days or frozen up to 2 months. Once cooked, they can be refrigerated up to 3 days.

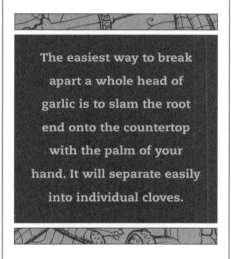

The easiest way to break apart a whole head of garlic is to slam the root end onto the countertop with the palm of your hand. It will separate easily into individual cloves.

Italian Chicken and Olive Sausage

Makes 2 pounds

Active time:
1 hour, including
30 minutes to
chill meat

Start to finish:
2 hours

There are lots of lusty flavors in this sausage, including garlic, olives, and plenty of Italian herbs. This sausage is great with a pasta dish or topping a pizza.

Medium hog sausage casings
(optional)
2 pounds boneless chicken or turkey
thigh meat with skin attached
2 tablespoons fennel seeds
¼ cup dry red wine
¼ cup chopped Kalamata olives
3 garlic cloves, minced
2 tablespoons chopped fresh parsley
1 tablespoon anchovy paste
1½ teaspoons Italian seasoning
½ teaspoon crushed red pepper
flakes

1. If using sausage casings, prepare them as directed on page 21.

2. Cut chicken into 1-inch cubes. Place cubes on a sheet of plastic wrap on a plate and freeze for 30 minutes, or until very firm. While chicken chills, grind fennel seeds in a mortar and pestle or in a spice or clean coffee grinder. Set aside.

3. Grind chicken through the coarse disk of a meat grinder, or in small batches in a food processor

VARIATIONS

*Substitute
1½ pounds
pork butt and
½ pound pork
fat for chicken.
Cook sausages
to an internal
temperature
of 160°F.*

*Omit anchovy
paste and add
1½ teaspoons
kosher salt.*

*Substitute
pimiento-stuffed
green olives for
Kalamata olives.*

fitted with the steel blade using the on-and-off pulse button. If using a food processor, do not process into a paste, but ingredients should be very finely chopped.

4. Combine chicken, fennel seeds, wine, olives, garlic, parsley, anchovy paste, Italian seasoning, and red pepper flakes in a mixing bowl, and knead mixture until well blended. Fry 1 tablespoon of mixture in a small skillet over medium-high heat. Taste and adjust seasoning, if necessary.

5. Stuff mixture into casings as described on page 24, if using, and twist off into 5-inch links; prick air bubbles with a straight pin or skewer. If time permits, arrange links on a wire rack over a baking sheet and air-dry uncovered in the refrigerator for 1 day before cooking. Alternately, if keeping sausage in bulk, refrigerate mixture for at least 30 minutes to blend flavors.

6. Cook sausages as directed on page 31 to an internal temperature of 165°F when pierced with

an instant-read thermometer or as directed in a specific recipe.

Note: Sausages can be refrigerated up to 2 days or frozen up to 2 months. Once cooked, they can be refrigerated up to 3 days.

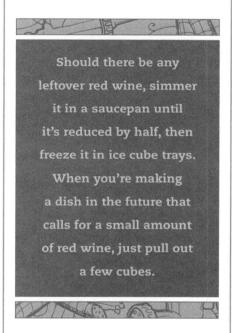

Should there be any leftover red wine, simmer it in a saucepan until it's reduced by half, then freeze it in ice cube trays. When you're making a dish in the future that calls for a small amount of red wine, just pull out a few cubes.

Greek Chicken and Pistachio Sausage

Makes 2 pounds

Active time:
1 hour, including
30 minutes to
chill meat

Start to finish:
1½ hours

VARIATIONS

Substitute 1½ pounds veal shoulder and ½ pound pork fat for chicken. Cook sausages to an internal temperature of 160ºF.

Substitute oregano for dill.

Crunchy nuts, aromatic dill, and sharp feta cheese are the accent flavors in this robust sausage. Serve it topped with Herbed Marinara Sauce (page 478) alongside a Greek salad.

Medium hog sausage casings
2 pounds boneless chicken or turkey
*   thigh meat with skin attached*
2 tablespoons olive oil
½ small onion, chopped
3 garlic cloves, minced
¾ cup crumbled feta cheese
¼ cup chopped shelled pistachio
*   nuts*
¼ cup chopped sun-dried tomatoes
¼ cup tomato sauce
¼ cup chopped fresh dill
1½ teaspoons kosher salt
½ teaspoon freshly ground
*   black pepper*
½ teaspoon dried oregano

1. Prepare sausage casings as directed on page 21.

2. Cut chicken into 1-inch cubes. Place cubes on a sheet of plastic wrap on a plate and freeze for 30 minutes, or until very firm.

3. While chicken chills, heat oil in a small skillet over medium-high heat. Add onion and garlic, and cook, stirring frequently, for 3 minutes, or until onion is translucent. Set aside.

4. Grind chicken through the coarse disk of a meat grinder, or in small batches in a food processor fitted with the steel blade using the on-and-off pulse button. If using a food processor, do not process into

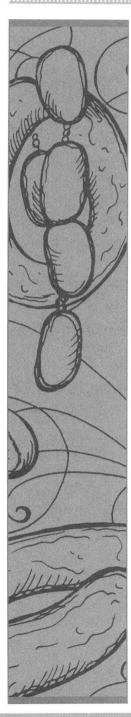

a paste, but ingredients should be very finely chopped.

5. Combine chicken, onion mixture, cheese, pistachio nuts, sun-dried tomatoes, tomato sauce, dill, salt, pepper, and oregano in a mixing bowl, and knead mixture until well blended. Fry 1 tablespoon of mixture in a small skillet over medium-high heat. Taste and adjust seasoning, if necessary.

6. Stuff mixture into casings as described on page 24 and twist off into 5-inch links; prick air bubbles with a straight pin or skewer. If time permits, arrange links on a wire rack over a baking sheet and air-dry uncovered in the refrigerator for 1 day before cooking.

7. To poach sausages, bring a large pot of salted water to a boil over high heat. Add sausages, and maintain water at a bare simmer. Cook sausages for 20 to 25 minutes, or until firm. Remove one sausage to a plate with tongs and insert an instant-read thermometer. If the temperature is 165°F, sausages are done. If not, return to the pot and continue cooking. Remove sausages from the pan with tongs, and serve immediately or cool to room temperature, lightly covered with plastic wrap, and refrigerate.

Note: Sausages can be refrigerated up to 2 days or frozen up to 2 months. Once cooked, they can be refrigerated up to 3 days.

Native to the Middle East, pistachios are one of the oldest flowering nut trees; archaeological discoveries in Turkey show that humans were munching on these healthful nuts as early as 7000 BCE. Legend has it that the Queen of Sheba decreed that pistachios were food for royals only. There are also reports that pistachio trees grew in the hanging gardens of Babylon.

Provençal Chicken Sausage

Makes 2 pounds

Active time:
1 hour, including 30 minutes to chill meat

Start to finish:
2 hours

Bright flavors like sun-dried tomatoes, capers, and orange zest characterize the cuisine of this sun-drenched region of France. Those are what you'll find in this sausage, too. Serve them with some Easy Aïoli (page 485).

Thin sheep sausage casings (optional)
2 pounds boneless chicken or turkey thigh meat with skin attached
2 tablespoons olive oil
1 large shallot, finely chopped
2 garlic cloves, minced
3 tablespoons dry white wine
⅓ cup finely chopped sun-dried tomatoes
2 tablespoons chopped fresh parsley
2 tablespoons nonpareil capers, rinsed
2 teaspoons herbes de Provence
1½ teaspoons grated orange zest
1½ teaspoons kosher salt
½ teaspoon freshly ground black pepper

1. If using sausage casings, prepare them as directed on page 21.

2. Cut chicken into 1-inch cubes. Place cubes on a sheet of plastic wrap on a plate and freeze for 30 minutes, or until very firm.

3. While chicken chills, heat oil in a small skillet over medium-high heat. Add shallot and garlic, and cook, stirring frequently, for 3 minutes, or until shallot is translucent. Set aside.

4. Grind chicken through the coarse disk of a meat grinder, or in small batches in a food processor fitted with the steel blade using the on-and-off pulse button. If using a

VARIATIONS

*Substitute
1½ pounds veal
shoulder or
boneless veal
breast and
½ pound pork
fat for chicken.
Cook sausages
to an internal
temperature of
160ºF.*

*Substitute Italian
seasoning
for herbes de
Provence, and
substitute ¼ cup
freshly grated
Parmigiano-
Reggiano for
capers.*

food processor, do not process into a paste, but ingredients should be very finely chopped.

5. Combine chicken, shallot mixture, wine, sun-dried tomatoes, parsley, capers, herbes de Provence, orange zest, salt, and pepper in a mixing bowl, and knead mixture until well blended. Fry 1 tablespoon of mixture in a small skillet over medium-high heat. Taste and adjust seasoning, if necessary.

6. Stuff mixture into casings as described on page 24, if using, and twist off into 5-inch links; prick air bubbles with a straight pin or skewer. If time permits, arrange links on a wire rack over a baking sheet and air-dry uncovered in the refrigerator for 1 day before cooking. Alternately, if keeping sausage in bulk, refrigerate mixture for at least 30 minutes to blend flavors.

7. Cook sausages as directed on page 31 to an internal temperature of 165°F when pierced with an instant-read thermometer or as directed in a specific recipe.

Note: Sausages can be refrigerated up to 2 days or frozen up to 2 months. Once cooked, they can be refrigerated up to 3 days.

Capers are the flower bud of a low bush native to the Mediterranean. They're sun-dried after being harvested, then dried and pickled in vinegar or preserved in salt. The best capers are the tiny ones from France. Always rinse capers well before using them.

Garlicky Chicken and Rosemary Sausage

Makes 2 pounds

- -

**Active time:
1 hour, including
30 minutes to
chill meat**

- -

**Start to finish:
2 hours**

VARIATIONS

*Substitute
chopped fresh
oregano for
rosemary.*

*Add ½ to 1
teaspoon crushed
red pepper flakes
for spicy sausage.*

*Add ½ cup freshly
grated Parmesan
to chicken
mixture.*

My favorite way to roast a chicken is with lemon, rosemary, and garlic, so why not make sausage with the same winning combination?

Medium hog sausage casings
    (optional)
2 pounds boneless chicken or turkey
    thigh meat with skin attached
2 tablespoons olive oil
1 large shallot, chopped
3 garlic cloves, minced
¼ cup chopped fresh rosemary
3 tablespoons white vermouth
    or dry white wine
1½ teaspoons grated lemon zest
1½ teaspoons kosher salt
½ teaspoon freshly ground
    black pepper

1. If using sausage casings, prepare them as directed on page 21.

2. Cut chicken into 1-inch cubes. Place cubes on a sheet of plastic wrap on a plate and freeze for 30 minutes, or until very firm.

3. While chicken chills, heat oil in a small skillet over medium-high heat. Add shallot and garlic, and cook, stirring frequently, for 3 minutes, or until shallot is translucent.

4. Grind chicken through the coarse disk of a meat grinder, or in small batches in a food processor fitted with the steel blade using the on-and-off pulse button. If using a food processor, do not process into a paste, but ingredients should be very finely chopped.

5. Combine chicken, shallot mixture, rosemary, vermouth, lemon zest, salt, and pepper in a mixing

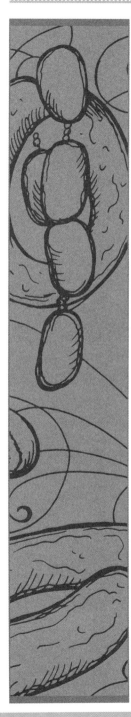

bowl, and knead mixture until well blended. Fry 1 tablespoon of mixture in a small skillet over medium-high heat. Taste and adjust seasoning, if necessary.

6. Stuff mixture into casings as described on page 24, if using, and twist off into 5-inch links; prick air bubbles with a straight pin or skewer. If time permits, arrange links on a wire rack over a baking sheet and air-dry uncovered in the refrigerator for 1 day before cooking. Alternately, if keeping sausage in bulk, refrigerate mixture for at least 30 minutes to blend flavors.

7. Cook sausages as directed on page 31 to an internal temperature of 165°F when pierced with an instant-read thermometer or as directed in a specific recipe.

Note: Sausages can be refrigerated up to 2 days or frozen up to 2 months. Once cooked, they can be refrigerated up to 3 days.

The attitude toward garlic varied wildly among different groups. Greeks and Egyptians embraced garlic's alleged aphrodisiac properties, but Tibetan monks were forbidden from entering the monasteries if they had eaten garlic as it was thought to inflame passions.

Chicken and Wild Mushroom Sausage

Makes 2 pounds

Active time:
1 hour, including
30 minutes to
chill meat

Start to finish:
2 hours

The earthiness of wild mushrooms—both dried and fresh in this sausage—gives this dish a heartiness that belies the delicacy of the chicken forming its base. Add some to a quiche or frittata.

Medium hog sausage casings (optional)
2 pounds boneless chicken or turkey thigh meat with skin attached
½ cup Chicken Stock (page 296) or purchased low-sodium stock
⅓ cup dried porcini mushrooms
2 fresh Portobello mushroom caps
3 tablespoons unsalted butter
2 tablespoons olive oil
1 large shallot, chopped
2 garlic cloves, minced
2 tablespoons heavy cream
2 tablespoons chopped fresh parsley
1½ teaspoons kosher salt
½ teaspoon freshly ground black pepper
½ teaspoon dried thyme

1. If using sausage casings, prepare them as directed on page 21.

2. Cut chicken into 1-inch cubes. Place cubes on a sheet of plastic wrap on a plate and freeze for 30 minutes, or until very firm.

3. While chicken chills, bring stock to a boil in a small saucepan. Add dried porcini mushrooms, pressing with the back of a spoon to push them down into stock. Soak mushrooms for 10 minutes, then drain mushrooms, reserving soaking liquid. Finely chop mushrooms, and strain liquid through a sieve lined with a paper coffee filter or paper towel. Set aside. Peel Portobello

Substitute 1 pound veal shoulder or boneless veal breast, ½ pound pork butt, and ½ pound pork fat for chicken. Cook sausages to an internal temperature of 160°F.

Substitute 1½ pounds beef chuck and ½ pound beef fat for chicken, and substitute dry red wine for cream. Cook sausages to an internal temperature of 160°F.

mushroom caps, cut off dark gills from underside, and chop finely in a food processor using the on-and-off pulse button.

4. Heat butter and oil in a medium skillet over medium-high heat. Add fresh mushrooms, shallots, and garlic, and cook, stirring frequently, for 3 to 5 minutes, or until mushrooms soften. Set aside.

5. Grind chicken through the fine disk of a meat grinder, or in small batches in a food processor fitted with the steel blade using the on-and-off pulse button. If using a food processor, do not process into a paste, but ingredients should be very finely chopped.

6. Combine chicken, fresh mushroom mixture, dried mushrooms, 2 tablespoons mushroom soaking liquid, cream, parsley, salt, pepper, and thyme in a mixing bowl, and knead mixture until well blended. Fry 1 tablespoon of mixture in a small skillet over medium-high heat. Taste and adjust seasoning, if necessary.

7. Stuff mixture into casings as described on page 24, if using, and twist off into 5-inch links; prick air bubbles with a straight pin or skewer. If time permits, arrange links on a wire rack over a baking sheet and air-dry uncovered in the refrigerator for 1 day before cooking. Alternately, if keeping sausage in bulk, refrigerate mixture for at least 30 minutes to blend flavors.

8. Cook sausages as directed on page 31 to an internal temperature of 165°F when pierced with an instant-read thermometer or as directed in a specific recipe.

Note: Sausages can be refrigerated up to 2 days or frozen up to 2 months. Once cooked, they can be refrigerated up to 3 days.

Spinach and Gruyère Chicken Sausage

Makes 2 pounds

Active time:
1 hour, including
30 minutes to
chill meat

Start to finish:
2 hours

Vibrant green spinach and nutty, creamy cheese in this sausage goes well with some stewed white beans or a tossed salad.

Medium hog sausage casings

2 pounds boneless chicken or turkey
    thigh meat with skin attached

2 tablespoons unsalted butter

2 large shallots, chopped

2 cups firmly packed baby spinach
leaves, rinsed, dried, and chopped

3 tablespoons dry vermouth or
    dry white wine

1 cup grated Gruyère

2 tablespoons chopped fresh parsley

1½ teaspoons kosher salt

½ teaspoon freshly ground
    black pepper

¼ teaspoon dried thyme

¼ teaspoon freshly grated nutmeg

1. Prepare sausage casings as directed on page 21.

2. Cut chicken into 1-inch cubes. Place cubes on a sheet of plastic wrap on a plate and freeze for 30 minutes, or until very firm.

VARIATIONS

Substitute 1½ pounds veal shoulder and ½ pound pork fat for chicken. Cook sausages to an internal temperature of 160°F.

Substitute cheddar or Swiss cheese for Gruyère.

Add 2 garlic cloves, minced, to the skillet with shallots.

3. While chicken chills, heat butter in a medium skillet over medium-high heat. Add shallots and cook for 3 minutes, stirring occasionally, or until shallots are translucent. Add spinach, and cook for 2 minutes, or until spinach wilts. Set aside.

4. Grind chicken through the coarse disk of a meat grinder, or in small batches in a food processor fitted with the steel blade using the on-and-off pulse button. If using a food processor, do not process into a paste, but ingredients should be very finely chopped.

5. Combine chicken, spinach mixture, vermouth, cheese, parsley, salt, pepper, thyme, and nutmeg in a mixing bowl, and knead mixture until well blended. Fry 1 tablespoon of mixture in a small skillet over medium-high heat. Taste and adjust seasoning, if necessary.

6. Stuff mixture into casings as described on page 24 and twist off into 4-inch links; prick air bubbles with a straight pin or skewer. If time permits, arrange links on a wire rack over a baking sheet and air-dry uncovered in the refrigerator for 1 day before cooking.

7. Cook sausages as directed on page 31 to an internal temperature of 165°F when pierced with an instant-read thermometer or as directed in a specific recipe.

Note: Sausages can be refrigerated up to 2 days or frozen up to 2 months. Once cooked, they can be refrigerated up to 3 days.

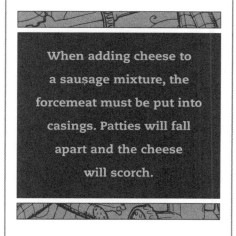

When adding cheese to a sausage mixture, the forcemeat must be put into casings. Patties will fall apart and the cheese will scorch.

Chicken Sausage with Leeks and Blue Cheese

Makes 2 pounds

Active time:
1 hour, including
30 minutes to
chill meat

Start to finish:
2 hours

Leeks have the sweetest flavor of any vegetable in the onion family, which contrasts nicely with bits of sharp blue cheese in this sausage. These sausages need no sauce or mustard to enjoy.

Medium hog sausage casings
2 pounds boneless chicken or turkey
　thigh meat with skin attached
3 large leeks
3 tablespoons unsalted butter
2 garlic cloves, minced
½ cup Chicken Stock (page 296) or
　purchased low-sodium stock
¾ cup crumbled blue cheese
2 tablespoons chopped fresh parsley
1 tablespoon fresh thyme or
　1 teaspoon dried

1½ teaspoons kosher salt
½ teaspoon freshly ground
　black pepper

1. Prepare sausage casings as directed on page 21.

2. Cut chicken into 1-inch cubes. Place cubes on a sheet of plastic wrap on a plate and freeze for 30 minutes, or until very firm.

3. While chicken chills, heat butter in a small skillet over medium-high heat. Add leeks and garlic, and cook, stirring frequently, for 5 minutes, or until leeks soften. Add chicken stock to the skillet, and continue to cook, stirring frequently, for 5 minutes, or until only 3 tablespoons of liquid remains. Set aside.

4. Grind chicken through the fine disk of a meat grinder, or in small batches in a food processor fitted with the steel blade using the on-

VARIATIONS

*Substitute
1½ pounds veal
shoulder or
boneless veal
breast and
½ pound pork
fat for chicken.
Cook sausages
to an internal
temperature
of 160°F.*

*Substitute 1 large
or 2 medium sweet
onions, such
as Bermuda or
Vidalia, for leeks.*

and-off pulse button. If using a food processor, do not process into a paste, but ingredients should be very finely chopped.

5. Combine chicken, leek mixture, blue cheese, parsley, thyme, salt, and pepper in a mixing bowl, and knead mixture until well blended. Fry 1 tablespoon of mixture in a small skillet over medium-high heat. Taste and adjust seasoning, if necessary.

6. Stuff mixture into casings as described on page 24 and twist off into 4-inch links; prick air bubbles with a straight pin or skewer. If time permits, arrange links on a wire rack over a baking sheet and air-dry uncovered in the refrigerator for 1 day before cooking.

7. Cook sausages as directed on page 31 to an internal temperature of 165°F when pierced with an instant-read thermometer or as directed in a specific recipe.

Note: Sausages can be refrigerated up to 2 days or frozen up to 2 months. Once cooked, they can be refrigerated up to 3 days.

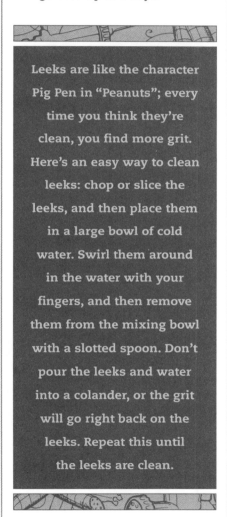

Leeks are like the character Pig Pen in "Peanuts"; every time you think they're clean, you find more grit. Here's an easy way to clean leeks: chop or slice the leeks, and then place them in a large bowl of cold water. Swirl them around in the water with your fingers, and then remove them from the mixing bowl with a slotted spoon. Don't pour the leeks and water into a colander, or the grit will go right back on the leeks. Repeat this until the leeks are clean.

Curried Chicken Sausage with Dried Fruit

Makes 2 pounds

Active time:
1 hour, including
30 minutes to
chill meat

Start to finish:
2 hours

I add some sort of dried fruit when making curry dishes, and this sausage is no exception. Serve with Orange Mustard Sauce (page 476).

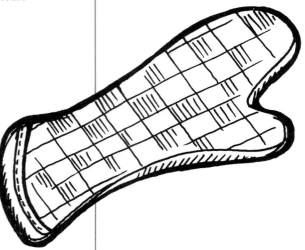

Medium hog sausage casings
   (optional)
2 pounds boneless chicken or turkey
   thigh meat with skin attached
½ cup finely chopped dried apricots
2 tablespoons plain yogurt
2 tablespoons curry powder
1½ teaspoons kosher salt
½ teaspoon ground ginger
½ teaspoon cayenne

1. If using sausage casings, prepare them as directed on page 21.

2. Cut chicken into 1-inch cubes. Place cubes on a sheet of plastic wrap on a plate and freeze for 30 minutes, or until very firm.

3. Grind chicken through the coarse disk of a meat grinder, or in small batches in a food processor fitted with the steel blade using the on-and-off pulse button. If using a food processor, do not process into

VARIATIONS

Substitute 1½ pounds pork butt or boneless country ribs and ½ pound pork fat for chicken. Cook sausages to an internal temperature of 160ºF.

Substitute raisins or dried cranberries for dried apricots.

Increase curry powder to 3 tablespoons and cayenne to 1 teaspoon for spicy sausage.

a paste, but ingredients should be very finely chopped.

4. Combine chicken, dried apricots, curry powder, salt, ginger, and cayenne in a mixing bowl, and knead mixture until well blended. Fry 1 tablespoon of mixture in a small skillet over medium-high heat. Taste and adjust seasoning, if necessary.

5. Stuff mixture into casings as described on page 24, if using, and twist off into 5-inch links; prick air bubbles with a straight pin or skewer. If time permits, arrange links on a wire rack over a baking sheet and air-dry uncovered in the refrigerator for 1 day before cooking. Alternately, if keeping sausage in bulk, refrigerate mixture for at least 30 minutes to blend flavors.

6. Cook sausages as directed on page 31 to an internal temperature of 165°F when pierced with an instant-read thermometer or as directed in a specific recipe.

Note: Sausages can be refrigerated up to 2 days or frozen up to 2 months. Once cooked, they can be refrigerated up to 3 days.

Curry powder is a blend of as many as 20 spices. Using fresh spices, make your own to suit your personal taste. Here's a basic formula: ¾ cup curry powder = 3 tablespoons ground coriander, 2 tablespoons crushed red pepper flakes, 2 tablespoons ground cumin, 2 tablespoons ground fenugreek seeds, 1 tablespoon ground ginger, 1 tablespoon turmeric, 1 tablespoon ground mustard seeds, 1 teaspoon freshly ground black pepper, and 1 teaspoon ground cinnamon. Store in a jar away from sunlight.

Japanese Chicken and Scallion Boudin

Makes 2 pounds

Active time:
1 hour, including
30 minutes to
chill meat

Start to finish:
2 hours

VARIATION

Substitute 1½ pounds pork butt or boneless country ribs and ½ pound pork fat for chicken. Cook sausages to an internal temperature of 160ºF.

While I may be taking some liberties with my recipe titles, I decree that any sausage containing rice can be called boudin. Subtle Japanese seasonings and a bit of fiery wasabi give these sausages a decidedly Asian flavor.

Medium hog sausage casings

2 pounds boneless chicken or turkey
  thigh meat with skin attached

1 cup cooked white rice

1 bunch scallions, white parts and
  4 inches of green tops, chopped

3 garlic cloves, minced

¼ cup reduced-sodium Japanese
  soy sauce

2 tablespoons Asian sesame oil

2 teaspoons grated fresh ginger

½ teaspoon freshly ground
  black pepper

½ teaspoon wasabi powder

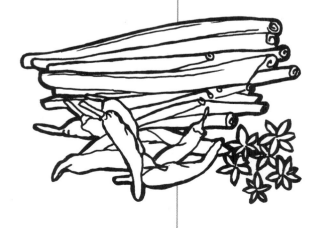

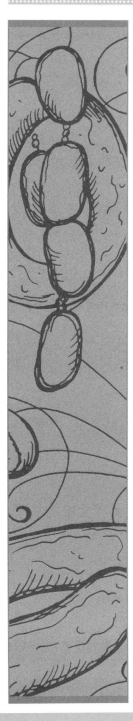

1. Prepare sausage casings as directed on page 21.

2. Cut chicken into 1-inch cubes. Place cubes on a sheet of plastic wrap on a plate and freeze for 30 minutes, or until very firm.

3. Grind chicken through the fine disk of a meat grinder, or in small batches in a food processor fitted with the steel blade using the on-and-off pulse button. If using a food processor, do not process into a paste, but ingredients should be very finely chopped.

4. Combine chicken, rice, scallions, garlic, soy sauce, sesame oil, pepper, and wasabi powder in a mixing bowl, and knead mixture until well blended. Fry 1 tablespoon of mixture in a small skillet over medium-high heat. Taste and adjust seasoning, if necessary.

5. Stuff mixture into casings as described on page 24 and twist off into 5-inch links; prick air bubbles with a straight pin or skewer. If time permits, arrange links on a wire rack over a baking sheet and air-dry uncovered in the refrigerator for 1 day before cooking.

6. Cook sausages as directed on page 31 to an internal temperature of 165°F when pierced with an instant-read thermometer or as directed in a specific recipe.

Note: Sausages can be refrigerated up to 2 days or frozen up to 2 months. Once cooked, they can be refrigerated up to 3 days.

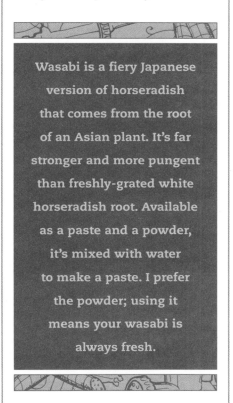

Wasabi is a fiery Japanese version of horseradish that comes from the root of an Asian plant. It's far stronger and more pungent than freshly-grated white horseradish root. Available as a paste and a powder, it's mixed with water to make a paste. I prefer the powder; using it means your wasabi is always fresh.

Asian Duck and Shiitake Mushroom Sausage

Makes 2 pounds

Active time:
1 hour, including
30 minutes to
chill meat

Start to finish:
2 hours

Here's an Asian-inspired sausage that goes with any stir-fried vegetable filling the other side of the plate. The mixture can also be shaped into meatballs, cooked, and served as an hors d'oeuvre.

Medium hog sausage casings
    (optional)
1½ pounds boneless chicken or
    turkey thigh meat with
    skin attached
½ pound boneless duck breast
    without skin
½ cup Chicken Stock (page 296) or
    purchased low-sodium stock
½ cup dried shiitake mushrooms
2 tablespoons Asian sesame oil
1 tablespoon vegetable oil

¼ pound fresh shiitake mushrooms,
    wiped with a damp paper towel,
    stemmed, and chopped
3 scallions, white parts and 4 inches
    of green tops, chopped
2 garlic cloves, minced
1 tablespoon grated fresh ginger
3 tablespoons Chinese oyster sauce
1 tablespoon reduced-sodium
    soy sauce
1½ teaspoons Chinese chile paste
    with garlic

1. If using sausage casings, prepare them as directed on page 21.

2. Cut chicken and duck into 1-inch cubes. Place cubes on a sheet of plastic wrap on a plate and freeze for 30 minutes, or until very firm.

3. While chicken and duck chill, bring stock to a boil in a small saucepan. Add dried shiitake mushrooms, pressing with the

VARIATIONS

Substitute hoisin sauce for oyster sauce, and add ½ teaspoon five-spice powder.

Substitute an additional ½ pound boneless chicken or thigh meat, with skin attached, for duck.

Substitute 1½ pounds pork butt or boneless country rib and ½ pound pork fat for chicken and duck. Cook sausages to an internal temperature of 160°F.

Increase Chinese chile paste with garlic to 1½ tablespoons for spicy sausage.

back of a spoon to push them down into stock. Soak mushrooms for 10 minutes, then drain mushrooms, reserving soaking liquid. Discard stems, and finely chop mushrooms. Strain liquid through a sieve lined with a paper coffee filter or paper towel. Set aside.

4. Heat sesame oil and vegetable oil in a medium skillet over medium-high heat. Add fresh shiitake mushrooms, scallions, garlic, and ginger. Cook, stirring frequently, for 3 to 4 minutes, or until mushrooms soften. Set aside.

5. Grind chicken and duck through the coarse disk of a meat grinder, or in small batches in a food processor fitted with the steel blade using the on-and-off pulse button. If using a food processor, do not process into a paste, but ingredients should be very finely chopped.

6. Combine chicken and duck, dried mushrooms, fresh mushroom mixture, oyster sauce, soy sauce, chile paste, and 2 tablespoons mushroom soaking liquid in a mixing bowl, and knead mixture until well blended. Fry 1 tablespoon of mixture in a small skillet over medium-high heat. Taste and adjust seasoning, if necessary.

7. Stuff mixture into casings as described on page 24, if using, and twist off into 5-inch links; prick air bubbles with a straight pin or skewer. If time permits, arrange links on a wire rack over a baking sheet and air-dry uncovered in the refrigerator for 1 day before cooking. Alternately, if keeping sausage in bulk, refrigerate mixture for at least 30 minutes to blend flavors.

8. Cook sausages as directed on page 31 to an internal temperature of 165°F when pierced with an instant-read thermometer or as directed in a specific recipe.

Note: Sausages can be refrigerated up to 2 days or frozen up to 2 months. Once cooked, they can be refrigerated up to 3 days.

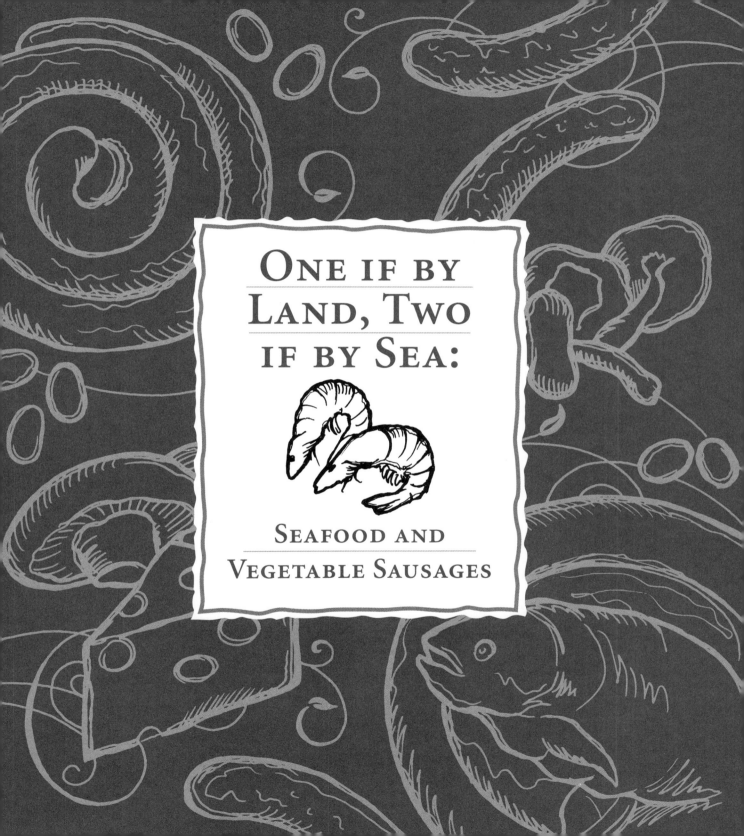

ONE IF BY LAND, TWO IF BY SEA:

SEAFOOD AND VEGETABLE SAUSAGES

While poultry sausages are available, sausages made with seafood and vegetables are harder to find and it's easy to make your own.

There's very little difference between a fish sausage and a quenelle, a classic French seafood dumpling. These sausages are made with a puree of eggs, cream, and seafood.

Buy seafood where the supply is fresh and displayed on chipped ice. Avoid seafood that has been prepackaged, unless it's frozen. Fish should be kept at even a lower temperature than meats. Fish fillets or steaks should look bright, lustrous, and moist, with no signs of discoloration or drying.

When making your selection, keep a few simple guidelines in mind: Ask to smell the fish. If it smells "fishy," pass on it. Fresh fish has the mild, clean scent of the sea—nothing more. If buying whole fish, look for bright, shiny colors in the fish scales, because as a fish sits, its skin becomes more pale and dull looking. Then peer into the eyes; they should be black and beady. If they're milky or sunken, the fish has been out of the water too long and isn't fresh. And if the fish isn't behind glass, gently poke its flesh. If the indentation remains, the fish is old.

Rinse all fish under cold running water before cutting or cooking.

A vegetable peeler and a pair of tweezers are the best ways to get rid of those pesky little bones in fish fillets. Run a peeler down the center of the fillet, starting at the tail end. It will catch the larger pin bones, and with a twist of your wrist, you can pull them out. For finer bones, use your fingers to rub the flesh lightly and then pull out the bones with the tweezers.

POACHING IN PLASTIC WRAP

Whether a vegetarian or simply have an aversion to using animal casings, you can wrap seafood and vegetable sausages in plastic wrap and poach them in simmering water, which results in sausages with a delicate texture.

Many articles have been written about cooking with plastic wrap and the potential dangers of imparting unwanted chemicals from the plastic to the food. My research shows that all of those studies have been done with plastic-wrapped food cooked in the microwave, which subjects them to very high temperatures.

I have found no studies that warn of any danger from cooking food in plastic wrap at lower temperatures. The sausages in the following recipes are poached in water slightly below a simmer (about 180°F).

Shrimp and Leek Sausage

Makes 2 pounds

Active time:
30 minutes

Start to finish:
1 hour

VARIATIONS

Substitute scallops for shrimp; if using large sea scallops, cut them into sixths for poaching.

Substitute Italian seasoning for herbes de Provence.

Add 2 tablespoons nonpareil capers, rinsed, to mixture and reduce salt to ½ teaspoon.

Blushing pink and dotted with light green, these sausages are elegant enough for a special dinner party. Serve them with Tartar Sauce (page 486).

1½ pounds peeled and deveined raw shrimp, divided
2 tablespoons unsalted butter
1 leek, white part only, chopped
2 large egg whites
¾ cup heavy cream
1½ teaspoons kosher salt
1 teaspoon herbes de Provence
¼ teaspoon freshly ground white pepper
Pinch freshly grated nutmeg

1. Bring a small saucepan of salted water to a boil over high heat. Add ½ pound shrimp, cover the pan, then remove the pan from the stove. Drain after 3 to 5 minutes, depending on the size of shrimp; shrimp will not be totally cooked. When cool enough to handle, chop shrimp, and set aside.

2. While shrimp poaches, heat butter in a small skillet over medium heat. Add leek, tossing to coat. Reduce the heat to low, cover the pan, and cook leek, stirring occasionally, for 5 to 7 minutes, or until leek softens. Set aside.

3. Combine remaining shrimp, egg whites, cream, salt, herbes de Provence, pepper, and nutmeg in a food processor fitted with the steel blade or in a blender. Puree until smooth. Scrape mixture into a mixing bowl, and stir in chopped shrimp and leeks. Cook 1 tablespoon of mixture on a microwave-safe dish for 30 seconds, covered with plastic wrap. Taste and adjust seasoning, if necessary.

4. Place a 12 x 12-inch sheet of plastic wrap on the counter in front

of you. Place ⅙ of fish mixture in a line 6 inches long that begins 2 inches from the bottom edge of the plastic wrap. Roll up plastic wrap and squeeze seafood mixture to form a cylinder. Twist ends of plastic wrap tightly, and tie shut with kitchen string. Wrap entire sausage in a second sheet of plastic wrap. Repeat with remaining fish mixture to form a total of 6 sausages.

5. To poach sausages, bring a large pot of water to a boil over high heat. Add sausages, reduce the heat to medium-low, and maintain water at a bare simmer of 180°F; attach a candy thermometer to the side of the pan or take the temperature of the water frequently with an instant-read thermometer. Cook sausages for 20 to 25 minutes, or until firm. Remove one sausage to a plate with tongs and insert an instant-read thermometer. If the temperature is 155°F, sausages are done. If not, return to the pot and continue cooking. Remove sausages from the pan with tongs, and allow sausages to sit for 5 minutes. Then cut off plastic wrap, and serve immediately, or cool to room tem-perature still in the plastic wrap, and refrigerate.

Note: Sausages can be refriger-ated up to a day; they should not be frozen. Once cooked, they can be refrigerated for 2 days. Reheat them by lowering them into sim-mering water for 5 minutes, or in a microwave oven at 45-second intervals on Medium (50 percent power) until hot.

To prevent recipes where the shrimp are only partially cooked in the beginning, poach them briefly in boiling water. To cook shrimp com-pletely, season them with Old Bay seasoning, wrap them in a foil packet and bake them in a 450°F oven for 5 to 8 minutes, depending on the size of the shrimp.

Seafood Scampi Sausage

Makes 2 pounds

- - - - - - - - - - - -

Active time:
30 minutes

- - - - - - - - - - - -

Start to finish:
1 hour

VARIATIONS

*Substitute
¾ pound firm
white-fleshed
fish fillets for
¾ pound scallops.*

*Substitute
½ pound lump
crabmeat for
shrimp. Crab
needs no further
cooking, but
should be picked
over to discard
shell fragments.*

Scampi is the Italian word for shrimp. Scampi has also become synonymous as a baked shrimp dish with the bold flavors of garlic and herbs. Top the shrimp sausages with Herbed Marinara Sauce (page 478).

1 pound bay scallops, or sea scallops
    cut into 6 parts, rinsed, divided
½ pound raw peeled and deveined
    shrimp
2 tablespoons unsalted butter
1 large shallot, chopped
5 garlic cloves, minced
2 large egg whites
½ cup heavy cream
1½ teaspoons kosher salt
½ teaspoon freshly ground
    black pepper
3 tablespoons chopped fresh parsley
1 tablespoon chopped fresh basil

1. Bring a small saucepan of salted water to a boil over high heat. Add ¼ pound scallops and shrimp, cover the pan, then remove the pan from the stove. Drain after 3 to 5 minutes, depending on the size of pieces; the seafood will not be totally cooked. When cool enough to handle, chop scallops and shrimp, and set aside.

2. While seafood poaches, heat butter in a small skillet over medium heat. Add shallot and garlic, and cook, stirring frequently, for 3 to 5 minutes, or until shallot softens. Set aside.

3. Combine remaining scallops, egg whites, cream, salt, and pepper in a food processor fitted with the steel blade or in a blender. Puree until smooth. Scrape mixture into a mixing bowl, and stir in chopped seafood, shallot mixture, parsley, and basil. Cook 1 tablespoon of mixture on a microwave-safe dish for 30 seconds, covered with plastic

wrap. Taste and adjust seasoning, if necessary.

4. Place a 12 x 12-inch sheet of plastic wrap on the counter in front of you. Place ⅙ of fish mixture in a line 6 inches long that begins 2 inches from the bottom edge of the plastic wrap. Roll up plastic wrap and squeeze seafood mixture to form a cylinder. Twist ends of plastic wrap tightly, and tie shut with kitchen string. Wrap entire sausage in a second sheet of plastic wrap. Repeat with remaining fish mixture to form a total of 6 sausages.

5. To poach sausages, bring a large pot of water to a boil over high heat. Add sausages, reduce the heat to medium-low, and maintain water at a bare simmer of 180°F; attach a candy thermometer to the side of the pan or take the temperature of the water frequently with an instant-read thermometer. Cook sausages for 20 to 25 minutes, or until firm. Remove one sausage to a plate with tongs and insert an instant-read thermometer. If the temperature is 155°F, sausages are done. If not, return to the pot and continue cooking. Remove sausages from the pan with tongs, and allow sausages to sit for 5 minutes. Then cut off plastic wrap, and serve immediately, or cool to room temperature still in the plastic wrap, and refrigerate.

Note: Sausages can be refrigerated up to a day; they should not be frozen. Once cooked, they can be refrigerated for 2 days. Reheat them by lowering them into simmering water for 5 minutes, or in a microwave oven at 45-second intervals on Medium (50 percent power) until hot.

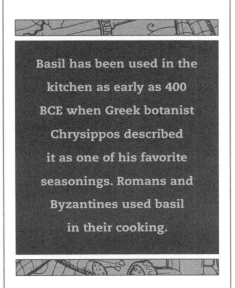

Basil has been used in the kitchen as early as 400 BCE when Greek botanist Chrysippos described it as one of his favorite seasonings. Romans and Byzantines used basil in their cooking.

Cajun Shrimp Boudin

Makes 2 pounds

Active time:
30 minutes

Start to finish:
1 hour

In Louisiana's bayou country this spicy treat is made with crawfish tails. Since they're not readily accessible in other parts of the country, here's an easy version made with shrimp. Serve with red beans and rice, of course.

4 tablespoons (½ stick) unsalted butter
2 leeks, white parts only, chopped and rinsed
3 garlic cloves, minced
1 celery rib, chopped
½ red bell pepper, seeds and ribs removed, and chopped
2 large eggs
¼ cup heavy cream
1 tablespoon tomato paste
1 tablespoon Cajun seasoning

1 tablespoon paprika
½ teaspoon cayenne
½ teaspoon dried thyme
1¼ pounds cooked peeled and deveined shrimp, coarsely chopped
1½ cups cooked white rice
3 tablespoons chopped fresh parsley

1. Heat butter in a medium skillet over medium-high heat. Add leeks, garlic, celery, and red bell pepper. Cook, stirring frequently, for 3 minutes, or until leeks are translucent. Set aside, and cool for 5 minutes.

2. Combine eggs, cream, tomato paste, Cajun seasoning, paprika, cayenne, and thyme in a mixing bowl. Whisk well. Stir in vegetable mixture, shrimp, rice, and parsley. Cook 1 tablespoon of mixture on a microwave-safe dish for 30 seconds, covered with plastic wrap. Taste and adjust seasoning, if necessary.

3. Place a 12 x 12-inch sheet of plastic wrap on the counter in front of you. Place ⅙ of fish mixture in a line 6 inches long that begins 2 inches from the bottom edge of the plastic wrap. Roll up plastic wrap and squeeze seafood mixture to form a cylinder. Twist ends of plastic wrap tightly, and tie shut with kitchen string. Wrap entire sausage in a second sheet of plastic wrap. Repeat with remaining fish mixture to form a total of 6 sausages.

4. To poach sausages, bring a large pot of water to a boil over high heat. Add sausages, reduce the heat to medium-low, and maintain water at a bare simmer of 180°F; attach a candy thermometer to the side of the pan or take the temperature of the water frequently with an instant-read thermometer. Cook sausages for 20 to 25 minutes, or until firm. Remove one sausage to a plate with tongs and insert an instant-read thermometer. If the temperature is 165°F, sausages are done. If not, return to the pot and continue cooking. Remove sausages from the pan with tongs, and allow sausages to sit for 5 minutes.

Then cut off plastic wrap, and serve immediately, or cool to room temperature still in the plastic wrap, and refrigerate.

Note: Sausages can be refrigerated up to a day; they should not be frozen. Once cooked, they can be refrigerated for 2 days. Reheat them by lowering them into simmering water for 5 minutes, or in a microwave oven at 45-second intervals on Medium (50 percent power) until hot.

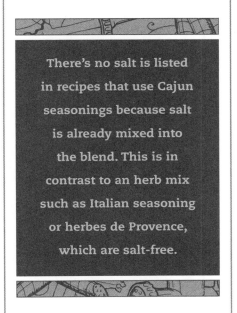

There's no salt is listed in recipes that use Cajun seasonings because salt is already mixed into the blend. This is in contrast to an herb mix such as Italian seasoning or herbes de Provence, which are salt-free.

Scallop Sausage Provençal

VARIATION

Substitute shrimp or lobster meat for scallops.

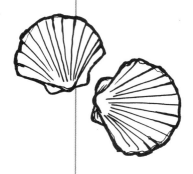

Olives, sun-dried tomatoes, capers, and herbs flavor this seafood sausage. Serve with ratatouille and saffron rice.

1½ pounds bay scallops or sea scallops cut into 6 pieces each, divided
2 tablespoons unsalted butter
1 large shallot, chopped
2 garlic cloves, minced
2 large egg whites
¼ cup heavy cream
2 tablespoons mayonnaise
2 teaspoons herbes de Provence
1½ teaspoons kosher salt
½ teaspoon freshly ground black pepper
¼ cup chopped oil-cured black olives
¼ cup chopped sun-dried tomatoes
2 tablespoons chopped fresh parsley
2 tablespoons small capers, drained and rinsed

1. Bring a small saucepan of salted water to a boil over high heat. Add ½ pound scallops, cover the pan, then remove the pan from the stove. Drain after 3 minutes; scallops will not be totally cooked. When cool enough to handle, chop scallops, and set aside.

2. While scallops poach, heat butter in a small skillet over medium heat. Add shallot and garlic, and cook, stirring frequently, for 3 minutes, or until shallot is translucent. Set aside.

3. Combine remaining scallops, egg whites, cream, and mayonnaise, herbes de Provence, salt, and pepper in a food processor fitted with the steel blade or in a blender. Puree until smooth. Scrape mixture into a mixing bowl, and stir in chopped scallops, shallot mixture, olives, tomatoes, parsley, and capers. Cook 1 tablespoon of mixture on a microwave-safe dish for 30 seconds, covered with plastic

wrap. Taste and adjust seasoning, if necessary.

4. Place a 12 x 12-inch sheet of plastic wrap on the counter in front of you. Place ⅙ of fish mixture in a line 6 inches long that begins 2 inches from the bottom edge of the plastic wrap. Roll up plastic wrap and squeeze seafood mixture to form a cylinder. Twist ends of plastic wrap tightly, and tie shut with kitchen string. Wrap entire sausage in a second sheet of plastic wrap. Repeat with remaining fish mixture to form a total of 6 sausages.

5. To poach sausages, bring a large pot of water to a boil over high heat. Add sausages, reduce the heat to medium-low, and maintain water at a bare simmer of 180°F; attach a candy thermometer to the side of the pan or take the temperature of the water frequently with an instant-read thermometer. Cook sausages for 20 to 25 minutes, or until firm. Remove one sausage to a plate with tongs and insert an instant-read thermometer. If the temperature is 155°F, sausages are done. If not, return to the pot and continue cooking. Remove sausages from the pan with tongs, and allow sausages to sit for 5 minutes. Then cut off plastic wrap, and serve immediately, or cool to room temperature still in the plastic wrap, and refrigerate.

Note: Sausages can be refrigerated up to a day; they should not be frozen. Once cooked, they can be refrigerated for 2 days. Reheat them by lowering them into simmering water for 5 minutes, or in a microwave oven at 45-second intervals on Medium (50 percent power) until hot.

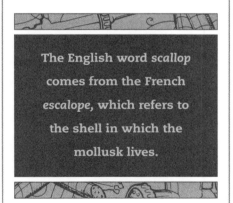

The English word *scallop* comes from the French *escalope*, which refers to the shell in which the mollusk lives.

Southwestern Crab Sausage

Cilantro and chili powder are folded into a base of smooth crabmeat mousse. A bowl of guacamole and one of salsa complete the meal.

1 pound mild-flavored white fish
   fillets, such as halibut, cod,
   or sole
3 tablespoons unsalted butter
4 scallions, white parts and 3 inches
   of green tops, chopped
½ red bell pepper, seeds and ribs
   removed, and chopped
2 garlic cloves, peeled and minced
½ cup heavy cream
1 large egg
3 tablespoons plain breadcrumbs
3 tablespoons chopped fresh cilantro
1 tablespoon paprika
1 tablespoon chili powder
2 teaspoons Worcestershire sauce
1½ teaspoons kosher salt
½ teaspoon dried oregano
½ teaspoon cayenne

¾ *pound lump crabmeat, picked over to remove shell fragments*

1. Rinse fish, pat dry with paper towels, remove any bones, and cut into 1-inch pieces. Place cubes on a sheet of plastic wrap, and freeze for 20 to 30 minutes, or until firm but not frozen solid.

2. Heat butter in a small skillet over medium-high heat. Add scallions, bell pepper, and garlic, and cook, stirring frequently, for 3 to 5 minutes, or until vegetables soften. Set aside.

3. Combine fish cubes, cream, and egg in a food processor fitted with the steel blade or in a blender. Puree until smooth. Scrape mixture into a mixing bowl, and stir in breadcrumbs, cilantro, paprika, chili powder, Worcestershire sauce, salt, oregano, and cayenne. Whisk until smooth, then gently fold in crab and vegetable mixture. Cook 1 tablespoon of mixture on a

microwave-safe dish for 30 seconds, covered with plastic wrap. Taste and adjust seasoning, if necessary.

4. Place a 12 x 12-inch sheet of plastic wrap on the counter in front of you. Place ⅙ of fish mixture in a line 6 inches long that begins 2 inches from the bottom edge of the plastic wrap. Roll up plastic wrap and squeeze seafood mixture to form a cylinder. Twist ends of plastic wrap tightly, and tie shut with kitchen string. Wrap entire sausage in a second sheet of plastic wrap. Repeat with remaining fish mixture to form a total of 6 sausages.

5. To poach sausages, bring a large pot of water to a boil over high heat. Add sausages, reduce the heat to medium-low, and maintain water at a bare simmer of 180°F; attach a candy thermometer to the side of the pan or take the temperature of the water frequently with an instant-read thermometer. Cook sausages for 20 to 25 minutes, or until firm. Remove one sausage to a plate with tongs and insert an instant-read thermometer. If the temperature is 155°F, sausages are done. If not, return to the pot and continue cooking. Remove sausages from the pan with tongs, and allow sausages to sit for 5 minutes. Then cut off plastic wrap, and serve immediately, or cool to room temperature still in the plastic wrap, and refrigerate.

Note: Sausages can be refrigerated up to a day; they should not be frozen. Once cooked, they can be refrigerated for 2 days. Reheat them by lowering them into simmering water for 5 minutes, or in a microwave oven at 45-second intervals on Medium (50 percent power) until hot.

To ensure that no shell fragments find their way into a dish, spread out the crab on a dark-colored plate. You'll see shell fragments against the dark background so you can pick them out easily.

Italian Fish and Spinach Sausage

Makes 2 pounds

Active time:
30 minutes

Start to finish:
1 hour

VARIATIONS

Substitute salmon, halibut, or haddock for cod.

Reduce cod to 1½ pounds, and fold in ½ pound lump crabmeat after other ingredients have been blended.

Heady Parmesan, creamy mozzarella, herbs, and bright green spinach are all combined into this easy-to-prepare sausage. Serve with risotto and a tossed salad in a garlicky dressing.

1½ pounds fresh cod fillet
½ (10-ounce) package frozen chopped spinach, thawed
¼ cup heavy cream
1 large egg
1 large egg white
1 garlic clove, minced
¼ cup grated whole-milk mozzarella
3 tablespoons freshly grated Parmesan
3 tablespoons chopped fresh parsley
1 tablespoon chopped fresh oregano or 1 teaspoon dried
1½ teaspoons kosher salt
½ teaspoon freshly ground black pepper

1. Rinse cod, pat dry with paper towels, and cut into 1-inch pieces. Place cod cubes on a sheet of plastic wrap, and freeze for 20 to 30 minutes, or until firm but not frozen solid. Place spinach in a colander and press with the back of a spoon to extract as much liquid as possible. Set aside.

2. Combine fish cubes, cream, egg, egg white, and garlic in a food processor fitted with the steel blade or in a blender. Puree until smooth. Scrape mixture into a mixing bowl, and stir in spinach, mozzarella, Parmesan, parsley, oregano, salt, and pepper. Stir well. Cook 1 tablespoon of mixture on a microwave-safe dish for 30 seconds, covered with plastic wrap. Taste and adjust seasoning, if necessary.

3. Place a 12 x 12-inch sheet of plastic wrap on the counter in front of you. Place ⅙ of fish mixture in a line 6 inches long that begins 2 inches from the bottom

edge of the plastic wrap. Roll up plastic wrap and squeeze seafood mixture to form a cylinder. Twist ends of plastic wrap tightly, and tie shut with kitchen string. Wrap entire sausage in a second sheet of plastic wrap. Repeat with remaining fish mixture to form a total of 6 sausages.

4. To poach sausages, bring a large pot of water to a boil over high heat. Add sausages, reduce the heat to medium-low, and maintain water at a bare simmer of 180°F; attach a candy thermometer to the side of the pan or take the temperature of the water frequently with an instant-read thermometer. Cook sausages for 20 to 25 minutes, or until firm. Remove one sausage to a plate with tongs and insert an instant-read thermometer. If the temperature is 155°F, sausages are done. If not, return to the pot and continue cooking. Remove sausages from the pan with tongs, and allow sausages to sit for 5 minutes. Then cut off plastic wrap, and serve immediately, or cool to room temperature still in the plastic wrap, and refrigerate.

Note: Sausages can be refrigerated up to a day; they should not be frozen. Once cooked, they can be refrigerated for 2 days. Reheat them by lowering them into simmering water for 5 minutes, or in a microwave oven at 45-second intervals on Medium (50 percent power) until hot.

Cod are so important to the history of New England fishing that Cape Cod became the official name for the sandbar. Cod are omnivorous, bottom-dwelling fish that are caught both in Nantucket Sound as well as in offshore waters. Scrod is a fancier term for small cod, since the fillets are thinner and can be sautéed better than those taken from larger fish. In some restaurants, scrod can also be haddock, and the two are similar.

Dilled Salmon Sausage

Makes 2 pounds

Active time:

30 minutes

Start to finish:

1 hour

VARIATIONS

Substitute cod, halibut, or monkfish for salmon.

Substitute a combination of parsley and tarragon for dill.

This dish has northern European inspirations with its use of fresh herb and contrasting sharp mustard. Serve with Green Mustard Sauce (page 471).

1¾ pounds skinned salmon fillet
1 large egg
1 large egg white
¼ cup mayonnaise
¼ cup heavy cream
3 tablespoons Dijon mustard
3 tablespoons chopped fresh dill
3 tablespoons plain breadcrumbs
1½ teaspoons kosher salt
¼ teaspoon freshly ground
   black pepper

1. Rinse salmon, pat dry with paper towels, remove any bones, and cut into 1-inch pieces. Place salmon cubes on a sheet of plastic wrap, and freeze for 20 to 30 minutes, or until firm but not frozen solid.

2. While fish chills, whisk egg, egg white, mayonnaise, cream, and mustard in a mixing bowl. Add dill, breadcrumbs, salt, and pepper, and whisk well.

3. Chop salmon in a food processor fitted with a steel blade using the on-and-off pulse button. Add salmon to the mixing bowl, and knead mixture until well blended. Cook 1 tablespoon of mixture on a microwave-safe dish for 30 seconds, covered with plastic wrap. Taste and adjust seasoning, if necessary.

4. Place a 12 x 12-inch sheet of plastic wrap on the counter in front of you. Place ⅙ of fish mixture in a line 6 inches long that begins 2

inches from the bottom edge of the plastic wrap. Roll up plastic wrap and squeeze seafood mixture to form a cylinder. Twist ends of plastic wrap tightly, and tie shut with kitchen string. Wrap entire sausage in a second sheet of plastic wrap. Repeat with remaining fish mixture to form a total of 6 sausages.

5. To poach sausages, bring a large pot of water to a boil over high heat. Add sausages, reduce the heat to medium-low, and maintain water at a bare simmer of 180°F; attach a candy thermometer to the side of the pan or take the temperature of the water frequently with an instant-read thermometer. Cook sausages for 20 to 25 minutes, or until firm. Remove one sausage to a plate with tongs and insert an instant-read thermometer. If the temperature is 155°F, sausages are done. If not, return to the pot and continue cooking. Remove sausages from the pan with tongs, and allow sausages to sit for 5 minutes. Then cut off plastic wrap, and serve immediately, or cool to room temperature still in the plastic wrap, and refrigerate.

Note: Sausages can be refrigerated up to a day; they should not be frozen. Once cooked, they can be refrigerated for 2 days. Reheat them by lowering them into simmering water for 5 minutes, or in a microwave oven at 45-second intervals on Medium (50 percent power) until hot.

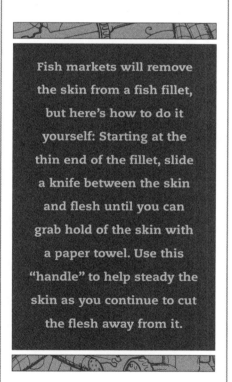

Fish markets will remove the skin from a fish fillet, but here's how to do it yourself: Starting at the thin end of the fillet, slide a knife between the skin and flesh until you can grab hold of the skin with a paper towel. Use this "handle" to help steady the skin as you continue to cut the flesh away from it.

Middle Eastern Lentil Sausage

Makes 2 pounds

Active time:
20 minutes

Start to finish:
1¼ hours, including
30 minutes to
chill mixture

Substitute
either green or
yellow split peas
for lentils.

Flavored with aromatic spices, tomato, and harissa, these sausages also have a crunchy texture from pine nuts. You can also make them as miniatures and serve them as a hors d'oeuvre. Serve with Greek Feta Sauce (page 488).

4 cups lentils, picked over, rinsed,
    and drained
1½ cups pine nuts
¼ cup olive oil
1 large onion, chopped
4 garlic cloves, minced
1 tablespoon ground coriander
2 teaspoons ground cumin
2 large eggs
¼ cup tomato juice
2 tablespoons tomato paste
1 tablespoon harissa

1 cups plain breadcrumbs
1½ teaspoons kosher salt
¾ teaspoon freshly ground black
    pepper to taste
Vegetable oil spray

1. Place lentils in a 4-quart saucepan, and cover with 2 quarts water. Bring to a boil over medium-high heat, then reduce the heat to low and simmer lentils, covered, for 15 minutes. Add salt, and cook for an additional 10 minutes, or until tender. Drain, and set aside.

2. While lentils simmer, place pine nuts in a small dry skillet over medium-high heat. Toast nuts, shaking the pan frequently, for 2 to 3 minutes, or until browned. Remove nuts from the pan, and set aside.

3. Heat oil in the same small skillet over medium-high heat. Add onion and garlic, and cook, stirring frequently, for 3 minutes,

or until onion is translucent. Add coriander and cumin, and cook for 1 minute, stirring constantly.

4. Whisk eggs, tomato juice, tomato paste, and harissa in a mixing bowl, add breadcrumbs, and mix well. Add lentils and onion mixture, and stir well.

5. Puree ½ cup pine nuts and 1 cup lentil mixture in a food processor fitted with a metal blade. Scrape mixture back into mixing bowl, and add remaining pine nuts. Season to taste with salt and pepper. Refrigerate lentil mixture for at least 30 minutes.

6. Preheat the oven to 450°F, line a rimmed baking sheet with heavy-duty aluminum foil, and spray the foil with vegetable oil spray. Divide sausage mixture in half, and arrange each half in a cylinder 1½-inches high; alternately, divide mixture into 4 to 6 patties 1½-inches high. Spray tops of sausages with vegetable oil spray.

7. Bake lentil sausages for 12 to 15 minutes, or until cooked through. Remove the pan from the oven, and serve immediately.

Note: The lentil mixture can be prepared up to a day in advance and refrigerated, tightly covered. Also, the sausages can be baked up to 2 days in advance and refrigerated, tightly covered. Reheat them in a 350°F oven, covered, for 10 to 12 minutes, or until hot.

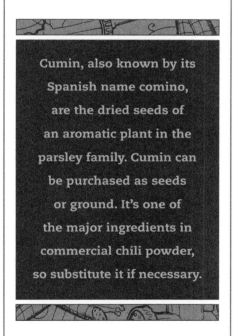

Cumin, also known by its Spanish name comino, are the dried seeds of an aromatic plant in the parsley family. Cumin can be purchased as seeds or ground. It's one of the major ingredients in commercial chili powder, so substitute it if necessary.

Southwestern Black Bean Sausages

Makes 1½ pounds

Active time:
25 minutes

Start to finish:
1 hour, including 30 minutes to chill mixture

Substitute kidney beans, garbanzo beans, or small navy beans for black beans.

Substitute 2 chipotle chiles in adobo sauce, finely chopped, for fresh chiles

These sausages can be put together in no time, because canned beans are used. The traditional pantheon of Southwestern ingredients—chili powder, chiles, and cilantro—are included. Serve with Mexican Tomato Sauce (page 479).

2 tablespoons olive oil
1 large onion, chopped
3 garlic cloves, minced
2 jalapeño or serrano chiles, seeds and ribs removed, and chopped
2 tablespoons chili powder
1½ tablespoons ground cumin
2 (15-ounce) cans black beans, drained and rinsed
½ cup chopped fresh cilantro
1 teaspoon kosher salt
½ teaspoon freshly ground black pepper
2 large eggs, beaten
Vegetable oil spray

1. Heat olive oil in a heavy large skillet over medium-high heat. Add onion, garlic, and chiles, and cook, stirring frequently, for 3 minutes, or until onion is translucent. Add chili powder and cumin and cook for 1 minute, stirring constantly. Add black beans, cilantro, and ½ cup water. Bring to a boil

and simmer mixture, stirring frequently, for 3 minutes.

2. Transfer mixture to a food processor fitted with a steel blade or to a blender, and puree. Scrape mixture into a mixing bowl, and season with salt and pepper. Refrigerate mixture for 30 minutes. Mix in eggs, and knead well.

3. Preheat the oven to 450°F, line a rimmed baking sheet with heavy-duty aluminum foil, and spray the foil with vegetable oil spray. Divide sausage mixture in half, and arrange each half in a cylinder 1½-inches high; alternately, divide mixture into 4 to 6 patties 1½-inches high. Spray tops of sausages with vegetable oil spray.

4. Bake bean sausages for 12 to 15 minutes, or until cooked through. Remove the pan from the oven, and serve immediately.

Note: The black bean mixture can be prepared for baking up to a day in advance and refrigerated, tightly covered. They can also be baked in advance; reheat them in a 400°F oven for 5 to 7 minutes, or until hot and crusty again.

To make your own chili powder, combine 2 tablespoons ground red chile, 2 tablespoons paprika, 1 tablespoon ground coriander, 1 tablespoon garlic powder, 1 tablespoon onion powder, 2 teaspoons ground cumin, 2 teaspoons ground red pepper or cayenne, 1 teaspoon ground black pepper, and 1 teaspoon dried oregano in a jar. Cover, shake to blend, and store with other spices.

Kidney Bean and Sweet Potato Sausages

Makes 1½ pounds

Active time:
30 minutes

Start to finish:
1 hour

These colorful sausages combine brightly colored orange sweet potatoes with deep red beans. The seasoning is mild, and they make a great side dish with grilled meats and poultry, too.

¾ *pound sweet potatoes, scrubbed and cut into 2-inch pieces*

3 *scallions, white parts and 3 inches of green tops, chopped*

2 *tablespoons chopped fresh parsley*

1 *tablespoon chopped fresh sage or 1 teaspoon dried*

1 *(15-ounce) can kidney beans, drained and rinsed*

2 *large eggs*

2 *garlic cloves, peeled*

1½ *teaspoons kosher salt*

½ *teaspoon freshly ground black pepper*

1. Cover sweet potatoes with salted water, and bring to a boil over high heat. Reduce the heat to medium, and cook potatoes for 15 minutes, or until tender. Drain potatoes, and when cool enough to handle, peel potatoes and place them in a mixing bowl.

2. Add scallions, parsley, and sage to the bowl, and mash potatoes with a potato masher until smooth.

3. Combine beans, eggs, garlic, salt, and pepper in the work bowl of a food processor fitted with a steel blade. Process until the mixture forms a smooth paste, scraping the sides of the work bowl as necessary. Add mixture to the mixing bowl, and mix well. Cook 1 tablespoon of mixture on a microwave-safe dish for 30 seconds, covered with plastic wrap. Taste and adjust seasoning, if necessary.

4. Place a 12 x 12-inch sheet of plastic wrap on the counter in front of you. Place ⅙ of mixture in a line 6 inches long that begins 2 inches from the bottom edge of the plastic wrap. Roll up plastic wrap and squeeze mixture to form a cylinder. Twist ends of plastic wrap tightly, and tie shut with kitchen string. Wrap entire sausage in a second sheet of plastic wrap. Repeat with remaining mixture to form a total of 6 sausages.

5. To poach sausages, bring a large pot of water to a boil over high heat. Add sausages, reduce the heat to medium-low, and maintain water at a bare simmer of 180°F; attach a candy thermometer to the side of the pan or take the temperature of the water frequently with an instant-read thermometer. Cook sausages for 20 to 25 minutes, or until firm. Remove one sausage to a plate with tongs and insert an instant-read thermometer. If the temperature is 155°F, sausages are done. If not, return to the pot and continue cooking. Remove sausages from the pan with tongs, and allow sausages to sit for 5 minutes. Then cut off plastic wrap, and serve immediately, or cool to room temperature still in the plastic wrap, and refrigerate.

Note: Sausages can be refrigerated up to a day; they should not be frozen. Once cooked, they can be refrigerated for 3 days. Reheat them by lowering them into simmering water for 5 minutes, or in a microwave oven at 45-second intervals on Medium (50 percent power) until hot.

The sweet potato provides proof for Thor Heyerdahl's theory that it was South American navigators who first crossed the Pacific. The Maoris of New Zealand have a tradition that the sweet potato, native to the tropical Americas, came to them from "the country of our ancestors."

Tofu-Mushroom Sausages

Makes 1½ pounds

Active time:
30 minutes

Start to finish:
1 hour

VARIATION

Make the balls with fresh portobello mushrooms for an even earthier flavor.

The meatiness in these vegetarian sausages comes from the sautéed mushrooms. Top spaghetti with sliced sausages, or serve them with Herbed Marinara Sauce (page 478).

3 tablespoons olive oil
1 large onion, diced
3 garlic cloves, minced
2 cups diced mushrooms
1½ teaspoons kosher salt
½ teaspoon freshly ground
    black pepper
1 (14-ounce) package extra-firm
    tofu, drained and crumbled
1 large egg
¼ cup Italian breadcrumbs
3 tablespoons chopped fresh parsley
2 tablespoons chopped fresh
    rosemary or 2 teaspoons dried
Vegetable oil spray

1. Heat oil in a medium skillet over medium-high heat. Add onion and garlic and cook, stirring frequently, for 3 minutes, or until onion is translucent. Add mushrooms, sprinkle with salt and pepper, and cook, stirring frequently, for 5 minutes, or until mushrooms give off water and it then evaporates. Scrape mixture into a mixing bowl, and set aside.

2. Combine tofu, egg, breadcrumbs, parsley, and rosemary in a food processor fitted with a steel blade, and puree until smooth. Scrape mixture into the mixing bowl with mushrooms, and season to taste with salt and pepper. Mix well. Cook 1 tablespoon of mixture on a microwave-safe dish for 30 seconds, covered with plastic wrap. Taste and adjust seasoning, if necessary.

4. Place a 12 x 12-inch sheet of plastic wrap on the counter in front of you. Place ⅙ of mixture in a line 6 inches long that begins 2 inches from the bottom edge of

the plastic wrap. Roll up plastic wrap and squeeze mixture to form a cylinder. Twist ends of plastic wrap tightly, and tie shut with kitchen string. Wrap entire sausage in a second sheet of plastic wrap. Repeat with remaining mixture to form a total of 6 sausages.

5. To poach sausages, bring a large pot of water to a boil over high heat. Add sausages, reduce the heat to medium-low, and maintain water at a bare simmer of 180°F; attach a candy thermometer to the side of the pan or take the temperature of the water frequently with an instant-read thermometer. Cook sausages for 20 to 25 minutes, or until firm. Remove one sausage to a plate with tongs and insert an instant-read thermometer. If the temperature is 155°F, sausages are done. If not, return to the pot and continue cooking. Remove sausages from the pan with tongs, and allow sausages to sit for 5 minutes. Then cut off plastic wrap, and serve immediately, or cool to room temperature still in the plastic wrap, and refrigerate.

Note: Sausages can be refrigerated up to a day; they should not be frozen. Once cooked, they can be refrigerated for 3 days. Reheat them by lowering them into simmering water for 5 minutes, or in a microwave oven at 45-second intervals on Medium (50 percent power) until hot.

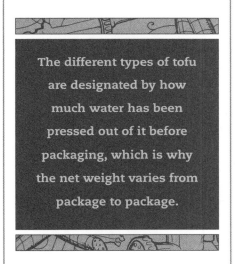

The different types of tofu are designated by how much water has been pressed out of it before packaging, which is why the net weight varies from package to package.

Sausages by Other Names:

Terrines, Pâtés, and Scrapple

All sausage mixtures are classified as forcemeat. Forcemeat is a mixture of lean meat, fat, and other ingredients that are then ground up; the word comes from the French "to stuff." In the previous chapters, the forcemeat was usually stuffed into a sausage casing of some sort to create a cylinder, or in some cases, the mixture could be shaped into patties and fried.

In this chapter you'll be making similar forcemeat to sausage, but in most cases, the mixture will shaped into a loaf and baked. Both pâtés and terrines are drawn from the French charcuterie tradition, which dates back to the fifteenth century. To differentiate the two, most culinary experts agree that a pâté is a smooth mixture that's spreadable on a cracker or toast point, while a terrine has a coarser texture and is usually eaten with a fork.

In America we have similar loaf versions, although they're not as fancy as French ones. In the Mid-Atlantic States during the seventeenth century, German immigrants combined meat with cornmeal, which is known as scrapple. It is based on a dish from their homeland called *ponhaus*. A similar dish further west in Cincinnati, Ohio, is called *goetta*, which is made with oats, rather than cornmeal.

The recipes in this chapter range from plain and hearty for breakfast or elegant and delicate for a sophisticated dinner.

Country Pork Terrine

Makes 8 to 10 servings

Active time:
1 hour, including
30 minutes to
chill meat

Start to finish:
8 hours

VARIATIONS

*Substitute
½ pound fatty
veal for ½ pound
of pork.*

*Substitute
½ pound finely
chopped raw
chicken livers
for ham.*

*Substitute
Calvados for
brandy.*

Coarsely ground meat, seasoned with a range of herbs and spices along with some brandy and cream make a classic pork terrine. Serve the slices with bread, mustard, and cornichons (or other pickles).

1¼ pounds pork butt or boneless
    country ribs, cut into 1-inch cubes
¼ pound pork fat, cut into 1-inch
    cubes
4 tablespoons (½ stick) unsalted
    butter
1 large onion, finely chopped
3 garlic cloves, mined
2 tablespoons chopped fresh parsley
1 teaspoon dried thyme
¼ teaspoon freshly grated nutmeg
¼ teaspoon ground allspice
Salt and freshly ground black
    pepper to taste
½ cup heavy cream

3 tablespoons brandy
2 large eggs, beaten
½ pound baked ham, cut into
    ¼-inch dice
¾ pound bacon

1. Place pork and pork fat on a sheet of waxed paper, and freeze for 30 minutes, or until stiff. Grind pork and pork fat through a meat grinder or chop finely in a food processor fitted with the steel blade, using the on-and-off pulse button.

2. While meats chill, heat butter in a small skillet over medium-high heat. Add onion and garlic, and cook, stirring frequently, for 3 minutes, or until onion is translucent. Scrape mixture into a mixing bowl, and add parsley, thyme, nutmeg, allspice, salt, pepper, cream, brandy, and eggs. Stir well.

3. Preheat the oven to 325°F and bring a kettle of water to a boil. Add ground meats to the mixing bowl, and beat with a spoon until well

blended. Stir in ham cubes. Fry 1 tablespoon of mixture in a small skillet over medium-high heat. Taste and adjust seasoning, if necessary.

4. Line the bottom and sides of a 9 x 5-inch loaf pan with bacon strips, reserving some strips for the top. Fill the pan with meat mixture, rapping it on the counter to remove any air bubbles. Cover the top with bacon strips, and wrap entire pan with heavy-duty aluminum foil. Place the loaf pan into a roasting pan and pour in boiling water to come halfway up the sides of the pan.

5. Bake for 1¾ to 2 hours, or until an instant-read thermometer inserted into the center of the loaf registers 160°F. Remove the pan from the oven, discard the foil, and allow it to sit on a rack for 30 minutes.

6. Place the terrine in the sink, and place another loaf pan of the same size on top of it. Press down to extract excess liquid, and then add 3 pounds of weights, such as 3 (15-ounce) cans, into the top loaf pan. Refrigerate terrine, with weights, for 4 hours, or until chilled; it is preferable for the terrine to chill overnight to blend the flavors.

7. To serve, remove the terrine from the refrigerator, and place it into a pan of very hot tap water for 3 minutes. Run a knife around the sides of the loaf pan, and then invert the terrine onto a cutting board or serving platter. Discard any liquid, and cut the terrine into ½-inch slices.

Note: The terrine can be made up to 2 days in advance and refrigerated, tightly covered.

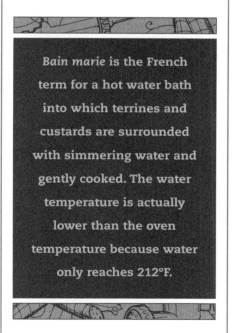

Bain marie is the French term for a hot water bath into which terrines and custards are surrounded with simmering water and gently cooked. The water temperature is actually lower than the oven temperature because water only reaches 212°F.

Ham and Apple Terrine

Makes 8 to 10 servings

Active time:
1 hour, including 30 minutes to chill meat

Start to finish:
8 hours

Here is an Americanized version of a terrine based on a dish I enjoyed many years ago when New American Cuisine was in its infancy and Bradley Ogden was chef at the Campton Place Hotel in San Francisco. The sweetness from apples, dried fruit, and Port is a welcome change from the classic savory mix.

1½ pounds pork butt or boneless country ribs

½ pound pork fat

¼ cup dried currants

¾ cup ruby Port

½ cup heavy cream

2 tablespoons brandy

1 large egg, beaten

2 Golden Delicious apples, peeled and chopped

½ teaspoon ground allspice

½ teaspoon dried thyme

Pinch freshly grated nutmeg

Salt and freshly ground black pepper to taste

3/4 pound bacon

¼ pound baked ham, sliced ¼-inch thick and cut into ¼-inch strips

1. Place pork and pork fat on a sheet of waxed paper, and freeze for 30 minutes, or until stiff. Soak dried currants in Port for 30 minutes.

2. Preheat the oven to 325°F and bring a kettle of water to a boil. Grind meat and fat through the coarse disk of a meat grinder, or in small batches in a food processor fitted with the steel blade using the on-and-off pulse button. If using a food processor, do not process into a paste, but ingredients should be very finely chopped.

3. Combine pork, currants, Port, cream, brandy, egg, apple, allspice, thyme, nutmeg, salt, and pepper in a mixing bowl. Beat with a spoon until well blended. Fry 1 tablespoon of mixture in a small skillet over medium-high heat. Taste and adjust seasoning, if necessary.

4. Line the bottom and sides of a 9 x 5-inch loaf pan with bacon strips, reserving some strips for the top. Fill the pan with ⅓ meat mixture, and top with ½ of ham strips. Repeat with another ⅓ of meat mixture and remaining ham, ending with the last ⅓ of meat mixture. Rap the loaf pan on the counter to remove any air bubbles. Cover the top with bacon strips, and wrap the entire pan with heavy-duty aluminum foil. Place the loaf pan into a roasting pan and pour in boiling water to come halfway up the sides of the pan.

5. Bake for 1¾ to 2 hours, or until an instant-read thermometer inserted into the center of the loaf registers 160°F. Remove the pan from the oven, discard the foil, and allow it to sit on a rack for 30 minutes.

6. Place the terrine in the sink, and place another loaf pan of the same size on top of it. Press down to extract excess liquid, and then add 3 pounds of weights, such as 3 (15-ounce) cans, into the top loaf pan. Refrigerate terrine, with weights, for 4 hours, or until chilled; it is preferable for the terrine to chill overnight to blend the flavors.

7. To serve, remove the terrine from the refrigerator, and place it into a pan of very hot tap water for 3 minutes. Run a knife around the sides of the loaf pan, and then invert the terrine onto a cutting board or serving platter. Discard any liquid, and cut the terrine into ½-inch slices.

Note: The terrine can be made up to 2 days in advance and refrigerated, tightly covered.

Chicken and Mushroom Terrine

Makes 8 to 10
servings

Active time:
1 hour, including
30 minutes to
chill meat

Start to finish:
8 hours

VARIATIONS

*Substitute pork
butt or boneless
country ribs
for chicken.*

*Substitute
Calvados or
Grand Marnier
for brandy.*

This terrine is lighter than most because it's made with chicken and woodsy mushrooms. It goes nicely with Green Mustard Sauce (page 471).

1 pound boneless chicken thigh
    meat with skin attached
¼ pound pork fat
6 tablespoons (¾ stick) unsalted
    butter, divided
1 medium onion, chopped
2 garlic cloves, minced
½ pound white mushrooms,
    wiped with a damp paper towel,
    and chopped
½ pound fresh shiitake mushrooms,
    stemmed, wiped with a damp
    paper towel, and chopped
½ cup dry white wine
3 tablespoons brandy
1 large egg, beaten
½ cup heavy cream
2 tablespoons chopped fresh parsley
1 teaspoon herbes de Provence

Salt and freshly ground black
    pepper to taste
Vegetable oil spray

1. Cut chicken and pork fat into 1-inch cubes. Place cubes on a sheet of waxed paper, and freeze for 30 minutes, or until stiff.

2. While meats chill, heat 2 tablespoons butter in a large skillet over medium-high heat. Add onion and garlic, and cook, stirring frequently, for 3 minutes, or until onion is translucent. Scrape mixture into a mixing bowl.

3. Heat remaining butter in the skillet and add white mushrooms and shiitake mushrooms. Cook, stirring frequently, for 5 minutes, or until mushrooms soften. Add wine and brandy and cook over high heat, stirring frequently, until liquid evaporates. Scrape mushrooms into the bowl with the onion and garlic.

4. Preheat the oven to 350°F and bring a kettle of water to a boil. Grind meat and fat through the coarse disk of a meat grinder, or in small batches in a food processor fitted with the steel blade using the on-and-off pulse button. If using a food processor, do not process into a paste, but ingredients should be very finely chopped.

5. Add meats, egg, cream, parsley, herbes de Provence, salt, and pepper to the mixing bowl, and beat with a spoon until well blended. Fry 1 tablespoon of mixture in a small skillet over medium-high heat. Taste and adjust seasoning, if necessary.

6. Grease the bottom and sides of a 9 x 5-inch loaf pan with vegetable oil spray. Fill the pan with meat mixture, rapping it on the counter to remove any air bubbles. Wrap the entire pan with heavy-duty aluminum foil. Place the loaf pan into a roasting pan and pour in boiling water to come halfway up the sides of the pan.

7. Bake for 1½ to 1¾ hours, or until an instant-read thermom-eter inserted into the center of the loaf registers 165°F. Remove the pan from the oven, discard the foil, and allow it to sit on a rack for 30 minutes.

8. Place the terrine in the sink, and place another loaf pan of the same size on top of it. Press down to extract excess liquid, and then add 3 pounds of weights, such as 3 (15-ounce) cans, into the top loaf pan. Refrigerate terrine, with weights, for 4 hours, or until chilled; it is preferable for the terrine to chill overnight to blend the flavors.

9. To serve, remove the terrine from the refrigerator, and place it into a pan of very hot tap water for 3 minutes. Run a knife around the sides of the loaf pan, and then invert the terrine onto a cutting board or serving platter. Discard any liquid, and cut the terrine into ½-inch slices.

Note: The terrine can be made up to 2 days in advance and refrigerated, tightly covered.

Smoked Fish Terrine

Makes 8 to 10 servings

Active time: 1 hour, including 30 minutes to chill fish

Start to finish: 6 hours

VARIATION

Substitute raw shrimp or scallops for fish.

Its shape determines a terrine, and the actual pan in which it's cooked is also called a terrine. But the actual food can be anything. In this it's a combination of fresh and smoked fish.

1 pound firm-fleshed white fish fillets such as cod, flounder, or halibut, rinsed and cut into 1-inch cubes

⅓ pound smoked whitefish fillet

2 large eggs

¾ cup heavy cream

⅓ cup chopped fresh parsley

Salt and freshly ground black pepper to taste

¾ pound smoked salmon, thickly sliced

¾ pound smoked sturgeon, thickly sliced

Vegetable oil spray

1. Place fish cubes on a sheet of waxed paper, and freeze for 30 minutes, or until stiff. Grease the inside of a 9 x 5-inch loaf pan lightly with vegetable oil spray.

2. Preheat the oven to 350°F and bring a kettle of water to a boil.

3. Combine fresh fish, smoked whitefish, eggs, and cream in a food processor fitted with the steel blade, and puree until smooth. Scrape mixture into a mixing bowl and stir in parsley, salt, and pepper.

4. Fill the pan with ⅓ fish mousse mixture, and top with smoked salmon slices. Repeat with another ⅓ of fish mousse and smoked sturgeon slices, meat mixture and remaining ham, ending with the last ⅓ of fish mousse. Wrap the loaf pan on the counter to remove any air bubbles, and wrap the entire pan with heavy-duty aluminum foil. Place the loaf pan into a roasting pan and pour in boiling water to come halfway up the sides of the pan.

5. Bake for 45 to 55 minutes, or until a skewer inserted into the center comes out clean. Remove the pan from the oven, discard the foil, and allow it to sit on a rack for 30 minutes. Pour out any accumulated liquid from the pan, and refrigerate until cold, tightly covered with plastic wrap. To serve, unmold the terrine onto a serving platter and cut off ¾-inch slices.

Note: The terrine can be made up to 2 days in advance and refrigerated, tightly covered.

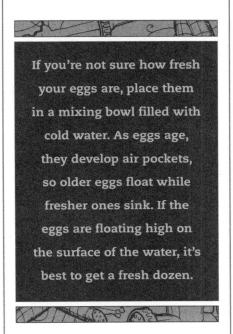

If you're not sure how fresh your eggs are, place them in a mixing bowl filled with cold water. As eggs age, they develop air pockets, so older eggs float while fresher ones sink. If the eggs are floating high on the surface of the water, it's best to get a fresh dozen.

Creole Chicken Liver Pâté

Makes 6 to 8 servings

Active time: 20 minutes

Start to finish: 2 hours, including 1½ hours to chill

VARIATION

Add 1 jalapeño or serrano chile, seeds and ribs removed, and finely chopped, to the skillet along with the scallions and garlic.

Butter imparts a velvety texture to this pate, which is made in a matter of minutes.

½ pound chicken livers
4 tablespoons (½ stick) unsalted butter
3 scallions, white parts and 3 inches of green tops, sliced
2 garlic cloves, minced
1 tablespoon chopped fresh parsley
½ teaspoon dried thyme
¼ teaspoon dried sage
Pinch ground allspice
½ pound chicken livers
1 tablespoon bourbon
Salt and freshly ground black pepper to taste
Crackers or toast points for serving

1. Rinse chicken livers in a sieve, and trim them of all fat. Cut livers into ¾-inch pieces, and drain on paper towels.

2. Melt butter in a large skillet over medium-high heat. Add scallions and garlic, and cook, stirring frequently, for 2 minutes. Add parsley, thyme, sage, and allspice, and cook for an additional 1 minute, or until scallions are translucent.

3. Add livers, and cook, stirring frequently, for 4 to 6 minutes, or until livers are just slightly pink in the center. Sprinkle with bourbon. Puree in a food processor fitted with the steel blade or in a blender. Season to taste with salt and pepper.

4. Line a small mixing bowl with plastic wrap, and scrape mixture into the bowl. Chill pâté for at least 1½ hours, or until cold. To serve, unmold onto a platter.

Note: The pâté can be made up to 2 days in advance and refrigerated, tightly covered.

Glazed Chicken Liver Pâté with Dried Fruit

Makes 6 to 8 servings

Active time:
20 minutes

Start to finish:
2 hours, including 1½ hours to chill

VARIATION

Substitute chopped dried figs and fig preserves for the apricots and apricot preserves.

Chicken livers are combined with dried fruit and jam in this easy pâté.

½ pound chicken livers
4 tablespoons (½ stick) unsalted butter
1 medium onion, peeled and chopped
¼ cup Port
½ cup apricot preserves, divided
¼ teaspoon ground cinnamon
Salt and freshly ground black pepper to taste
½ cup finely chopped dried apricots
Crackers or toast points for serving

1. Rinse chicken livers in a sieve, and trim them of all fat. Cut livers into ¾-inch pieces, and drain on paper towels.

2. Melt butter in a large skillet over medium-high heat. Add onion, and cook, stirring frequently, for 3 minutes, or until onion is translucent.

3. Add livers, and cook, stirring frequently, for 4 to 6 minutes, or until livers are just slightly pink in the center. Transfer liver mixture to a food processor fitted with the steel blade or to a blender.

4. Add Port, 2 tablespoons apricot preserves, and cinnamon to the skillet, and cook for 1 minute, stirring constantly. Add liquid to livers, and puree until smooth. Season to taste with salt and pepper.

5. Line a small mixing bowl with plastic wrap, and scrape mixture into the bowl. Chill pâté for at least 1½ hours, or until cold. To serve, unmold onto a platter, and spread top of pâté with remaining apricot preserves.

Note: The pâté can be made up to 2 days in advance and refrigerated, tightly covered.

Apple-Walnut-Chicken Liver Pâté

Makes 6 to 8 servings

Active time: 20 minutes

Start to finish: 2 hours, including 1½ hours to chill

VARIATION

Substitute almonds or pecans for the walnuts.

A pâté that gets its light texture from the addition of apples and walnuts to the puree. A splash of Calvados, French apple brandy, boosts the apple flavor. I serve this as the first course of a game dinner in the fall.

½ cup chopped walnuts
½ pound chicken livers
5 tablespoons unsalted butter, divided
1 McIntosh apple, peeled, cored, and thinly sliced
1 teaspoon sugar
1 tablespoon Calvados or apple brandy
Salt and freshly ground black pepper to taste
Crackers and toast points for serving

1. Preheat the oven to 350°F, and line a baking sheet with foil. Bake walnuts for 5 to 7 minutes, or until lightly browned. Set aside. Rinse chicken livers in a sieve, and trim them of all fat. Cut livers into ¾-inch pieces, and drain on paper towels.

2. Melt 2 tablespoons butter in a large skillet over medium-high heat. Add livers, and cook, stirring frequently, for 4 to 6 minutes, or

until livers are just slightly pink in the center. Transfer liver mixture to a food processor fitted with the steel blade or to a blender.

3. Add remaining butter to the skillet, add apple slices, and sprinkle apples with sugar. Cook for 4 to 6 minutes, or until apples are tender. Add brandy, and cook for 1 minute more.

4. Add apples and walnuts to the livers, and puree until smooth. Season to taste with salt and pepper.

5. Line a small mixing bowl with plastic wrap, and scrape mixture into the bowl. Chill pâté for at least 1½ hours, or until cold. To serve, unmold onto a platter, and spread top of pâté with remaining apricot preserves.

Note: The pâté can be made up to 2 days in advance and refrigerated, tightly covered.

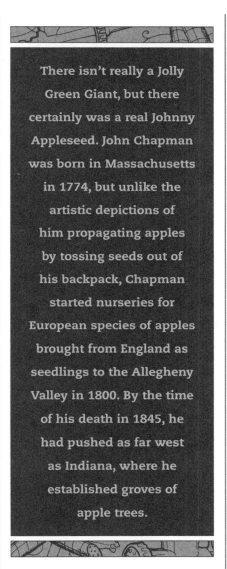

There isn't really a Jolly Green Giant, but there certainly was a real Johnny Appleseed. John Chapman was born in Massachusetts in 1774, but unlike the artistic depictions of him propagating apples by tossing seeds out of his backpack, Chapman started nurseries for European species of apples brought from England as seedlings to the Allegheny Valley in 1800. By the time of his death in 1845, he had pushed as far west as Indiana, where he established groves of apple trees.

Quick Sausage Scrapple

Makes 8 to 10 servings

Active time:
25 minutes

Start to finish:
5 hours, including
4 hours to chill

VARIATIONS

Substitute bulk Sweet Italian Sausage (page 52) or purchased sausage for the American Breakfast Sausage.

Add 1 teaspoon dried thyme or dried sage to mixture.

Here's an easy way to make scrapple; all the flavors and seasonings are in the sausage itself.

1 pound bulk American Breakfast Sausage (page 46) or purchased sausage

3 cups Chicken Stock (page 296) or purchased low-sodium stock

1¼ cups polenta

Salt and freshly ground black pepper to taste

¼ cup all-purpose flour

½ cup vegetable oil for frying

Vegetable oil spray

1. Crumble sausage into a 4-quart saucepan, and cook over medium-high heat, breaking up lumps with a fork, for 3 to 5 minutes, or until sausage browns.

2. Pour stock into the pan, bring to a boil over medium-high heat, and pour in polenta in a slow stream, whisking constantly so no lumps form. Reduce the heat to medium, and continue to whisk for 2 minutes. Cover the pan, reduce the heat to the lowest setting, and stir with a heavy spoon every 8 to 10 minutes for 30 seconds, or until polenta is smooth again. Continue to cook for 30 minutes, or until very thick.

3. Line a 9 x 5-inch loaf pan with heavy-duty aluminum foil, and grease the foil with vegetable oil spray. Pack cornmeal mixture into the loaf pan, rapping it on the counter to remove any air bubbles. Chill scrapple for at least 4 hours, or until chilled.

4. Invert loaf onto a cutting board, and pull off foil. Cut scrapple into 1-inch slices, and dust slices with flour.

5. Heat oil in a large skillet over medium-high heat. Add scrapple slices and cook for 2 to 3 minutes per side, or until crusty and brown, turning slices with a slotted spatula. Blot slices with paper towels, and serve immediately.

Note: The loaf can be made up to 2 days in advance and refrigerated, tightly covered. Slice it and sauté it just prior to serving.

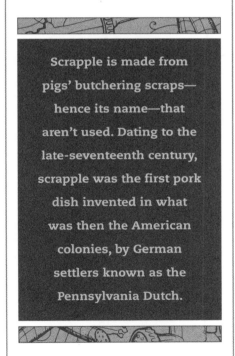

Scrapple is made from pigs' butchering scraps—hence its name—that aren't used. Dating to the late-seventeenth century, scrapple was the first pork dish invented in what was then the American colonies, by German settlers known as the Pennsylvania Dutch.

Updated Scrapple

Makes 8 to 10
servings

Active time:
25 minutes

Start to finish:
6½ hours,
including
4 hours to chill

VARIATIONS

*Substitute ¼
pound baked ham,
diced, for ¼ pound
of the pork. Stir
the ham into the
scrapple mixture
before chilling.*

*Substitute
1 teaspoon
dried thyme and
1 teaspoon dried
marjoram for
the dried sage.*

This recipe uses the traditional technique of cooking the pork and then making the corn mixture with the resulting broth. The pork parts used are identifiable here, not the scraps.

1¼ *pounds boneless pork butt*
  or boneless country ribs,
  cut into 1-inch cubes
3½ *cups Chicken Stock (page 296)*
  or purchased low-sodium stock
2 *teaspoons dried sage*
1 *teaspoon freshly ground*
  black pepper
½ *teaspoon cayenne*
Salt *to taste*
1 *small onion*
3 *whole cloves*
2 *garlic cloves, peeled*
1¼ *cups polenta*
¼ *cup all-purpose flour*
½ *cup vegetable oil for frying*
Vegetable oil spray

1. Combine pork cubes, stock, sage, pepper, cayenne and salt in a saucepan. Press cloves into onion, and add to the pan along with garlic cloves. Bring to a boil over medium-high heat, then cover the pan, reduce the heat to low, and simmer pork for 1½ to 1¾ hours, or until pork is very tender.

Substitute blue cornmeal for the polenta, and add 1 jalapeño or serrano chile, halved, to the stock while cooking the pork, and substitute 2 teaspoons ground cumin for the sage.

Reduce the amount of stock to 2½ cups, and stir ¾ cup grated sharp cheddar, Gruyère, or crumbled blue cheese into the polenta after it's cooked.

2. Remove pork from the pan with a slotted spoon, and shred with 2 forks. Set aside. Strain broth, pressing with the back of a spoon to extract as much liquid as possible, and measure stock. Add additional stock or water to make 3 cups of liquid. Return stock to the saucepan.

3. Bring stock into a boil over medium-high heat, and pour in polenta in a slow stream, whisking constantly so no lumps form. Reduce the heat to medium, and continue to whisk for 2 minutes. Cover the pan, reduce the heat to the lowest setting, and stir with a heavy spoon every 8 to 10 minutes for 30 seconds, or until polenta is smooth again. Continue to cook for 30 minutes, or until very thick.

4. Line a 9 x 5-inch loaf pan with heavy-duty aluminum foil, and grease the foil with vegetable oil spray. Stir pork into cornmeal mixture, and season to taste with salt and pepper. Pack mixture into the loaf pan, rapping it on the counter to remove any air bubbles. Chill scrapple for at least 4 hours, or until chilled.

5. Invert loaf onto a cutting board, and pull off foil. Cut scrapple into 1-inch slices, and dust slices with flour.

6. Heat oil in a large skillet over medium-high heat. Add scrapple slices and cook for 2 to 3 minutes per side, or until crusty and brown, turning slices with a slotted spatula. Blot slices with paper towels, and serve immediately.

Note: The loaf can be made up to 2 days in advance and refrigerated, tightly covered. Slice it and sauté it just prior to serving.

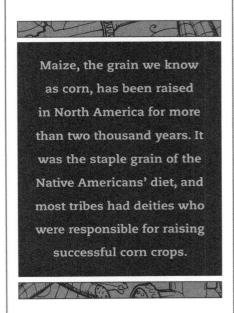

Maize, the grain we know as corn, has been raised in North America for more than two thousand years. It was the staple grain of the Native Americans' diet, and most tribes had deities who were responsible for raising successful corn crops.

Goetta

Makes 8 to 10 servings

Active time: 1 hour

Start to finish: 5½ hours, including 4 hours for chilling

VARIATIONS

Substitute bulk Sweet Italian Sausage (page 52) for American Breakfast Sausage.

Substitute allspice for thyme.

Add 2 garlic cloves, minced, to the pan along with onions.

Goetta (pronounced GET-uh), a culinary curiosity found only around Cincinnati, Ohio, arrived with the large wave of German immigrants in the late nineteenth century. It's a first cousin of scrapple, but it's made with oats rather than cornmeal, and my updated version contains lots of herbs for additional flavor.

2 tablespoons bacon grease or vegetable oil
1 medium onion, finely chopped
1 pound bulk American Breakfast Sausage (page 46) or purchased sausage
4 cups Chicken Stock (page 296) or purchased low-sodium stock
1½ cups steel-cut oats
2 bay leaves
½ teaspoon dried thyme
Salt and freshly ground black pepper to taste
¼ cup all-purpose flour
Additional bacon grease or vegetable oil *for frying*
Vegetable oil spray

1. Heat bacon grease in a 4-quart saucepan over medium-high heat. Add onion and cook, stirring frequently, for 3 minutes, or until onion is translucent. Crumble sausage into the saucepan and cook, breaking up lumps with a fork, for 3 to 5 minutes, or until browned.

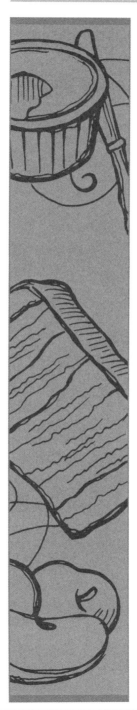

2. Add stock to the pan, and bring to a boil over medium-high heat, stirring occasionally. Reduce the heat to low, and simmer mixture for 10 minutes.

3. Stir oats into the pan and cook over low heat, covered, for 45 to 55 minutes, or until very thick. Stir often toward the end of the cooking time to prevent sticking. Remove and discard bay leaves, and season to taste with salt and pepper.

4. Line a 9 x 5-inch loaf pan with heavy-duty aluminum foil, and grease the foil with vegetable oil spray. Pack goetta mixture into the loaf pan, rapping it on the counter to remove any air bubbles. Chill goetta for at least 4 hours, or until chilled.

5. Invert loaf onto a cutting board, and pull off foil. Cut goetta into 1-inch slices, and dust slices with flour. Heat bacon grease in a large skillet over medium-high heat. Add goetta slices and cook for 2 to 3 minutes per side, or until crusty and brown, turning slices with a slotted spatula. Blot slices with paper towels, and serve immediately.

Note: The loaf can be made up to 2 days in advance and refrigerated, tightly covered. Slice it and sauté it just prior to serving.

Findlay Market in Cincinnati's Over-the-Rhine district has been in continuous operation since its founding in 1852. While Glier's is the largest commercial producer of goetta, fans of Eckerlin Meats travel to Findlay Market just to purchase the homemade version from this long-time purveryor. There are also endless discussions among locals regarding the merits of each firm's goetta.

PART II:

COOKING WITH SAUSAGE

Perhaps you'll never make sausage, but since you enjoy the complex flavor that sausage imparts to many dishes, here are recipes that can be prepared with homemade or store-bought sausage. None of the recipes require that you make the sausages in the previous chapters, although there are references to which sausage recipes to use. There are ready-made sausages to use for each one.

Because so many herbs and spices are used in the forcemeat mixture, cooking with sausages is a quick way to prepare many dishes. Only a handful of these recipes require more than twenty minutes of your hands-on, active time in the kitchen.

These recipes are divided by dish forms, dominant ingredients, and—in the case of grilling—how the dishes are cooked. There are chapters for sausage soups, pasta and rice dishes, sausages cooked with beans and vegetables, sausages cooked in specific sauces, and lots of appetizers and side dishes glorified with sausage. A chapter on sausages and eggs can take home cooks from breakfast to brunch to dinner. The last chapter includes sauces that go with various sausages to take you beyond mustard.

Natural Partners:

Sausages and Eggs

As long as you have some eggs in the house you'll never go hungry. Eggs are mildly flavored and take to endless seasoning combinations and other ingredients. Like sausages. There are sausage quiches, variations on the Italian frittata, and stratas, a fancy name for a savory bread pudding.

CUTTING CHOLESTEROL

Eggs have gotten a bad nutritional reputation because of the fat and cholesterol in the yolk, not for the white. The white is what gives eggs their ability to bind, and it is made up primarily of protein and water.

If you want to be judicious about cutting cholesterol you can use any of the egg substitute products on the market; the best-known brand is Egg Beaters. Egg substitutes are egg whites tinted yellow. But you can also make your own by using two egg whites for each whole egg, or if a recipe calls for several eggs use two egg whites and one whole egg for every two whole eggs listed. There are few recipes in this chapter that require whole eggs, so feel free to experiment.

EGG-CETERA

There are times that you might want an egg and sausage sandwich, or serve a patty of sausage under poached eggs. Here are a few tricks I've developed:

Poaching eggs in plastic: Making poached eggs for a crowd is easy using this method, and you can have them ready to poach up to a day in advance of cooking them. Press a 12-inch-square sheet of plastic wrap into the bottom of a ramekin, place a few thin pats of butter on top of the plastic wrap, and sprinkle the butter with salt and freshly ground black pepper. Break an egg onto the plastic in the cup, twist the plastic wrap around the egg, and then tie the packet closed with a piece of kitchen twine. Repeat until you've created plastic pouches for all the eggs you intend to cook. To poach the eggs, bring a large pot of water to a boil over high heat. Add the egg pouches, reduce the heat to medium-low, and maintain the water at a bare simmer of 180°F; attach a candy thermometer to the side of the pan or take the temperature of the water frequently with an instant-read thermometer. Cook the eggs for 3 minutes for runny, up to 5 minutes for almost hard cooked. Remove the egg packets from the pan, and cut off the twine and top of the plastic wrap. You can then coax the egg out of the plastic and onto a plate, sausage patty, or slice of toast.

Eggs for English muffin sandwiches: A tuna can is just about the same diameter as an English muffin. Save a few cans and remove any paper wrappers. Use a can opener to remove the other side of the cans and wash them well. Grease the inside of the rings with vegetable oil spray. Place the rings in a skillet, and put a pat of butter inside each one. Heat the skillet over medium heat, then break an egg into each ring, and sprinkle it with salt and freshly ground black pepper. Cover the skillet, reduce the heat to low, and cook the egg for 3 to 5 minutes, or until done to your liking. Run a spatula under the egg, and remove it with the ring. Place the egg on the English muffin, and then gently pull off the ring.

Mexican Frittata

Makes 4 to 6 servings

Active time: 25 minutes

Start to finish: 55 minutes

VARIATIONS

Substitute Sweet Italian Sausage (page 52), Hot Italian Sausage (page 54), or Luganega (page 58) for Fresh Mexican Chorizo.

Substitute herbes de Provence or Italian seasoning for cumin and oregano.

This frittata is a first cousin to a Spanish *tortilla*, which is an omelet served at tapas bars, not the flatbread we associate with soft tacos or burritos. Keep any leftovers from this dish; refrigerate, and cut into small squares to serve as a snack.

2 tablespoons olive oil

¼ pound bulk Fresh Mexican Chorizo (page 66), Linguiça (page 68), or purchased chorizo or linguiça

1 large red-skinned potato, scrubbed and cut into ½-inch dice

1 red bell pepper, seeds and ribs removed, and chopped

1 large sweet onion, such as Bermuda or Vidalia, diced

2 garlic cloves, minced

Salt and freshly ground black pepper to taste

6 large eggs

¼ cup freshly grated Parmesan

¼ cup grated whole-milk mozzarella

1 teaspoon ground cumin

1 teaspoon dried oregano

2 tablespoons unsalted butter

1. Heat olive oil in a large skillet over medium-high heat. Crumble sausage into the skillet and cook, breaking up lumps with a fork, for 3 to 5 minutes, or until browned. Remove sausage from the skillet with a slotted spoon, and set

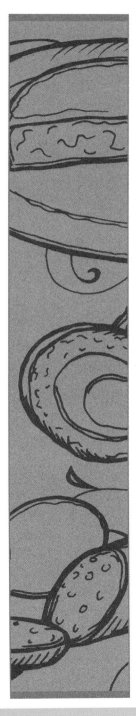

aside. Discard all but 2 tablespoons grease from the skillet.

2. Add potato to the skillet, and cook, stirring occasionally, for 5 minutes, or until potatoes are browned. Add red bell pepper, onion, and garlic to the skillet. Cook, stirring frequently, for 3 minutes, or until onion is translucent. Return sausage to the skillet, reduce the heat to low, cover the pan, and cook vegetable mixture for 15 minutes, or until vegetables are tender. Season to taste with salt and pepper, and allow mixture to cool for 10 minutes.

2. Preheat the oven to 425°F. Whisk eggs well, stir in Parmesan, mozzarella, and Italian seasoning. Stir cooled vegetable mixture into eggs.

3. Heat butter in a large, oven-proof skillet over medium heat. Add egg mixture and cook for 4 minutes, or until the bottom of cake is lightly brown. Transfer the skillet to the oven, and bake for 10 to 15 minutes, or until top is browned.

4. Run a spatula around the sides of the skillet and under the bottom of the cake to release it. Slide cake gently onto a serving platter, and cut it into wedges. Serve immediately, or at room temperature.

Note: The sausage mixture can be cooked up to a day in advance and refrigerated, tightly covered. Reheat the vegetables to room temperature in a microwave-safe dish, or over low heat, before completing the dish.

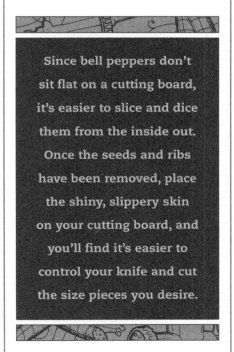

Since bell peppers don't sit flat on a cutting board, it's easier to slice and dice them from the inside out. Once the seeds and ribs have been removed, place the shiny, slippery skin on your cutting board, and you'll find it's easier to control your knife and cut the size pieces you desire.

Andouille and Swiss Chard Frittata

Makes 4 to 6 servings

Active time:
20 minutes

Start to finish:
50 minutes

VARIATIONS

Substitute jalepeño Jack for Monterey Jack for a spicier dish.

Substitute Smoked Kielbasa (page 126) or French Garlic Sausage (page 72) for Andouille.

This a colorful dish, contrasting slices of pink sausage with bright green Swiss chard. The greens balance very well with the spicy sausage, and a tossed salad alongside completes the plate.

2 tablespoons olive oil

1 small onion, diced

2 garlic cloves, minced

½ pound Andouille Sausage (page 62) or purchased cooked andouille, thinly sliced

½ pound Swiss chard, stems and center ribs discarded, rinsed, and chopped

6 large eggs

⅓ cup grated Monterey Jack

Salt and freshly ground black pepper to taste

2 tablespoons unsalted butter

1. Heat oil in a large skillet over medium-high heat. Add onion and garlic, and cook, stirring frequently, for 3 minutes, or until onion is translucent. Add sausage, and cook for 2 minutes. Add half of Swiss chard, and toss to wilt before adding remainder. Increase the heat to high, and cook for 2 minutes, or until liquid from Swiss chard evaporates. Allow mixture to cool for 10 minutes.

2. Preheat the oven to 425°F. Whisk eggs well, stir in Monterey Jack, and season to taste with salt and pepper. Stir cooled vegetable mixture into eggs.

3. Heat butter in a large, oven-proof skillet over medium heat. Add egg mixture and cook for 4 minutes, or until the bottom of cake is lightly brown. Transfer the skillet to the oven, and bake for 10 to 15 minutes, or until top is browned.

4. Run a spatula around the sides of the skillet and under the bottom of the cake to release it. Slide cake gently onto a serving platter, and cut it into wedges. Serve immediately, or at room temperature.

Note: The sausage and vegetable mixture can be cooked up to a day in advance and refrigerated, tightly covered. Reheat the vegetables to room temperature in a microwave-safe dish, or over low heat, before completing the dish.

A frittata is an open-faced Italian omelet. While I find it easier to bake frittatas, Italians fry them. The Italian word frittata is derived from the Latin *frigere*, which means "to fry." It's easier to make one large frittata than four separate omelets.

Herbed Sausage and Tomato Quiche

Makes 4 to 6 servings

Active time: 20 minutes

Start to finish: 50 minutes

VARIATIONS

Substitute Italian seasoning for herbes de Provence.

Add ½ cup pitted and chopped olives to custard.

Quiche got a bad reputation after the publication in 1982 of Bruce Feirstein's satirical look at masculinity, *Real Men Don't Eat Quiche*. I can assure you that the men around my table gobble up this hearty custard pie loaded with sausage and herbs.

1 (9-inch single) Basic Piecrust (page 260) or purchased pie shell, thawed if frozen

1 tablespoon olive oil

¾ pound bulk Sweet Italian Sausage (page 52), Herbed Turkey and White Wine Sausage (page 156), or purchased sausage

1 small onion, chopped

3 garlic cloves, minced

1 (14.5-ounce) can petite cut canned tomatoes, drained

2 teaspoons herbes de Provence

3 large eggs

¾ cup heavy cream

Salt and freshly ground black pepper to taste

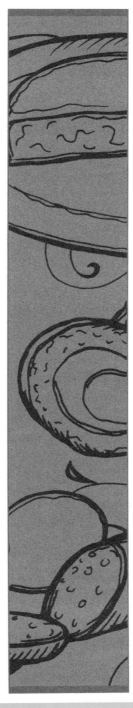

1. Preheat the oven to 400°F. Prick pie shell all over with the tines of a fork and bake for 8 to 10 minutes, or until pastry is set and just starting to brown. Remove crust from the oven, and set aside.

2. While crust bakes, heat oil in a large skillet over medium-high heat. Crumble sausage into the skillet and cook, breaking up lumps with a fork, for 3 to 5 minutes, or until browned. Remove sausage from the skillet with a slotted spoon, and set aside. Add onion and garlic and cook, stirring frequently, for 3 minutes, or until onion is translucent. Add tomatoes and cook, stirring occasionally, for 5 to 7 minutes, or until tomato juice has evaporated. Cool mixture for 5 minutes.

3. Reduce the oven temperature to 375°F. Whisk eggs with cream, stir in sausage and vegetable mixture, and season to taste with salt and pepper. Pour custard into prepared piecrust.

4. Bake quiche for 25 to 30 minutes, or until it is browned and eggs are set. Serve immediately.

Note: The filling can be prepared a day in advance and refrigerated, tightly covered. Add 5 to 7 minutes to the baking time if filling is chilled.

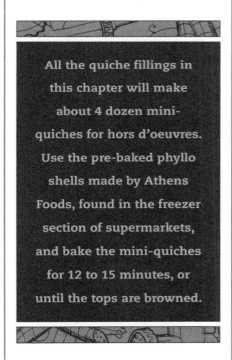

All the quiche fillings in this chapter will make about 4 dozen mini-quiches for hors d'oeuvres. Use the pre-baked phyllo shells made by Athens Foods, found in the freezer section of supermarkets, and bake the mini-quiches for 12 to 15 minutes, or until the tops are browned.

Quiche Provençal

Makes 4 to 6 servings

Active time: 20 minutes

Start to finish: 50 minutes

VARIATION

Substitute ½ cup grated whole-milk mozzarella and ¼ cup freshly grated Parmesan for Gruyère.

Colorful vegetables, salty olives, and herbs—reminiscent of the south of France—complement the filling of this quiche, made with a light chicken sausage. Oven-roasted potatoes are a nice accompaniment.

1 (9-inch single) Basic Piecrust (page 260) or purchased pie shell, thawed if frozen

1 tablespoon olive oil

¾ pound bulk Garlicky Chicken and Rosemary Sausage (page 164) or purchased poultry sausage

½ small onion, diced

1 small zucchini, thinly sliced

1 cup sliced mushrooms

3 large eggs

¾ cup heavy cream

¾ cup grated Gruyère

¼ cup chopped sun-dried tomatoes

¼ cup chopped pitted Kalamata olives

2 tablespoons chopped fresh basil

2 tablespoons chopped fresh parsley

¾ teaspoons herbes de Provence

Salt and freshly ground black pepper to taste

1. Preheat the oven to 400°F. Prick pie shell all over with the tines of a fork and bake for 8 to 10 minutes, or until pastry is set and just starting to brown. Remove crust from the oven, and set aside.

2. While crust bakes, heat oil in a large skillet over medium-high heat. Crumble sausage into the skillet and cook, breaking up lumps with a fork, for 3 to 5 minutes, or until browned. Remove sausage from the skillet with a slotted spoon, and set aside.

3. Add onion, zucchini, and mushrooms to the skillet. Cook, stirring frequently, for 5 to 7 minutes, or until vegetables soften. Set aside.

4. Reduce the oven temperature to 375°F. Whisk eggs with cream in a mixing bowl. Stir in sausage, vegetable mixture, Gruyère, sun-dried tomatoes, olives, basil, parsley, and herbes de Provence. Season to taste with salt and pepper. Pour custard into prepared piecrust.

5. Bake quiche for 25 to 30 minutes, or until it is browned and eggs are set. Serve immediately.

Note: The filling can be prepared a day in advance and refrigerated, tightly covered. Add 5 to 7 minutes to the baking time if filling is chilled.

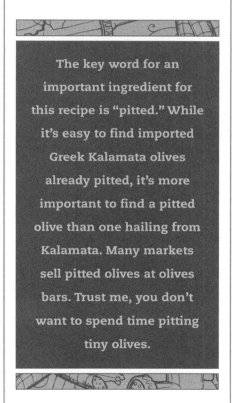

The key word for an important ingredient for this recipe is "pitted." While it's easy to find imported Greek Kalamata olives already pitted, it's more important to find a pitted olive than one hailing from Kalamata. Many markets sell pitted olives at olives bars. Trust me, you don't want to spend time pitting tiny olives.

Quiche Mexicana

Makes 4 to 6 servings

Active time: 20 minutes

Start to finish: 50 minutes

VARIATION

Substitute Monterey Jack for all or some of jalapeño Jack for a milder flavor.

Although quiche is a French dish, there are similar custards in other cuisines, especially Mexican cooking. The herbs, spices, and vegetables give vibrant flavor to this dish.

1 (9-inch single) Basic Piecrust (page 260) or purchased pie shell, thawed if frozen

1 tablespoon olive oil

⅓ pound bulk Fresh Mexican Chorizo (page 66), Linguiça (page 68), or purchased sausage

1 medium onion, peeled and chopped

2 garlic cloves, minced

1 teaspoon ground cumin

½ teaspoon dried oregano

3 large eggs

2 cups half-and-half

1½ cups grated jalapeño Jack cheese

2 tablespoons chopped fresh cilantro

Salt and freshly ground black pepper to taste

½ cup frozen corn kernels, cooked according to package directions and drained well

¼ cup sliced pimiento-stuffed green olives

1. Preheat the oven to 400°F. Prick pie shell all over with the tines of a fork and bake for 8 to 10 minutes, or until pastry is set and just starting to brown. Remove crust from the oven, and set aside.

2. While crust bakes, heat oil in a large skillet over medium-high heat. Crumble sausage into the skillet and cook, breaking up lumps with a fork, for 3 to 5 minutes, or until browned. Remove sausage from the skillet with a slotted spoon, and set aside. Discard all but 2 tablespoons grease from the skillet.

3. Add onion and garlic to the skillet, and cook, stirring frequently, for 5 minutes, or until onion softens. Stir in cumin and oregano, and cook for 1 minute, stirring constantly.

4. Reduce the oven temperature to 375°F. Whisk eggs with half-and-half in a mixing bowl. Stir in sausage, cheese, and cilantro, and season to taste with salt and pepper. Stir corn, olives, and onion

mixture into custard. Pour custard into prepared piecrust.

5. Bake quiche for 25 to 30 minutes, or until it is browned and eggs are set. Serve immediately.

Note: The filling can be prepared a day in advance and refrigerated, tightly covered. Add 5 to 7 minutes to the baking time if filling is chilled.

Half-and-half is almost identical to light cream, and it can be replicated by using half heavy cream and half whole milk in any recipe. If you only have milk on hand, add 2 tablespoons melted butter to every cup milk to achieve the same level of fat as half-and-half.

Sausage Cornbread Strata

Makes 4 to 6 servings

Active time:

15 minutes

Start to finish:

1 hour

The cornbread base makes this a more home-y strata than most. Accompany it with some fried green tomatoes.

6 large eggs

2½ cups whole milk

Salt and freshly ground black pepper to taste

1 tablespoon dried sage

1 cup grated Monterey Jack

6 cups finely diced cornbread

1 tablespoon olive oil

½ pound bulk American Breakfast Sausage (page 46) or purchased sausage

3 tablespoons unsalted butter

1 medium onion, peeled and diced

1 green bell pepper, seeds and ribs removed, and finely chopped

1 carrot, peeled and finely chopped

1 celery rib, rinsed, trimmed, and finely chopped

Vegetable oil spray

1. Preheat the oven to 350°F, and grease a 9 x 13-inch baking pan with vegetable oil spray.

2. Combine eggs, milk, salt, pepper, and sage in mixing bowl, and whisk well. Stir in cheese. Arrange cornbread pieces in the prepared

pan, and pour egg mixture over them, pressing down so that bread will absorb liquid.

3. Heat oil in a medium skillet over medium-high heat. Crumble sausage into the skillet and cook, breaking up lumps with a fork, for 3 to 5 minutes, or until browned. Remove sausage from the skillet with a slotted spoon, and discard fat from the skillet.

4. Reduce the heat to medium, and heat butter. Add onion, bell pepper, carrot, and celery. Cook, stirring frequently, for 5 to 7 minutes, or until vegetables soften. Stir vegetables and sausage into bread mixture.

5. Cover the baking pan with aluminum foil, and bake in the center of the oven for 30 minutes. Remove the foil, and bake for an additional 15 to 20 minutes, or until a toothpick inserted in the center comes out clean and the top is lightly browned. Allow to rest for 5 minutes, and then serve.

Note: The strata can be prepared for baking up to a day in advance and refrigerated, tightly covered. Add 10 minutes to the covered baking time if the strata is cold. Also, the strata can be baked up to 3 days in advance; reheat it in a 325°F oven, covered, for 20 to 25 minutes, or until hot.

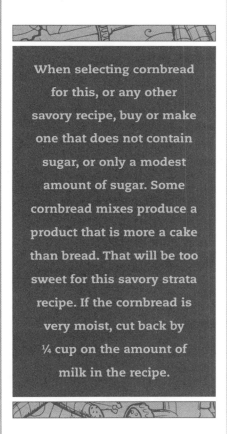

When selecting cornbread for this, or any other savory recipe, buy or make one that does not contain sugar, or only a modest amount of sugar. Some cornbread mixes produce a product that is more a cake than bread. That will be too sweet for this savory strata recipe. If the cornbread is very moist, cut back by ¼ cup on the amount of milk in the recipe.

Jalapeño Jack Strata with Chorizo and Vegetables

Makes 4 to 6 servings

Active time: 15 minutes

Start to finish: 1 hour

VARIATIONS

Substitute Monterey Jack for jalapeño Jack for a milder dish.

Substitute 1 (15-ounce) can kidney beans, drained and rinsed, for corn.

Jalapeño Jack is Monterey Jack cheese combined with finely minced jalapeño peppers. It's a real cheese and the same price as its milder cousin. Serve this with some diced tomatoes tossed with balsamic vinegar, salt, and pepper.

6 large eggs

2½ cups whole milk

Salt and freshly ground black pepper to taste

1 cup grated jalapeño Jack cheese

½ pound loaf French or Italian bread, cut into ½-inch slices

1 tablespoon vegetable oil

1 pound bulk Fresh Mexican Chorizo (page 66) or purchased sausage

1 medium onion, diced

2 garlic cloves, minced

½ green bell pepper, seeds and ribs removed, and chopped

¾ cup frozen corn, thawed and drained

Vegetable oil spray

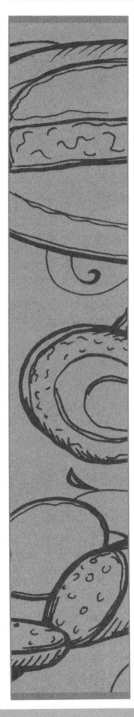

1. Preheat the oven to 350°F, and grease a 9 x 13-inch baking pan with vegetable oil spray.

2. Combine eggs, milk, salt, and pepper in mixing bowl, and whisk well. Stir in cheese. Arrange bread slices in the prepared pan, and pour egg mixture over them, pressing down so that bread will absorb liquid.

3. Heat oil in a medium skillet over medium-high heat. Crumble sausage into the skillet and cook, breaking up lumps with a fork, for 3 to 5 minutes, or until browned. Add onion, garlic, and bell pepper, and cook, stirring frequently, for 5 minutes, or until vegetables soften. Stir mixture and corn into bread mixture.

4. Cover the baking pan with aluminum foil, and bake in the center of the oven for 30 minutes. Remove the foil, and bake for an additional 15 to 20 minutes, or until a toothpick inserted in the center comes out clean and the top is lightly browned. Allow to rest for 5 minutes, and then serve.

Note: The strata can be prepared for baking up to a day in advance and refrigerated, tightly covered. Add 10 minutes to the covered baking time if the strata is cold. Also, the strata can be baked up to 3 days in advance; reheat it in a 325°F oven, covered, for 20 to 25 minutes, or until hot.

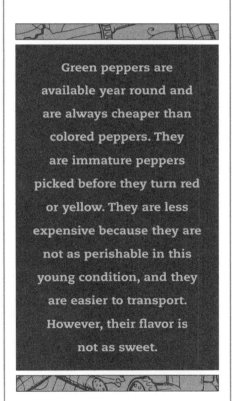

Green peppers are available year round and are always cheaper than colored peppers. They are immature peppers picked before they turn red or yellow. They are less expensive because they are not as perishable in this young condition, and they are easier to transport. However, their flavor is not as sweet.

Sausage and Apple Strata

Makes 4 to 6 servings

Active time:
15 minutes

Start to finish:
1 hour

VARIATIONS

Substitute dried cranberries or chopped dried apricots for raisins.

Substitute hoisin sauce for maple syrup.

American breakfast sausage can be used as an accent in a sweet dish or as the star of a savory dish. In this strata, a touch of sweetness comes from the fruit and maple syrup, and the sausage balances them nicely.

6 large eggs
2½ cups whole milk
2 tablespoons pure maple syrup
2 teaspoons dried sage
¾ teaspoon ground cinnamon
Pinch of freshly ground nutmeg
Salt and freshly ground black
    pepper to taste
1 cup grated Monterey Jack
½ cup raisins
½ pound loaf French or Italian
    bread, cut into ½-slices

1 tablespoon vegetable oil
¾ pound bulk Turkey, Apple and
    Sage Sausage (page 150),
    American Breakfast Sausage
    (page 46), Breakfast Sausage
    with Dried Fruit (page 50),
    or purchased sausage
2 tablespoons unsalted butter
1 small onion, peeled and diced
1 large McIntosh or Golden Delicious
    apple, peeled, cored, quartered,
    and chopped
Vegetable oil spray

1. Preheat the oven to 350°F, and grease a 9x13-inch baking pan with vegetable oil spray.

2. Combine eggs, milk, maple syrup, sage, cinnamon, nutmeg, salt, and pepper in mixing bowl, and whisk well. Stir in cheese and raisins. Arrange bread in the prepared pan, and pour egg mixture over them, pressing down so that the bread will absorb the liquid.

3. Heat oil in a large skillet over medium-high heat. Crumble sausage into the skillet and cook, breaking up lumps with a fork, for 3 to 5 minutes, or until browned. Remove sausage from the skillet with a slotted spoon, and add to bread mixture. Discard sausage grease.

4. Return the skillet to the stove, and reduce the heat to medium. Add butter and onion. Cook, stirring frequently, for 2 minutes. Add apple, and cook, stirring frequently, for 3 minutes, or until apple softens. Stir contents of the skillet into bread mixture.

5. Cover the baking pan with aluminum foil, and bake in the center of the oven for 30 minutes. Remove the foil, and bake for an additional 15 to 20 minutes, or until a toothpick inserted in the center comes out clean and the top is lightly browned. Allow to rest for 5 minutes, and then serve.

Note: The strata can be prepared for baking up to a day in advance and refrigerated, tightly covered. Add 10 minutes to the covered baking time if the strata is cold. Also, the strata can be baked up to 3 days in advance; reheat it in a 325°F oven, covered, for 20 to 25 minutes, or until hot.

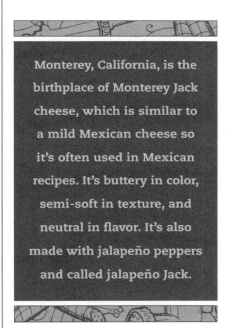

Monterey, California, is the birthplace of Monterey Jack cheese, which is similar to a mild Mexican cheese so it's often used in Mexican recipes. It's buttery in color, semi-soft in texture, and neutral in flavor. It's also made with jalapeño peppers and called jalapeño Jack.

Sausage, Egg, and Arugula Salad

Makes 4 to 6 servings

Active time:
15 minutes

Start to finish:
20 minutes

VARIATIONS

Substitute Fresh Mexican Chorizo (page 66) or Chaurice (page 64) for Sweet Italian Sausage.

Substitute frisée or watercress for arugula.

The soft, creamy eggs, the peppery sharpness of arugula, and the hearty sausage makes this a versatile salad that can be served at brunch or dinner. Serve it with garlic bread or olive bread.

Salad:

1 tablespoon olive oil

½ pound bulk Sweet Italian Sausage (page 52), Hot Italian Sausage (page 54), Luganega (page 58), or purchased sausage

2 tablespoons unsalted butter

8 to 10 large eggs

⅓ cup sour cream

Salt and freshly ground black pepper to taste

6 cups arugula leaves, rinsed, stems removed

Dressing:

2 tablespoons balsamic vinegar

1 small shallot, chopped

1 garlic clove, minced

2 teaspoons Dijon mustard

Salt and freshly ground black pepper to taste

¼ cup olive oil

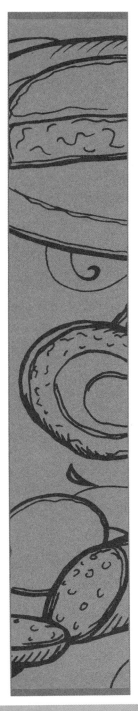

1. Heat oil in a large skillet over medium-high heat. Crumble sausage into the skillet and cook, breaking up lumps with a fork, for 3 to 5 minutes, or until browned. Remove sausage from the skillet with a slotted spoon, and set aside. Discard grease from the skillet.

2. Melt butter in the same skillet over low heat. Whisk eggs with sour cream, salt, and pepper. When butter melts, add eggs to the pan, then cover the pan. After 3 minutes, stir eggs and cover the pan again. Cook until the eggs are ¾ set.

3. While eggs cook, make dressing. Combine vinegar, shallot, garlic, mustard, salt, and pepper in a jar with a tight-fitting lid, and shake well. Add oil, and shake well again. Set aside.

4. Place arugula in a salad bowl, and toss with vinaigrette. Add reserved sausage and hot eggs to the salad bowl, and toss gently. Serve immediately.

Note: The dressing can be made 2 days in advance and refrigerated, tightly covered.

We all drop eggs on the floor, and they're a mess to clean up. Instead of rushing with a roll of paper towels, sprinkle the mess with lots of salt and let stand for 20 minutes. After that time, the eggs should be solid enough to sweep into a dust pan.

Sausage and Pepper Hash with Baked Eggs

Makes 4 to 6 servings

Active time: 20 minutes

Start to finish: 1 hour

VARIATION

Substitute bulk Sweet Italian Sausage (page 52) for American Breakfast Sausage.

This hash, a perfect brunch dish for brisk fall and winter days, is as colorful as it is appealing, with bright peppers and herbs. Serve it with crisp oven-roasted potatoes and a Caesar salad.

1 tablespoon olive oil

1¼ pounds bulk American Breakfast Sausage (page 46), Sweet Italian Sausage (page 52), or purchased sausage

10 shallots, minced

6 garlic cloves, minced

1 yellow bell pepper, seeds and ribs removed, finely chopped

1 red bell pepper, seeds and ribs removed, finely chopped

1 green bell pepper, seeds and ribs removed, finely chopped

1 jalapeño or serrano chile, seeds and ribs removed, finely chopped

1 tablespoon chopped fresh sage or 1 teaspoon dried

1 tablespoon fresh thyme leaves or 1 teaspoon dried

1 tablespoon chopped fresh rosemary leaves or 1 teaspoon dried

2 teaspoons chopped fresh oregano or ½ teaspoon dried

½ cup chopped fresh parsley

2 bay leaves

Salt and freshly ground black pepper to taste

8 to 12 large eggs

1. Heat oil in a large skillet over medium-high heat. Crumble sausage into the skillet and cook, breaking up lumps with a fork, for 3 to 5 minutes, or until browned. Remove sausage from the skillet with a slotted spoon, and set aside.

2. Add shallots, garlic, yellow bell pepper, red bell pepper, green bell pepper, and chile to the skillet. Cook, stirring frequently, for 3 minutes, or until the shallots are translucent. Return sausage to the pan and add sage, thyme, rosemary, oregano, parsley, and bay leaves. Simmer mixture over low heat for 20 to 30 minutes, or until vegetables are very soft. Remove and discard bay leaves. Tilt the pan and skim off as much grease as possible. Season to taste with salt and pepper.

3. Preheat the oven to 375°F. Spread sausage mixture in a 9 x 13-inch baking dish. Make 8 to 12 indentations in the mixture with the back of a spoon and break 1 egg into each. Sprinkle eggs with salt and pepper and bake for 12 to 15 minutes, or until the whites are set. Serve immediately.

Note: Sausage mixture can be made 2 days in advance and refrigerated, tightly covered. Reheat it over low heat or in a microwave oven before adding the eggs and baking the dish.

Hash is a general term for food that is finely chopped. The English word first appeared in the mid-seventeenth century and came from the French word *hacher*, which means to chop. Since hash was frequently made with leftovers, inexpensive restaurants became known as "hash houses."

Scotch Eggs

Makes 6 servings

Active time:
25 minutes

Start to finish:
1 hour

Scotch eggs, hard-cooked eggs coated with flavorful sausage and then fried, are popular in the British Isles as a picnic and brunch treat.

8 large eggs, divided
1 pound bulk American Breakfast Sausage (page 46), Garlicky Chicken and Rosemary Sausage (page 164), or purchased sausage
2 tablespoons chopped fresh parsley
2 tablespoons chopped fresh chives
2 teaspoons dried sage
½ teaspoon dried thyme
Cayenne to taste
2 tablespoons Dijon mustard
½ cup all-purpose flour
1 cup plain breadcrumbs
Vegetable oil for frying

1. Place 6 eggs in a saucepan, and cover with cold water by 2 inches. Bring to a boil over high heat, uncovered. Boil for 1 minute, cover the pan, and remove the pan from the heat. Allow eggs to sit for 15 minutes, covered. Drain eggs, and fill pan with cold running water for 3 minutes to stop the cooking action. Allow eggs to sit in cold water for 10 minutes, then peel eggs.

2. Combine sausage, parsley, chives, sage, thyme, and cayenne in a mixing bowl. Beat remaining 2 eggs with mustard in a shallow bowl. Place flour on a sheet of plastic wrap or waxed paper, and place breadcrumbs on another sheet of plastic wrap or waxed paper.

3. Dust peeled eggs with flour, then using wet hands, pat ⅙ of sausage mixture around each egg. Dip coated eggs into egg mixture, and then roll in breadcrumbs, pressing gently to get crumbs to adhere. Refrigerate eggs for 30 minutes.

4. Heat 2 inches of oil in a deep-sided saucepan to a temperature of 350°F. Add 3 eggs to hot oil, and fry for 6 to 8 minutes, turning them gently with a slotted spoon occasionally, or until eggs are dark brown and sausage is cooked through. Remove eggs from the pan with a slotted spoon, and drain well on paper towels. Repeat with remaining 3 eggs. When cool enough to handle, cut eggs in half lengthwise. Serve at room temperature or chilled.

Note: The eggs can be prepared for frying up to a day in advance and refrigerated, tightly covered. They can be fully cooked up to 2 days in advance, and refrigerated, tightly covered.

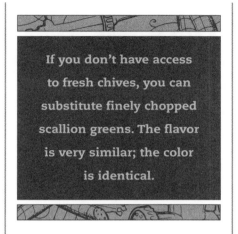

If you don't have access to fresh chives, you can substitute finely chopped scallion greens. The flavor is very similar; the color is identical.

Mexican Scrambled Eggs

Makes 4 to 6 servings

**Active time:
25 minutes**

**Start to finish:
25 minutes**

While the chiles were a bit much for me to handle at 7 a.m. when I was served this dish in Mexico, I knew this scrambled egg dish, called *migas*, would make a great supper dish. Serve with some sliced avocados and tomatoes.

4 (6-inch) corn tortillas

1 tablespoon olive oil

½ pound bulk Fresh Mexican Chorizo (page 66), Linguiça (page 68), or purchased sausage

½ small red onion, peeled and finely chopped

2 garlic cloves, peeled and minced

1 small jalapeño or serrano chile, seeds and ribs removed, and finely chopped

½ red bell pepper, seeds and ribs removed, and finely chopped

4 ripe plum tomatoes, rinsed, cored, seeded, and coarsely chopped

½ teaspoon ground cumin

4 large eggs, lightly beaten

½ cup grated Monterey Jack or mild cheddar

Salt and freshly ground black pepper to taste

1. Tear tortillas into 1-inch pieces, and set aside. Heat oil in a large skillet over medium-high heat. Crumble sausage into the skillet and cook, breaking up lumps with a fork, for 3 to 5 minutes, or until browned. Remove sausage from the skillet with a slotted spoon, and set aside. Discard all but 3 tablespoons bacon grease from the skillet.

2. Add tortilla pieces a handful at a time to the skillet and fry them, turning them frequently with tongs, for 2 to 3 minutes, or until pale golden. Transfer to paper towels to drain.

3. Add onion, garlic, chile, and red bell pepper to the skillet and cook, stirring frequently, for 5 minutes, or until onion softens. Return sausage to the skillet, and add tomatoes and cumin. Cook, stirring occasionally, for 2 to 3 minutes, or until tomatoes begin to soften.

4. Add tortilla pieces and stir until well combined. Pour eggs over tortilla mixture and stir in cheese. Season to taste with salt and pepper. Reduce heat to low, and cover pan. Cook for 2 minutes, then stir, recover pan, and cook for an additional 1 to 2 minutes, or until eggs are just set and cheese is melted. Serve immediately.

Note: The dish can be prepared up to the end of Step 3 up to a day in advance and refrigerated, tightly covered. Reheat it in the skillet before completing Step 4.

This method for making scrambled eggs results in very light and fluffy eggs. Use it whenever scrambled eggs are called for. To make scrambled eggs for a crowd, bake, covered with aluminum foil, in a 350°F oven for 15 minutes. Stir, recover the pan, and cook at 10-minute intervals until the eggs reach the proper consistency.

Huevos Rancheros

Makes 4 to 6 servings

Active time:
20 minutes

Start to finish:
30 minutes

VARIATION

Substitute jalapeño Jack for Monterey Jack for a spicier dish.

Mexican fried eggs with chorizo and salsa are popular all over America, especially as a brunch dish. Prepare the tomato sauce in advance and the dish can be on the table in a matter of minutes. Serve it with fried potato slices or Mexican rice.

2 tablespoons olive oil, divided

¾ pound bulk Fresh Mexican Chorizo (page 66), Chaurice (page 64), or purchased sausage

1 large onion, diced

4 garlic cloves, minced

3 tablespoons chili powder

1 tablespoon smoked Spanish paprika

1 (15-ounce) can tomato sauce

Salt and cayenne to taste

8 to 12 (6-inch) corn tortillas

2 cups grated Monterey Jack

2 tablespoons unsalted butter

8 to 12 large eggs

Freshly ground black pepper to taste

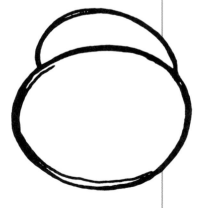

1. Preheat the oven broiler. Heat 1 tablespoon oil in a heavy 2-quart saucepan over medium-high heat. Crumble chorizo into the pan, and cook, stirring frequently, for 3 to 5 minutes, or until sausage browns. Remove sausage from the pan with a slotted spoon, and discard grease from the pan.

2. Return the pan to the stove, and add remaining oil. Add onion and garlic, and cook, stirring frequently, for 3 minutes, or until onion is translucent. Stir in chili powder and paprika, and cook for 1 minute, stirring constantly.

3. Add tomato sauce and sausage, and bring to a boil, stirring occasionally. Reduce the heat to low and simmer sauce, uncovered, for 10 minutes, stirring occasionally. Season to taste with salt and cayenne. Keep warm.

4. While sauce simmers, arrange tortillas on a baking sheet, and sprinkle each with cheese. Broil for 1 to 2 minutes, or until cheese melts. Remove the pan from the broiler, and set aside.

5. Melt butter in a heavy 12-inch skillet over medium heat. Break eggs into the skillet, and season eggs to taste with salt and pepper. Cook eggs to desired doneness. To serve, place 1 egg on each tortilla and top with chorizo sauce. Serve immediately.

Note: The sauce can be prepared up to 3 days in advance and refrigerated, tightly covered. Reheat over low heat before continuing.

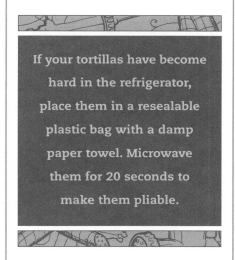

If your tortillas have become hard in the refrigerator, place them in a resealable plastic bag with a damp paper towel. Microwave them for 20 seconds to make them pliable.

Basic Piecrust

Active time:

15 minutes

Start to finish:

15 minutes

Piecrust is nothing more than flour, salt, and fat, mixed with a little water. The method remains constant; what changes is the proportion of ingredients.

Proportions for Piecrust				
Size	Flour	Salt	Unsalted Butter	Ice Water
8 to 10-inch single	1⅓ cups	¼ teaspoon	½ cup	3 to 4 tablespoons
8 to 9-inch double	2 cups	½ teaspoon	¾ cup	5 to 6 tablespoons
10-inch double	2⅔ cups	¾ teaspoon	1 cup	7 to 8 tablespoons

1. Place flour in a mixing bowl. Cut butter into cubes the size of lima beans, and cut into flour using a pastry blender, two knives, or your fingertips until mixture forms pea-sized chunks. This can also be done in a food processor fitted with the steel blade using the on-and-off pulse button.

2. Sprinkle mixture with water, 1 tablespoon at a time. Toss lightly with fork until dough will form a ball. If using a food processor, process until mixture holds together when pressed between two fingers; if it is processed until it forms a ball too much water has been added.

3. Depending on if it is to be a 1- or 2-crust pie, form dough into 1 or 2 (5- to 6-inch) "pancakes." Flour "pancake" lightly on both sides, and, if time permits, refrigerate dough before rolling it to allow more even distribution of the moisture.

4. Either roll dough between 2 sheets of waxed paper or inside a lightly floured jumbo plastic bag. Use the former method for piecrust dough that will be used for formed pastries such as empanadas, and the latter to make circles suitable for lining or topping a pie pan. For a round circle, make sure dough starts out in the center of the bag, and then keep turning it in ¼ turns until the circle is 1-inch larger in diameter than the inverted pie plate. Either remove the top sheet of wax paper or cut the bag open on the sides. You can either begin to cut out shapes or invert the dough into a pie plate, pressing it into the bottom and up the sides, and extending the dough 1 inch beyond the edge of the pie plate.

5. If you want to partially or totally bake the pie shell before adding a filling, prick bottom and sides with a fork, press in a sheet of waxed paper or aluminum foil, and fill the pie plate with dried beans, rice, or the metal pie stones sold in cookware stores. Bake crust in a 375° F oven for 10 to 15 minutes. The shell is now partially baked.

To complete baking, remove the weights and wax paper, and bake an additional 15 to 20 minutes, or until golden brown. Otherwise, fill pie shell. If you want a double-crust pie, roll out the second dough "pancake" the same way you did the first half, and invert it over the top, crimping the edges and cutting in some steam vents with the tip of a sharp knife.

Note: The crust can be prepared up to 3 days in advance and refrigerated, tightly covered. Both dough rounds and rolled out sheets can be frozen up to 3 months.

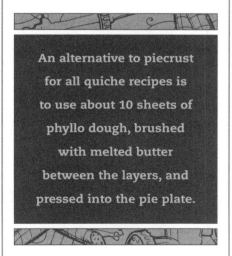

An alternative to piecrust for all quiche recipes is to use about 10 sheets of phyllo dough, brushed with melted butter between the layers, and pressed into the pie plate.

THE
BOUNTIFUL
BOWL:

SOUPS WITH SAUSAGE

Both sausages and hearty soups qualify as comfort food, and when the two are joined, the results warm both the soul and the tummy on the coldest winter nights.

At the end of the chapter are a few recipes for homemade stocks. Homemade stock makes soups, stews, and sauces taste better. A long-simmered stock can be frozen and taken out of the freezer as needed. And if you save chicken and beef bones, the stock is almost free, too.

To dress up bowls of soup, add a sprinkling of the same chopped herb used in the recipe. Chopped parsley always adds bright color. Or, cut stale bread into croutons and bake until crisp.

Another alternative is to add some crunchy croutons. Traditionally croutons were sautéed in butter in a skillet, but it's easier to bake them in the oven. Preheat the oven to 375°F. Arrange the bread cubes in a single layer on a baking sheet and spray them with garlic-flavored vegetable oil spray. Sprinkle with some dried herbs, salt, and pepper, and bake for 5 to 10 minutes, or until brown.

Southwestern Chorizo and Vegetable Soup

Makes 4 to 6 servings

Active time:
20 minutes

Start to finish:
40 minutes

VARIATIONS

Substitute sweet potatoes for red-skinned potatoes.

Omit hot chile for milder soup.

A clear broth that's loaded with vegetables, chiles, sausage, and herbs needs nothing more than some warm cornbread as an accompaniment.

1 tablespoon olive oil

¾ pound bulk Fresh Mexican Chorizo (page 66), Chaurice (page 64), or purchased sausage

1 large onion, diced

1 small poblano chile, seeds and ribs removed, and chopped

2 garlic cloves, minced

1 jalapeño or serrano chile, seeds and ribs removed, and finely chopped

2 teaspoons ground cumin

1 teaspoon dried oregano

5 cups Chicken Stock (page 296) or purchased low-sodium stock

¾ pound red-skinned potatoes, scrubbed and cut into ¾-inch cubes

1 (15-ounce) can red kidney beans, drained and rinsed

1 (10-ounce) package frozen mixed vegetables, thawed

¼ cup chopped fresh cilantro

Salt and freshly ground black pepper to taste

For garnish: lime wedges

1. Heat oil in a 4-quart saucepan over medium-high heat. Crumble sausage into the skillet and cook, breaking up lumps with a fork, for 3 to 5 minutes, or until browned. Remove sausage from the pan with a slotted spoon, and set aside. Discard all but 2 tablespoons grease from the pan.

2. Add onion, poblano chile, garlic, and jalapeño chile. Cook, stirring frequently, for 3 minutes, or until onion is translucent. Add cumin and oregano, and cook for 1 minute, stirring constantly.

2. Return sausage to the pan, stir in stock, and add potatoes. Bring to a boil over high heat, then reduce the heat to low, cover the pan, and cook for 12 to 15 minutes, or until potatoes are tender.

3. Stir in beans, mixed vegetables, and cilantro. Bring back to a boil and simmer, covered, for 3 minutes. Season to taste with salt and pepper, and serve immediately, garnishing each serving with lime wedges.

Note: The soup can be prepared up to 2 days in advance and refrigerated, tightly covered. Reheat it over low heat, covered, until hot, stirring occasionally.

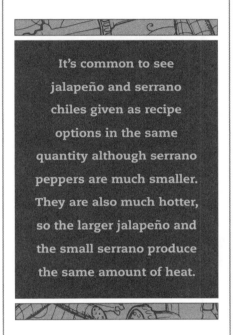

It's common to see jalapeño and serrano chiles given as recipe options in the same quantity although serrano peppers are much smaller. They are also much hotter, so the larger jalapeño and the small serrano produce the same amount of heat.

Acorn Squash and Sausage Chowder

Makes 4 to 6 servings

Active time: 20 minutes

Start to finish: 1½ hours

VARIATION

Substitute 2 (15-ounce) cans solid pack pumpkin for squash.

Serve this filling soup from late summer through the winter when fresh winter squash comes to the market. Although acorn squash is listed, any winter squash—butternut, hubbard, acorn—can be used. Serve it with some coleslaw.

2 (2-pound) acorn squash

¼ cup vegetable oil, divided

2 tablespoons unsalted butter

1 medium onion, diced

1 celery rib, diced

1 large carrot, diced

6 cups Chicken Stock (page 296) or purchased low-sodium stock, divided

3 tablespoons pure maple syrup

2 tablespoons chopped fresh parsley

2 tablespoons bourbon

1 teaspoon dried sage

½ pound bulk American Breakfast Sausage (page 46), Turkey, Apple, and Sage Sausage (page 150), or purchased sausage

1 cup fresh corn kernels or frozen corn kernels

½ cup fresh peas or frozen peas

⅔ cup heavy cream

Salt and freshly ground black pepper to taste

1. Preheat the oven to 425°F, and line a baking pan with heavy-duty aluminum foil. Cut squash in half, and discard seeds. Rub cut surfaces with 2 tablespoons oil, and place cut side down in the pan. Bake squash for 35 to 45 minutes, or until very tender when pierced with a knife.

2. While squash bakes, heat butter in a 4-quart skillet over medium-high heat. Add onion, celery, and carrot. Cook, stirring frequently, for 3 minutes, or until onion is translucent. Stir in 4 cups stock, maple syrup, parsley, bourbon, and sage. Bring to a boil and simmer soup, partially covered, for 20 minutes, or until vegetables are tender.

3. While soup simmers, heat remaining oil in a skillet over medium-high heat. Crumble sausage into the skillet and cook, breaking up lumps with a fork, for 3 to 5 minutes, or until browned. Set aside.

4. Scrape squash from the shell, and puree with remaining stock in a food processor fitted with the steel blade or in a blender; this may have to be done in batches.

5. Add squash and sausage to soup, and simmer for 10 minutes. Add corn and peas, and simmer for 5 minutes. Season to taste with salt and pepper, and serve immediately.

Note: The soup can be made up to 2 days in advance and refrigerated, tightly covered. Reheat it over low heat, covered.

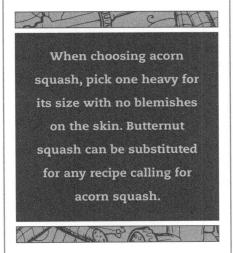

When choosing acorn squash, pick one heavy for its size with no blemishes on the skin. Butternut squash can be substituted for any recipe calling for acorn squash.

Italian Sausage and Chestnut Soup

Makes 4 to 6 servings

Active time:
20 minutes

Start to finish:
50 minutes

VARIATION

Substitute golden sherry for Marsala.

Creamy, earthy chestnuts and herbed sausage laced with a bit of heady Marsala wine makes a warming winter soup. Serve with an arugula salad and a garlicky dressing.

3 tablespoons unsalted butter

1 small onion, chopped

1 celery rib, chopped

1 small carrot, chopped

1 garlic clove, minced

6 cups Chicken Stock (page 296) or purchased low-sodium stock

2 tablespoons chopped fresh parsley

1 tablespoon chopped fresh rosemary or 1 teaspoon dried

1 bay leaf

1 (15-ounce) jar cooked chestnuts, chopped

⅓ cup Marsala

1 tablespoon olive oil

½ pound bulk Sweet Italian Sausage (page 52), Porchetta-Style Sausage (page 56), or purchased sausage

½ cup heavy cream

Salt and freshly ground black pepper to taste

1. Heat butter in a 4-quart saucepan over medium-high heat. Add onion, celery, carrot, and garlic. Cook, stirring frequently, for 3 minutes, or until onion is translucent.

2. Add stock, parsley, rosemary, chestnuts, and Marsala to the pan, and bring to a boil over medium-high heat, stirring occasionally. Cover the pan, reduce the heat to low, and simmer soup for 20 minutes, or until vegetables are soft.

3. While soup simmers, heat oil in a skillet over medium-high heat. Crumble sausage into the skillet and cook, breaking up lumps with a fork, for 3 to 5 minutes, or until browned. Set aside.

4. Remove and discard bay leaf. Puree soup with an immersion blender, a food processor fitted with the steel blade, or in a blender; this will have to be done in batches unless using an immersion blender.

5. Add sausage and cream to soup, and bring to a boil over medium heat. Simmer soup for 10 minutes, uncovered, over low heat. Season to taste with salt and pepper, and serve immediately.

Note: The soup can be made up to 2 days in advance and refrigerated, tightly covered. Reheat it over low heat, covered.

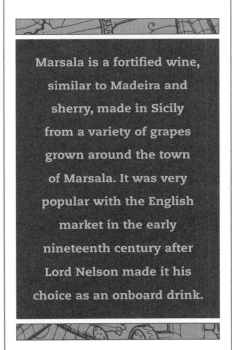

Marsala is a fortified wine, similar to Madeira and sherry, made in Sicily from a variety of grapes grown around the town of Marsala. It was very popular with the English market in the early nineteenth century after Lord Nelson made it his choice as an onboard drink.

Linguiça and Kale Soup

Makes 4 to 6 servings

Active time: 20 minutes

Start to finish: 1 hour

VARIATION

Substitute escarole or Swiss chard for kale.

Garlicky sausage, dark, leafy greens, and potatoes are combined in this soup served in cafés and home kitchens throughout Portugal. Serve it with a loaf of crusty bread.

1 tablespoon olive oil

¾ pound bulk Portuguese Linguiça (page 68), Fresh Mexican Chorizo (page 66), or purchased linguiça

1 large onion, diced

2 garlic cloves, minced

1½ pounds boiling potatoes, peeled and diced

5½ cups Chicken Stock (page 296) or purchased low-sodium stock

¾ pound kale

Salt and freshly ground black pepper to taste

1. Heat oil in a 4-quart saucepan over medium-high heat. Add sausage and cook, stirring frequently, for 3 to 5 minutes, or until browned. Remove sausage from the pan with a slotted spoon, and set aside. Discard all but 2 tablespoons grease from the pan.

2. Add onion and garlic, and cook, stirring frequently, for 3 minutes, or until onion is translucent. Add potatoes and stock to the pan, and bring to a boil over medium-high heat. Simmer soup, partially covered, for 20 to 25 minutes, or until potatoes are tender.

3. While soup simmers, prepare kale. Rinse kale and discard stems and center of ribs. Cut leaves crosswise into thin slices.

4. Drain soup through a sieve placed over a mixing bowl. Transfer solids to a food processor fitted with the steel blade or to a blender, and puree until smooth.

5. Return liquid to the saucepan, and stir in vegetable puree, sausage, and kale. Bring to a boil over medium heat, stirring occasionally. Reduce the heat to low, and simmer soup for 20 to 30 minutes, or until kale is cooked and tender. Season to taste with salt and pepper, and serve immediately.

Note: The soup can be prepared up to 2 days in advance and refrigerated, tightly covered. Reheat it over low heat, covered, until hot, stirring occasionally.

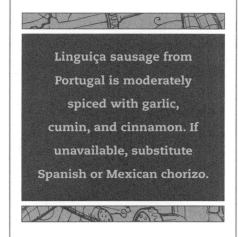

Linguiça sausage from Portugal is moderately spiced with garlic, cumin, and cinnamon. If unavailable, substitute Spanish or Mexican chorizo.

Italian Wedding Soup with Sausage Meatballs

Makes 4 to 6 servings

Active time:
20 minutes

Start to finish:
45 minutes

Tasty greens, swirls of egg, lots of heady Parmesan and flavorful meatballs are what you'll find in this easy-to-prepare soup. Serve with a loaf of garlic bread and your meal is complete.

Meatballs:

1 large egg

⅓ cup Italian breadcrumbs

¼ cup whole milk

1 pound bulk Sweet Italian Sausage (page 52) or purchased sausage

½ cup freshly grated Parmesan

Soup:

6 cups Chicken Stock (page 296) or purchased low-sodium stock

1 pound curly endive, rinsed, cored, and coarsely chopped

2 large eggs

½ cup freshly grated Parmesan, divided

Salt and freshly ground black pepper to taste

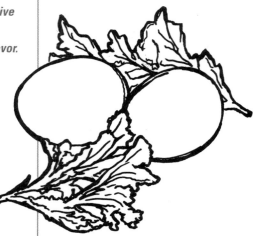

1. Combine egg, breadcrumbs, milk, sausage, and Parmesan, and mix well into a paste.

2. Combine stock and endive in a 4-quart saucepan, and bring to a boil over medium-high heat. Reduce the heat to low, and simmer soup, uncovered, for 10 minutes.

3. Using wet hands, form meatball mixture into 1-inch balls, and drop them into simmering soup. Cook for 7 to 10 minutes, or until cooked through and no longer pink.

4. Whisk eggs with 2 tablespoons cheese. Stir soup and gradually add egg mixture to form thin strands. Season to taste with salt and pepper, and serve immediately, passing remaining cheese separately.

Note: The soup can be made up to 2 days in advance and refrigerated, tightly covered. Reheat it over low heat, covered.

Wedding soup is an Italian-American dish, rather than one traditionally Italian. The name is a mistranslation of *minestra maritata*, which has nothing to do with nuptials, but is a reference to the fact that green vegetables and meats go well together.

Two Mushroom, Barley, and Beef Sausage Soup

Makes 6 to 8 servings

Active time: 20 minutes

Start to finish: 1½ hours

Mushroom-barley soup is most closely identified with Eastern European countries such as Poland and Russia. Adding sausage to the soup makes it a one-dish meal. The combination of aromatic and flavorful dried mushrooms with the delicate flavor and texture of fresh mushrooms makes it a winner. Serve with some dark and dense pumpernickel.

¼ cup dried porcini mushrooms

2 tablespoons vegetable oil, divided

1 pound Smoked Kielbasa
   (page 126) links, or purchased
   cooked beef sausage, cut into
   ½-inch dice

1 large onion, diced

2 carrots, sliced

2 celery ribs, sliced

1 pound white mushrooms, wiped
   with a damp paper towel,
   trimmed, and sliced

7 cups Beef Stock (page 299) or
   purchased low-sodium stock

¾ cup whole barley, rinsed well

3 tablespoons chopped fresh parsley

1 tablespoon fresh thyme or
   1 teaspoon dried

Salt and freshly ground black
   pepper to taste

VARIATIONS

Substitute fresh Portobello mushrooms for white mushrooms. Peel them and remove brown gills from under the caps, and then cut into ½-inch dice.

Substitute chicken stock for the beef stock, and substitute a poultry sausage for the beef sausage.

1. Combine porcini mushrooms and ½ cup boiling water, pushing down on the mushrooms with the back of a spoon. Soak for 10 minutes, then drain mushrooms, reserving soaking liquid, and chop mushrooms. Strain soaking liquid through a paper coffee filter or a paper towel. Set aside.

2. Heat 1 tablespoon oil in a 4-quart saucepan over medium-high heat. Add sausage slices and cook, stirring frequently, for 3 to 5 minutes, or until sausage browns. Remove sausage from the pan with a slotted spoon, and set aside.

3. Add remaining oil to the pan, add onion and cook, stirring frequently, for 3 minutes, or until onion is translucent. Add carrots, celery, mushrooms, stock, barley, parsley, thyme, chopped porcini, and reserved mushroom liquid, and bring to a boil over medium-high heat. Reduce the heat to low, and simmer soup, covered, for 40 minutes.

4. Return sausage to the pan, and simmer for an additional 20 minutes, or until vegetables and barley are tender. Season to taste with salt and pepper, and serve immediately.

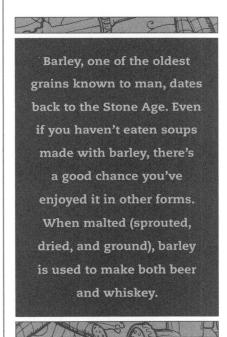

Barley, one of the oldest grains known to man, dates back to the Stone Age. Even if you haven't eaten soups made with barley, there's a good chance you've enjoyed it in other forms. When malted (sprouted, dried, and ground), barley is used to make both beer and whiskey.

Potato Soup with Sausage and Gorgonzola

Makes 4 to 6 servings

Active time: 20 minutes

Start to finish: 45 minutes

VARIATION

Substitute blue cheese or Stilton for Gorgonzola.

Serve small cups of this potato-sausage soup laced with Gorgonzola as the first course of an elegant dinner, or large bowls as a meal accompanied by a salad of bitter greens.

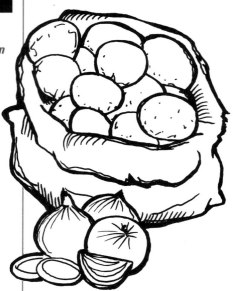

1 tablespoon olive oil

¾ pound bulk Sweet Italian Sausage (page 52), Luganega (page 58), or purchased sausage

1 large onion, chopped

1 large carrot, chopped

1 celery rib, chopped

2 garlic cloves, minced

¾ cup dry white wine

5 cups Chicken Stock (page 296) or purchased low-sodium stock

2 tablespoons chopped fresh parsley

1 bay leaf

1 pound Russet potatoes, peeled and chopped

1 cup crumbled Gorgonzola cheese

1 cup half-and-half or whole milk

Salt and freshly ground black pepper to taste

1. Heat oil in a 4-quart saucepan over medium-high heat. Crumble sausage into the skillet and cook, breaking up lumps with a fork, for 3 to 5 minutes, or until browned. Remove sausage from the pan with a slotted spoon, and set aside. Discard all but 2 tablespoons grease from the pan.

2. Add onion, carrot, celery, and garlic to the pan, and cook, stirring frequently, for 3 minutes, or until onion is translucent. Return sausage to the pan, add wine, and cook for 2 minutes. Add stock, parsley, bay leaf, and potato. Bring to a boil over high heat, stirring occasionally.

3. Reduce the heat to low, cover the pan, and cook for 15 to 20 minutes, or until vegetables are very soft. Remove and discard bay leaf.

4. Remove 1 cup of solids from the pan with a slotted spoon. Combine solids and cheese in a food processor fitted with the steel blade or in a blender. Puree until smooth, and stir puree back into soup. Season to taste with salt and pepper, and serve immediately.

Note: The soup can be prepared up to 2 days in advance and refrigerated, tightly covered. Reheat it over low heat, covered, until hot, stirring occasionally.

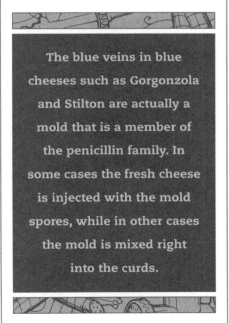

The blue veins in blue cheeses such as Gorgonzola and Stilton are actually a mold that is a member of the penicillin family. In some cases the fresh cheese is injected with the mold spores, while in other cases the mold is mixed right into the curds.

Sausage Gumbo Z'herbes

Makes 4 to 6
servings

Active time:
30 minutes

Start to finish:
1 hour

This traditional Cajun gumbo is made with andouille sausage and a number of leafy greens. The darker the greens—think kale, collards, mustards—the more nutrients they have, and their bitter flavors contrast with the spicy sausage. Serve this over a scoop of rice and with a bowl of coleslaw on the side.

½ cup vegetable oil, divided
⅔ cup all-purpose flour
¾ Andouille Sausage (page 62) or purchased sausage, cut into ½-inch dice
3 tablespoons unsalted butter
1 large onion, diced

2 celery ribs, diced
5 garlic cloves, minced
2 tablespoons filé powder
4 cups Chicken Stock (page 296) or purchased low-sodium stock, divided
4 cups sliced collard greens, rinsed well
4 cups sliced mustard greens, rinsed well
½ cup chopped fresh parsley
1 teaspoon dried thyme
2 bay leaves
Hot red pepper sauce to taste
Salt and freshly ground black pepper to taste
2 to 3 cups cooked white or brown rice, hot

1. Preheat the oven to 450°F. Combine ⅓ cup oil and flour in a Dutch oven, and place the pan in the oven. Bake roux for 20 to 30 minutes, or until walnut brown, stirring occasionally.

2. While roux bakes, heat remaining oil in a large skillet over medium-high heat. Add sausage and cook, stirring frequently, for 3 to 5 minutes, or until browned. Remove sausage from the pan with a slotted spoon, and set aside. Discard grease from the skillet.

3. Melt butter in the skillet, and add onion, celery, and garlic. Cook, stirring frequently, for 3 minutes, or until onion is translucent. Add filé powder, and cook for 30 seconds, stirring constantly. Add 1½ cups stock, collard greens, mustard greens, parsley, thyme, and bay leaves. Bring to a boil over medium-high heat, then cover the pan and cook, covered, over low heat for 12 to 15 minutes, or until greens are tender.

4. Remove and discard bay leaves. Transfer mixture to a food processor fitted with the steel blade or to a blender. Puree until smooth.

5. Remove roux from the oven, and place the pan on the stove over medium heat. Whisk in remaining stock, and whisk constantly, until mixture comes to a boil and thickens. Add vegetable puree and sausage, and cook for an additional 10 minutes.

6. Season to taste with hot red pepper sauce, salt, and pepper. Serve immediately over rice.

Note: The soup can be prepared up to 2 days in advance and refrigerated, tightly covered. Reheat it over low heat, covered, until hot, stirring occasionally.

Filé is a powder made from ground sassafras leaves and can be used as an alternative thickener to okra for gumbo. It's available in the spice section of most supermarkets.

Red Lentil and Sausage Soup

Makes 4 to 6 servings

**Active time:
20 minutes**

**Start to finish:
50 minutes**

VARIATION

Substitute green or yellow split peas for lentils.

Lentils come in a rainbow of colors— green, brown, yellow, orange. Red lentils add body and flavor to this Middle Eastern soup. Serve with a Greek salad.

3 tablespoons olive oil

1 small onion, finely chopped

1 carrot, finely chopped

1 celery rib, finely chopped

3 garlic cloves, minced

1 tablespoon ground turmeric

2 teaspoons ground cumin

1 teaspoon ground coriander

6 cups Chicken Stock (page 296) or
    purchased low-sodium stock

1 pound red lentils, rinsed

3 tablespoons chopped fresh parsley

1 pound Merguez (page 92) links,
    North African Lamb Sausage
    (page 100) links, or purchased
    hearty sausage

Salt and freshly ground black
    pepper to taste

1. Heat olive oil in a 3-quart saucepan over medium-high heat. Add onion, carrot, celery, and garlic, and cook, stirring frequently, for 3 minutes, or until onion is translucent. Add turmeric, cumin, and coriander, and cook for 1 minute, stirring constantly.

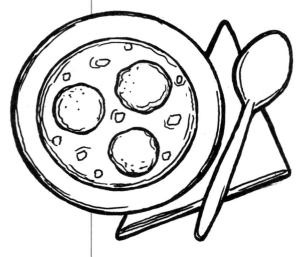

2. Stir in stock, lentils, and parsley, and bring to a boil over medium-high heat, stirring occasionally. Reduce the heat to low, and simmer soup, uncovered, for 20 to 25 minutes, or until lentils are tender. Remove soup from the heat, and set aside.

3. While soup simmers, preheat the oven broiler and line a broiler pan with heavy-duty aluminum foil. Prick sausages on all sides, and broil 4 to 6 inches from the broiler element for 5 to 7 minutes, or until cooked through and no longer pink, turning them with tongs to brown on all sides. Allow sausages to sit for 5 minutes, then cut them into ½-inch pieces, and cover sausage to foil to keep warm.

4. Puree soup with an immersion blender, a food processor fitted with the steel blade, or in a blender; this will have to be done in batches unless using an immersion blender. Return soup to the pan, if necessary.

5. Add sausage to soup, and bring to a boil over medium heat. Reduce the heat to low and simmer soup for 5 minutes. Season to taste with salt and pepper, and serve immediately.

Note: The soup can be made up to 2 days in advance and refrigerated, tightly covered. Reheat it over low heat, covered.

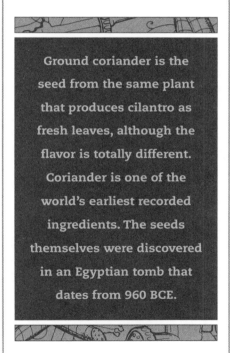

Ground coriander is the seed from the same plant that produces cilantro as fresh leaves, although the flavor is totally different. Coriander is one of the world's earliest recorded ingredients. The seeds themselves were discovered in an Egyptian tomb that dates from 960 BCE.

Spicy Lentil and Sausage Soup

Makes 4 to 6 servings

Active time:
20 minutes

Start to finish:
50 minutes

VARIATION

Substitute green or yellow split peas for lentils.

This classic soup needs nothing more than some olive or other crusty bread as an accompaniment.

3 tablespoons olive oil, divided

1 medium onion, finely chopped

1 large carrot, finely chopped

2 celery ribs, finely chopped

3 garlic cloves, minced

1½ cups French green lentils, rinsed well

7 cups Chicken Stock (page 296) or purchased low-sodium stock

2 tablespoons chopped fresh parsley

2 teaspoons herbes de Provence

¾ pound bulk Chaurice (page 64), Linguiça (page 68), or purchased hot Italian sausage

1 tablespoon cider vinegar

Salt and freshly ground black pepper to taste

1. Heat 2 tablespoons oil in a 4-quart saucepan over medium-high heat. Add onion, carrot, celery, and garlic. Cook, stirring frequently, for 3 minutes, or until onion is translucent. Add lentils, stock, parsley, and herbes de Provence. Bring to a boil over medium-high heat, stirring occasionally.

2. Cover the pan, reduce the heat to low, and simmer soup for 20 minutes, or until lentils are almost tender.

3. While soup simmers, heat remaining oil in a skillet over medium-high heat. Crumble sausage into the skillet and cook, breaking up lumps with a fork, for 3 to 5 minutes, or until browned. Set aside.

4. Remove ⅔ cup solids from the saucepan with a slotted spoon and puree in a food processor fitted with the steel blade or in a blender. Stir puree and sausage into the soup, and simmer, covered, for an additional 10 minutes, or until lentils are very tender. Stir in vinegar, and season to taste with salt and pepper. Serve immediately.

Note: The soup can be made up to 2 days in advance and refrigerated, tightly covered. Reheat it over low heat, covered.

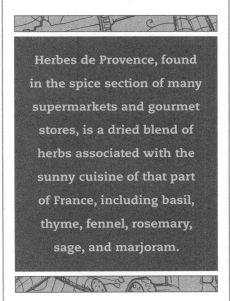

Herbes de Provence, found in the spice section of many supermarkets and gourmet stores, is a dried blend of herbs associated with the sunny cuisine of that part of France, including basil, thyme, fennel, rosemary, sage, and marjoram.

Tuscan White Bean and Sausage Soup

Makes 4 to 6 servings

Active time:
20 minutes

Start to finish:
45 minutes

VARIATION

Substitute kidney beans for white beans.

Using canned beans means that no soaking is required, so dinner can be on the table in no time. Accompany with a tossed salad.

⅔ pound bulk Sweet Italian Sausage (page 52), Porchetta-Style Sausage (page 56), or purchased sausage

2 medium onions, diced

3 garlic cloves, minced

2 celery ribs, diced

1 large carrot, diced

1 (6-inch-square) Parmesan rind (optional)

4 cups Chicken Stock (page 296) or purchased low-sodium stock, divided

2 (15-ounce) cans white beans, drained and rinsed

¼ cup chopped fresh parsley

1 teaspoon dried thyme

1 bay leaf

½ pound Swiss chard, rinsed, stemmed, and thinly sliced

½ cup freshly grated Parmesan

Salt and freshly ground black pepper to taste

1. Place a heavy 4-quart saucepan over medium-high heat. Crumble sausage into the skillet and cook, breaking up lumps with a fork, for 3 to 5 minutes, or until browned. Remove sausage from the pan with a slotted spoon, and set aside. Discard all but 2 tablespoons sausage fat from the pan.

2. Add onion, garlic, celery, and carrot to the pan. Cook for 3 minutes, stirring frequently, or until onion is translucent. Add sausage, Parmesan rind (if using), 3½ cups stock, half of beans, parsley, thyme, and bay leaf to the pan. Bring to a boil over medium heat, and simmer, partially covered, for 20 minutes, or until vegetables soften.

3. While soup simmers, combine reserved beans and remaining stock in a food processor fitted with the steel blade or in a blender. Puree until smooth, and stir mixture into soup.

4. Add Swiss chard to soup, and simmer for 5 minutes. Remove and discard bay leaf and Parmesan rind (if using), and stir Parmesan into soup. Season to taste with salt and pepper, and serve immediately.

Note: The soup can be prepared up to 2 days in advance and refrigerated, tightly covered. Reheat it over low heat, covered, until hot, stirring occasionally.

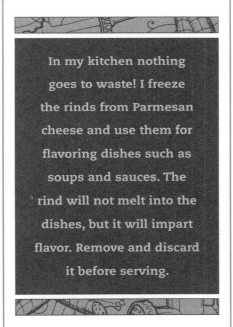

In my kitchen nothing goes to waste! I freeze the rinds from Parmesan cheese and use them for flavoring dishes such as soups and sauces. The rind will not melt into the dishes, but it will impart flavor. Remove and discard it before serving.

Chorizo Chili Soup with Beans

Makes 4 to 6 servings

Active time:
20 minutes

Start to finish:
1 hour

Substitute 1 or 2 fresh jalapeño or serrano chiles for canned chiles for spicier soup. Cook fresh chiles with onion mixture in Step 2.

Try this soup version of chili con carne with some warm corn or whole-wheat tortillas and sliced tomatoes and avocados.

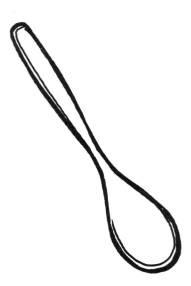

Soup:

3 tablespoons olive oil, divided

¾ pound bulk Fresh Mexican Chorizo (page 66), Chaurice (page 64), or purchased sausage

1 large onion, diced

1 large green bell pepper, seeds and ribs removed, and diced

1 celery rib, diced

3 garlic cloves, minced

2 tablespoons chili powder

2 teaspoons ground cumin

4 cups Beef Stock (page 299) or purchased low-sodium stock

1 (14.5-ounce) can diced tomatoes, undrained

1 (4-ounce) can diced mild green chiles, drained

2 (15-ounce) cans red kidney beans, drained and rinsed

Salt and freshly ground black pepper to taste

Garnish:

½ to ¾ cup grated cheddar

½ to ¾ cup sour cream or plain yogurt

¼ to ½ cup chopped onion

1. Heat 1 tablespoon oil in a 4-quart saucepan over medium-high heat. Crumble sausage into the skillet and cook, breaking up lumps with a fork, for 3 to 5 minutes, or until browned. Remove sausage from the pan with a slotted spoon, and set aside. Discard fat from the pan.

2. Heat remaining oil over medium-high heat. Add onion, green bell pepper, celery, and garlic. Cook, stirring frequently, for 3 minutes, or until onion is translucent. Add chili powder and cumin, and cook for 1 minute, stirring constantly.

3. Return sausage to the pan and add stock, tomatoes, chiles, and tomato paste. Stir well to dissolved tomato paste, and bring to a boil over medium-high heat.

4. Reduce the heat to low, and simmer soup, covered, for 20 minutes. Add beans, and cook for an additional 20 minutes. Season to taste with salt and pepper, and serve immediately, passing bowls of cheddar, sour cream, and onion separately.

Note: The soup can be prepared up to 2 days in advance and refrigerated, tightly covered. Reheat it over low heat, covered, until hot, stirring occasionally.

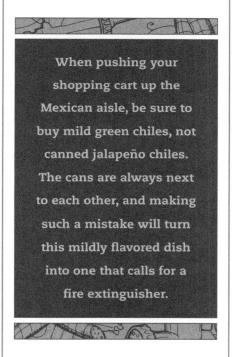

When pushing your shopping cart up the Mexican aisle, be sure to buy mild green chiles, not canned jalapeño chiles. The cans are always next to each other, and making such a mistake will turn this mildly flavored dish into one that calls for a fire extinguisher.

Sausage Provençal, Bean, and Barley Soup

Makes 4 to 6 servings

Active time: 20 minutes

Start to finish: 1 hour

VARIATION

Substitute Sweet Italian Sausage for the turkey sausage and substitute Italian seasoning for the herbes de Provence. Add ½ cup freshly grated Parmesan to soup before seasoning with salt and pepper.

Joining grains and legumes is part of the tradition in much of Mediterranean cooking, and the beans and barley in this soup create a silky texture. The sausage adds its own complexity too. Serve with a raw fennel salad.

1 pound Garlicky Chicken and Rosemary (page 164) links, Provençal Chicken Sausage (page 162) links, or purchased turkey or pork sausage

3 tablespoons olive oil

1 large onion, diced

3 garlic cloves, minced

2 celery ribs, sliced

2 carrots, sliced

1 red bell pepper, seeds and ribs removed, and diced

¾ cup pearl barley, rinsed well

5 cups Chicken Stock (page 296) or purchased low-sodium stock

1 (15-ounce) can cannellini beans, drained and rinsed

1 (14.5-ounce) can diced tomatoes, undrained

1 (8-ounce) can tomato sauce

2 tablespoons chopped fresh parsley

2 teaspoons herbes de Provence

1 bay leaf

Salt and freshly ground black pepper to taste

1. Preheat the oven broiler, and line a broiler pan with heavy-duty aluminum foil. Prick sausages on all sides, and broil 4 to 6 inches from the broiler element for 5 to 7 minutes, or until cooked through and no longer pink, turning them with tongs to brown on all sides. Allow sausages to sit for 5 minutes, then cut them into ¾-inch dice, and cover sausage to foil to keep warm.

2. Heat oil in a 4-quart saucepan over medium-high heat. Add onion, garlic, celery, carrot, and red bell pepper, and cook, stirring frequently, for 3 minutes, or until onion is translucent.

3. Add barley, stock, beans, tomatoes, tomato sauce, parsley, herbes de Provence, and bay leaf. Stir well. Bring to a boil, then reduce the heat to low and simmer soup, covered, for 15 minutes. Add sausage, and simmer for an additional 25 to 30 minutes, or until vegetables and barley are tender.

4. Remove and discard bay leaf. Season to taste with salt and pepper, and serve immediately.

Note: The soup can be prepared up to 2 days in advance and refrigerated, tightly covered. Reheat it over low heat, covered, until hot, stirring occasionally.

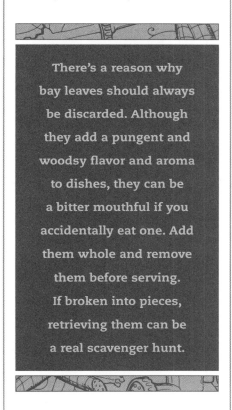

There's a reason why bay leaves should always be discarded. Although they add a pungent and woodsy flavor and aroma to dishes, they can be a bitter mouthful if you accidentally eat one. Add them whole and remove them before serving. If broken into pieces, retrieving them can be a real scavenger hunt.

Middle Eastern Garbanzo Bean and Sausage Soup

Makes 4 to 6 servings

Active time:
15 minutes

Start to finish:
2½ hours, including 1 hour to soak beans

Garbanzo beans are used extensively in the Middle East—there'd be no hummus without them. They're also used in soups, much like this one. The flavors from the sausage and spices turn this soup into a vibrant dish. Serve with some pita bread.

2 cups dried garbanzo beans

3 tablespoons olive oil

1 large onion, diced

6 garlic cloves, minced

1 large carrot, chopped

2 celery ribs, minced

2 tablespoons ground cumin

1 tablespoon ground coriander

1 (14.5-ounce) can diced tomatoes, drained

6½ cups Chicken Stock (page 296) or purchased low-sodium stock

3 tablespoons chopped fresh parsley

1 pound Lamb Sausage with Sun-Dried Tomatoes and Pine Nuts (page 96) links, Greek Chicken and Pistachio Sausage (page 160) links, or purchased uncooked sausage

Salt and freshly ground black pepper to taste

VARIATION

The same basic formulation can also become a Latin American soup. Substitute red kidney beans for garbanzo beans, cilantro for parsley, and Fresh Mexican Chorizo (page 66) links for lamb sausage. Omit ground coriander, and add 2 teaspoons dried oregano to soup.

1. Rinse beans in a colander and place them in a mixing bowl covered with cold water. Allow beans to soak overnight. Or place beans into a saucepan and bring to a boil over high heat. Boil 1 minute. Turn off the heat, cover the pan, and soak beans for 1 hour. With either soaking method, drain beans, discard soaking water, and begin cooking as soon as possible.

2. Heat olive oil in a 4-quart saucepan over medium-high heat. Add onion, garlic, carrot, and celery, and cook, stirring frequently, for 3 minutes, or until onion is translucent. Add cumin and coriander, and cook for 1 minute, stirring constantly. Stir in tomatoes, stock, and parsley.

3. Bring to a boil, then reduce the heat to low and simmer soup, covered, for 1¼ to 1½ hours, or until beans are tender.

4. While soup simmers, preheat the oven broiler, and line a broiler pan with heavy-duty aluminum foil. Prick sausages on all sides, and broil 4 to 6 inches from the broiler element for 5 to 7 minutes, or until cooked through and no longer pink, turning them with tongs to brown on all sides. Allow sausages to sit for 5 minutes, then cut them into ¾-inch dice, and cover sausage to foil to keep warm.

5. Using a slotted spoon, transfer ¾ cup of solids to a food processor fitted with a metal blade or a blender, and puree until smooth. Stir puree back into soup, add sausage, season to taste with salt and pepper, and serve immediately.

Note: The soup can be made up to 2 days in advance and refrigerated, tightly covered. Reheat it over low heat, covered.

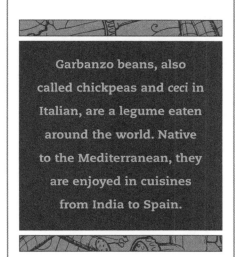

Garbanzo beans, also called chickpeas and *ceci* in Italian, are a legume eaten around the world. Native to the Mediterranean, they are enjoyed in cuisines from India to Spain.

Canadian Yellow Split Pea and Sausage Soup

Makes 4 to 6 servings

Active time: 15 minutes

Start to finish: 1 hour

VARIATION

Substitute green or red lentils for split peas.

While green split pea soup is the norm, I prefer the lighter color of its first cousin made with yellow split peas. This is the way the dish is traditionally made in Canada. Serve with crusty bread.

2 tablespoons vegetable oil

¾ pound Smoked Kielbasa (page 126), Smoky Mettwurst (page 128), or purchased smoked sausage, cut into ½-inch dice

1 large onion, finely chopped

1 carrot, finely chopped

1 celery rib, finely chopped

2 garlic cloves, minced

1 pound yellow split peas, rinsed

6 cups Chicken Stock (page 296) or purchased low-sodium stock

3 tablespoons chopped fresh parsley

1 teaspoon dried thyme

1 bay leaf

Salt and freshly ground black pepper to taste

1. Heat oil in a 4-quart saucepan over medium-high heat. Add sausage and cook, stirring frequently, for 3 to 5 minutes, or until browned. Remove sausage from the pan with a slotted spoon, and set aside. Add onion, carrot, celery, and garlic to the pan. Cook, stirring frequently, for 3 minutes, or until onion is translucent.

2. Return sausage to the pan, and add split peas, stock, parsley, thyme, and bay leaf. Stir well, and bring to a boil over medium-high heat. Reduce the heat to low and simmer soup, covered, for 40 to 50 minutes, or until split peas have disintegrated. Remove and discard bay leaf, season to taste with salt and pepper, and serve immediately.

Note: The soup can be made up to 2 days in advance and refrigerated, tightly covered. Reheat it over low heat, covered.

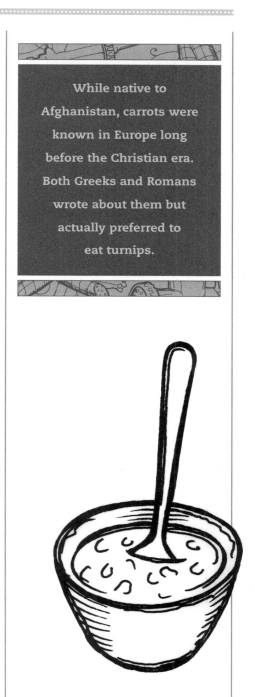

While native to Afghanistan, carrots were known in Europe long before the Christian era. Both Greeks and Romans wrote about them but actually preferred to eat turnips.

Chicken Stock

Makes 3 quarts

Active time:
10 minutes

Start to finish:
3½ hours

Richly flavored, homemade chicken stock is as important as good olive oil in my kitchen, and it's as easy to make as boiling water.

6 quarts water

5 pounds chicken bones, skin, and trimmings

4 celery ribs, rinsed and cut into thick slices

2 onions, trimmed and quartered

2 carrots, trimmed, scrubbed, and cut into thick slices

2 tablespoons whole black peppercorns

6 garlic cloves, peeled

4 sprigs parsley

4 sprigs thyme or 1 teaspoon dried

2 bay leaves

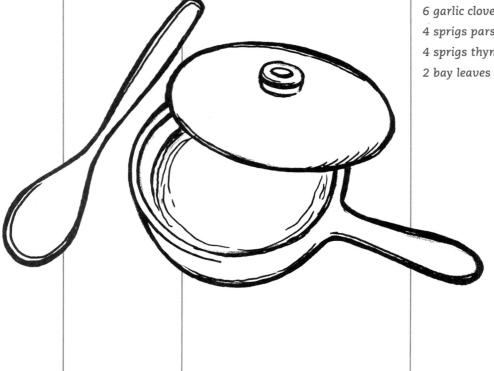

1. Place water and chicken in a large stockpot, and bring to a boil over high heat. Reduce the heat to low, and skim off foam that rises during the first 10 to 15 minutes of simmering. Simmer stock, uncovered, for 1 hour, then add celery, onions, carrots, peppercorns, garlic, parsley, thyme, and bay leaves. Simmer for 2½ hours.

2. Strain stock through a fine-meshed sieve, pushing with the back of a spoon to extract as much liquid as possible. Discard solids, spoon stock into smaller containers, and refrigerate. Remove and discard fat from surface of stock.

Note: The stock can be refrigerated and used within 3 days, or it can be frozen up to 6 months.

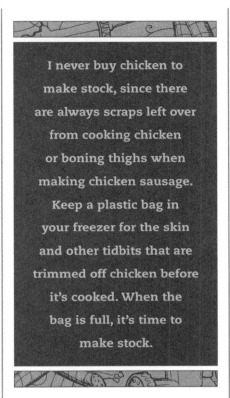

I never buy chicken to make stock, since there are always scraps left over from cooking chicken or boning thighs when making chicken sausage. Keep a plastic bag in your freezer for the skin and other tidbits that are trimmed off chicken before it's cooked. When the bag is full, it's time to make stock.

Quick Chicken Stock

Makes 2 quarts

Active time:
10 minutes

Start to finish:
30 minutes

It's happened to me, too. I go to the freezer for a quart of chicken stock and discover that the frozen larder is bare. Here's a way to make a reasonable facsimile of stock in just a few minutes.

2 quarts canned low-sodium
   chicken stock
4 celery ribs, rinsed and finely
   chopped
1 onion, peeled and diced
2 carrots, trimmed, scrubbed, and
   finely chopped
2 tablespoons whole black
   peppercorns
6 garlic cloves, peeled
4 sprigs parsley
4 sprigs thyme or 1 teaspoon dried
2 bay leaves

1. Combine stock, celery, onion, carrots, peppercorns, garlic, parsley, thyme, and bay leaves in a large stockpot, and bring to a boil over high heat. Reduce the heat to low, cover the pan, and simmer 20 minutes.

2. Strain stock through a fine-meshed sieve, pressing with the back of a spoon to extract as much liquid as possible. Spoon stock into smaller containers, and refrigerate when cool.

Note: The stock can be refrigerated and used within 3 days, or it can be frozen up to 6 months.

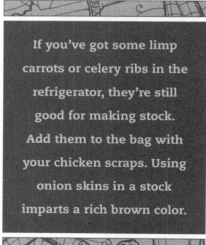

If you've got some limp carrots or celery ribs in the refrigerator, they're still good for making stock. Add them to the bag with your chicken scraps. Using onion skins in a stock imparts a rich brown color.

Beef Stock

Makes 2 quarts

Active time:
15 minutes

Start to finish:
3½ hours

Browning the meat before adding liquid turns the stock dark brown and slightly caramelizes the flavor.

2 pounds beef shank (or 1 pound
    beef stew meat or chuck roast)
2 quarts water
1 carrot, trimmed, scrubbed, and
    cut into thick slices
1 medium onion, peeled and sliced
1 celery rib, trimmed and sliced
1 tablespoon whole black
    peppercorns
3 sprigs fresh parsley
3 sprigs fresh thyme or
    1 teaspoon dried
2 garlic cloves, peeled
1 bay leaf

1. Preheat the oven broiler, and line a broiler pan with heavy-duty aluminum foil. Broil beef for 3 minutes per side, or until browned. Transfer beef to a large stockpot, and add water. Bring to a boil over high heat. Reduce the heat to low, and skim off foam that rises during the first 10 to 15 minutes of simmering. Simmer for 1 hour, uncovered, then add carrot, onion, celery, peppercorns, parsley, thyme, garlic, and bay leaves. Simmer for 3 hours.

2. Strain stock through a fine-meshed sieve, pushing with the back of a spoon to extract as much liquid as possible. Discard solids, and spoon stock into smaller containers. Refrigerate, remove and discard fat from surface of stock.

Note: The stock can be refrigerated and used within 3 days, or it can be frozen up to 6 months.

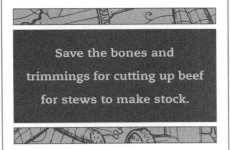

Save the bones and
trimmings for cutting up beef
for stews to make stock.

THE SIDE SHOW:

APPETIZERS, SIDES,
AND SALADS

Sometimes it's the little touches that can make a meal special, especially if the entrée is a simple piece of grilled or roasted food. These dishes are for small bites or accompaniments, from hors d'oeuvre to serve before dinner to all range of side dishes.

Also included are a few recipes for sausage stuffings, or dressings, depending on where you live. Stuffings are side dishes that shouldn't be limited to Thanksgiving or the occasional chicken dinner, but should be served more frequently with any roasts or grilled meats and seafood.

If you do stuff a bird, never do so in advance of cooking. Warm, moist stuffing provides a great breeding ground for bacteria, especially nasty ones as such salmonella and E. coli. (That's why I never buy one of the pre-stuffed chickens or chicken breasts in the supermarket.)

To stuff a roasting chicken or turkey, make the mixture just before putting the bird in the oven. The stuffing will be warm and pass through the danger zone of 40°F to 140°F as quickly as possible once it goes into the oven. If the stuffing was made in advance, reheat it in a microwave oven and then stuff the chicken. Make sure the stuffing reaches the same 165°F as the bird before it's taken out of the oven. Also, use two to three fewer tablespoons of stock because juices are absorbed from the bird too.

Merguez-Stuffed Grape Leaves

Makes 50 grape leaves

Active time:
1 hour

Start to finish:
5 hours, including
3 hours to chill

Grape leaves stuffed with lamb sausage and dressed with a lemony sauce are a perfect appetizer to serve with any Middle Eastern meal.

⅔ cup long-grain rice
1 (1-pound) jar brine-packed
     grape leaves
½ cup pine nuts
½ pound bulk Merguez Sausage
     (page 92) or purchased
     merguez or hot Italian sausage
⅓ cup olive oil, divided
1 medium onion, finely chopped
3 tablespoons chopped fresh dill
2 tablespoons chopped fresh parsley
¼ cup freshly squeezed lemon juice,
     divided
Salt and freshly ground black
     pepper to taste
2 cups Chicken Stock (page 296) or
     purchased low-sodium stock, hot
Vegetable oil spray

1. Bring 1⅓ cups salted water to a boil in a small saucepan. Stir in rice, cover the pan, reduce the heat to low, and cook rice for 15 to 17 minutes, or until water is absorbed. Scrape rice into a large mixing bowl.

2. While rice cooks, bring a large pot of water to a boil. Drain grape leaves and rinse them under cold running water in a flat colander. Blanch leaves for 3 minutes, then plunge them into ice water to stop the cooking action. Drain well, and set aside.

3. Toast pine nuts in a dry skillet over medium heat for 2 to 3 minutes, or until browned. Add nuts to the bowl with the rice.

4. Return the skillet to the stove, and heat 1 tablespoon oil over medium-high heat. Crumble sausage into the skillet and cook, breaking up lumps with a fork, for 3 to 5 minutes, or until browned.

VARIATIONS

Substitute chopped fresh mint for dill.

Substitute chopped Spanish chorizo for fresh sausage.

Add ½ cup crumbled feta or goat cheese to filling.

Add ¼ cup chopped dried apricots, raisins, or dried currants to filling.

Remove sausage from the skillet with a slotted spoon, and add to the mixing bowl. Discard all but 2 tablespoons grease from the skillet, add onion and cook, stirring frequently, for 3 minutes, or until onion is translucent.

5. Add onion to the mixing bowl, and add dill, parsley, and 2 tablespoons lemon juice. Mix well, and season to taste with salt and pepper.

6. Preheat the oven to 375°F, and grease 2 (9 x 13-inch) baking pans lightly with vegetable oil spray. Place 1 grape leaf, vein side up, on a plate or cutting board. Trim stem at base of leaf. Place 1 tablespoon rice mixture in center of leaf at widest part. Fold bottom of leaf over filling. Fold sides in. Roll up. Place seam side down in prepared dish. Repeat with remaining leaves and rice mixture, arranging in single layer in the dishes.

7. Combine stock with remaining oil and remaining lemon juice, and divide mixture into the dishes. Cover the pans with foil, and bake for 40 to 50 minutes, or until grape leaves are tender. Cool to room temperature. Remove grape leaves from the dishes with a slotted spatula, and refrigerate until cold.

Note: The dish can be prepared up to 3 days in advance and refrigerated, tightly covered. Also the filling can be made up to 2 days in advance of rolling and cooking the grape leaves.

Making stuffed grape leaves, which are always a hit at Mediterranean parties, is not difficult, but it does take far less time if you enlist some friends or your kids to help you with the rolling process.

Sausage and Puff Pastry Bites

Makes 24 pieces

Active time:
20 minutes

Start to finish:
1¼ hours,
including 30
minutes to chill

These easy-to-make crispy swirls disappear at every party.

1 tablespoon olive oil
½ cup finely chopped onion
¼ cup Italian breadcrumbs
2 tablespoons whole milk
½ pound bulk Sweet Italian Sausage
   (page 52), Luganega (page 58),
   or purchased sausage
2 large eggs, divided
½ teaspoon Italian seasoning
2 tablespoons all-purpose flour
½ pound frozen puff pastry, thawed
Vegetable oil spray

1. Lightly grease a baking sheet with vegetable oil spray. Heat oil in a small skillet over medium-high heat. Add onion and cook, stirring frequently, for 3 minutes, or until onion is translucent. Set aside. Combine breadcrumbs with milk, and stir well.

2. Combine onion, breadcrumbs mixture, sausage, 1 egg, and Italian seasoning in a food processor fitted with the steel blade and combine well, using the on-and-off pulse button. This can also be done by hand.

3. Dust a counter with flour, and unfold puff pastry. Roll pastry with a lightly floured rolling pin into a rectangle that is 12 x 10 inches. Then cut the rectangle into 3 strips that are 4 inches wide. Lightly beat remaining egg in a small cup, and brush each pastry strip with egg wash.

VARIATIONS

Substitute bulk Fresh Mexican Chorizo (page 66) for Italian sausage, substitute plain breadcrumbs for Italian breadcrumbs, and substitute 1 teaspoon ground cumin and 1 teaspoon dried oregano for Italian seasoning.

Add 1 or 2 garlic cloves to the skillet along with onion.

4. Divide sausage mixture into a thin line down the center of each puff pastry strip. Pull up sides of pastry, and crimp it in the center to enclose filling. Arrange rolls seam side down on the prepared baking sheet, and refrigerate for at least 30 minutes, or until firm.

5. Preheat the oven to 425°F. Cut each roll into 8 even sections, and arrange them on the baking sheet. Moisten tops of slices with beaten egg.

6. Bake for 20 minutes, or until pastry is puffed and golden. Serve immediately.

Note: The dish can be prepared for baking up to a day in advance and refrigerated, tightly covered.

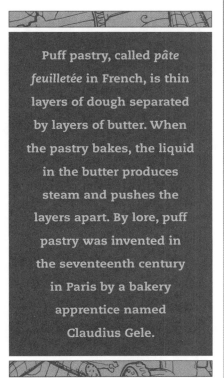

Puff pastry, called *pâte feuilletée* in French, is thin layers of dough separated by layers of butter. When the pastry bakes, the liquid in the butter produces steam and pushes the layers apart. By lore, puff pastry was invented in the seventeenth century in Paris by a bakery apprentice named Claudius Gele.

Sausage-Stuffed Mushrooms Au Gratin

Makes 20 mushrooms

Active time: 20 minutes

Start to finish: 45 minutes

VARIATION

Substitute sharp cheddar for both Gruyère and Parmesan.

Stuffed mushrooms can either be served as an hors d'oeuvre or as a side dish with some baked chicken or beef. Two cheeses make the filling soft and creamy.

20 large mushrooms, wiped with a damp paper towel, trimmed, and stemmed

6 tablespoons (¾ stick) unsalted butter, melted, divided

Salt and freshly ground black pepper to taste

1 tablespoon olive oil

1 large shallot, finely chopped

1 garlic clove, minced

¼ cup dry white wine

⅓ pound bulk Veal Sausage Marengo (page 106), Porchetta-Style Sausage (page 56), or purchased sweet Italian sausage

¼ cup plain breadcrumbs

½ cup grated Gruyère, divided

¼ cup freshly grated Parmesan

3 tablespoons chopped fresh parsley

1 teaspoon dried tarragon

3 tablespoons heavy cream

Vegetable oil spray

1. Preheat the oven to 375°F, and grease a 10 x 14-inch baking pan with vegetable oil spray. Remove mushroom stems, and set aside. Arrange mushrooms in the prepared pan cap side down. Brush inside of caps with 2 tablespoons butter, and sprinkle with salt and pepper.

2. Chop mushroom stems finely in a food processor fitted with the steel blade using the on-and-off pulse button. Heat remaining butter and oil in a large skillet over medium-high heat. Add shallot and garlic and cook, stirring frequently, for 3 minutes, or until shallot is translucent. Add chopped mushroom stems and cook, stirring frequently, for 3 to 5 minutes, or until mushrooms soften. Add wine to the skillet, and cook over high heat for 2 to 3 minutes, or until wine is almost evaporated. Scrape mixture into a mixing bowl.

3. Crumble sausage into the skillet and cook, breaking up lumps with a fork, for 3 to 5 minutes, or until browned. Scrape sausage into the mixing bowl.

4. Add breadcrumbs, ¼ cup Gruyère, Parmesan, parsley, tarragon, and cream, and mix well. Season to taste with salt and pepper. Stuff mushrooms with filling, mounding it slightly in the center. Top mushrooms with remaining Swiss cheese.

5. Bake mushrooms for 15 to 20 minutes, or until mushrooms are tender. Allow to cool for 5 minutes, then serve.

Note: The dish can be prepared for baking up to a day in advance and refrigerated, tightly covered.

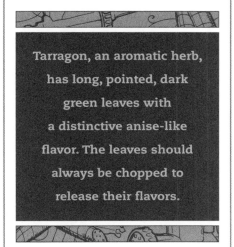

Tarragon, an aromatic herb, has long, pointed, dark green leaves with a distinctive anise-like flavor. The leaves should always be chopped to release their flavors.

Stuffed Mushrooms Siciliana

Makes 24 mushrooms

Active time:
20 minutes

Start to finish:
45 minutes

Toasted pine nuts, salty olives, and succulent dried currants offer the traditional salty and sweet flavors often found in Sicilian food.

20 large white mushrooms, wiped with a damp paper towel, and stemmed

⅓ cup olive oil, divided

Salt and freshly ground black pepper to taste

½ cup pine nuts

½ pound bulk Sweet Italian Sausage (page 52), Porchetta-Style Sausage (page 56), or purchased Italian sausage

½ cup chopped fresh parsley

⅓ cup finely chopped pimiento-stuffed green olives

3 tablespoons dried currants

2 tablespoons capers, drained and rinsed

⅔ cup plain breadcrumbs, divided

Vegetable oil spray

VARIATIONS

Substitute slivered blanched almonds, toasted and chopped, for pine nuts, and substitute bulk Fresh Mexican Chorizo (page 66) for Sweet Italian Sausage. Omit dried currants from filling.

Add ½ to ¾ teaspoon crushed red pepper flakes to filling for a spicier dish.

1. Preheat the oven to 400°F, and grease a 10 x 14-inch baking pan with vegetable oil spray. Arrange mushrooms in the prepared pan cap side down. Brush inside of caps with 2 tablespoons olive oil, and sprinkle with salt and pepper. Toast pine nuts in a dry skillet over medium heat for 2 to 3 minutes, or until browned.

2. Combine pine nuts, sausage, parsley, olives, currants, capers, 3 tablespoons breadcrumbs, and 1 tablespoon remaining oil in a mixing bowl. Mix well, and season to taste with salt and pepper. Fry 1 tablespoon of mixture in a small skillet over medium-high heat. Taste and adjust seasoning, if necessary.

3. Stuff mushrooms with filling, mounding it slightly in the center. Combine remaining breadcrumbs and olive oil in a small bowl, and pat mixture onto tops of mushrooms.

4. Bake mushrooms for 20 minutes, or until stuffing is cooked through and crumbs are brown. Allow to cool for 5 minutes, then serve.

Note: The dish can be prepared for baking up to a day in advance and refrigerated, tightly covered. If using purchased sausage, add 2 tablespoons finely chopped sun-dried tomatoes to the filling.

Pine nuts are called *piñon* in Spanish and *pignoli* in Italian, and they are sometimes found by those names in ethnic markets where they are generally less expensive. The nuts are located inside the pinecones of various species of evergreen, and to remove them the pine cones must be heated, and then the nuts, which are in thin shells, are pulled out by hand. This labor-intensive method is why they are so expensive.

Vietnamese Sausage Rolls

Makes 36 pieces

Active time:
25 minutes

Start to finish:
1 hour

*C*ha gio, crispy Vietnamese spring rolls wrapped in rice paper, are baked instead of fried, which makes them quicker to prepare and lighter.

5 large dried shiitake mushrooms
1 ounce bean thread (cellophane)
    noodles
⅓ pound Sweet Chinese Sausage
    (page 74) or purchased cooked
    Chinese sausage, finely chopped
¼ pound ground pork
1 cup fresh bean sprouts, rinsed
    and cut into 1-inch lengths
1 small carrot, peeled and grated
5 scallions, white parts and 4 inches
    of green tops, chopped
6 garlic cloves, minced
3 tablespoons fish sauce (nam pla)
2 large eggs, lightly beaten
1 teaspoon sugar
Freshly ground black pepper to taste
18 (8-inch) rice paper pancakes
Vegetable oil spray

1. Soak dried mushrooms and bean thread noodles in separate bowls of very hot tap water for 15 minutes. Drain mushrooms, and squeeze well to extract as much water as possible. Discard stems, and finely chop mushrooms. Drain bean thread noodles. Place them on a cutting board in a long log shape, and cut into 1-inch pieces. Measure out ½ cup, and discard any additional.

2. Preheat the oven to 400°F, cover a baking sheet with heavy-duty aluminum foil, and grease the foil with vegetable oil spray.

3. Place mushrooms and noodles in a mixing bowl, and add sausage, pork, bean sprouts, carrot, scallions, garlic, fish sauce, eggs, and sugar. Season to taste with pepper, and mix well.

4. Fill a wide mixing bowl with very hot tap water. Place a damp tea towel in front of you on the

counter. Place rice paper pancakes on a plate, and cover with a barely damp towel.

5. Fill 1 rice paper pancake at a time, keeping remainder covered. Totally immerse pancake in the hot water for 2 seconds. Remove it and place it on the damp tea towel; it will become pliable within a few seconds. Gently fold the front edge of the pancake ⅓ of the way to the top. Place about 2 tablespoons filling on the folded-up portion, and shape it into a log, leaving a 2-inch margin on each side. Lightly spray the unfilled part of the pancake with vegetable oil spray. Fold the sides over the filling, and roll tightly but gently, beginning with the filled side. Place roll on the prepared baking sheet, and continue until all rice paper pancakes are filled. Spray tops and sides of rolls with vegetable oil spray.

6. Bake for 12 minutes, then turn rolls gently with tongs, and bake an additional 10 to 12 minutes, or until rolls are browned. Remove the pan from the oven, and blot rolls with paper towels. Slice each in half on the diagonal, and serve immediately.

Note: The rolls can be baked up to 2 days ahead and refrigerated, tightly covered. Reheat them, uncovered, in a 375°F oven for 5 to 7 minutes, or until hot. Do not slice them prior to reheating.

Brittle rice paper pancakes are made from rice that is finely milled into rice flour. Used extensively in Vietnamese and Thai cooking, they must be soaked briefly in water to make them supple enough to roll. The pancakes when filled, rolled, and chilled are called summer rolls. Rice paper pancakes are an excellent substitution for spring roll wrappers when cooking for someone who is gluten intolerant.

Sausage Rice Balls

Makes 36 balls

Active time:
45 minutes

**Start to finish:
3 hours, including
2 hours to chill
mixture**

VARIATIONS

Add ½ teaspoon crushed saffron to stock; the rice will take on a bright yellow color.

Cook ⅓ pound chopped wild mushrooms in 2 tablespoons unsalted butter and add them to risotto as it cooks.

*A*rancini means "little oranges" in Italian. These stuffed rice balls are a classic in Sicilian cooking. Make them when you have leftover risotto.

Risotto:
3 tablespoons unsalted butter
1 medium onion, peeled and chopped
2 garlic cloves, peeled and minced
2 cups arborio rice
¾ cup white wine
5 cups Chicken Stock (page 296) or
    purchased low-sodium stock,
    heated to just below simmer
¾ cup freshly grated Parmesan
Salt and freshly ground black
    pepper to taste

Rice balls:
¼ pound Sweet Italian Sausage
    (page 52) links, Italian Chicken
    and Olive Sausage (page 158)
    links, or purchased sausage
2 large eggs
2 cups risotto, chilled
½ cup freshly grated Parmesan
1½ cups seasoned Italian
    breadcrumbs, divided
3 cups vegetable oil for frying

1. Place butter in a heavy saucepan over medium-high heat. Add onion and garlic, and cook, stirring frequently, for 3 minutes, or until onion is translucent. Add rice, and stir to coat with butter.

2. Raise the heat to high, add wine, and cook for 2 minutes, stirring constantly. Reduce the heat to medium, and ladle 1 cup hot stock over rice. Stir constantly and wait for rice to absorb stock before adding next 1 cup. Repeat with stock until all 5 cups have been absorbed; this should take 12 to 15 minutes.

3. Stir Parmesan into rice, and season to taste with salt and pepper. Scrape rice into a 9 x 13-inch baking pan, and chill for at least 2 hours.

Add 2 cups chopped fresh spinach or ½ of a 10-ounce package of frozen chopped spinach to risotto as it cooks.

Stir 1 cup pureed cooked asparagus into stock while making risotto.

Add ¼ cup chopped fresh herbs (some combination of parsley, basil, oregano, thyme, and rosemary) to risotto as it cooks.

4. While rice chills, preheat the oven broiler and line a broiler pan with heavy-duty aluminum foil. Prick sausages on all sides, and broil 4 to 6 inches from the broiler element for 5 to 7 minutes, or until cooked through and no longer pink, turning them with tongs to brown on all sides. Allow sausages to sit for 5 minutes, then cut them into ½-inch cubes, and set aside.

4. For rice balls, whisk eggs in a mixing bowl, and stir in risotto, cheese, and ½ cup breadcrumbs. Place remaining 1 cup breadcrumbs in a shallow bowl.

5. Measure out 1 tablespoon of rice mixture into your hand, and press a sausage cube into it. Top with another 1 tablespoon of rice mixture, and form into a ball; be careful to totally enclose sausage cube. Roll balls in breadcrumbs, and repeat until all of rice mixture is used.

6. Heat oil in a deep-sided saucepan or deep-fryer to a temperature of 375°F. Preheat the oven to 150°F, and line a baking sheet with paper towels.

7. Add rice balls, being careful not to crowd the pan. Cook rice balls for 3 to 4 minutes, or until browned. Remove rice balls from the pan with a slotted spoon, and drain well on paper towels. Keep fried rice balls warm in the oven while frying remaining balls. Serve immediately.

Note: The rice balls can be prepared for frying up to a day in advance and refrigerated, tightly covered. They can also be fried in advance; reheat them in a 400°F oven for 5 to 7 minutes or until hot and crusty again.

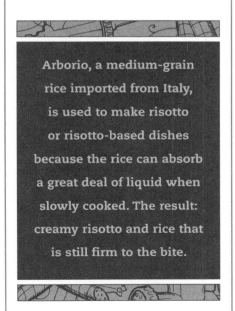

Arborio, a medium-grain rice imported from Italy, is used to make risotto or risotto-based dishes because the rice can absorb a great deal of liquid when slowly cooked. The result: creamy risotto and rice that is still firm to the bite.

Chile con Queso

Makes 8 servings

Active time:
15 minutes

Start to finish:
30 minutes

*Substitute
1 chipotle chile
in adobo sauce,
finely chopped,
for fresh chile.
Add it along with
other ingredients
in Step 2.*

Celery ribs and cucumber slices make good dippers to accompany this chorizo and chili dip in place of tortilla chips.

1 tablespoon olive oil
1 small onion, peeled and diced
2 garlic cloves, peeled and minced
1 jalapeño or serrano chile, seeds and ribs removed, and finely chopped

½ pound bulk Fresh Mexican Chorizo (page 66), Linguiça (page 68), or purchased chorizo
2 ripe plum tomatoes, rinsed, cored, seeded, and chopped
¼ cup heavy cream
1 cup grated Monterey Jack
1 cup grated cheddar
2 teaspoons cornstarch
Freshly ground black pepper to taste

1. Heat oil in a large heavy skillet over medium-high heat. Add onion, garlic, and chile. Add sausage and cook, breaking up lumps with a fork, for 3 to 5 minutes, or until browned. Add tomatoes and chipotle chiles, and cook for an additional 3 minutes. Remove the contents of the skillet with a slotted spoon, and discard grease from the skillet.

2. Return mixture to the skillet, and add cream, Monterey Jack, and cheddar. Cook over low heat, stirring frequently, for 3 minutes, or until cheeses melt and are bubbly.

3. Combine cornstarch and 1 tablespoon cold water in a small bowl, and stir to dissolve cornstarch. Add mixture to dip and bring to a simmer, stirring constantly. Cook over low heat for 1 to 2 minutes, or until dip thickens. Season to taste with pepper.

Note: The dip can be prepared up to 2 days in advance and refrigerated, tightly covered. Reheat it over how heat, covered, until hot, stirring occasionally.

Take care when cooking hot chilies that the steam from the pan doesn't get in your eyes. The potent oils in the peppers can be transmitted in the vapor.

Pasta Salad with Sausage and Stir-Fried Vegetables

Makes 6 to 8 servings

Active time: 20 minutes

Start to finish: 50 minutes

VARIATION

Substitute 2 cups cooked rice for pasta.

The bits of spicy sausage joined with crunchy vegetables in a Parmesan-laced dressing makes this side dish quite the treat.

Salad:

½ pound penne pasta

1 tablespoon olive oil

¼ pound bulk Sweet Italian Sausage (page 52), Luganega (page 58), or purchased sausage

½ small red onion, diced

2 garlic cloves, minced

1 small zucchini, cut into ½-inch dice

1 small carrot, thinly sliced

½ red bell pepper, seeds and rib removed, and thinly sliced

1 teaspoon Italian seasoning

Salt and freshly ground black pepper to taste

2 ripe plum tomatoes, cored, seeded, and diced

⅓ cup sliced pitted Kalamata olives

Dressing:

¼ cup white wine vinegar

2 garlic cloves, minced

Salt and crushed red pepper flakes to taste

⅓ cup freshly grated Parmesan

⅓ cup olive oil

1. Bring a large pot of salted water to a boil over high heat. Add pasta, and cook according to package directions until al dente. Drain pasta, and run it under cold tap water to cool. Drain again, place pasta in a mixing bowl, and refrigerate.

2. While water heats, heat oil in a large skillet over medium-high heat. Crumble sausage into the skillet and cook, breaking up lumps with a fork, for 3 to 5 minutes, or until browned. Remove sausage from the skillet with a slotted spoon, and set aside. Discard all but 2 tablespoons grease from the skillet.

3. Add onion, garlic, zucchini, carrot, and red bell pepper to the skillet, and sprinkle with Italian seasoning. Cook, stirring frequently, for 5 minutes, or until vegetables are crisp-tender. Season to taste with salt and pepper, and add vegetables and sausage to pasta along with tomato and olives.

4. Combine vinegar, garlic, salt, crushed red pepper flakes, and Parmesan in a jar with a tight-fitting lid, and shake well. Add oil, and shake well again.

5. To serve, toss salad with dressing and serve immediately at room temperature or chill.

Note: The dish and the dressing can be prepared up to a day in advance and refrigerated, tightly covered. Do not dress the salad until just prior to serving.

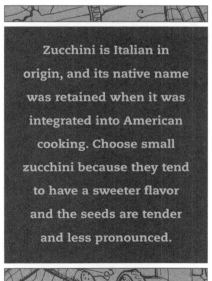

Zucchini is Italian in origin, and its native name was retained when it was integrated into American cooking. Choose small zucchini because they tend to have a sweeter flavor and the seeds are tender and less pronounced.

Warm German Potato Salad with Kielbasa

Makes 4 to 6 servings

Active time:
20 minutes

Start to finish:
45 minutes

Substitute sweet potatoes for white potatoes.

German potato salad with mustard seed and vegetables has always been one of my favorite side dishes, and one I frequently serve with sausage. It's even better with the sausage in the dish.

2 pounds large red-skinned
   potatoes, scrubbed
2 tablespoons vegetable oil
½ pound Smoked Kielbasa
   (page 126), Smoky Mettwurst
   (page 128), or purchased cooked
   sausage, thinly sliced
1 medium onion, chopped
2 celery ribs, diced
2 tablespoons all-purpose flour
⅓ cup cider vinegar
2 tablespoons chopped fresh parsley
1 tablespoon Dijon mustard
1 tablespoon sugar
1 teaspoon celery seeds
1 teaspoon mustard seeds
¼ cup chopped dill pickles
4 scallions, white parts and 4 inches
   of green tops, thinly sliced
Salt and freshly ground black
pepper to taste

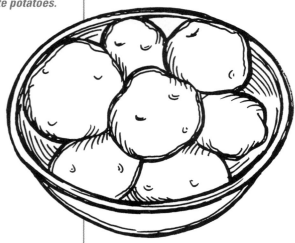

1. Cut potatoes into ¾-inch dice, and steam over boiling water for 12 to 15 minutes, or until tender when pierced with the tip of a paring knife. Transfer potatoes to a mixing bowl, and set aside.

2. While potatoes steam, heat oil in a large skillet over medium-high heat. Add sausage and cook for 3 to 4 minutes, or until browned. Remove sausage from the skillet with a slotted spoon, and set aside.

3. Add onion and celery to the skillet and cook, stirring frequently, for 3 minutes, or until onion is translucent. Reduce the heat to low, stir in flour, and cook for 2 minutes, stirring constantly. Add ½ cup water and vinegar, and bring to a boil over medium heat, whisking constantly. Stir parsley, mustard, sugar, celery seeds, and mustard seeds into the skillet.

4. Pour dressing over potatoes, and then add sausage, pickles, and scallions. Season to taste with salt and pepper, and serve warm or at room temperature.

Note: The dish can be prepared up to a day in advance and refrigerated, tightly covered. Allow it to reach room temperature before serving.

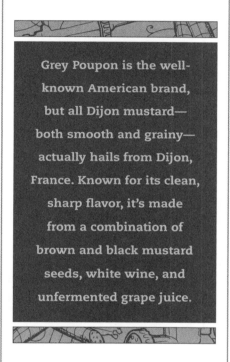

Grey Poupon is the well-known American brand, but all Dijon mustard—both smooth and grainy—actually hails from Dijon, France. Known for its clean, sharp flavor, it's made from a combination of brown and black mustard seeds, white wine, and unfermented grape juice.

Louisiana Potato Salad

Makes 6 to 8 servings

- - - - - - - - - - - - -

Active time: 20 minutes

- - - - - - - - - - - - -

Start to finish: 1¼ hours

Substitute sweet potatoes for red-skinned potatoes. Cut sweet potatoes into quarters, or sixths, if large.

Add ½ to 1 teaspoon cayenne to dressing for a spicy dish.

The assertive seasoning of Cajun cooking is addictive, and the andouille sausage in this salad adds sparkling flavor to a mayonnaise-dressed mix of potatoes and crunchy vegetables.

Salad:

2 pounds small red-skinned potatoes, scrubbed

⅓ pound Andouille Sausage (page 62) or purchased sausage

½ green bell pepper, seeds and ribs removed, and chopped

2 celery ribs, diced

6 scallions, white parts and 3 inches of green tops, sliced

½ cup mayonnaise

Salt and freshly ground black pepper to taste

Dressing:

½ cup distilled white vinegar

2 garlic cloves, minced

2 tablespoons chopped fresh parsley

1 tablespoon sugar

2 tablespoons Creole or Dijon mustard

½ teaspoon dried thyme

Salt and freshly ground black pepper to taste

2 tablespoons olive oil

1. Place potatoes in a large pot of salted water and bring to a boil over high heat. Reduce the heat to medium, and boil potatoes for 12 to 16 minutes, depending on size, or when tender when pierced with the tip of a paring knife. Drain potatoes, and run them under cold running water.

2. While potatoes cook, make dressing. Combine vinegar, garlic, parsley, sugar, mustard, thyme, salt, and pepper in a jar with a tight-fitting lid, and shake well. Add oil, and shake well again.

3. Cut sausage links into quarters lengthwise, and then cut into ½-inch slices. Heat oil in a skillet over medium-high heat. Add sausage and cook, stirring frequently, for 2 to 3 minutes, or until browned. Remove sausage from the skillet with a slotted spoon, and set aside.

4. When potatoes are cool enough to handle, dice potatoes into ¾-inch cubes and place them in a mixing bowl. Toss with dressing, and allow potatoes to marinate for 30 minutes, tossing them occasionally.

5. Add sausage, green bell pepper, celery, scallions, and mayonnaise to salad, and mix gently. Serve immediately at room temperature, or chill.

Note: The dish can be prepared up to 2 days in advance and refrigerated, tightly covered.

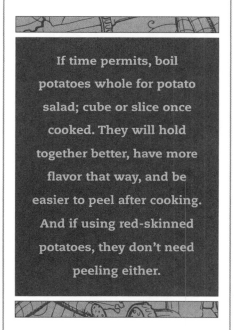

If time permits, boil potatoes whole for potato salad; cube or slice once cooked. They will hold together better, have more flavor that way, and be easier to peel after cooking. And if using red-skinned potatoes, they don't need peeling either.

Grilled Corn and Sausage Salad

Makes 4 to 6 servings

**Active time:
20 minutes**

**Start to finish:
45 minutes**

It's not an August meal at my table if fresh corn in some form isn't part of it. This salad combines sausage, grilled corn, and a simple dressing. Serve with any grilled meat or poultry, or in larger portions for a light supper.

1 cup hickory or mesquite chips

4 ears fresh corn, unshucked

¾ pound bulk American Breakfast
  Sausage (page 46), Loukanika
  (page 138), or purchased
  sausage

½ red bell pepper, seeds and ribs
  removed, and chopped

3 scallions, white parts and 3 inches
  of the green tops, finely chopped

3 tablespoons olive oil

2 tablespoons freshly squeezed
  lime juice

2 tablespoons pure maple syrup

Salt and freshly ground black
  pepper to taste

3 tablespoons chopped fresh cilantro

1. Light a charcoal or gas grill. If using a charcoal grill, soak the hickory chips in cold water to cover for 20 minutes. If using a gas grill, create a packet of heavy-duty aluminum foil to enclose the chips, and poke holes in the foil.

2. While grill heats, remove all but one layer of husks from corn and pull out as much of corn silks as possible. Soak corn in cold water to cover for 10 minutes. Drain hickory chips and place on the fire. Grill corn for 10 to 15 minutes, turning with tongs occasionally.

3. When cool enough to handle, discard husks, and cut kernels off of cobs, using a sharp serrated knife.

4. Crumble sausage into the skillet and cook, breaking up lumps with a fork, for 3 to 5 minutes, or until browned. Combine sausage and its fat with corn, red bell pepper, and scallions in a mixing bowl. Combine olive oil, lime juice, maple syrup, and salt and pepper in a jar with a tight-fitting lid. Shake well, and toss with the corn mixture. Toss with the cilantro and serve at room temperature.

Note: The salad can be made up to a day in advance and refrigerated, tightly covered with plastic wrap. Allow it to sit at room temperature for a few hours to take the chill off. Do not add the cilantro until just prior to serving.

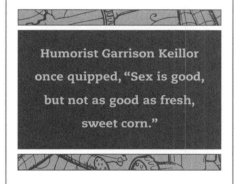

Humorist Garrison Keillor once quipped, "Sex is good, but not as good as fresh, sweet corn."

Sausage, Spinach, and Fennel Salad

Makes 4 to 6
servings

Active time:
15 minutes

Start to finish:
20 minutes

VARIATION

*Substitute arugula
or watercress
for spinach.*

Crunchy fennel with its slight anise flavor is becoming more popular in American kitchens. Serve with any simple entrée.

½ pound Sweet Italian Sausage
   (page 52) links, Provençal
   Chicken Sausage (page 162)
   links, or purchased sausage
3 tablespoons freshly squeezed
   lemon juice
3 tablespoons chopped fresh parsley
Salt and freshly ground black
   pepper to taste
⅓ cup olive oil
4 to 6 cups baby spinach leaves,
   rinsed and stemmed if necessary
1 large fennel bulb, cored, quartered,
   and thinly sliced
4 scallions, white parts and 3 inches
   of green tops, sliced
¾ cup freshly grated Parmesan

1. Preheat the oven broiler, and line a broiler pan with heavy-duty aluminum foil. Prick sausages on all sides, and broil 4 to 6 inches from the broiler element for 5 to 7 minutes, or until cooked through and no longer pink, turning them with tongs to brown on all sides. Allow sausages to sit for 5 minutes, then cut them into ½-inch pieces, and cover sausage to foil to keep warm.

2. While sausage broils, combine lemon juice, parsley, salt, and pepper in a jar with a tight-fitting lid and shake well. Add olive oil, and shake well again. Set aside.

3. Combine spinach, fennel, scallions, and Parmesan in a mixing bowl. Toss with dressing, and divide among plates. Top each portion with sausage, and serve immediately.

Note: The dressing can be prepared and the sausage can be cooked up to a day in advance and refrigerated, tightly covered. Reheat the sausage until warm before serving.

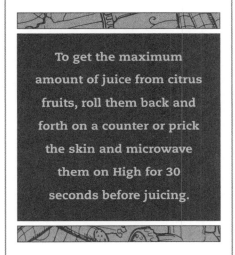

To get the maximum amount of juice from citrus fruits, roll them back and forth on a counter or prick the skin and microwave them on High for 30 seconds before juicing.

Greek Garbanzo Bean and Sausage Salad

Makes 6 to 8 servings

Active time: 15 minutes

Start to finish: 45 minutes, including 30 minutes to chill

VARIATIONS

Substitute kidney beans or black beans for garbanzo beans.

Substitute bulk Sweet Italian Sausage (page 52), North African Lamb Sausage (page 100), or Lugangega (page 58) for Lukanika.

Lemon and oregano, a classic Greek combination, are added to the dressing for this colorful salad with dotted with tomatoes, bell pepper, and scallions.

Dressing:
¼ cup freshly squeezed lemon juice
3 garlic cloves, minced
2 teaspoons dried oregano
1 teaspoon sugar
Salt and freshly ground black
    pepper to taste
½ cup olive oil

Salad:
1 tablespoon olive oil
⅓ pound bulk Loukanika (page 138),
    Hot Italian Sausage (page 54),
    or purchased hearty sausage
2 (15-ounce) cans garbanzo,
    drained and rinsed
½ red bell pepper, seeds and ribs
    removed, and chopped
3 scallions, white parts and 3 inches
    of green tops, sliced
2 ripe plum tomatoes, cored, seeded,
    and diced
½ cup crumbled feta cheese

1. For dressing, combine lemon juice, garlic, oregano, sugar, salt, and pepper in a jar with a tight-fitting lid and shake well. Add olive oil, and shake well again.

2. For salad, heat oil in a medium skillet over medium-high heat. Crumble sausage into the skillet and cook, breaking up lumps with a fork, for 3 to 5 minutes, or until browned.

3. Combine sausage, beans, red bell pepper, scallions, tomatoes, and feta in a mixing bowl, and toss with dressing. Refrigerate for 30 minutes to blend flavors.

Note: The dish can be prepared up to a day in advance and refrigerated, tightly covered. Allow it to reach room temperature before serving.

Feta cheese is a Greek cheese traditionally made from sheep or goat milk, although today it's often made with cow's milk. White, crumbly, and rindless, feta is usually pressed into square cakes. It has a rich, tangy flavor and can range in texture from soft to semidry.

Tabbouleh with Lamb Sausage

Makes 6 to 8 servings

Active time:
20 minutes

Start to finish:
2 hours, including
1 hour to chill

VARIATION

Add ½ cup crumbled feta cheese along with the vegetables.

Tabbouleh is served as an accompaniment to many Middle Eastern dishes. The basic ingredients are bulgur, lots of parsley, and lemon juice. From there, it's open to endless interpretations.

1 pound bulgur wheat

¾ cup freshly squeezed lemon juice

¼ pound bulk North African Lamb Sausage (page 100), Loukanika (page 138), or purchased hearty sausage

1 cucumber, peeled, halved, seeded, and chopped

4 ripe plum tomatoes, rinsed, cored, seeded, and chopped

1 small red onion, chopped

2 garlic cloves, minced

1 cup chopped fresh parsley

3 tablespoons chopped fresh mint

½ cup olive oil

Salt and freshly ground black pepper to taste

1. Place bulgur in a large mixing bowl and add lemon juice and 3 cups of very hot tap water. Cover the bowl with plastic wrap, and let stand for 30 minutes or until bulgur is tender. Drain off any excess liquid.

2. While bulgur soaks, heat a skillet over medium-high heat. Crumble sausage into the skillet and cook, breaking up lumps with a fork, for 3 to 5 minutes, or until browned. Remove sausage from the skillet with a slotted spoon, and set aside.

3. Add sausage, cucumbers, tomatoes, onion, garlic, parsley, and mint to bulgur and toss to combine. Add olive oil a few tablespoons at a time to make salad moist but not runny. Season to taste with salt and pepper.

4. Refrigerate tabbouleh for at least 1 hour. Serve cold or at room temperature.

Note: The dish can be prepared up to a day in advance and refrigerated, tightly covered.

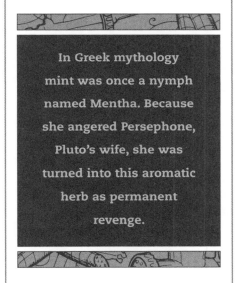

In Greek mythology mint was once a nymph named Mentha. Because she angered Persephone, Pluto's wife, she was turned into this aromatic herb as permanent revenge.

All-Purpose Herbed Sausage Stuffing

Makes 6 to 8 servings

Active time: 25 minutes

Start to finish: 1¼ hours

VARIATIONS

Add ½ pound cooked chopped chestnuts.

Add ½ pound mushrooms, wiped with a damp paper towel, trimmed, and chopped, to the skillet along with onion and celery.

Here's my blueprint for creating a wide range of great stuffings. The basic proportions and method are here along with many variations. But feel free to personalize the ingredients to suit your family's taste.

¾ pound bulk American Breakfast Sausage (page 46), Turkey, Apple, and Sage Italian Sausage (page 150), or purchased sausage

6 tablespoons (¾ stick) unsalted butter

1 large onion, diced

3 celery ribs, diced

1¼ cups Chicken Stock (page 296) or purchased low-sodium stock

3 tablespoons chopped fresh parsley

1 tablespoon dried sage

1 teaspoon dried thyme

3 cups herb stuffing cubes

Salt and freshly ground black pepper to taste

1. Preheat the oven to 350°F, and grease a 9 x 13-inch baking pan if not using stuffing inside a turkey or chicken. For safety instructions for stuffed poultry, see page 302.

2. Heat a large, covered skillet over medium-high heat. Crumble sausage into the skillet and cook, breaking up lumps with a fork, for 3 to 5 minutes, or until browned. Remove sausage from the skillet with a slotted spoon, and set aside.

3. Heat butter in the skillet over medium-high heat. Add onion and celery, and cook, stirring frequently, for 3 minutes, or until onion is translucent. Return sausage to the skillet, and add stock, parsley, sage, and thyme, and bring to a boil, stirring occasionally. Reduce the heat to low, cover the skillet, and simmer mixture for 15 minutes, or until vegetables are tender.

4. Stir in stuffing cubes, and season to taste with salt and pepper. Transfer stuffing to the prepared pan. Cover the pan with aluminum foil, and bake for 30 minutes. Remove the foil, and bake for an additional 10 minutes, or until slightly crisp.

Note: The stuffing can be prepared for baking up to 2 days in advance and refrigerated, tightly covered. Add 15 minutes to the covered baking time if mixture is chilled.

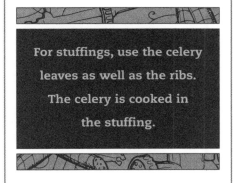

For stuffings, use the celery leaves as well as the ribs. The celery is cooked in the stuffing.

Sausage and Fruit Cornbread Stuffing

Makes 6 to 8 servings

Active time: 25 minutes

Start to finish: 1¼ hours

Here's a stuffing from the Southern cooking tradition, although the cranberries are a New England addition. Try it with grilled pork chops or chicken.

¾ pound bulk American Breakfast Sausage (page 46), Breakfast Sausage with Dried Fruit (page 50), Turkey, Apple, and Sage Sausage (page 150), or purchased sausage

6 tablespoons (¾ stick) unsalted butter

1 large onion, diced

2 celery ribs, diced

1¼ cups Chicken Stock (page 296) or purchased low-sodium stock

2 Golden Delicious apples, peeled, cored, and diced

½ cup chopped dried apricots

¼ cup dried cranberries

2 tablespoons chopped fresh parsley

1 teaspoon dried thyme

3 cups cornbread stuffing cubes

Salt and freshly ground black pepper to taste

VARIATIONS

Substitute chopped dried apple for dried apricots and dried cranberries, and add ½ teaspoon ground cinnamon to the skillet with other ingredients.

Substitute 3 fresh peaches, peeled and diced, for Golden Delicious apples.

Add ½ pound cooked and diced sweet potatoes along with stuffing cubes.

1. Preheat the oven to 350°F, and grease a 9 x 13-inch baking pan if not using stuffing inside a turkey or chicken. For safety instructions for stuffed poultry, see page 302.

2. Heat a large, covered skillet over medium-high heat. Crumble sausage into the skillet and cook, breaking up lumps with a fork, for 3 to 5 minutes, or until browned. Remove sausage from the skillet with a slotted spoon, and set aside.

3. Heat butter in the skillet over medium-high heat. Add onion and celery, and cook, stirring frequently, for 3 minutes, or until onion is translucent. Return sausage to the skillet, and add stock, apples, dried apricots, dried cranberries, parsley, and thyme, and bring to a boil, stirring occasionally. Reduce the heat to low, cover the skillet, and simmer mixture for 15 minutes, or until vegetables are tender.

4. Stir in stuffing cubes, and season to taste with salt and pepper. Transfer stuffing to the prepared pan. Cover the pan with aluminum foil, and bake for 30 minutes. Remove the foil, and bake for an additional 10 minutes, or until slightly crisp.

Note: The stuffing—without the addition of the apples—can be prepared for baking up to 2 days in advance and refrigerated, tightly covered. Add 15 minutes to the covered baking time if mixture is chilled.

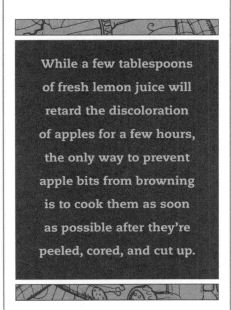

While a few tablespoons of fresh lemon juice will retard the discoloration of apples for a few hours, the only way to prevent apple bits from browning is to cook them as soon as possible after they're peeled, cored, and cut up.

Southwestern Sausage and Cornbread Stuffing

Makes 6 to 8 servings

Active time:
25 minutes

Start to finish:
1¼ hours

Cornbread is traditional in many parts of the United States, from New England to the South and the Southwest. This stuffing contains some of the hearty flavors of traditional Southwestern cooking.

¾ pound bulk Fresh Mexican Chorizo (page 66), Chaurice (page 64), or purchased sausage

6 tablespoons (¾ stick) unsalted butter

1 large red onion, diced

½ green bell pepper, seeds and ribs removed, and chopped

1 celery rib, diced

2 garlic cloves, minced

1 tablespoon ground cumin

1 teaspoon dried oregano

1¼ cups Chicken Stock (page 296) or purchased low-sodium stock

¼ cup chopped fresh cilantro

2 tablespoons canned chopped mild green chiles, drained

3 cups cornbread stuffing cubes

Salt and freshly ground black pepper to taste

Add 2 chipotle chiles in adobo sauce, finely chopped, to the skillet along with other ingredients for a spicy stuffing.

Add 1 small zucchini, rinsed, trimmed, and diced to the skillet when sautéing onion and celery.

Add ¾ cup cooked corn kernels to the skillet along with stuffing cubes.

1. Preheat the oven to 350°F, and grease a 9 x 13-inch baking pan if not using stuffing inside a turkey or chicken. For safety instructions for stuffed poultry, see page 302.

2. Heat a large, covered skillet over medium-high heat. Crumble sausage into the skillet and cook, breaking up lumps with a fork, for 3 to 5 minutes, or until browned. Remove sausage from the skillet with a slotted spoon, and set aside.

3. Heat butter in the skillet over medium-high heat. Add onion, green bell pepper, celery, and garlic, and cook, stirring frequently, for 3 minutes, or until onion is translucent. Add cumin and oregano, and cook for 1 minute, stirring constantly. Return sausage to the skillet, and add stock, cilantro, and chiles, and bring to a boil, stirring occasionally. Reduce the heat to low, cover the skillet, and simmer mixture for 15 minutes, or until vegetables are tender.

4. Stir in stuffing cubes, and season to taste with salt and pepper. Transfer stuffing to the prepared pan. Cover the pan with aluminum foil, and bake for 30 minutes. Remove the foil, and bake for an additional 10 minutes, or until slightly crisp.

Note: The stuffing can be prepared for baking up to 2 days in advance and refrigerated, tightly covered. Add 15 minutes to the covered baking time if mixture is chilled.

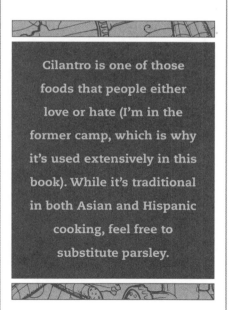

Cilantro is one of those foods that people either love or hate (I'm in the former camp, which is why it's used extensively in this book). While it's traditional in both Asian and Hispanic cooking, feel free to substitute parsley.

Sausage and Cheese Grits

Makes 4 to 6 servings

Active time: 15 minutes

Start to finish: 1 hour

VARIATIONS

Substitute Swiss cheese, jalapeño Jack, or a combination of mozzarella and freshly grated Parmesan for cheddar.

Substitute thyme for sage.

Grits, a form of coarsely ground corn, is beloved in Southern cooking, especially when cheese is added. Adding sausage turns this breakfast classic into a side dish for dinner.

½ pound bulk American Breakfast Sausage (page 46), Sweet Italian Sausage (page 52), or purchased sausage
2¼ cups water
⅔ cup quick-cooking white grits
½ teaspoon dried sage
Salt and cayenne to taste
1 cup grated sharp cheddar
2 tablespoons unsalted butter
½ cup milk
2 large eggs, lightly beaten
Vegetable oil spray

1. Preheat the oven to 350°F, and grease a 9 x 13-inch baking pan with vegetable oil spray.

2. Bring water to a boil in a heavy saucepan over high heat. Whisk in grits, sage, salt, and cayenne. Reduce heat to medium-low, cover pan, and cook, stirring occasionally, for 15 minutes, or until very thick. Remove the pan from the heat, and stir in ⅔ cup cheddar and butter. Allow mixture to cool for 10 minutes, uncovered, stirring occasionally.

3. While grits cook, heat a medium skillet over medium-high heat. Crumble sausage into the skillet and cook, breaking up lumps with a fork, for 3 to 5 minutes, or until browned. Remove sausage from the skillet with a slotted spoon, and set aside.

Substitute Chaurice (page 64) or Linguiça (page 68) for American Breakfast Sausage.

Add 1 cup chopped tomato to the casserole.

Add ½ pound mushrooms, wiped with a damp paper towel, trimmed, and sliced, and then sautéed in 2 tablespoons unsalted butter and 1 tablespoon olive oil until browned.

4. Stir sausage, milk, and eggs into grits, and spoon mixture into the prepared pan. Cover the pan with aluminum foil, and bake for 30 minutes. Uncover the pan, sprinkle with remaining ⅓ cup cheese, and bake for an additional 15 minutes, or until set and top browns. Let stand for 5 minutes, then serve immediately.

Note: The grits can be prepared for baking up to a day in advance and refrigerated, tightly covered. Add 12 to 15 minutes to the initial baking time if mixture is chilled.

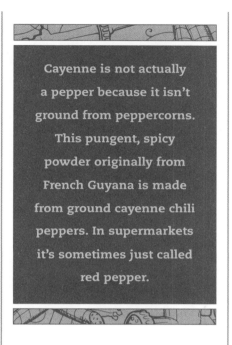

Cayenne is not actually a pepper because it isn't ground from peppercorns. This pungent, spicy powder originally from French Guyana is made from ground cayenne chili peppers. In supermarkets it's sometimes just called red pepper.

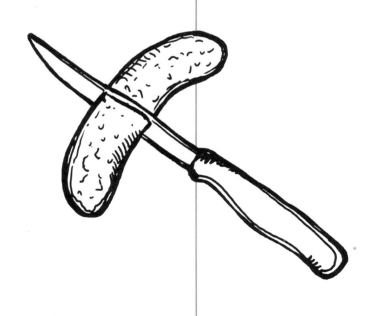

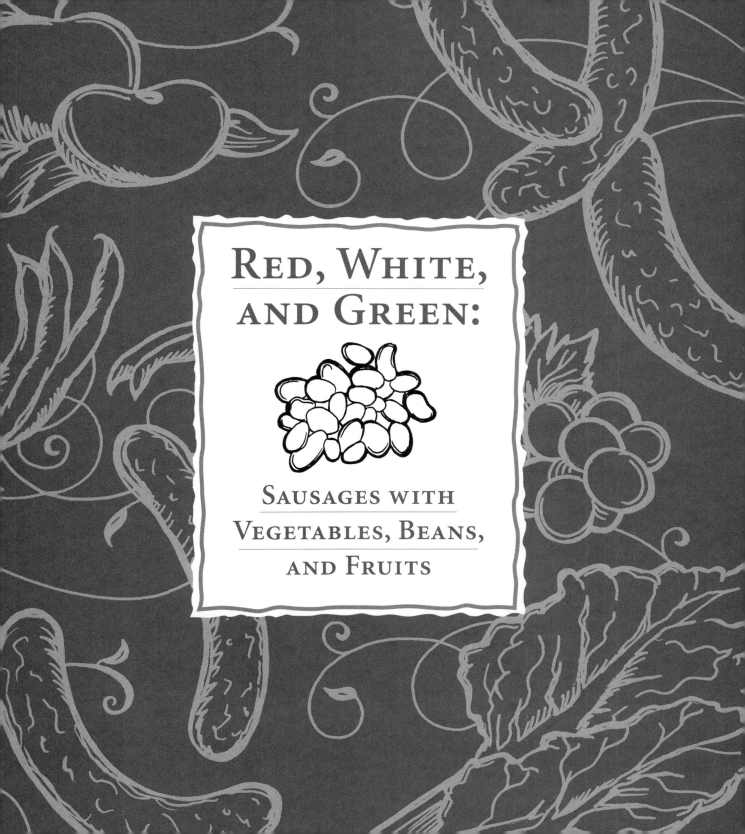

RED, WHITE, AND GREEN:

SAUSAGES WITH VEGETABLES, BEANS, AND FRUITS

While sausage and beans are a well-known tradition, sausages paired with vegetables and fruit are new classics.

Beans are available dried and canned. Dried beans are less expensive; they don't have the high sodium count of canned beans, you can monitor their texture, and you can flavor them as you wish. Canned beans are cooked and ready to use but should be rinsed and drained before using.

Two-thirds cup dry beans, when cooked, is equal to the contents of 1 (15-ounce) can cooked beans. So calculate accordingly. Add canned beans at the end of the cooking time since they're already cooked.

BEAN SUBSTITUTION CHART

Beans are very accommodating; one variety can easily be substituted for another in most recipes, as explained in the following chart. When substituting, also use color, texture, and flavor when making a choice.

BEAN	WHAT TO SUBSTITUTE
Black (also called Turtle)	Kidney
Black-eyed Peas	Kidney
Cannellini	Navy
Cranberry	Kidney
Fava (broad beans)	Large Lima
Flageolet	Navy
Kidney (pink and red, pinto)	Navy
Lentils (red, brown, green)	Split peas
Split peas	Lentils

Warm French Lentil and Sausage Salad

Makes 4 to 6 servings

Active time: 20 minutes

Start to finish: 35 minutes

VARIATION

Substitute 2 (15-ounce) cans white beans or garbanzo beans, drained, and rinsed, for lentils, and omit carrot from recipe.

Frequently found on bistro menus in France, lentils are cooked with carrots and herbs, then dressed with a light vinaigrette before being topped with sausage.

2½ cups French green lentils
1 large carrot, diced
2 tablespoons herbes de Provence, divided
1 bay leaf
Salt and freshly ground black pepper to taste
½ cup olive oil, divided
1 small onion, diced
3 garlic cloves, minced
1 pound French Garlic Sausage (page 72), Smoked Kielbasa (page 126), or purchased cooked sausage
¼ cup red wine vinegar

2 tablespoons chopped fresh parsley
1 tablespoon Dijon mustard
1 teaspoon sugar

1. Rinse lentils under cold running water. Bring 2 quarts water to a boil in a saucepan, and add lentils, carrot, 1 tablespoon herbes de Provence, and bay leaf. Cover the pan, reduce the heat to low, and simmer for 15 minutes. Add salt and pepper, and simmer for an additional 3 to 5 minutes, covered, or until lentils are tender. Remove and discard bay leaf, and drain lentils. Return lentils to the saucepan.

2. While lentils simmer, heat 2 tablespoons olive oil in a small skillet over medium heat. Add onion and garlic, and cook, stirring frequently, for 5 to 7 minutes, or until vegetables soften. Add vegetables to the saucepan with drained lentils.

3. Preheat the oven broiler, and line a broiler pan with heavy-duty aluminum foil. Broil sausages 4 to 6 inches from the broiler element for 3 to 5 minutes, turning them with tongs to brown on all sides. Cut them into ½-inch pieces, and cover sausage with foil to keep warm.

4. Combine vinegar, remaining 1 tablespoon herbes de Provence, parsley, mustard, sugar, salt, and pepper in a jar with a tight-fitting lid. Shake well, add remaining olive oil, and shake well again. Pour half of dressing over lentils, and mix gently. Reheat lentils to warm, if necessary.

5. To serve, mound lentils onto plates and top with sausage slices. Serve immediately, passing remaining dressing separately.

Note: The lentils can be cooked and the dressing can be prepared up to 2 days in advance and refrigerated, tightly covered. Reheat lentils in a 350°F oven, covered, for 10 to 12 minutes, or until warm, before dressing them.

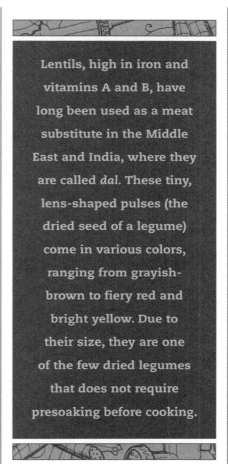

Lentils, high in iron and vitamins A and B, have long been used as a meat substitute in the Middle East and India, where they are called *dal*. These tiny, lens-shaped pulses (the dried seed of a legume) come in various colors, ranging from grayish-brown to fiery red and bright yellow. Due to their size, they are one of the few dried legumes that does not require presoaking before cooking.

Red Lentils with Sausage and Greens

Makes 4 to 6 servings

Active time:
20 minutes

Start to finish:
45 minutes

VARIATION

Substitute green lentils or yellow split peas for red lentils.

Nutrient-rich kale, filling lentils, and succulent sausage are perfect for supper on a bitterly cold night. A crusty olive bread goes well with this dish.

2½ cups red lentils

1 pound kale

1 tablespoon olive oil

¾ pound bulk Sweet Italian Sausage (page 52), bulk Luganega (page 58), or purchased sausage

1 large onion, chopped

1 large carrot, chopped

3 garlic cloves, minced

3 cups Chicken Stock (page 296) or purchased low-sodium stock

2 tablespoons chopped fresh parsley

1 tablespoon chopped fresh oregano or 1 teaspoon dried

1 bay leaf

Salt and freshly ground black pepper to taste

1. Rinse lentils well, and set aside. Rinse kale, discard stems and center of ribs. Cut leaves crosswise into thin slices.

2. Heat oil in a large saucepan over medium-high heat. Crumble sausage into the pan and cook, breaking up lumps with a fork, for 3 to 5 minutes, or until browned. Remove sausage from the pan with a slotted spoon, and discard all but 2 tablespoons grease. Add onion, carrot, and garlic, and cook, stirring frequently, for 3 minutes, or until onion is translucent.

3. Add lentils, stock, parsley, oregano, and bay leaf to the pan. Bring to a boil over medium-high heat, stirring occasionally. Cover the pan, reduce the heat to low, and simmer for 10 minutes.

4. Add sausage and kale to the pan, and cook for an additional 10 to 15 minutes, or until lentils are tender and kale is crisp-tender. Add more stock or water if mixture seems dry. Remove and discard bay leaf, and season to taste with salt and pepper. Serve immediately.

Note: The dish can be prepared up to 2 days in advance and refrigerated, tightly covered. Reheat it, covered, in a 350°F oven for 20 to 25 minutes, or over low heat, stirring occasionally, until hot.

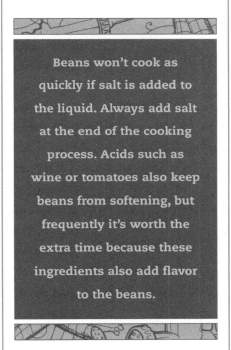

Beans won't cook as quickly if salt is added to the liquid. Always add salt at the end of the cooking process. Acids such as wine or tomatoes also keep beans from softening, but frequently it's worth the extra time because these ingredients also add flavor to the beans.

Cassoulet

Makes 6 to 8 servings

Active time: 30 minutes

Start to finish: 4½ hours, including 1 hour to soak beans

It isn't winter unless this dish appears at least once on my table. Serve with a salad of bitter greens and a mustardy vinaigrette— and plenty of red wine.

1 pound flageolet or other small beans such as navy beans
2 tablespoons olive oil
2 large onions, diced
5 garlic cloves, minced
2 cups Chicken Stock (page 296) or purchased low-sodium stock
1 cup dry white wine
1 (14.5-ounce) can diced tomatoes, undrained
3 tablespoons tomato paste
1 tablespoon herbes de Provence or 1 teaspoon dried thyme, 1 teaspoon dried rosemary, and 1 teaspoon dried oregano
1 bay leaf
1 pound stewing lamb, cut into 1-inch cubes
1 pound Fresh Kielbasa (page 70) links, or purchased fresh sausage, cut into ¾-inch slices
1 pound Boudin Blanc (page 118) or purchased bratwurst, cut into ¾-inch slices
Salt and freshly ground black pepper to taste

1. Rinse beans in a colander and place them in a mixing bowl covered with cold water. Allow beans to soak overnight. Or place beans in a saucepan and bring to a boil over high heat. Boil 1 minute. Turn off the heat, cover the pan, and soak beans for 1 hour. Using either soaking method, drain beans, discard soaking water, and begin cooking as soon as possible.

2. Heat oil in a Dutch oven over medium-high heat. Add onions and garlic, and cook, stirring frequently, for 3 minutes, or until onions are translucent.

3. Add drained beans, stock, wine, tomatoes, tomato paste, herbes de Provence, and bay leaf to the pan. Bring to a boil over medium-high heat, reduce the heat to low, and simmer beans, covered, for 45 minutes.

4. While beans cook, preheat the oven broiler, and line a broiler pan with heavy-duty aluminum foil. Broil lamb, kielbasa, and boudin blanc for 3 minutes per side, or until browned. Stir meats into the pan, along with any juices in the pan. Cook for an additional 1½ to 2 hours, or until lamb and beans are tender. Remove and discard bay leaf, and season to taste with salt and pepper. Serve immediately.

Note: The dish can be prepared up to 2 days in advance and refrigerated, tightly covered. Reheat it, covered, in a 350°F oven for 25 to 40 minutes, or until hot.

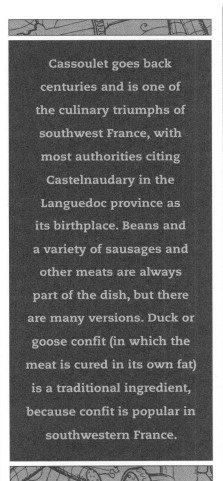

Cassoulet goes back centuries and is one of the culinary triumphs of southwest France, with most authorities citing Castelnaudary in the Languedoc province as its birthplace. Beans and a variety of sausages and other meats are always part of the dish, but there are many versions. Duck or goose confit (in which the meat is cured in its own fat) is a traditional ingredient, because confit is popular in southwestern France.

Feijoada

Makes 6 to 8 servings

**Active time:
25 minutes**

**Start to finish:
3 hours, including
1 hour to soak
beans**

This sausage and black bean stew scented with orange is the national dish of Brazil. It has as many variations as there are cooks in Brazil.

1 pound dried black beans
½ pound Fresh Kielbasa (page 70) links, or purchased sausage, cut into 1-inch pieces
½ pound Fresh Mexican Chorizo (page 66) links or purchased chorizo, cut into 1-inch pieces
½ pound Bratwurst (page 120) or purchased bratwurst, cut into 1-inch pieces
½ pound ham steak, trimmed of fat and cut into 1-inch pieces
3 large onions, diced
5 garlic cloves, minced
1 red bell pepper, seeds and ribs removed, and chopped
5 cups water
1 navel orange, cut into quarters
3 bay leaves

Salt and freshly ground black pepper to taste
3 to 4 cups cooked rice, hot

For garnish:
1 navel orange, sliced
1 cup homemade or refrigerated tomato salsa
1 cup shredded green cabbage, blanched for 5 minutes

1. Rinse beans in a colander and place them in a mixing bowl covered with cold water. Allow beans to soak overnight. Alternatively, place beans in a saucepan and bring to a boil over high heat; boil 1 minute; turn off the heat, cover the pan, and soak beans for 1 hour. Using either soaking method, drain beans, discard soaking water, and begin cooking as soon as possible.

2. Place kielbasa, chorizo, boudin blanc, and ham in a Dutch oven over medium-high heat. Cook, stirring frequently, until sausages are browned. Remove meat from the

pan with a slotted spoon, and set aside. Add onions, garlic, and red bell pepper to the pan. Cook, stirring frequently, for 3 minutes, or until onion is translucent.

3. Return meats to the pan, and add beans, water, orange, and bay leaves. Bring to a boil over medium-high heat, cover the pan, reduce the heat to low, and simmer for 1½ hours, or until beans are tender. Remove and discard orange quarters and bay leaves.

4. Transfer 1 cup of beans and ½ cup of cooking liquid to food processor fitted with the steel blade or to a blender. Puree until smooth, and stir mixture back into the pot. Season to taste with salt and pepper. Serve immediately on rice, passing bowls of garnish foods separately.

Note: The dish can be prepared up to 2 days in advance and refrigerated, tightly covered. Reheat it, covered, in a 350°F oven for 20 to 25 minutes, or over low heat, stirring occasionally, until hot.

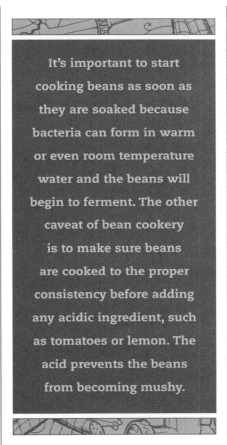

It's important to start cooking beans as soon as they are soaked because bacteria can form in warm or even room temperature water and the beans will begin to ferment. The other caveat of bean cookery is to make sure beans are cooked to the proper consistency before adding any acidic ingredient, such as tomatoes or lemon. The acid prevents the beans from becoming mushy.

Italian Sausage with Garbanzo Beans and Spinach

Makes 6 to 8 servings

Active time:
15 minutes

Start to finish:
50 minutes

VARIATION

Substitute 1 pound blanched broccoli rabe for spinach.

Take this crowd-pleasing dish—beans, bright green spinach, and sausage with a bit of lemon—to your potluck dinner.

1½ pounds Sweet Italian Sausage (page 52) links, Hot Italian Sausage (page 54) links, or purchased sausage

2 tablespoons olive oil

1 small red onion, finely chopped

2 garlic cloves, minced

1 (10-ounce) package frozen chopped spinach, thawed

1 (15-ounce) can garbanzo beans, drained and rinsed

¾ cup evaporated milk

¾ cup freshly grated Parmesan, divided

1 teaspoon grated lemon zest

1 tablespoon freshly squeezed lemon juice

¼ teaspoon ground nutmeg

Salt and freshly ground black pepper to taste

⅓ cup fine dry bread crumbs

2 tablespoons unsalted butter, melted

1. Preheat the oven broiler, and grease a 9 x 13-inch baking pan.

2. Prick sausages on all sides, and broil 4 to 6 inches from the broiler element for 5 to 7 minutes, or until cooked through and no longer pink, turning them with tongs to brown on all sides. Allow sausages to sit for 5 minutes, then cut them into 1-inch pieces, and cover sausage to foil to keep warm.

3. While sausages broil, heat oil in a large skillet over medium-high heat. Add onion and garlic and cook, stirring frequently, for 3 minutes, or until onion is translucent. Place spinach in colander, and press with the back of a spoon to extract as much liquid as possible.

4. Preheat the oven to 375°F. Combine sausage, onion mixture, spinach, beans, evaporated milk, ½ cup Parmesan, lemon zest, lemon juice, and nutmeg in a mixing bowl. Season to taste with salt and pepper, and spread mixture into the prepared pan.

5. For topping, combine breadcrumbs, remaining ¼ cup Parmesan, and butter in a small mixing bowl. Sprinkle on top of casserole. Bake, covered with foil, for 15 minutes. Uncover, and bake for an additional 20 minutes, or until bubbly. Serve immediately.

Note: The dish can be prepared up to 2 days in advance and refrigerated, tightly covered. Reheat it, covered, in a 350°F oven for 20 to 25 minutes, or until hot.

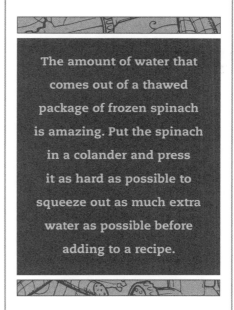

The amount of water that comes out of a thawed package of frozen spinach is amazing. Put the spinach in a colander and press it as hard as possible to squeeze out as much extra water as possible before adding to a recipe.

Hoppin' John with Sausage and Collard Greens

Makes 4 to 6 servings

Active time:
15 minutes

Start to finish:
2½ hours

Both black-eyed peas and collard greens own their parentage to Africa and were brought over by slaves in the seventeenth and eighteenth centuries. The herbs and chiles make this a vibrantly flavored stew; serve over rice and with a bowl of coleslaw.

1½ cups dried black-eyed peas

3 tablespoons vegetable oil, divided

1 large onion, chopped

2 garlic cloves, minced

6 to 7 cups Chicken Stock (page 296) or purchased stock

1 pound collard greens, stemmed, rinsed well, and thinly sliced

1 chipotle chile in adobo sauce, finely chopped

2 tablespoons chopped fresh parsley

1 teaspoon dried thyme

1 teaspoon dried sage

1 bay leaf

1 pound Hot Italian Sausage (page 54) links, or purchased spicy sausage

Salt and freshly ground black pepper to taste

2 to 3 cups cooked white or brown rice, hot

1. Place black-eyed peas in a sieve, and rinse well under cold running water. Discard any broken black-eyed peas.

2. Heat 2 tablespoons oil in a 4-quart saucepan over medium-high heat. Add onion and garlic, and cook, stirring frequently, for 3 minutes, or until onion is translucent.

3. Add black-eyed peas, stock, collard greens, chile, parsley, thyme, and sage to the pan, and bring to a boil over high heat. Reduce the heat to low, and simmer beans, covered, for 1½ hours, or until beans are tender but not mushy.

4. While beans simmer, prick sausages on all sides. Heat remaining oil in a large skillet over medium-high heat. Add sausages and brown on all sides, turning them with tongs. Add sausages to beans after beans have cooked for 30 minutes.

5. Remove and discard bay leaf, season to taste with salt and pepper, and serve immediately over rice.

Note: The dish can be cooked up to 2 days in advance and refrigerated, tightly covered. Reheat it over low heat, covered, until hot, stirring occasionally.

Hoppin' John dates to the colonial era in the Carolinas and is still eaten to bring good luck on New Year's Day. The black-eyed peas, called pigeon peas in Africa, were brought over with the slaves in the seventeenth century, and the first recipe for Hoppin' John comes from *The Carolina Housewife,* published in 1847.

Kidney Beans and Vegetables with Sausage

Makes 4 to 6 servings

Active time:
20 minutes

Start to finish:
40 minutes

VARIATION

Substitute garbanzo beans for kidney beans, and substitute Merguez (page 92) for sausages listed.

This easy-to-prepare dish is a variation on the classic Cajun red beans and rice. It has other vegetables added to the mix, and it's not quite as spicy.

1 tablespoon olive oil

1 pound Chaurice (page 64) links or purchased sausage

½ pound Hot Italian Sausage (page 54) links or purchased sausage

1 medium onion, chopped

1 celery rib, chopped

½ green bell pepper, seeds and ribs removed, chopped

3 garlic cloves, minced

1¾ cups Chicken Stock (page 296) or purchased low-sodium stock

1 (14.5-ounce) can diced tomatoes, undrained

1 (15-ounce) can kidney beans, drained and rinsed

1 (10-ounce) package frozen cut green beans, thawed

2 tablespoons chopped fresh parsley

1 tablespoon fresh thyme or 1 teaspoon dried

1 bay leaf

Salt and freshly ground black pepper to taste

Hot red pepper sauce to taste

2 to 3 cups cooked white rice, hot

1. Heat oil in a deep skillet over medium-high heat. Prick sausages, and add them to the skillet. Brown sausages well on all sides, turning frequently with tongs. Remove sausages from the skillet, and set aside.

2. Add onion, celery, green bell pepper, and garlic to the skillet. Cook over medium-high heat, stirring frequently, for 3 minutes, or until onion is translucent.

3. Add stock, tomatoes, beans, parsley, thyme, and bay leaf, and bring to a boil over medium-high heat. Return sausages to the skillet, bring to a boil, and simmer over low heat, uncovered, for 10 minutes, or until sausages are cooked through. Add green beans, and simmer 5 minutes. Remove and discard bay leaf, and season to taste with salt, pepper, and hot red pepper sauce. Serve immediately over rice.

Note: The dish can be prepared up to 2 days in advance and refrigerated, tightly covered. Reheat it, covered, in a 350°F oven for 20 to 25 minutes, or over low heat, stirring occasionally, until hot.

Out of all the ways I've read to lessen the tear factor when slicing and chopping onions, the best one I know is to chill them well in advance. The volatile chemicals that cause all the tears do not escape as readily from a cold onion as they do from one at room temperature.

Maque Choux with Sausage

Makes 4 to 6
servings

Active time:
20 minutes

Start to finish:
40 minutes

VARIATION

Substitute green bell pepper and carrot for red bell pepper and celery.

Maque choux (pronounced "mock shoe") is a staple of Southern Louisiana; both the name and the ingredients are an amalgam of Native American and French ingredients and dishes. While it always includes corn and bell peppers, the other ingredients vary widely; adding sausage transforms this side dish into an entrée.

1 tablespoon olive oil

¾ pound bulk Chaurice (page 64), Hot Italian Sausage (page 54), or purchased sausage

1 large onion, chopped

1 red bell pepper, seeds and ribs removed, chopped

1 celery rib, chopped

1 jalapeño or serrano chile, seeds and ribs removed, chopped

2 garlic cloves, minced

1 tablespoon smoked Spanish paprika

1 teaspoon dried oregano

½ teaspoon dried thyme

2 tablespoons chopped fresh parsley

1 bay leaf

¾ cup heavy cream

2 cups fresh or frozen and thawed corn kernels

Salt and freshly ground black pepper to taste

Hot red pepper sauce to taste

1. Heat oil in a large deep skillet over medium-high heat. Add sausage and brown well. Remove sausage from the skillet with a slotted spoon, and set aside.

2. Add onion, red bell pepper, celery, chile, and garlic to the skillet. Cook over medium-high heat, stirring frequently, for 3 minutes, or until onion is translucent. Add paprika, oregano, and thyme, and cook for 1 minute, stirring constantly.

3. Stir parsley, bay leaf, and cream into the skillet, and bring to a boil, stirring frequently. Return sausage to the skillet, cover the skillet, reduce the heat to low, and simmer for 10 minutes, or until vegetables soften. Add corn, and simmer for an additional 3 minutes uncovered.

4. Season to taste with salt, pepper, and hot red pepper sauce. Serve immediately.

Note: The dish can be prepared up to 2 days in advance and refrigerated, tightly covered. Reheat it, covered, over low heat, stirring occasionally, until hot.

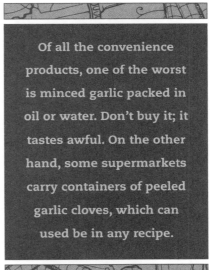

Of all the convenience products, one of the worst is minced garlic packed in oil or water. Don't buy it; it tastes awful. On the other hand, some supermarkets carry containers of peeled garlic cloves, which can used be in any recipe.

Bangers and Mashed with Onion Gravy

Makes 4 to 6 servings

Active time:
20 minutes

Start to finish:
50 minutes

VARIATIONS

Substitute cauliflower florets for potatoes; mash them in the same way.

Substitute Bratwurst (page 120), Bockwurst (page 122), or Hungarian Sausage (page 124) for British Bangers.

This book would be incomplete without a recipe for England's favorite way to serve sausages. A sweet onion gravy covers the sausages and potatoes.

Gravy:
2 tablespoons unsalted butter
2 tablespoons vegetable oil
4 large onions, peeled and thinly
*   sliced*
Salt and freshly ground black
*   pepper to taste*
2 teaspoons sugar
½ cup dry white wine
2 cups Chicken Stock (page 296) or
*   purchased low-sodium stock*
2 tablespoons chopped fresh parsley
2 teaspoons fresh thyme or
*   ½ teaspoon dried*
2 teaspoons cornstarch

Potatoes:
2 pounds Yukon Gold potatoes,
*   peeled and cut into 1-inch cubes*
2 teaspoons kosher salt
⅔ cup half-and-half or whole milk
4 tablespoons (½ stick) unsalted
*   butter*
Freshly ground black pepper to taste

Dish:
1½ pounds British Bangers
*   (page 48) or purchased*
*   cooked sausages*
2 tablespoons vegetable oil
2 tablespoons chopped fresh parsley

1. For gravy, heat oil and butter in a large skillet over medium heat. Add onions, and toss to coat. Cover the pan, and cook onions for 10 minutes, stirring occasionally. Sprinkle onions with salt, pepper, and sugar, and raise the heat to medium-high. Cook onions for 15 to 20 minutes, stirring occasionally, or until brown. Add wine, and cook

over high heat for 1 minute, stirring constantly. Add stock, parsley, and thyme, and bring to a boil over medium-high heat. Reduce the heat to low, and simmer sauce, uncovered, for 15 minutes.

2. Combine cornstarch and 1 tablespoon cold water in a small bowl, and stir well. Add mixture to sauce, and cook for an additional 2 minutes, or until slightly thickened. Season sauce to taste with salt and pepper, and set aside.

3. While onions brown, combine potatoes, 6 cups cold water, and salt in a 3-quart saucepan, and bring to a boil over high heat. Reduce the heat to medium, and cook potatoes, partially covered, for 10 to 15 minutes, or until very tender.

4. Drain potatoes in a colander, shaking the colander over the sink. Return potatoes to the pan. Cook over medium heat for 2 minutes, shaking the pan frequently. Transfer potatoes to a mixing bowl.

5. Heat half-and-half and butter in the saucepan until butter is melted. Pour mixture over potatoes, and mash with a potato masher until desired consistency is reached. Season to taste with salt and pepper, and keep hot.

6. Heat oil in a large skillet over medium heat. Add sausages, and brown on all sides, turning them gently with tongs. To serve, arrange sausages and potatoes on plates, and top both with gravy.

Note: The gravy can be prepared up to 3 days in advance and refrigerated, tightly covered. Reheat it over low heat, stirring occasionally. The potatoes can be kept at room temperature for 6 hours; reheat them, covered, over low heat.

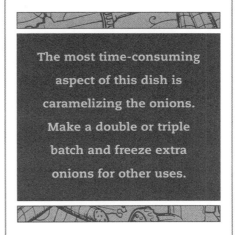

The most time-consuming aspect of this dish is caramelizing the onions. Make a double or triple batch and freeze extra onions for other uses.

Italian Sausages with Broccoli Rabe

Makes 4 to 6 servings

Active time: 20 minutes

Start to finish: 35 minutes

Substitute Swiss chard for broccoli rabe; simmer stems for 10 minutes and leaves, which should be cut into 2-inch ribbons, for 2 minutes.

Broccoli rabe, also called *rapini*, has longer, thinner stems and smaller florets than traditional broccoli. Serve with or without pasta.

1 pound Sweet Italian Sausage
(page 52) links, Hot Italian
Sausage (page 54) links,
Luganega (page 58) links,
or purchased sausage
2 pounds broccoli rabe
¼ cup olive oil
4 garlic cloves, minced
Salt and freshly ground black
pepper to taste
½ cup freshly grated Parmesan

1. Preheat the oven broiler, and line a broiler pan with heavy-duty aluminum foil. Bring a large pot of salted water to a boil, and have a bowl of ice water handy.

2. Prick sausages on all sides, and broil 4 to 6 inches from the broiler element for 5 to 7 minutes, or until cooked through and no longer pink, turning them with tongs to brown on all sides. Allow sausages to sit for 5 minutes, then cut them into 1-inch pieces, and cover sausage in foil to keep warm.

3. Rinse broccoli rabe, and cut it into 1-inch pieces. Blanch broccoli rabe in boiling water for 4 to 5 minutes, depending on the thickness of the stalks. Drain, and plunge into ice water to stop the cooking action. Drain again, and place broccoli rabe in a colander. Squeeze out as much water as possible with the back of a spoon. Set aside.

4. Heat oil in a large skillet over medium-high heat. Add garlic and cook, stirring constantly, for 45 seconds. Add broccoli rabe, separating pieces with tongs, and heat through. Add sausage, and heat through. Season dish to taste with salt and pepper, and serve immediately, passing Parmesan separately.

Note: Both the broccoli rabe and the sausage can be cooked a day in advance and refrigerated separately. Sauté the garlic and reheat the other elements of the dish just before serving.

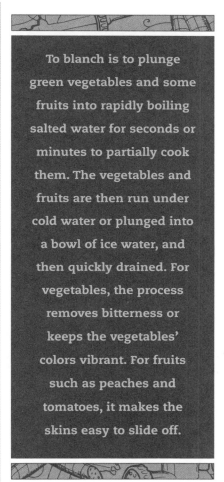

To blanch is to plunge green vegetables and some fruits into rapidly boiling salted water for seconds or minutes to partially cook them. The vegetables and fruits are then run under cold water or plunged into a bowl of ice water, and then quickly drained. For vegetables, the process removes bitterness or keeps the vegetables' colors vibrant. For fruits such as peaches and tomatoes, it makes the skins easy to slide off.

Kielbasa and Sauerkraut Cakes

Makes 4 to 6 servings

Active time: 20 minutes

Start to finish: 30 minutes

VARIATIONS

Substitute chopped ham for kielbasa.

Add ½ cup grated cheese, such as cheddar or smoked cheddar.

Sauerkraut cakes are part of the German tradition brought to the Midwestern states in the nineteenth century, although few German cookbooks contain them. Adding sausage takes the cakes from a side dish to a main event.

1 pound Russet potatoes, peeled
1 pound sauerkraut, well drained
1 tablespoon olive oil
½ pound Smoked Kielbasa (page 126), Smoky Mettwurst (page 128), or purchased smoked sausage, chopped
2 large eggs
¾ cup whole grain Dijon mustard, divided
3 scallions, white parts and 3 inches of green tops, chopped
2 tablespoons chopped fresh parsley
1 tablespoon crushed caraway seeds
Salt and freshly ground black pepper to taste
1 cup plain breadcrumbs
3 cups vegetable oil for frying
½ cup mayonnaise
½ cup sour cream

1. Dice potatoes into 1-inch cubes, and boil in salted water for 10 to 15 minutes, or until very tender. Drain potatoes, shaking in a colander to get out as much water as possible. Mash potatoes until smooth, and set aside.

2. While potatoes boil, soak sauerkraut in cold water, changing the water every 3 minutes. Drain sauerkraut, pressing with the back of a spoon to extract as much liquid as possible, and coarsely chop sauerkraut.

3. While sauerkraut soaks, heat oil in a medium skillet over medium-high heat. Add kielbasa and cook, stirring frequently, for 3 minutes,

or until sausage browns. Remove sausage from the skillet with a slotted spoon, and set aside.

4. Whisk eggs and ¼ cup mustard in a mixing bowl, and add potatoes, sauerkraut, sausage, scallions, parsley, and caraway seeds. Mix well, and season to taste with salt and pepper.

5. Place breadcrumbs in a shallow bowl. Divide mixture into 8 to 12 portions, and form into balls. Flatten balls into 1-inch-thick patties, and pat with breadcrumbs on both sides.

6. Heat oil in a deep-sided skillet to a temperature of 375°F. Preheat the oven to 150°F, and line a baking sheet with paper towels.

7. While oil heats, mix remaining ½ cup mustard with mayonnaise and sour cream, and whisk well. Set aside.

8. Add patties, being careful not to crowd the pan. Cook patties for 2 to 3 minutes per side, or until browned. Remove patties from the pan with a slotted spatula, and drain well on paper towels. Keep fried sauerkraut patties warm in the oven while frying remaining patties. Serve immediately, passing sauce separately.

Note: The sauerkraut patties can be prepared for frying up to a day in advance and refrigerated, tightly covered. They can also be fried in advance; reheat them in a 375°F oven for 5 to 7 minutes, or until hot and crusty again.

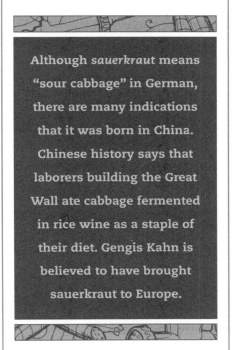

Although *sauerkraut* means "sour cabbage" in German, there are many indications that it was born in China. Chinese history says that laborers building the Great Wall ate cabbage fermented in rice wine as a staple of their diet. Gengis Kahn is believed to have brought sauerkraut to Europe.

Choucroute Garnie

Makes 6 to 8 servings

Active time: 25 minutes

Start to finish: 2¼ hours

VARIATION

Substitute Smoky Mettwurst (page 128) for Smoked Kielbasa, and substitute Boudin Blanc (page 118) for Bratwurst.

In this traditional Alsatian dish, the sauerkraut is soaked and then braised to render it sweet and silky. Serve with some boiled potatoes or buttered egg noodles.

3 pounds sauerkraut

2 tablespoons unsalted butter

1 large onion, thinly sliced

1 carrot, thinly sliced

1 cup Chicken Stock (page 296) or purchased low-sodium stock

1 cup dry white wine

¼ cup gin (or 10 whole juniper berries tied in cheesecloth)

¼ cup chopped fresh parsley

2 teaspoons fresh thyme or ¾ teaspoon dried

1 bay leaf

1 pound smoked pork butt, cut into 1-inch cubes

½ pound Smoked Kielbasa (page 126) or purchased smoked sausage, cut into ¾-inch slices

½ pound Bratwurst (page 120) or purchased bratwurst, cut into ¾-inch slices

Salt and freshly ground black pepper to taste

For serving: ¾ cup whole grain mustard

1. Preheat the oven to 350°F. Drain sauerkraut in a colander. Place sauerkraut into a large mixing bowl of cold water for 10 minutes. Drain and repeat the soaking. Press out as much water as possible from sauerkraut, and set aside.

2. Heat butter in a Dutch oven over medium-high heat. Add onion and carrot, and cook, stirring frequently, for 3 minutes, or until onion is translucent. Add sauerkraut, stock, wine, gin, parsley, thyme, and bay leaf. Mix well. Add pork and kielbasa. Press meats down into sauerkraut. Bring to a boil over medium-high heat, stirring occasionally.

3. Cover the pan, and transfer it to the oven. Bake for 1¾ to 2 hours, or until meats are tender and sauerkraut is soft. Remove and discard bay leaf, and season to taste with salt and pepper. Serve immediately, passing mustard separately.

Note: The dish can be prepared up to 2 days in advance and refrigerated, tightly covered. Reheat it, covered, in a 350°F oven for 20 to 25 minutes, or over low heat, stirring occasionally, until hot.

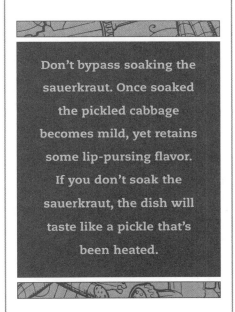

Don't bypass soaking the sauerkraut. Once soaked the pickled cabbage becomes mild, yet retains some lip-pursing flavor. If you don't soak the sauerkraut, the dish will taste like a pickle that's been heated.

Sauerkraut with Dried Fruit and Sausages

Makes 4 to 6 servings

Active time: 20 minutes

Start to finish: 2½ hours

VARIATION

Substitute dried cranberries for dried apricots and dried currants for raisins.

Similar to choucroute with braised sauerkraut as its base, but the pickled cabbage is balanced by succulent dried fruits. Accompany with some buttered egg noodles or steamed potatoes.

2 pounds refrigerated sauerkraut

2 tablespoons unsalted butter

1 large onion, chopped

1 large carrot, chopped

2 cups Chicken Stock (page 296)
 or purchased low-sodium stock

¾ cup dry white wine

½ cup raisins

½ cup chopped dried apricots

2 tablespoons chopped fresh parsley

2 teaspoons fresh thyme or
 ½ teaspoon dried

1½ pounds Turkey, Apple, and Sage
 Sausage (page 150) links,
 Herbed Turkey and White
 Wine Sausage (page 156) links,
 or purchased sausage

Salt and freshly ground black
 pepper to taste

1. Preheat the oven to 350°F. Drain sauerkraut in a colander. Place sauerkraut into a large mixing bowl of cold water for 10 minutes. Drain and repeat the soaking. Press out as much water as possible from sauerkraut, and set aside.

2. Heat butter in a Dutch oven over medium-high heat. Add onion and carrot, and cook, stirring frequently, for 3 minutes, or until onion is translucent. Add sauerkraut, stock, wine, raisins, dried apricots, parsley, thyme, and bay leaf. Mix well.

3. Prick sausages on all sides, and add sausage to the pan, pressing them down into sauerkraut. Bring to a boil over medium-high heat, stirring occasionally.

4. Cover the pan, and transfer it to the oven. Bake for 1¾ to 2 hours, or until meats are tender and sauerkraut is soft. Remove and discard bay leaf, and season to taste with salt and pepper. Serve immediately.

Note: The dish can be prepared up to 2 days in advance and refrigerated, tightly covered. Reheat it, covered, in a 350°F oven for 20 to 25 minutes, or over low heat, stirring occasionally, until hot.

If your dried fruit has hardened into little bullets, add them to a long-simmered sauce without soaking them. In a recipe that cooks quickly, soak the hard fruit in ½ cup boiling water for 10 to 15 minutes to soften before using.

Boudin Blanc with Apples and Onions

Makes 4 to 6 servings

Active time: 20 minutes

Start to finish: 45 minutes

VARIATION

Add 2 tablespoons Calvados or applejack brandy to sauce.

The cooking of Normandy in northwestern France is characterized by the use of apples and cream. Those ingredients along with some caramelized onions create a rich sauce for these delicate sausages. Serve atop buttered egg noodles.

3 tablespoons unsalted butter

¼ cup olive oil, divided

2 large onions, diced

Salt and freshly ground black pepper to taste

1 teaspoon sugar

½ teaspoon dried thyme

1½ pounds Boudin Blanc (page 370), Bockwurst (page 122), or purchased fully-cooked sausages, cut into 1-inch pieces

2 Golden Delicious apples, peeled, cored, and cut into ½-inch slices

1¼ cups Chicken Stock (page 296) or purchased low-sodium stock

½ cup heavy cream

1. Melt butter and 2 tablespoons oil in a large skillet over medium heat. Add onions, salt, pepper, and sugar, and toss to coat onions. Cover the skillet, and cook for 10 minutes, stirring occasionally. Uncover the skillet, add thyme, and cook over medium-high heat for 12 to 15 minutes, or until onions are medium brown, stirring occasionally and stirring browned bits from the skillet into the onions.

2. While onions cook, heat remaining oil in another large skillet over medium-high heat. Add sausages and brown lightly on all sides. Remove the pan from the heat.

3. Add apples and stock to onions, and bring to a boil. Simmer mixture over medium heat, uncovered, for 8 to 10 minutes, or until apples soften, stirring occasionally. Add cream, and cook for 2 minutes.

4. Stir sausages into mixture to reheat, season to taste with salt and pepper, and serve immediately.

Note: The dish can be prepared up to 2 days in advance and refrigerated, tightly covered. Reheat it, covered, in a 350°F oven for 20 to 25 minutes, or over low heat, stirring occasionally, until hot.

Some time-honored methods of cutting up fruits and vegetables make sense when professional chefs have plenty of extra helpers on hand, but not for home cooks. If it matters how the apples in the dish look, then peeling, coring, and then slicing each half or quarter is still the best method. But if the apples are going to be hidden as in this dish, there's a faster way: Peel the apple and keep turning it in your hand as you cut off slices. Soon all you'll be left with is the core, which you can discard.

Sausages with Grapes Al Forno

Makes 4 to 6 servings

Active time:
15 minutes

Start to finish:
45 minutes

VARIATION

Substitute Fresh Kielbasa (page 70) links for sausages listed.

Al Forno restaurant put my adopted home city of Providence, Rhode Island, on the culinary map. The owners, my friends Johanne Killeen and George Germon, continue to dazzle diners at their restaurant. Here is an adaptation of one of their signature dishes, which is served with rich mashed potatoes.

¾ *pound Sweet Italian Sausage (page 52) links or purchased sausage*
¾ *pound Hot Italian Sausage (page 54) links or purchased sausage*
2 *tablespoons unsalted butter*
4 *cups seedless green or red grapes, or some combination of the two, rinsed*
3 *tablespoons aged balsamic vinegar*
Salt and freshly ground black pepper to taste

1. Preheat the oven to 500°F, and bring a large pot of water to a boil.

2. Prick sausages on all sides, and lower them into the boiling water. Reduce the heat to low, and simmer sausages, uncovered, for 8 minutes.

3. While sausages simmer, melt butter in a roasting pan over low heat. Add grapes, and toss to coat with butter. Add sausages, and roast, uncovered, for a total of 20 to

25 minutes, turning sausages and stirring grapes gently a few times.

4. Remove the pan from the oven, and remove sausages and grapes from the pan with a slotted spoon. Cover with foil to keep food warm.

5. Place the roasting pan over a burner, and stir in vinegar. Cook for 2 to 3 minutes, stirring to dislodge browned bits from the bottom of the pan, or until mixture is thick. To serve, spoon sauce over sausages and grapes.

Note: The dish can be prepared up to 2 days in advance and refrigerated, tightly covered. Reheat it, covered, in a 350°F oven for 20 to 25 minutes, or until hot.

Partially cooking sausages before roasting them accomplishes two things: It warms the meat, requiring a shorter roasting time, and it removes some of the fat.

Sausages with Plums and Wine Sauce

Makes 4 to 6 servings

Active time:
20 minutes

Start to finish:
1 hour

VARIATION

Substitute white wine vinegar for red wine vinegar, white wine for the red wine, and fresh apricots for the plums.

Make this dish in late summer or early autumn when plums are at their peak. Serve with rice pilaf to enjoy every drop of sauce.

¾ cup sugar

¾ cup red wine vinegar

½ cup dry red wine

1 (3-inch) cinnamon stick

4 whole cloves

6 ripe purple plums

1½ pounds Sweet Italian Sausage (page 52) links, Fresh Kielbasa (page 70) links, or purchased sausage

Salt and freshly ground black pepper to taste

2 teaspoons cornstarch

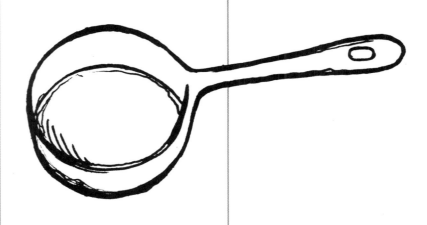

1. Combine sugar, vinegar, wine, cinnamon stick, and cloves in a non-reactive saucepan, and bring to a boil over medium-high heat, stirring occasionally. Simmer 5 minutes, then add plums, cover the pan, and simmer plums for 10 minutes over low heat. Remove plums from the pan with a slotted spoon, reserving poaching liquid. Strain poached liquid and return it to the pan. When cool enough to handle, remove and discard stones and slice fruit. Set aside.

2. While plums poach, prick sausages on all sides, and broil 4 to 6 inches from the broiler element for 5 to 7 minutes, or until cooked through and no longer pink, turning them with tongs to brown on all sides. Allow sausages to sit for 5 minutes, then cut them into 1-inch pieces, and cover sausage to foil to keep warm.

3. Add sausage slices to reserved poaching liquid. Bring to a boil, and simmer sausages, covered, over low heat, turning occasionally with a slotted spoon, for 15 minutes. Remove sausages from the pan with a slotted spoon, and add to plum slices.

6. Cook poaching liquid over medium-high heat until reduced by half. Mix cornstarch with 1 tablespoon cold water in a small bowl, and add to sauce. Cook for 1 minute, or until slightly thickened. Return sausages and plums to sauce to reheat, and serve immediately.

Note: The dish can be cooked up to 2 days in advance and refrigerated, tightly covered. Reheat it in a 350°F oven, covered, for 15 to 20 minutes, or until hot.

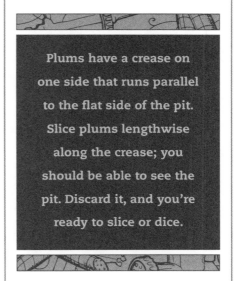

Plums have a crease on one side that runs parallel to the flat side of the pit. Slice plums lengthwise along the crease; you should be able to see the pit. Discard it, and you're ready to slice or dice.

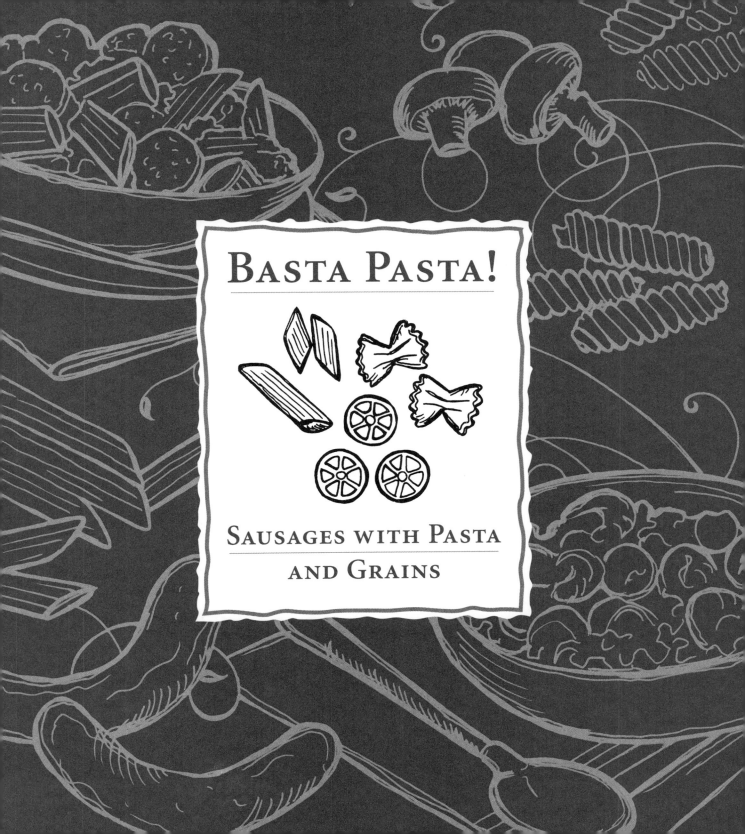

Basta Pasta!

Sausages with Pasta

and Grains

All of the dishes in this chapter qualify as one-dish meals. No need to worry about what goes with what; it's all right there in the pan.

Although pasta is synonymous with Italian cuisine, every cuisine has its noodles. Recipes range from Asian to Hispanic to lots of Italian fare.

At the end of the chapter are some dishes made with rice—the most popular grain in the world—and one homey polenta dish that shouts "comfort food."

PASTA PERFECT

Good-quality dried pasta is made with a high percentage of high-gluten semolina, the inner part of the grain of hard durum wheat. The gluten gives the pasta resilience and allows it to cook while remaining somewhat firm, what is known as *al dente*. As a general rule, pasta imported from Italy is superior to American factory-made products due to its higher semolina percentage. Try to purchase pasta that you can see wrapped in plastic or through the cellophane in a box. The pasta should be smooth and shiny, not crumbly.

Traditional dried Italian pastas are named by their shapes. For example, fusilli are twists and fiochetti are bows. You could fill an entire kitchen with different shaped pastas. If you happen to be out of a certain shape, here are some guidelines for substitutions.

A good rule to follow is to cook pasta according to the directions below if it's going to be sauced and served, and to undercook it by a few minutes if it's going to be baked. During the 20-plus minutes that a lasagne or baked ziti cooks in the oven, it will absorb moisture from the sauce and soften further.

NAMES	COOKING TIMES
Farfalle, Fiochetti, Fusilli, Orecchiette, Penne, Rigatoni, Ziti	10 to 12 minutes
Anelli, Cavatappi, Macaroni, Manicotti, Mostaccioli, Orzo, Rotelle	8 to 10 minutes
Fettuccine, Linguine, Spaghetti, Tagliatelli	6 to 9 minutes

The birthplace of pasta has always been a subject for culinary controversy. Legend had it that Marco Polo brought the idea of noodles back with him to Italy from China. The truth is that pasta existed in some form in both places independently long before Polo's expeditions. Archaeological evidence now substantiates that noodles probably originated in central Asia and date back to 1000 BCE.

FROM PADDY TO PAN

All 2,500 species of rice, the world's most popular grain, trace their lineage to India. Once rice is harvested, it is termed "paddy rice," and the non-edible hull must be removed before it can be eaten. Brown rice is whole or broken kernels of rice from which only the hull has been removed. For white rice, the grains are rubbed together to remove this natural bran.

Rice is classified primarily by the size of the grain. Long grains are five times longer than they are wide, and when cooked, the grains tend to remain separate. Medium grains are plump in shape, but not round, and when cooked, medium grain rice tends to be more moist and tender than long grain. Used for sushi and other Japanese dishes, short grain rice appears almost round in shape, and when cooked, it tends to cling together, which is why it's sometimes called sticky rice.

If rice is cooked at the bottom of the pot but raw at the top, too much steam is escaping. Give the rice a big stir, cover the pot either with foil or with a tea towel (be sure to fold the loose ends up over the top), replace the lid, and continue cooking.

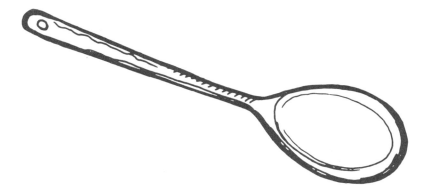

Pasta Primavera with Sausage

Makes 4 to 6 servings

Active time:
20 minutes

Start to finish:
55 minutes

VARIATION

Substitute summer squash for zucchini and cauliflower florets for broccoli.

Spaghetti is dotted with a cornucopia of colorful fresh vegetables and bits of sausage in a creamy sauce laced with cheese.

¾ pound Sweet Italian Sausage links (page 52) links, Porchetta-Style Sausage (page 56) links, or purchased sausage
⅔ pound thin spaghetti
⅓ cup olive oil, divided
1 small onion, finely chopped
3 garlic cloves, minced
1 small zucchini, rinsed, trimmed, and cut into ½-inch dice
⅓ pound mushrooms, wiped with a damp paper towel, trimmed, and thinly sliced
1 red bell pepper, seeds and ribs removed, and sliced
1 (14.5-ounce) can diced tomatoes, drained
1 cup Chicken Stock (page 296) or purchased low-sodium stock

1 cup heavy cream
¼ cup chopped fresh parsley
2 teaspoons Italian seasoning
1 cup broccoli florets
½ cup frozen peas, thawed
Salt and crushed red pepper flakes to taste
¾ cup freshly grated Parmesan

1. Preheat the oven broiler and line a broiler pan with heavy-duty aluminum foil. Prick sausages on all sides, and broil 4 to 6 inches from the broiler element for 5 to 7 minutes, or until cooked through and no longer pink, turning them with tongs to brown on all sides. Allow sausages to sit for 5 minutes, then cut them into ½-inch pieces, and cover sausage with foil to keep warm.

2. While sausages cook, bring a large pot of salted water to a boil. Add pasta, and cook according to package directions until al dente. Drain, toss with 2 tablespoons olive oil, and keep warm.

3. Heat remaining oil in a large skillet over medium-high heat. Add onion and garlic and cook, stirring frequently, for 3 minutes, or until onion is translucent. Add zucchini, mushrooms, and red bell pepper. Cook for 3 minutes, stirring frequently.

4. Add sausage slices, tomatoes, stock, cream, parsley, Italian seasoning, broccoli, and peas to the skillet. Bring to a boil over medium-high heat, and simmer, uncovered, for 3 minutes. Season to taste with salt and red pepper flakes, and simmer for an additional 2 minutes.

5. To serve, add drained pasta to skillet, and toss with cheese. Serve immediately.

Note: The sauce can be prepared up to 4 hours in advance and kept at room temperature. Reheat it over low heat to a simmer before adding the pasta.

Primavera is the Italian word for "springtime," and although this dish sounds quintessentially Italian, the original version was invented in New York City. Restaurateur Sirio Maccioni created it in the mid-1970s at his famed Le Cirque restaurant, and food writers popularized the dish nationally.

Sausage Carbonara

Makes 4 to 6 servings

Active time:
15 minutes

Start to finish:
35 minutes

VARIATION

Substitute ½ cup grated whole-milk mozzarella for ½ cup Parmesan.

While spaghetti carbonara is traditionally made with bacon, try this sausage version and you'll never cook this dish any other way. A colorful tossed salad with some diced tomatoes is all that's needed as an accompaniment.

⅔ pound spaghetti
¾ pound bulk Sweet Italian Sausage (page 52), Hot Italian Sausage (page 54), or purchased sausage
6 garlic cloves, peeled and minced
Freshly ground black pepper to taste (at least 1½ teaspoons)
6 large eggs, well beaten
1½ cups freshly grated Parmesan
Salt to taste

1. Bring a large pot of salted water to a boil. Add pasta, and cook according to package directions until al dente. Drain, and set aside.

2. While water heats, crumble sausage into a large heavy skillet medium-high heat. Cook, breaking up lumps with a fork, for 3 to 5 minutes, or until well browned. Remove sausage from the skillet with a slotted spoon, and set aside. Discard all but 2 tablespoons grease from the pan. Add garlic and black pepper, and cook for 30 seconds. Return sausage to the skillet, and turn off the heat.

3. Add drained pasta to the skillet, and cook over medium heat for 1 minute. Remove the pan from the stove, and stir in the eggs. Allow eggs to thicken but do not put the pan back on the stove or they will scramble. Add cheese, and season to taste with salt and additional pepper. Serve immediately.

Note: The sausage mixture can be cooked up to 3 hours in advance and kept in the skillet.

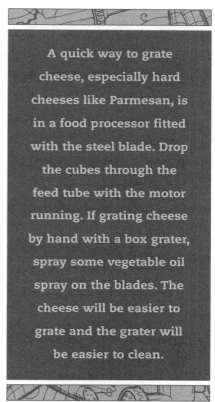

A quick way to grate cheese, especially hard cheeses like Parmesan, is in a food processor fitted with the steel blade. Drop the cubes through the feed tube with the motor running. If grating cheese by hand with a box grater, spray some vegetable oil spray on the blades. The cheese will be easier to grate and the grater will be easier to clean.

Baked Fusilli with Sausage and Three Cheeses

Makes 6 to 8 servings

Active time: 20 minutes

Start to finish: 1 hour

This is an incredibly rich baked pasta dish, with a combination of cheddar, Gorgonzola, and Brie in the sauce. A stir-fried or steamed green vegetable makes a nice contrast of color and texture.

1 pound Sweet Italian Sausage (page 52) links, Luganega (page 58) links, or purchased sausage

1 pound spinach fusilli

1 cup light cream

½ cup dry white wine

1½ cups grated sharp cheddar, divided

1 cup grated Gorgonzola

1 cup diced Brie, rinds removed

2 tablespoons chopped fresh sage or 2 teaspoons dried

1 tablespoon fresh thyme or 1 teaspoon dried

Salt and freshly ground black pepper to taste

4 ripe plum tomatoes, cored, seeded, and thinly sliced

½ cup Italian breadcrumbs

2 tablespoons chopped fresh parsley

VARIATIONS

Substitute tomato pasta for spinach pasta.

Add ½ cup chopped sun-dried tomatoes to sauce.

1. Preheat the oven broiler and line a broiler pan with heavy-duty aluminum foil. Prick sausages on all sides, and broil 4 to 6 inches from the broiler element for 5 to 7 minutes, or until cooked through and no longer pink, turning them with tongs to brown on all sides. Allow sausages to sit for 5 minutes, then cut them into ½-inch pieces, and cover sausage to foil to keep warm.

2. Preheat the oven to 350°F, and grease a 9 x 13-inch baking pan. Bring a large pot of salted water to a boil, and cook the pasta according to package directions for 2 minutes less than suggested. Drain, and return pasta to the pot.

3. Place cream and wine in a saucepan over medium heat and bring to a boil, stirring occasionally. Stir in 1 cup cheddar along with the Gorgonzola, Brie, sage, and thyme. Stir until cheeses melt, then reduce the heat to low, and simmer, uncovered, for 3 minutes.

4. Place half the fusilli in the prepared pan, and top with sausage slices and ½ of cheese sauce.

Sprinkle with remaining 1 cup cheddar cheese, and top with remaining pasta and sauce.

5. Cover the pan with aluminum foil, and bake for 15 minutes. Uncover the pan, and bake for 20 minutes. Arrange tomato slices on top, and sprinkle with breadcrumbs and parsley. Bake for an additional 15 minutes. Serve immediately.

Note: The dish can be prepared for baking up to 2 days in advance and refrigerated, tightly covered. Add 10 minutes to the initial cooking time if chilled.

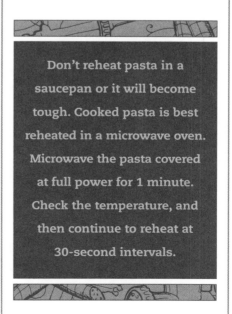

Don't reheat pasta in a saucepan or it will become tough. Cooked pasta is best reheated in a microwave oven. Microwave the pasta covered at full power for 1 minute. Check the temperature, and then continue to reheat at 30-second intervals.

Italian Baked Pasta, Sausage, and Beans

Nuggets of sausage and hearty beans are baked with pasta and tomato sauce. Serve with a Caesar salad or sliced tomatoes.

Makes 4 to 6 servings

Active time:
20 minutes

Start to finish:
1 hour

VARIATIONS

Substitute garbanzo beans for kidney beans.

Substitute ½ pound ground beef for ½ pound sausage.

½ to ¾ pound penne

1 pound bulk Sweet Italian Sausage (page 52), Luganega (page 58), or purchased sausage

1 medium onion, chopped

3 garlic cloves, minced

1 teaspoon dried oregano

½ teaspoon dried thyme

1 (28-ounce) can diced tomatoes, drained

2 tablespoons tomato paste

1 (15-ounce) can kidney beans, drained and rinsed

Salt and freshly ground black pepper to taste

½ cup freshly grated Parmesan

¼ cup chopped fresh parsley

1 cup grated fontina or provolone

1. Preheat the oven to 400°F, and grease a 9 x 13-inch baking pan. Bring a large pot of salted water to a boil. Boil pasta according to package directions until al dente. Drain, and place pasta in the prepared pan.

2. Heat a large skillet over medium-high heat. Add sausage, breaking up lumps with a fork, and brown well. Remove sausage from the skillet with a slotted spoon, discard all but 2 tablespoons of grease, and set aside.

3. Heat the skillet again, and add onion and garlic. Cook, stirring frequently, for 3 minutes, or until onion is translucent. Add oregano and thyme, and cook 1 minute, stirring constantly. Add tomatoes, tomato paste, kidney beans, and simmer 5 minutes. Season to taste with salt and pepper. Stir in Parmesan and parsley, and stir mixture into pasta.

4. Cover the pan with aluminum foil, and bake for 15 minutes. Uncover the pan, sprinkle with fontina, and bake for an additional 15 minutes, or until bubbly and cheese melts. Serve immediately.

Note: The dish can be prepared for baking up to 2 days in advance and refrigerated, tightly covered. Add 10 minutes to the covered baking if chilled.

Like many recipes, this one calls for just a few tablespoons of tomato paste. I buy tomato paste that comes in a tube, which will keep refrigerated for a few weeks. If you do open a can, freeze the remaining sauce in 1 tablespoon portions in an ice cube tray. Then store the small cubes in a plastic bag up to six months.

Baked Penne with Sausage and Wild Mushroom Ragout

Makes 6 to 8 servings

Active time: 25 minutes

Start to finish: 1 hour

VARIATIONS

Add 3 tablespoons tomato paste to sauce.

Add ¼ cup finely chopped sun-dried tomatoes to sauce.

Wild mushrooms in a cream sauce with sausage make a hearty baked pasta. Serve with a tossed salad or some baked tomatoes.

1 pound *Herbed Turkey and White Wine Sausage (page 156) links, Sweet Italian Sausage (page 52) links, or purchased sausage*
2 cups *Chicken Stock (page 296) or purchased low-sodium stock*
½ cup *dried porcini mushrooms*
½ to ¾ *pound penne*
6 tablespoons (¾ stick) *unsalted butter, divided*
2 *large onions, finely chopped*
½ *pound white mushrooms, wiped with a damp paper towel and sliced*
½ *pound fresh shiitake mushrooms, stemmed, wiped with a damp paper towel, and sliced*

3 tablespoons *all-purpose flour*
1½ cups *whole milk*
¾ cup *freshly grated Parmesan, divided*
½ cup *finely chopped fresh chives*
Salt and freshly ground black pepper to taste
½ cup *Italian breadcrumbs*

1. Preheat the oven broiler, and line a broiler pan with heavy-duty aluminum foil. Prick sausages on all sides, and broil 4 to 6 inches from the broiler element for 5 to 7 minutes, or until cooked through and no longer pink, turning them with tongs to brown on all sides. Allow sausages to sit for 5 minutes, then cut them into ½-inch pieces, and cover sausage to foil to keep warm.

2. While sausages cook, bring stock to a boil in a small saucepan over high heat. Add dried mushrooms, pushing them down into stock with the back of a spoon. Remove the pan

from the heat, and allow to sit for 10 minutes. Remove mushrooms from the pan with a slotted spoon, and chop finely. Strain stock through a coffee filter or paper towel, and set aside. Bring a large pot of salted water to a boil, and cook the pasta according to package directions for 2 minutes less than suggested. Drain, and return pasta to the pot.

3. Melt 3 tablespoons butter in heavy large skillet over medium-high heat. Add onions and cook, stirring frequently, for 3 minutes, or until onions are translucent. Add white and shiitake mushrooms and cook for 5 minutes, stirring frequently. Add chopped porcini and reserved soaking liquid, and simmer over medium-high heat for 10 minutes.

4. Melt remaining 3 tablespoons butter in a saucepan over low heat. Add flour and cook, stirring constantly, for 2 minutes. Gradually whisk in milk, raise the heat to medium, and cook, whisking constantly, until sauce thickens and boils. Stir sauce into mushroom mixture. Simmer 2 minutes, stirring occasionally. Stir in ½ cup Parmesan

and chives. Season to taste with salt and pepper. Set aside.

5. Preheat oven to 425°F, and grease a 9 x 13-inch baking pan. Add sausage and mushroom sauce to pasta, and toss well to coat. Transfer to prepared baking dish. Sprinkle breadcrumbs and remaining ¼ cup Parmesan. Bake casserole until heated through and light golden, about 25 minutes.

Note: The dish can be prepared for baking up to 2 days in advance and refrigerated, tightly covered. Cover the pan with foil and bake for 10 minutes before removing the foil for the 25 minute baking time if chilled.

To slice and dice mushrooms use an egg slicer. Slice them in one direction and then reverse the slices. The even slices will cook at the same rate.

Greek Pasta with Sausage, Oven-Roasted Tomatoes, and Feta

Makes 4 to 6 servings

Active time:
15 minutes

Start to finish:
1¼ hours

Kalamata olives, tomatoes, and sharp feta cheese are all used extensively in Greek cooking. Add some lamb sausages and you have the perfect Sunday night supper.

1 pound Loukanika (page 138) links, Lamb Sausage with Sun-Dried Tomatoes and Pine Nuts (page 96) links, or purchased hearty sausage, such as hot or sweet Italian

3 pounds ripe plum tomatoes, cored, seeded, and diced

⅓ cup olive oil

5 garlic cloves, minced

1 tablespoon balsamic vinegar

½ teaspoon crushed red pepper flakes

Salt and freshly ground black pepper to taste

3 tablespoons chopped fresh oregano or 1 tablespoon dried

3 tablespoons chopped fresh basil or 2 teaspoons dried

½ to ¾ pound linguine

½ cup pitted Kalamata olives, halved

½ pound feta, crumbled

1. Preheat the oven broiler and line a broiler pan with heavy-duty aluminum foil. Prick sausages on all sides, and broil 4 to 6 inches from the broiler element for 5 to 7 minutes, or until cooked through and no longer pink, turning them with tongs to brown on all sides. Allow sausages to sit for 5 minutes, then cut them into ½-inch pieces, and cover sausage with foil to keep warm.

2. Preheat the oven to 375°F. Combine tomatoes, oil, garlic, vinegar, and crushed red pepper in 9 x 13-inch baking pan. Season to taste with salt and pepper. Roast tomatoes for 45 minutes, or until tomatoes are tender and juicy, stirring occasionally. Stir in oregano and basil.

3. While tomatoes cook, bring a large pot of salted water to a boil over high heat. Cook linguine according to package directions until al dente. Return pasta to the pot, and add sausage, tomato mixture, olives, and feta. Stir over medium heat until heated through and feta melts, about 3 minutes. Serve immediately.

Note: The sauce can be prepared up to 2 days in advance and refrigerated, tightly covered. Reheat it, covered, over low heat, stirring occasionally, until hot.

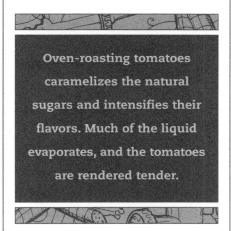

Oven-roasting tomatoes caramelizes the natural sugars and intensifies their flavors. Much of the liquid evaporates, and the tomatoes are rendered tender.

Angel Hair with Chorizo in Chile Sauce

Pasta and sausage are cooked in one skillet in a matter of minutes. Serve some guacamole and salsa on the side.

Makes 4 to 6 servings

Active time: 20 minutes

Start to finish: 45 minutes

VARIATIONS

Substitute jalapeño Jack for Monterey Jack for a spicier dish.

Substitute 2 tablespoons canned diced mild green chiles for chipotle chiles for a milder dish.

1 tablespoon olive oil

1 pound bulk Fresh Mexican Chorizo (page 66), Chaurice (page 64), or purchased sausage

2 medium onions, finely chopped

4 garlic cloves, minced

⅔ pound vermicelli or angel hair pasta, broken into 2-inch lengths

1 tablespoon dried oregano, preferably Mexican

1 teaspoon ground cumin

1 (14.5-ounce) can diced tomatoes, drained

1 (8-ounce) can tomato sauce

2 chipotle chiles in adobo, finely chopped

1½ cups Chicken Stock (page 296) or purchased low-sodium stock

Salt and freshly ground black pepper to taste

2 cups grated Monterey Jack

¼ cup chopped fresh cilantro

1. Heat oil in large covered skillet over medium-high heat. Crumble sausage into the skillet, and cook for 3 to 5 minutes, or until sausage browns. Remove sausage from the skillet with a slotted spoon, and set aside. Discard all but 2 tablespoons grease from the skillet.

2. Add onions and garlic to the skillet, and cook, stirring frequently, for 3 minutes, or until onions are translucent. Add pasta, oregano, and cumin. Cook, stirring constantly, for 2 to 3 minutes, or until pasta is lightly toasted.

3. Add tomatoes, tomato sauce, chipotle chiles, and stock to the pan, and bring to a boil over high heat, stirring occasionally. Return sausage to the skillet, reduce the heat to medium, and simmer for 8 to 10 minutes, or until pasta is soft and liquid has almost evaporated. Season to taste with salt and pepper, and stir in cheese. Sprinkle with cilantro, and serve immediately.

Note: The dish can be prepared up to 2 days in advance and refrigerated, tightly covered. Reheat it, covered, in a 350°F oven for 20 to 25 minutes, or until hot.

Toasting pasta, as in this recipe, is a technique used in much of Mexico and Latin America. Toasting keeps the pasta strands separate as they cook. Note that they take longer to cook after being toasted because the starch on the surface has hardened.

Couscous with Lamb Sausage and Dried Fruit

Makes 4 to 6 servings

Active time: 20 minutes

Start to finish: 2 hours

VARIATION

Substitute parsnips for carrots and chopped dried apricots for prunes.

Couscous is a tiny granular pasta, not a grain, that's used extensively in North African cooking. Here it serves as the base for a vegetable and fruit stew with nuggets of lamb sausage in an aromatic broth.

6 cups Beef Stock (page 299) or purchased low-sodium stock
2 tablespoons olive oil
6 sprigs fresh cilantro, rinsed
6 garlic cloves, peeled
3 (3-inch) cinnamon sticks
2 teaspoons ground cumin
2 teaspoons curry powder

1 pound North African Lamb Sausage (page 100) links, Merguez (page 92) links, or any hearty purchased sausage links
3 leeks, white parts only, halved lengthwise, and cut into 1-inch lengths
2 small carrots, halved lengthwise, and cut into 1-inch pieces
3 small onions, peeled and halved
1 small zucchini, ends trimmed, halved lengthwise, and cut into 1-inch lengths
2 ripe large tomatoes, cored, seeded, and cut into sixths
1 (15-ounce) can garbanzo beans, drained and rinsed
¾ cup pitted prunes, halved
¼ cup dried currants
3 tablespoons chopped fresh cilantro
Salt and freshly ground black pepper to taste
2½ to 4 cups couscous, prepared according to package directions, hot

1. Combine stock, oil, cilantro sprigs, garlic, cinnamon sticks, cumin, and curry powder in a Dutch oven. Bring to a boil over high heat, reduce the heat to low, and simmer, uncovered, for 30 minutes. Strain stock, pressing with the back of a spoon to extract as much liquid as possible. Discard solids, and return stock to the pan.

2. While stock simmers, preheat the oven broiler, line a broiler pan with heavy-duty aluminum foil, and prick sausages on all sides. Broil sausages 4 to 6 inches from the broiler element for 2 to 3 minutes per side, or until browned, turning them with tongs to brown on all sides. Allow sausages to sit for 5 minutes, then cut them into ½-inch pieces, and set aside.

3. Add leeks, carrots, and onions to stock. Bring to a boil over medium-high heat, reduce the heat to low, and simmer, uncovered, for 30 minutes.

4. Add sausage, zucchini, tomatoes, chickpeas, prunes, and dried currants. Simmer, uncovered, for an additional 15 minutes. Stir in chopped cilantro, and season to taste with salt and pepper. Spoon couscous into shallow bowls and top with sausage, vegetables, and broth. Serve immediately.

Note: The sausage mixture and couscous can be prepared up to 2 days in advance and refrigerated, tightly covered. Reheat it, covered, over low heat, stirring occasionally, until hot.

While it's a good idea to toss out any dried herb or spice that's been opened for more than six months, abbreviate the life of curry powder to two months. Like all spices once ground, this blend, made of as many as 20 herbs and spices, quickly loses its flavor and aroma.

Vegetable and Sausage Lo Mein

Makes 6 to 8 servings

Active time: 15 minutes

Start to finish: 30 minutes

VARIATIONS

Add 1 to 2 tablespoons Chinese chile paste with garlic for a spicy dish.

Substitute Chinese black bean sauce with garlic for oyster sauce for a more robust dish.

Making your own lo mein with lots of vegetables and Chinese sausage tastes better than any take-out version.

½ to ¾ *pound thin spaghetti, broken into 2-inch lengths*
1 *cup Chicken Stock (page 296) or purchased low-sodium stock*
8 *large dried shiitake mushrooms*
3 *tablespoons Asian sesame oil*
12 *scallions, white parts and 4 inches of green tops, sliced, divided*
4 *garlic cloves, peeled and minced*
2 *tablespoons grated fresh ginger*
1 *pound Sweet Chinese Sausage (page 74) or purchased cooked Asian sausage, thinly sliced*
2 *celery ribs, sliced on the diagonal*
1 *carrot, peeled and thinly sliced on the diagonal*
2 *cups thinly sliced Napa cabbage or bok choy*

⅓ *cup Chinese oyster sauce*
2 *tablespoons soy sauce*
¼ *pound snow peas, stemmed*
1 *cup fresh bean sprouts, rinsed*
Freshly ground black pepper to taste

1. Bring a large pot of salted water to a boil. Add spaghetti, and cook according to package directions until al dente. Drain, and set aside.

2. Bring stock to a boil in a small saucepan over high heat. Add mushrooms to stock, and push mushrooms down into liquid with the back of a spoon. Allow mushrooms to soak for 10 minutes, then drain, reserving stock. Discard mushroom stems, and slice thinly. Strain stock through a paper coffee filter or paper towel, and set aside.

3. Heat sesame oil in large skillet over medium-high heat. Add ⅓ of scallions, garlic, and ginger. Cook, stirring constantly, for 30 seconds,

or until fragrant. Add remaining scallions, sausage, celery, and carrot to the pan. Cook, stirring constantly, for 2 minutes.

4. Add reserved mushrooms, stock, oyster sauce, and soy sauce to the skillet. Cover and cook 5 minutes, or until vegetables are crisp-tender. Uncover the pan, stir in pasta, snow peas, and bean sprouts, and cook an additional 2 to 3 minutes, or until pasta is hot. Serve immediately.

Note: The dish can be prepped and the pasta can be cooked up to 6 hours in advance and refrigerated, tightly covered. Do not cook the dish until just prior to serving.

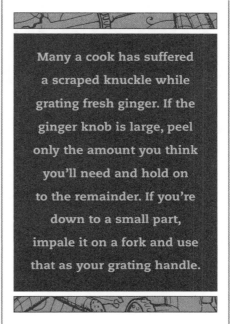

Many a cook has suffered a scraped knuckle while grating fresh ginger. If the ginger knob is large, peel only the amount you think you'll need and hold on to the remainder. If you're down to a small part, impale it on a fork and use that as your grating handle.

Cajun Red Beans and Rice with Andouille

Makes 4 to 6 servings

Active time:
20 minutes

Start to finish:
35 minutes

VARIATIONS

Omit chipotle chile for a milder dish.

Substitute Smoked Kielbasa (page 126) or other smoked sausage for andouille for a milder dish.

Jazz great Louis Armstrong used to sign his letters "red beans and ricely yours." You may adopt his phrase after trying this spicy version of the Louisiana classic. Serve with a bowl of cole slaw.

1 pound Andouille Sausage (page 62) or purchased andouille

2 tablespoons olive oil

2 medium onions, chopped

4 garlic cloves, minced

1 green bell pepper, seeds and ribs removed, and finely diced

1 tablespoon smoked Spanish paprika

1 (14.5-ounce) can diced tomatoes, undrained

1 (8-ounce) can tomato sauce

1 chipotle chile in adobo sauce, drained and finely chopped

2 (15-ounce) cans kidney beans, drained and rinsed

Salt and freshly ground black pepper to taste

2 to 3 cups cooked white rice, hot

1. Preheat the oven broiler and line a broiler pan with heavy-duty aluminum foil. Prick sausages on all sides, and broil 4 to 6 inches from the broiler element for 3 to 5 minutes, or until browned, turning them with tongs to brown on all sides; if using purchased uncooked andouille, cook for 5 to 7 minutes or until cooked through. Allow sausages to sit for 5 minutes, then cut them into ½-inch pieces, and cover sausage with foil to keep warm.

2. Heat oil in a large skillet over medium heat. Add onions, garlic, and green bell pepper, and cook, stirring frequently, for 8 to 10 minutes, or until vegetables soften. Add paprika, and cook 30 seconds, stirring constantly.

3. Mix in tomatoes, tomato sauce, chipotle, and kidney beans. Bring to a boil over medium-high heat, and simmer about 5 minutes. Add sausage, reduce the heat to low, and simmer mixture for an additional 5 minutes, stirring frequently, or until the mixture is slightly thickened. Serve immediately over rice.

Note: The dish can be prepared up to 2 days in advance and refrigerated, tightly covered. Reheat it over low heat, covered, stirring occasionally, until hot.

While chipotle chiles, smoked jalapeño peppers, are not part of the Cajun tradition, adding them gives dishes a slightly smoky flavor and a bit of heat.

Mexican Rice with Chorizo and Chicken

Makes 4 to 6 servings

Active time: 20 minutes

Start to finish: 1 hour

In this easy-to-put-together all-in-one dish, the rice cooks in the same savory Mexican sauce as the sausages and chicken.

2 to 3 (6 to 8-ounce) chicken breasts with skin and bones, cut in half crosswise

Salt and freshly ground black pepper to taste

3 tablespoons olive oil

¾ pound Fresh Mexican Chorizo (page 66) links, Chaurice (page 64) links, or purchased sausage

1 large onion, diced

3 garlic cloves, minced

1 cup long-grain white rice

1 (14.5-ounce) can diced tomatoes, drained

1 (4-ounce) can diced mild green chiles, drained

1¾ cups Chicken Stock (page 296) or purchased low-sodium stock

1 tablespoon ground cumin

2 teaspoons dried oregano

1 bay leaf

½ cup sliced pimiento-stuffed green olives

1 (10-ounce) package frozen peas, thawed

¼ cup chopped fresh cilantro

VARIATIONS

Substitute 1 or 2 chipotle chiles in adobo sauce, finely chopped, for mild green chiles for a spicier dish.

Substitute thin boneless pork chops for chicken.

Substitute 1 (15-ounce) can garbanzo beans or kidney beans, drained and rinsed, for peas.

1. Rinse chicken, pat dry with paper towels, and sprinkle chicken with salt and pepper. Heat oil in a large skillet over medium-high heat. Add chicken pieces to the pan, and brown well on all sides, turning gently with tongs, and being careful to not crowd the pan. Remove chicken from the pan, and set aside.

2. Add sausages to the skillet and brown sausages over medium-high heat, turning them with tongs to brown on all sides. Remove sausages from the skillet, and cut into 1-inch slices. Set aside.

3. Add onion and garlic to the pan, and cook, stirring frequently, for 3 minutes, or until onion is translucent. Add rice to the pan, and cook for 1 minute, stirring constantly. Add tomatoes, green chiles, stock, cumin, oregano, and bay leaf to the pan, and bring to a boil over high heat, stirring frequently.

4. Return chicken and sausage to the pan, cover the pan, reduce the heat to low, and cook for 25 to 35 minutes, or until chicken is tender and no longer pink, an instant-read thermometer registers 165°F when inserted into the center of the pieces, and almost all liquid has been absorbed.

5. Stir olives and peas into the pan, recover the pan, and cook for 2 to 3 minutes, or until hot and remaining liquid is absorbed. Remove and discard bay leaf, season to taste with salt and pepper, and serve immediately.

Note: The dish can be prepared up to 2 days in advance and refrigerated, tightly covered. Reheat it, covered, in a 350°F oven for 20 to 25 minutes, or until hot.

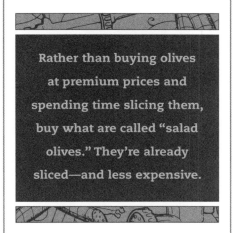

Rather than buying olives at premium prices and spending time slicing them, buy what are called "salad olives." They're already sliced—and less expensive.

Chicken and Sausage Jambalaya

Makes 6 to 8
servings

Active time:
20 minutes

Start to finish:
1 hour

VARIATION

*Substitute
Smoked Kielbasa
(page 126) for
Andouille for
a milder dish.*

Jambalaya is a staple of cooking in Louisiana, where culinary traditions of France, Spain, Italy, and the New World, among others, have long been blended together. Jambalaya was the local adaptation of the Spanish rice dish, paella, and became a favorite among Cajuns, French transplants who settled in the Louisiana bayous.

1 (3½–4-pound) frying chicken, cut into serving pieces, with each breast half cut in half crosswise

Salt and freshly ground black pepper to taste

3 tablespoons olive oil

½ pound Andouille Sausage (page 62) or purchased sausage, cut into ½-inch slices

2 celery ribs, diced

1 large onion, diced

½ red bell pepper, seeds and ribs removed, and diced

4 garlic cloves, minced

2 (5-ounce) packages yellow rice (such as Carolina brand)

1½ cups Chicken Stock (page 296) or purchased low-sodium stock

2 tablespoons chopped fresh parsley

1 teaspoon dried thyme

1 bay leaf

1 cup frozen green peas, thawed

1. Rinse chicken, pat dry with paper towels, and sprinkle chicken with salt and pepper. Heat oil in a large skillet over medium-high heat. Add chicken pieces to the skillet, and brown well on all sides, turning gently with tongs, and being careful not to crowd the pan. Remove chicken from the skillet, and set aside.

2. Add sausage, celery, onion, red bell pepper, and garlic to the skillet, and cook, stirring frequently, for 3 minutes, or until onion is translucent. Add rice to the skillet, and cook for 1 minute, stirring constantly. Add stock, parsley, thyme, and bay leaf to the skillet, and bring to a boil over high heat, stirring frequently.

3. Return chicken to the skillet, cover the skillet, reduce the heat to medium-low, and cook for 25 to 35 minutes, or until chicken is cooked through and no longer pink, and almost all liquid has been absorbed.

4. Stir peas into the skillet, recover the pan, and cook for 2 to 3 minutes, or until hot and remaining liquid is absorbed. Remove and discard bay leaf, and serve immediately.

Note: The dish can be cooked up to 2 days in advance and refrigerated, tightly covered. Reheat in a 350°F oven, covered, for 30 to 35 minutes, or until hot.

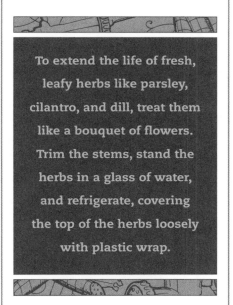

To extend the life of fresh, leafy herbs like parsley, cilantro, and dill, treat them like a bouquet of flowers. Trim the stems, stand the herbs in a glass of water, and refrigerate, covering the top of the herbs loosely with plastic wrap.

Baked Sausage and Wild Mushroom Risotto

Makes 6 to 8 servings

Active time: 20 minutes

Start to finish: 1 hour

VARIATIONS

Substitute red wine for white wine.

Substitute fresh shiitake mushrooms for Portobello mushrooms.

Risotto is a traditional Italian rice dish that dates back to the Renaissance. The key ingredient is Arborio rice, which is a short, fat-grained Italian rice with a high starch content that makes the dish creamy without the addition of stock or water. I discovered that it can be successfully baked in the oven rather than stirred laboriously on top of the stove.

4 cups Chicken Stock (page 296) or purchased low-sodium stock
½ cup dried porcini mushrooms
1 pound Portobello mushroom caps
4 tablespoons (½ stick) unsalted butter, divided
2 tablespoons olive oil
1 large onion, chopped
3 garlic cloves, minced
1 pound bulk Sweet Italian Sausage (page 52), Luganega (page 58), or purchased sausage
2 cups Arborio rice
½ cup dry white wine
¾ cup freshly grated Parmesan or more to taste
Salt and freshly ground black pepper to taste

1. Preheat the oven to 400°F, and grease a 10 x 14-inch baking pan. Bring stock to a boil over high heat. Add dried porcini, pushing them down into the stock with the back of a spoon. Allow mushrooms to soak for 10 minutes, then remove

mushrooms from stock with a slotted spoon, and chop. Set aside, and reserve stock.

2. Peel skin from Portobello mushrooms, and discard dark gills from the underside of caps. Dice mushrooms into ½-inch pieces.

3. Heat 2 tablespoons butter and oil in a large skillet over medium-high heat. Add diced mushrooms and cook, stirring constantly, for 3 to 5 minutes, or until mushrooms are browned and tender. Remove mushrooms from the skillet, and set aside.

4. Heat remaining butter in the skillet, and add onion and garlic. Cook, stirring frequently, for 3 minutes, or until onion is translucent. Crumble sausage into the skillet, and cook for 3 minutes, or until sausage browns.

5. Add rice to the pan, and cook for 2 minutes, stirring constantly. Add wine to the pan, raise the heat to high, and cook for 3 minutes, stirring constantly, or until wine is almost evaporated. Add reserved stock, and bring to a boil. Scrape mixture into the prepared pan, cover the pan with aluminum foil, and bake for 25 to 30 minutes, or until rice is soft and has absorbed liquid. Stir in Parmesan, season to taste with salt and pepper, and serve immediately.

Note: The dish can be prepared up to 2 days in advance and refrigerated, tightly covered. Reheat it, covered, in a 350°F oven for 20 to 25 minutes, or until hot.

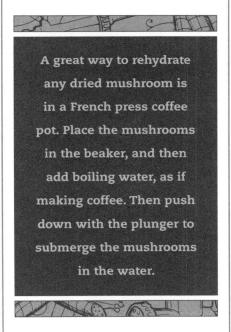

A great way to rehydrate any dried mushroom is in a French press coffee pot. Place the mushrooms in the beaker, and then add boiling water, as if making coffee. Then push down with the plunger to submerge the mushrooms in the water.

Baked Risotto with Greens and Sausage

Makes 4 to 6 servings

Active time: 20 minutes

Start to finish: 1 hour

VARIATIONS

Substitute Swiss chard or mustard greens for broccoli rabe.

Substitute hot sausage for sweet sausage.

Healthful greens are a wonderful ingredient in risotto and serve to balance the herbs and spices in the sausage. Serve this with a tossed salad, perhaps sprinkled with some Gorgonzola cheese and toasted walnuts.

1 pound broccoli rabe, cut into 2-inch lengths

2 tablespoons unsalted butter

2 tablespoons olive oil

1 large onion, chopped

3 garlic cloves, minced

1 pound bulk Sweet Italian Sausage (page 52), Luganega (page 58), or purchased sausage

2 cups Arborio rice

½ cup dry white wine

4 cups Chicken Stock (page 296) or purchased low-sodium stock

¾ cup freshly grated Parmesan or more to taste

Salt and freshly ground black pepper to taste

1. Preheat the oven to 400°F, and grease a 10 x 14-inch baking pan. Bring a large pot of salted water to a boil. Blanch broccoli rabe for 3 minutes. Drain, pressing with the back of a spoon to extract as much liquid as possible. Set aside.

3. Heat butter and oil in a large skillet over medium-high heat, and add onion and garlic. Cook, stirring frequently, for 3 minutes, or until onion is translucent. Crumble sausage into the skillet, and cook for 3 minutes, or until sausage browns.

5. Add rice to the pan, and cook for 2 minutes, stirring constantly. Add wine to the pan, raise the heat to high, and cook for 3 minutes, stirring constantly, or until wine is almost evaporated. Add stock, and bring to a boil. Scrape mixture into the prepared pan, cover the pan with aluminum foil, and bake for 10 minutes. Add reserved broccoli rabe, and bake for an additional 15 to 20 minutes, or until rice is soft and has absorbed liquid. Stir in Parmesan, season to taste with salt and pepper, and serve immediately.

Note: The dish can be prepared up to 2 days in advance and refrigerated, tightly covered. Reheat it, covered, in a 350°F oven for 20 to 25 minutes, or until hot.

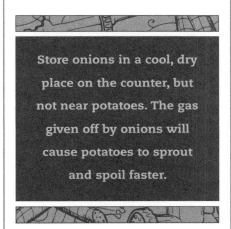

Store onions in a cool, dry place on the counter, but not near potatoes. The gas given off by onions will cause potatoes to sprout and spoil faster.

Creamy Polenta with Sausage and Red Wine Sauce

Makes 4 to 6 servings

Active time: 10 minutes

Start to finish: 45 minutes

Traditionally cooked polenta demands that the cook stir the cornmeal mixture continuously for 20 to 30 minutes. In this method, however, the polenta is covered, so there's less stirring and you can tend to other things.

Sausage Sauce:

1½ cups dry red wine

1 tablespoon olive oil

3/4 pound bulk Sweet Italian Sausage (page 52), Luganega (page 58), or purchased sausage

1 large shallot, chopped

2 garlic cloves, minced

½ pound mushrooms, wiped with a damp paper towel, trimmed, and sliced

1 (14.5-ounce) can petite diced tomatoes, undrained

2 tablespoons tomato paste

2 tablespoons chopped fresh parsley

1 tablespoon chopped fresh rosemary or 1 teaspoon dried

3 tablespoons unsalted butter

3 tablespoons all-purpose flour

¾ cup Beef Stock (page 299) or purchased low-sodium stock

Salt and freshly ground black pepper to taste

Polenta:

3 cups water

1 cup whole milk

1 teaspoon salt

1 cup polenta

2 tablespoons unsalted butter, cut into small bits

Freshly ground black pepper to taste

1. For sausage sauce, place wine in a small saucepan and bring to a boil over medium-high heat. Boil until reduced by half. Set aside.

VARIATIONS

Substitute chicken stock or vegetable stock for water.

Add 2 tablespoons chopped fresh parsley and ½ teaspoon Italian seasoning to water.

Add ½ to ¾ cup grated whole-milk mozzarella, a combination of whole-milk mozzarella and freshly grated Parmesan, or Swiss cheese, along with butter.

2. Heat oil in a saucepan over medium-high heat. Crumble sausage into the skillet, and cook for 3 to 5 minutes, or until sausage browns. Add shallot and garlic, and cook for 1 minute. Add mushrooms, and cook, stirring frequently, for 5 to 7 minutes, or until mushrooms soften.

3. Add reduced wine, tomatoes, tomato paste, parsley, and rosemary to the pan, and bring to a boil over medium-high heat. Reduce the heat to low, and simmer mixture, partially covered, for 10 minutes.

4. While sauce simmers, melt butter in a small saucepan over low heat. Add flour and cook, stirring constantly, for 2 minutes. Raise the heat to medium and whisk in stock. Bring to a boil, whisking frequently, until mixture boils and thickens. Pour mixture into the saucepan with sausage and wine mixture, and simmer for an additional 10 minutes, stirring occasionally. Season to taste with salt and pepper, and keep hot.

5. While sauce simmers, start polenta. Bring water, milk, and salt to a boil in a 3-quart saucepan over high heat. Whisk in polenta in a thin stream, whisking so no lumps form.

6. Reduce the heat to medium, and continue to whisk for 2 minutes. Cover the pan, reduce the heat to the lowest setting, and stir with a heavy spoon every 8 to 10 minutes for 30 seconds, or until polenta is smooth again. Continue to cook for 30 minutes.

7. Remove the pan from the heat, and stir in butter. Season to taste with salt and pepper, and serve immediately, topped with sausage sauce.

Note: The sauce can be prepared up to 2 days in advance and refrigerated, tightly covered. Reheat it over low heat, stirring occasionally, until simmering. The polenta can be prepared up to 20 minutes in advance. If holding it for longer than that time, add additional milk and butter to create a creamy consistency again.

Fiery Fare:

Grilled Sausage

Dishes

Time to fire up the barbie! There's nothing like the added aroma and flavor that grilling gives food, especially sausages. Featured are kebabs, grilled sandwiches, and sausage-topped salads. You'll also find some ingredients—from squid to steak—in which the sausage is used as a stuffing.

Charcoal grills ruled the world until the last decade. It was in the early 1950s that George Stephen invented the covered grill, now generically dubbed the Weber kettle.

Gas grills appeared about 30 years ago and have become increasingly popular due to their convenience. All you have to do is turn on the gas and the grill warms up in minutes, while a charcoal grill takes a good 30 minutes to reach the right temperature. With gas, though, you give up the luscious flavor and aroma of food cooked over charcoal.

TAKING YOUR GRILL'S TEMPERATURE

Ignore the thermometer sticking out of the grill's lid. All that's going to tell you is the temperature of the air in the upper part of the grill lid, and not the temperature at the grate level where the food is grilling. The best way to judge your grill's surface temperature is with the palm of your hand. Once the coals have a light coating of ash, place your hand, palm side down, about 4 to 5 inches above the cooking rack. Grilling is a high-heat cooking method, so if you can hold your hand over the coals for more than 7 seconds, it means you should be adding more coals or preheat the gas burners for longer.

Here are your readings:
- Hot grill: 2 seconds
- Medium-hot grill: 3 to 4 seconds
- Medium grill: 5 to 6 seconds
- Medium-low grill: 7 seconds

Sausage and Vegetable Kebabs

Makes 4 to 6 servings

Active time: 15 minutes

Start to finish: 1½ hours, including 1 hour for marinating

Substitute green or red bell pepper, cut into 1-inch squares, for onion.

Substitute red wine vinegar for lemon juice.

Kebabs are a dramatic way to present food. For these, vegetables are first marinated to boost their flavor, then skewered with the sausages.

8 to 12 bamboo skewers
3 tablespoons freshly squeezed lemon juice
2 garlic cloves, minced
1½ teaspoons dried oregano
½ teaspoon dried thyme
Salt and freshly ground black pepper to taste
⅓ cup olive oil
1 medium zucchini, halved lengthwise and cut into 1½-inch chunks
½ sweet onion, such as Vidalia or Bermuda, cut into wedges
¼ pound mushrooms, wiped with a damp paper towel, with stem trimmed flat to cap
1¼ pounds Sweet Italian Sausage (page 52) links, Luganega (page 58) links, Garlicky Chicken and Rosemary Sausage (page 164) links, or any purchased flavorful sausage, cut into 1-inch chunks
4 to 6 sprigs fresh rosemary, cut into 1½-inch lengths

1. Prepare a medium-hot charcoal or gas grill. Soak bamboo skewers in cold water for 30 minutes.

2. Combine lemon juice, garlic, oregano, thyme, salt, and pepper in a jar with a tight-fitting lid, and shake well. Add oil, and shake well again. Set aside.

3. Place zucchini, onion, and mushrooms in a heavy resealable plastic bag. Add dressing, turning the bag to coat. Marinate vegetables at room temperature for 1 hour, turning the bag occasionally. Remove vegetables from marinade, reserving marinade.

4. Thread sausage, marinated vegetables, and rosemary onto skewers. Brush each skewer with reserved dressing.

5. Grill skewers for 3 to 4 minutes per side, uncovered if using a charcoal grill, turning them gently with tongs. Serve immediately.

Note: The kebabs can be assembled up to a day in advance and refrigerated, tightly covered.

Many photographs in food magazines and cookbooks include kebabs with bright red cherry tomatoes. While they may look attractive, tomatoes cook so quickly that they will fall apart before sturdier vegetables like peppers, onion, and zucchini are done. Make separate tomato skewers and grill them briefly.

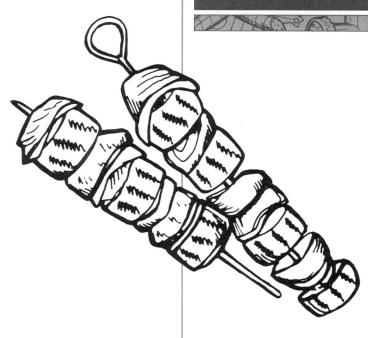

Sausage Spiedini

Makes 4 to 6 servings

Active time:
15 minutes

Start to finish:
45 minutes

VARIATIONS

Substitute ½-inch thick slices of zucchini and yellow squash for bell pepper.

Substitute wedges of red onion for 1 bell pepper.

Substitute herbes de Provence for Italian seasoning.

These Italian kebabs are made with large bread cubes and vegetables. The dressing used to brush them also lightly coats the accompanying salad greens.

8 to 12 bamboo skewers
¼ cup balsamic vinegar
2 tablespoons Dijon mustard
1 shallot, chopped
2 garlic cloves, minced
2 teaspoons Italian seasoning
Salt and freshly ground black
    pepper to taste
⅔ cup olive oil
1½ pounds French Garlic Sausage
    (page 72), Bockwurst (page 122),
    Boudin Blanc (page 118), or
    purchased fully-cooked sausage,
    cut into ¾-inch slices
16 to 24 (1-inch) cubes French or
    Italian bread
1 red bell pepper, seeds and ribs
    removed, and cut into 1-inch
    squares
1 orange or yellow bell pepper, seeds
    and ribs removed, and cut into
    1-inch squares
4 to 6 cups mixed salad greens,
    rinsed and dried

1. Prepare a medium-hot charcoal or gas grill. Soak bamboo skewers in cold water for 30 minutes.

2. Combine vinegar, mustard, shallot, garlic, Italian seasoning, salt, and pepper in a jar with a tight-fitting lid, and shake well. Add olive oil, and shake well again. Set aside.

3. Thread sausage, bread cubes, red bell pepper squares, and orange bell pepper squares onto skewers. Brush each skewer with 1 tablespoon dressing.

4. Grill skewers for 2 to 3 minutes per side, uncovered if using a charcoal grill, turning them gently with tongs.

5. Toss greens with some of remaining dressing. To serve, line a platter or individual plates with salad, and arrange kebabs on top. Serve immediately, passing remaining dressing separately.

Note: The dressing can be made and the kebabs can be assembled up to a day in advance and refrigerated, tightly covered. Allow dressing to sit at room temperature for 30 minutes.

The reason to make salad dressing in two stages is that granular seasonings such as salt or sugar dissolve in vinegar or other liquid but not in oil. Mix the acid and seasonings first, then add the olive oil.

Asian Sausage Kebabs

Makes 4 to 6 servings

Active time:
15 minutes

Start to finish:
45 minutes

VARIATIONS

Substitute broccoli or cauliflower florets for bok choy.

Add 1 to 2 teaspoons Chinese chile paste with garlic to dressing for a spicy dish.

Grilled meats, seafood, and vegetables on skewers are sold in open-air markets throughout Asia. These combine sausage with vegetables, which remain crunchy.

8 to 12 bamboo skewers

2 tablespoons reduced-sodium soy sauce

2 tablespoons dry sherry

2 tablespoons firmly packed dark brown sugar

1 tablespoon rice wine vinegar

2 garlic cloves, minced

1 tablespoon grated fresh ginger

Freshly ground black pepper to taste

1 tablespoon Asian sesame oil

3 tablespoons vegetable oil

1¼ pounds Thai-Style Pork Sausage (page 76) links, Asian Duck and Shiitake Mushroom Sausage (page 176) links, or purchased sausage with Asian flavoring, cut into 1-inch chunks

2 to 3 heads baby bok choy, stem and leaves trimmed, and cut into quarters through the core

¼ pound mushrooms, wiped with a damp paper towel, and stems trimmed flat with cap

1. Prepare a medium-hot charcoal or gas grill. Soak bamboo skewers in cold water for 30 minutes.

2. Combine soy sauce, sherry, garlic, ginger, and pepper in a jar with a tight-fitting lid, and shake well. Add sesame oil and vegetable oil, and shake well again. Set aside.

3. Thread sausage, bok choy, and mushrooms onto skewers. Brush each skewer with 1 tablespoon dressing.

4. Grill skewers for 3 to 4 minutes per side, uncovered if using a charcoal grill, turning them gently with tongs. Serve immediately.

Note: The dressing can be made and the kebabs can be assembled up to a day in advance and refrigerated, tightly covered. Allow dressing to sit at room temperature for 30 minutes.

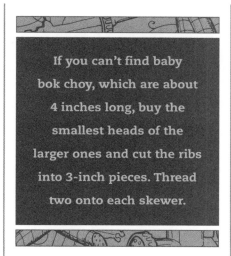

If you can't find baby bok choy, which are about 4 inches long, buy the smallest heads of the larger ones and cut the ribs into 3-inch pieces. Thread two onto each skewer.

Sausage-Stuffed Portobello Mushrooms

Makes 4 to 6 servings

Active time:
15 minutes

Start to finish:
45 minutes

VARIATIONS

Substitute Andouille Sausage (page 62) or Smoky Beef Summer Sausage (page 82) for Smoked Kielbasa.

Substitute cheddar or Parmesan for Gruyère.

Hearty and meaty Portobello mushrooms are enhanced with a sausage filling. Potato salad is a nice addition to this plate.

4 to 6 (4-inch wide) Portobello mushrooms, stems discarded and wiped with a damp paper towel.

¼ cup olive oil, divided

Salt and freshly ground black pepper to taste

1 large shallot, chopped

½ pound Smoked Kielbasa (page 126), French Garlic Sausage (page 72), or purchased cooked sausage, chopped

¾ cup plain breadcrumbs

¼ cup mayonnaise

1 teaspoon herbes de Provence

½ cup grated Gruyère

1. Prepare a medium-hot charcoal or gas grill.

2. Brush mushrooms with 2 tablespoons oil, and sprinkle with salt and pepper.

3. Heat remaining oil in a skillet over medium-high heat. Add shallot and sausage, and cook, stirring frequently, for 3 minutes, or until shallot is translucent. Scrape mixture into a mixing bowl, and add breadcrumbs and mayonnaise, and stir well. Season to taste with salt and pepper, and set aside.

4. Grill mushrooms stem side down for 5 minutes. Remove mushrooms from the grill and place them on a baking sheet. Divide sausage mixture into grilled side of mushrooms, and sprinkle with cheese.

5. Return mushrooms to the grill, stuffing side up, and grill, covered, for 3 to 5 minutes, or until cheese melts and mushrooms are tender. Serve immediately.

Note: The mushrooms can be pre-cooked and stuffed up to 6 hours in advance and refrigerated, tightly covered.

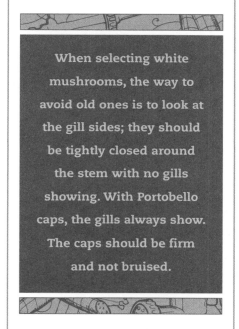

When selecting white mushrooms, the way to avoid old ones is to look at the gill sides; they should be tightly closed around the stem with no gills showing. With Portobello caps, the gills always show. The caps should be firm and not bruised.

Calamari Stuffed with Sausage

Makes 4 to 6 servings

Active time:
15 minutes

Start to finish:
45 minutes

VARIATION

Substitute Gulf Coast Chicken and Shrimp Sausage (page 136) for Italian Sausage, and substitute Cajun seasoning for salt and pepper.

When grilled, squid becomes tender and moist. Their delicate flavor is enhanced with a sausage stuffing. Serve with sliced tomatoes drizzled with olive oil.

12 wooden toothpicks

½ cup Italian breadcrumbs

3 tablespoons whole milk

3 tablespoons olive oil, divided

⅓ pound bulk Sweet Italian Sausage (page 52), Hot Italian Sausage (page 54), or purchased sausage

1 pound small cleaned squid bodies plus tentacles

Salt and freshly ground black pepper to taste

1. Prepare a medium-hot charcoal or gas grill. Soak toothpicks in cold water to cover. Mix breadcrumbs with milk in a small bowl, and set aside.

2. Heat 1 tablespoon oil in a skillet over medium-high heat. Crumble sausage into the skillet and cook, breaking up lumps with a fork, for 3 to 5 minutes, or until browned. Remove sausage from the skillet with a slotted spoon, and place it in a mixing bowl. Add breadcrumb mixture, and stir well.

3. Loosely stuff squid bodies with sausage mixture, leaving a ½-inch space at the top. Close tops with soaked toothpicks. Coat stuffed bodies and tentacles with remaining oil, and season to taste with salt and pepper.

4. Grill squid bodies, uncovered if using a charcoal grill, turning them gently with tongs, for 12 to 14 minutes, or until browned and an instant-read thermometer registers 160°F. Remove bodies from the grill, and then grill tentacles for 1 to 2 minutes, or until opaque. Sprinkle all with parsley, and serve immediately.

Note: The squid can be stuffed up to 6 hours in advance and refrigerated, tightly covered with plastic wrap. Add 1 to 2 minutes to the grilling time if chilled.

Fresh squid is very perishable. Cover it tightly and store it in the coldest section of your refrigerator or on a bed of ice. Fresh squid should be used within 2 days, or cleaned and frozen up to 3 months.

Sausage-Coated Lamb Chops with Sun-Dried Tomato Butter

Makes 4 to 6 servings

Active time:
15 minutes

Start to finish:
55 minutes

VARIATION

Substitute boneless rib-eye steaks for lamb chops.

After making a batch of Scotch Eggs (page 254), I figured that if sausage was a good coating for eggs, it would be even better for lamb chops. The flavors from the brandy-laced sausage enhance the richness of the lamb.

Dish:

4 to 6 (1½-inch thick) loin or rib lamb chops

Salt and freshly ground black pepper to taste

2 tablespoons olive oil

½ pound bulk Loukanika (page 138), North African Lamb Sausage (page 100), or purchased sausage

½ cup Italian breadcrumbs

1 large egg, lightly beaten

1 tablespoon brandy

Sauce:

6 tablespoons (¾ stick) unsalted butter, softened

2 garlic cloves, minced

2 teaspoons anchovy paste

2 tablespoons finely chopped sun-dried tomatoes

Freshly ground black pepper to taste

1. Prepare a medium-hot charcoal or gas grill.

2. Sprinkle lamb chops with salt and pepper. Heat oil in a large skillet or grill pan over high heat. Sear chops on both sides until brown, and set aside to cool.

3. While lamb cools, combine sausage, breadcrumbs, egg, and brandy in a mixing bowl. Knead well. For topping, combine butter, garlic, anchovy paste, sun-dried tomatoes, and pepper in a small bowl, and mix well. Form mixture into a cylinder on a sheet of plastic wrap or waxed paper, and refrigerate.

4. Divide sausage mixture into a portion for each chop, and wrap meat completely with sausage mixture; leave bones uncovered if using rib chops.

5. Grill chops for 10 minutes per side for medium-rare, 125°F on an instant-read thermometer, or to desired doneness. Allow chops to rest for 5 minutes. To serve, top each chop with a few slices of butter.

Note: The stuffing mixture and butter topping can be made up to a day in advance and refrigerated, tightly covered. Do not brown chops or coat with sausage until just prior to serving.

The reason to let meat sit before carving, often referred to as "resting," is so that the juices will be reabsorbed into the fibers. If meat is carved as soon as it comes out of the oven or off the grill, it will lose a lot of its juices and dry out faster. The amount of time that meat or poultry should rest relates to its size. A thin piece of meat can be carved after 5 minutes; a standing rib should sit for 15 minutes.

Pepper and Sausage Stuffed Flank Steak

Makes 4 to 6 servings

Active time: 25 minutes

Start to finish: 3¾ hours, including 3 hours for marinating

VARIATION

Substitute pork tenderloin for steak, stuffing mixture into the center. Grill pork over a medium-hot grill.

Flank steak is ideal for stuffing because its flat surface makes it easy to cut a nice, neat pocket. This sausage stuffing is made with some sautéed vegetables and Parmesan cheese.

1 (1½-pound) flank steak, cut from the thick end
1 cup dry red wine
1 shallot, chopped
4 garlic cloves, minced, divided
1 tablespoon herbes de Provence
¼ cup olive oil
Salt and freshly ground black pepper to taste
2 tablespoons unsalted butter
⅓ pound bulk Sweet Italian Sausage (page 52), Luganega (page 58), or purchased sausage
½ red bell pepper, seeds and ribs removed, and chopped
1 small onion, chopped
2 tablespoons Beef Stock (page 299) or purchased low-sodium stock
¼ cup freshly grated Parmesan
½ cup Italian breadcrumbs
2 tablespoons chopped fresh parsley
1 chopped fresh oregano or 1 teaspoon dried
1 fresh thyme or 1 teaspoon dried

1. Rinse flank steak and pat dry with paper towels. Score steak lightly in a diamond pattern on both sides. Cut a deep pocket in the center of steak that extends to within ½ inch of the sides of the meat. Combine wine, shallot, 2 garlic cloves, and herbes de Provence in a heavy resealable plastic bag. Season to taste with salt and pepper. Mix well, add olive oil, and mix well again. Add steak to marinade and marinate, refrig-

erated, for a minimum of 3 hours and up to 8 hours, turning the bag occasionally.

2. Prepare a hot charcoal or gas grill.

3. Melt butter in a skillet over medium-high heat. Crumble sausage into the skillet and cook, breaking up lumps with a fork, for 3 to 5 minutes, or until browned. Reduce the heat to medium, and add red bell pepper, onion, and remaining garlic. Cook, stirring frequently, for 10 minutes, or until vegetables soften. Remove the pan from the heat, and stir in stock, Parmesan, breadcrumbs, parsley, oregano, and thyme. Season to taste with salt and pepper, and mix well.

4. Remove steak from marinade, and discard marinade. Gently stuff sausage mixture into pocket of steak and skewer the opening closed with turkey-trussing skewers or wooden toothpicks soaked in water. Sprinkle meat with salt and pepper.

5. Grill steak over a hot grill, uncovered, for 3 to 4 minutes per side for medium-rare or to desired doneness. Allow steak to rest for 5 minutes, then slice. Serve immediately.

Note: The stuffing can be made up to 2 days in advance and refrigerated, tightly covered. Allow it to reach room temperature before stuffing steak.

Flank steak is a long, thin, and very fibrous cut of beef from the hindquarter. It's often tenderized by marinating it before grilling and should be sliced against the grain.

Sausage and Cheese-Stuffed Chicken Breasts

Makes 4 servings

Active time:
15 minutes

Start to finish:
55 minutes

Substitute cheddar, Swiss cheese, or Gouda for Gruyère.

Substitute 1½-inch thick pork chops for chicken breasts.

Bone-in chicken breasts are stuffed with nutty Gruyère and sausage, then basted while on the grill.

4 (8 to 10-ounce) chicken breast halves with skin and bones

Salt and freshly ground black pepper to taste

4 tablespoons (½ stick) unsalted butter, melted and divided

¼ pound bulk Garlicky Chicken and Rosemary Sausage (page 164), Provençal Chicken Sausage (page 162), or purchased poultry or pork sausage

¼ pound Gruyère, grated

¼ cup plain breadcrumbs

2 tablespoons freshly squeezed lemon juice

2 tablespoons Worcestershire sauce

1. Prepare a medium-hot charcoal or gas grill.

2. Rinse chicken and pat dry with paper towels. Insert a sharp paring knife into the thicker side of chicken breasts and cut a lengthwise pocket, being careful not to puncture the skin. Sprinkle chicken with salt and pepper, and set aside.

3. Heat 1 tablespoon butter in a small skillet over medium-high heat. Crumble sausage into the skillet and cook, breaking up lumps with a fork, for 3 to 5 minutes, or until browned. Scrape sausage into a mixing bowl, and add cheese and breadcrumbs.

4. Gently stuff mixture into pocket of chicken breasts, and secure openings with a wooden toothpick or metal skewer. Combine remaining butter, lemon juice, and Worcestershire sauce in a small bowl, and set aside.

5. Grill chicken, covered, for 10 to 12 minutes per side, basting it frequently with sauce. Do not baste for final 2 minutes of cooking, and discard any unused sauce. Chicken is cooked when it registers 165°F on an instant-read thermometer inserted into the thickest part. Serve immediately.

Note: The stuffing can be prepared up to a day in advance and refrigerated, tightly covered. Do not stuff chicken breasts until just prior to serving.

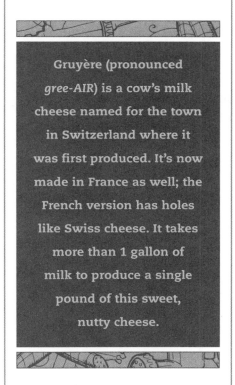

Gruyère (pronounced *gree-AIR*) is a cow's milk cheese named for the town in Switzerland where it was first produced. It's now made in France as well; the French version has holes like Swiss cheese. It takes more than 1 gallon of milk to produce a single pound of this sweet, nutty cheese.

Grilled Sausage and Vegetable Hoagies

Makes 4 to 6 servings

Active time:
15 minutes

Start to finish:
30 minutes

VARIATIONS

Substitute lavash or flour tortillas for rolls.

Add shredded provolone or fontina cheese over the sausages and vegetables.

Sausages redolent with herbs, spices, and garlic and topped with grilled vegetables are piled on hero rolls. Serve your favorite pasta salad on the side.

¼ cup olive oil

2 garlic cloves, minced

1 large red onion, peeled

1 green bell pepper, seeds and ribs removed, and cut into quarters

1 red bell pepper, seeds and ribs removed, and cut into quarters

1 tablespoon balsamic vinegar

Salt and freshly ground black pepper to taste

1½ pounds Sweet Italian Sausage (page 52) links, Hot Italian Sausage (page 54) links, Luganega (page 58) links, or purchased sausage

4 to 6 (7-inch) hoagie buns, split

1. Prepare a medium-hot charcoal or gas grill. Stir olive oil and garlic together in a small cup, and set aside.

2. Cut onion into slices ⅓-inch thick. Insert metal or bamboo skewers through slices. Brush

onion, green bell pepper, and red bell pepper with garlic oil.

3. Grill vegetables, uncovered, for 3 to 5 minutes per side, turning them gently with tongs and a slotted spatula. Remove vegetables from the grill, discard skewers, and thinly slice peppers. Toss vegetables with vinegar, and season to taste with salt and pepper. Keep warm.

4. Prick sausages with a fork, and grill, turning them gently with tongs, for 10 to 15 minutes, depending on diameter, or until cooked to an internal temperature of 160°F. Brush cut sides of buns with garlic oil, and grill, cut side down, until toasted.

5. To serve, arrange sausages on toasted buns and top with vegetable mixture. Serve immediately.

Note: The vegetables and sausages can be grilled up to a day in advance and refrigerated, tightly covered. Reheat them in a microwave oven until hot.

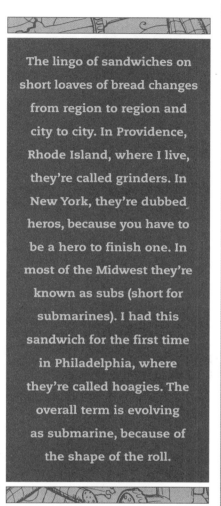

The lingo of sandwiches on short loaves of bread changes from region to region and city to city. In Providence, Rhode Island, where I live, they're called grinders. In New York, they're dubbed heros, because you have to be a hero to finish one. In most of the Midwest they're known as subs (short for submarines). I had this sandwich for the first time in Philadelphia, where they're called hoagies. The overall term is evolving as submarine, because of the shape of the roll.

Lamb Sausage and Yogurt Sauce Pita Pockets

Makes 4 to 6 servings

Active time: 15 minutes

Start to finish: 45 minutes

VARIATIONS

Substitute feta for goat cheese.

Add 2 tablespoons chopped fresh dill or fresh mint to sauce.

The ground spiced meat mixture for the traditional gyro is roasted on a vertical skewer that slowly spins like a gyroscope, then the meat is carved for the sandwich. It's much easier and faster to cook some lamb sausages. Serve this with a Greek salad.

1½ cups plain yogurt

1 ripe plum tomato, rinsed, cored, seeded, and chopped

½ cup chopped, peeled, and seeded cucumber

4 garlic cloves, minced and divided

Salt and freshly ground black pepper to taste

1½ pounds bulk Lukanika (page 138), North African Lamb Sausage (page 100), or purchased sausage

1 (3-ounce) log goat cheese

4 to 6 (7 or 8-inch) pita bread, top 1 inch discarded and pockets opened

1. Prepare a medium-hot charcoal or gas grill.

2. Place yogurt in a strainer set over a mixing bowl, and allow it to drain for 30 minutes. After draining, discard whey, and mix yogurt with tomato, cucumber, and 1 garlic clove. Season to taste with salt and

pepper, and refrigerate until ready to serve.

3. While yogurt drains, form sausage into 8 to 12 portions, and roll each into a ball. Flatten into a patty ½-inch thick. Cut goat cheese into 4 to 6 portions, and place one on top of lamb patties. Top with remaining patties, sealing to enclose cheese. Press with your thumb in the center of each burger to form an indentation.

4. Grill burgers with the indentation up, uncovered if using a charcoal grill, for a total time of 4 to 6 minutes per side, to an internal temperature of 125°F for medium rare, or to desired done-ness. To serve, fill each pita bread with lamb. Divide sauce on top of lamb, and serve immediately.

Note: The burgers and sauce can be prepared up to a day in advance and refrigerated, tightly covered.

It's amazing how much liquid yogurt contains. Draining it while the lamb is being prepared gives the sauce the consistency of one made with sour cream for a better texture.

Grilled Chicken Sausage Salad with Honey-Mustard Dressing

Makes 4 to 6 servings

Active time:
30 minutes

Start to finish:
55 minutes

VARIATION

Substitute Spicy Thai Sausage (page 144) for turkey sausage and substitute hoisin sauce for honey and rice vinegar for cider vinegar.

Nuggets of grilled chicken sausage atop a salad napped with an old-fashioned honey and mustard dressing. Serve with cornbread or biscuits.

Salad:
6 to 9 cups bite-sized pieces salad greens of your choice, rinsed and dried
2 carrots, peeled and cut into thin strips
1 green bell pepper, seeds and ribs removed, and cut into thin slices
1 small red onion, peeled, halved lengthwise, and cut into thin rings
1 pound Turkey, Apple and Sage Sausage (page 150) links, Thanksgiving Turkey Sausage (page 152) links, or purchased raw poultry sausage

Dressing:
3 tablespoons honey
3 tablespoons Dijon mustard
⅓ cup cider vinegar
Salt and freshly ground black pepper to taste
½ cup olive oil

1. Prepare a medium-hot charcoal or gas grill.

2. Arrange lettuce, carrots, green pepper, and onion on individual plates or on a serving platter. Combine honey, mustard, vinegar, salt, and pepper in a jar with a tight-fitting lid. Shake well, add olive oil, and shake well again. Set aside.

3. Prick sausages with a fork, and grill, turning them gently with tongs, for 10 to 15 minutes, depending on diameter, or until cooked to an internal temperature of 165°F. Allow sausages to rest for

5 minutes, and then cut into ½-inch thick slices.

4. To serve, arrange sausage pieces on top of the salad, and drizzle dressing over all.

Note: Sausage and dressing can be prepared a day in advance and refrigerated, tightly covered. Reheat sausage, uncovered, in a 375°F oven for 8 to 10 minutes, or until hot and crisp. Allow dressing to sit at room temperature for at least 30 minutes if chilled.

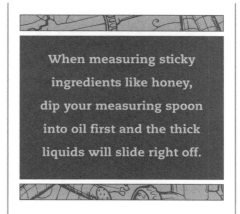

When measuring sticky ingredients like honey, dip your measuring spoon into oil first and the thick liquids will slide right off.

Chicken Sausage Provençal Salad

Makes 4 to 6 servings

Active time: 25 minutes

Start to finish: 55 minutes

Substitute Sweet Italian Sausage (page 52) links for Provençal Chicken Sausage and substitute Italian seasoning for herbes de Provence.

Both the sausages and the vegetables are grilled and then arranged on a bed of frisée, onions, and tomatoes.

⅓ cup red wine vinegar

2 shallots, chopped

2 garlic cloves, minced

1 tablespoon Dijon mustard

2 teaspoons sugar

2 teaspoons herbes de Provence

Salt and freshly ground black pepper to taste

1 cup olive oil

1 small zucchini, quartered lengthwise

2 Japanese eggplant, quartered lengthwise

1 small yellow squash, quartered lengthwise

1 red bell pepper, seeds and ribs removed, and cut into 1-inch strips

1¼ pounds Provençal Chicken Sausage (page 162) links, Italian Chicken and Olive Sausage (page 158) links, or purchased raw chicken or pork sausage links

1 large bunch frisée, broken into bite-sized pieces, rinsed and dried

1 small red onion, halved lengthwise and thinly sliced

½ pint cherry tomatoes, rinsed and halved

1. Prepare a medium-hot charcoal or gas grill.

2. To prepare dressing, combine vinegar, shallots, garlic, mustard, sugar, herbes de Provence, salt, and pepper in a jar with a tight-fitting lid, and shake well. Add olive oil, and shake well again. Set aside.

3. Brush dressing on zucchini, eggplant, yellow squash, and bell pepper.

4. Prick sausages with a fork, and grill, turning them gently with tongs, for 10 to 15 minutes, depending on diameter, or until cooked to an internal temperature of 165°F. Allow sausages to rest for 5 minutes, and then cut into ½-inch thick slices. Grill vegetables for 2 to 3 minutes per side, uncovered, or until vegetables are crisp-tender. Remove vegetables from the grill, and cut into bite-sized pieces.

6. To serve, combine frisée, onion, and cherry tomatoes in a mixing bowl, and toss with enough dressing to coat lightly. Mound mixture onto a serving platter or individual plates, and top with sausage and vegetable slices. Serve immediately, passing extra dressing separately.

Note: The dressing can be made up to a day in advance and refrigerated, tightly covered. Bring to room temperature before using.

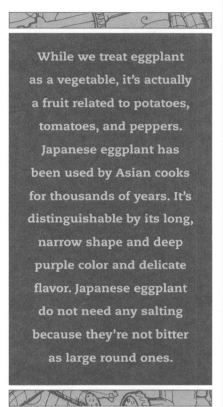

While we treat eggplant as a vegetable, it's actually a fruit related to potatoes, tomatoes, and peppers. Japanese eggplant has been used by Asian cooks for thousands of years. It's distinguishable by its long, narrow shape and deep purple color and delicate flavor. Japanese eggplant do not need any salting because they're not bitter as large round ones.

Middle Eastern Sausage Salad

Makes 4 to 6 servings

Active time: 25 minutes

Start to finish: 1¼ hours

VARIATION

Substitute brown rice for bulgur. Cook rice over low heat, covered, for 30 to 40 minutes, or until tender. Drain.

This salad is a one-dish meal with nutty bulgur and vegetables that serves as a base for nuggets of sausage.

1 cup bulgur

2 cups boiling water

1 (15-ounce) can garbanzo beans, drained and rinsed

2 large tomatoes, cored, seeded, and diced

1 cup chopped fresh parsley

1 bunch scallions, white parts and 2 inches of green tops, sliced

½ cup freshly squeezed lemon juice

¼ cup chopped fresh mint

¼ cup olive oil

Salt and freshly ground black pepper to taste

1¼ pounds Loukanika (page 138) links, Fresh Mexican Chorizo (page 66) links, or purchased Italian sausage links

½ head romaine lettuce, rinsed and dried

1. Place bulgur in a large mixing bowl. Stir in boiling water, cover the bowl, and allow bulgur to stand for 1 hour. Drain any remaining liquid from bulgur. Add beans, tomatoes, parsley, scallions, lemon juice, mint, olive oil, salt, and pepper to bulgur, and mix well. Refrigerate salad, tightly covered.

2. Prepare a medium-hot charcoal or gas grill.

3. Prick sausages with a fork, and grill, turning them gently with tongs, for 10 to 15 minutes, depending on diameter, or until cooked to an internal temperature of 160°F. Cut sausage into ½-inch slices.

4. To serve, line a platter or individual plates with lettuce leaves, and mound bulgur salad on top of lettuce. Top salad with sausage slices, and serve immediately.

Note: The bulgur salad can be made up to a day in advance and refrigerated, tightly covered.

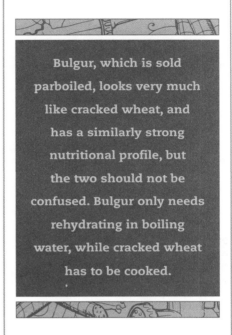

Bulgur, which is sold parboiled, looks very much like cracked wheat, and has a similarly strong nutritional profile, but the two should not be confused. Bulgur only needs rehydrating in boiling water, while cracked wheat has to be cooked.

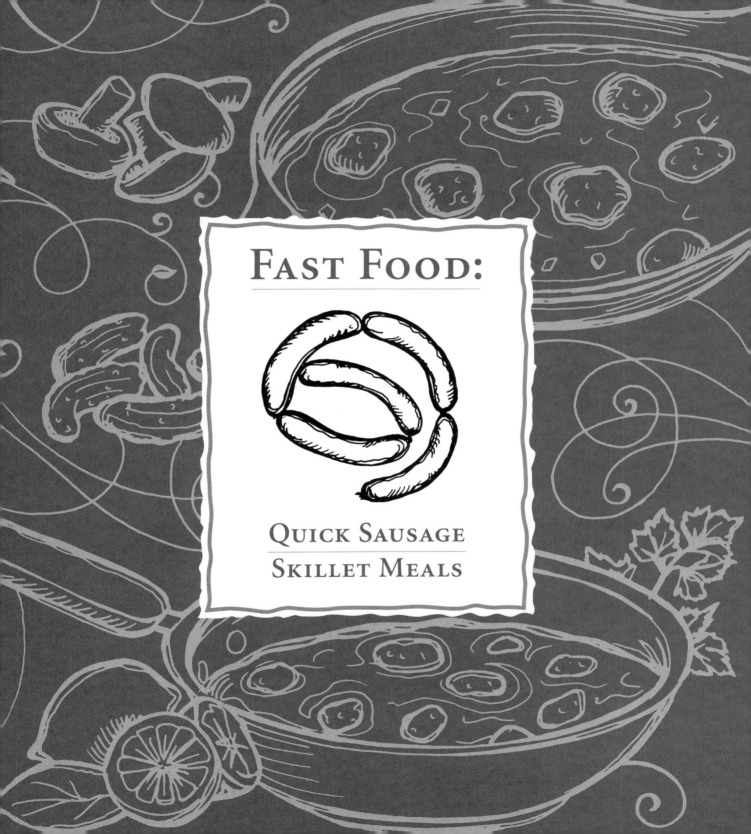

FAST FOOD:

QUICK SAUSAGE

SKILLET MEALS

Sausages cook quickly, especially when compared to the foods from which they're made. For example, a sausage made from beef chuck is cooked in less than 30 minutes while a stew made from the same meat takes almost 3 hours to cook to tenderness.

All of the dishes in this chapter can be on the table in less than 1 hour. And what comes to the table are moist, tender sausages cooked in a sauce specifically created for each recipe. While any sausage with Mediterranean flavors can be simmered in a tomato sauce with good results, a one-of-a-kind sausage-and-sauce pairing is better.

These hearty dishes are not one-dish meals like stews, because most vegetables usually found in stews—such as carrots and potatoes—take far longer to cook than these sausages.

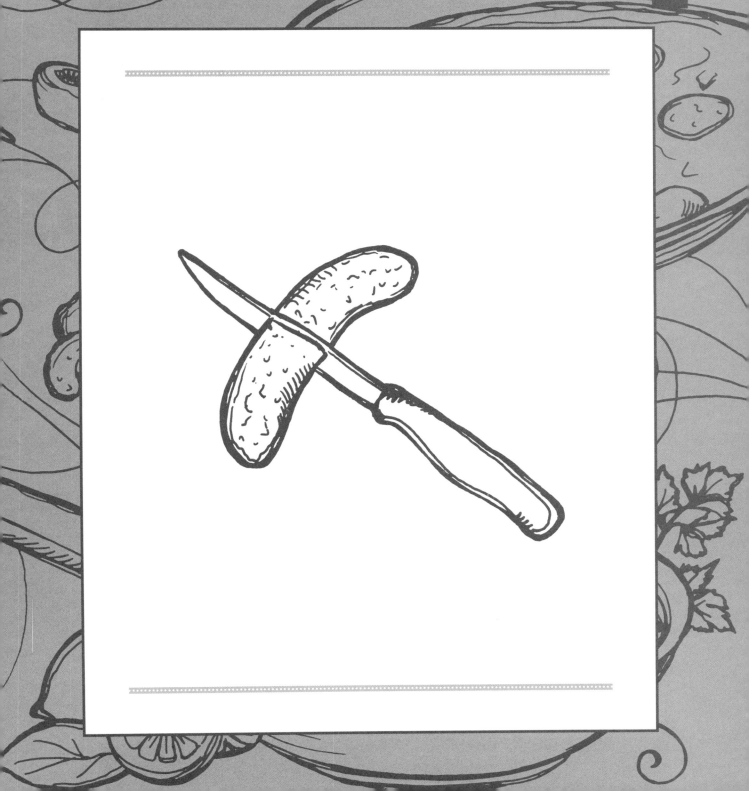

Seafood Sausage in Creole Sauce

Makes 4 to 6 servings

Active time: 20 minutes

Start to finish: 40 minutes

VARIATION

Add 1 or 2 chipotle chiles in adobo sauce, finely chopped, for a spicy dish.

A crowd-pleasing dish that can be served on a buffet table at a party, this is always a hit. It's easy to make and perfect served over a scoop of boiled white rice.

2 tablespoons olive oil

1 large onion, diced

3 garlic cloves, minced

1 celery rib, diced

½ red bell pepper, seeds and ribs removed, and diced

1 (28-ounce) can diced tomatoes, undrained

¾ cup bottled clam juice

2 tablespoons tomato paste

2 tablespoons chopped fresh parsley

1 tablespoon fresh thyme or 1 teaspoon dried

1 tablespoon chopped fresh oregano or 1 teaspoon dried

1 bay leaf

1½ pounds cooked Scallop Sausage Provençal (page 188), Shrimp and Leek Sausage (page 182), or purchased cooked seafood or fish sausage, cut into 1-inch slices

Salt and freshly ground black pepper to taste

1. Heat oil in large covered skillet over medium-high heat. Add onion, garlic, celery, and red bell pepper. Cook, stirring frequently, for 3 minutes, or until onion is translucent.

2. Add tomatoes, clam juice, tomato paste, thyme, oregano, and bay leaf to the skillet, and bring to a boil over medium-high heat, stirring occasionally. Simmer sauce, uncovered, for 15 minutes.

3. Add sausage slices to the skillet, and cook over low heat, covered, for 2 to 3 minutes, or until sausage is heated through. Remove and discard bay leaf, season to taste with salt and pepper, and serve immediately.

Note: The sauce can be made up to 3 days in advance and refrigerated, tightly covered. The dish can be made up to a day in advance and refrigerated, tightly covered. Reheat it over low heat or in a 350°F oven for 30 minutes, or until hot.

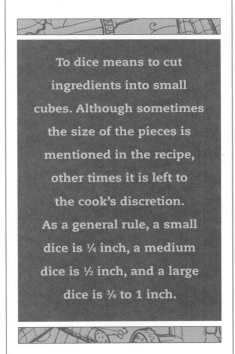

To dice means to cut ingredients into small cubes. Although sometimes the size of the pieces is mentioned in the recipe, other times it is left to the cook's discretion. As a general rule, a small dice is ¼ inch, a medium dice is ½ inch, and a large dice is ¾ to 1 inch.

Sausages in Bourbon Barbecue Sauce

Makes 4 to 6 servings

Active time:
15 minutes

Start to finish:
45 minutes

VARIATIONS

Add 1 or 2 jalapeño or serrano chiles to the skillet with onion and garlic for a spicy dish.

Substitute rum for bourbon.

In addition to creating a family-pleasing meal, you can also serve this dish as a snack at parties by cutting the links into one-inch sections after it's prepared. The sausage is simmered in a light barbecue sauce laced with bourbon.

1½ pounds Turkey, Apple, and Sage Sausage (page 150) links, American Breakfast Sausage (page 46) links, or purchased sausage

2 tablespoons vegetable oil

1 small onion, diced

2 garlic cloves, minced

1 cup Gingered Barbecue Sauce (page 481) or purchased barbecue sauce

¾ cup Chicken Stock (page 296) or purchased low-sodium stock

⅓ cup bourbon

¼ cup firmly packed light brown sugar

2 tablespoons whole grain Dijon mustard

2 teaspoons cornstarch

Salt and freshly ground black pepper to taste

1. Separate sausage into links, if necessary, and prick sausages with the tip of paring knife or the tines of a sharp meat fork.

2. Heat oil in the skillet over medium-high heat. Brown sausages on all sides, turning them gently with tongs. Remove sausages from the skillet, and set aside.

3. Add onion and garlic to the skillet, and cook, stirring frequently, for 3 minutes, or until onion is translucent. Add barbecue sauce, stock, bourbon, brown sugar, and mustard to the skillet. Bring to a boil over medium-high heat, stirring occasionally. Simmer sauce over low heat, uncovered, for 10 minutes.

4. Return sausages to the skillet, bring to a boil, and simmer sausages, covered, over low heat, turning occasionally with a slotted spoon, for 20 to 25 minutes, or until sausages are very tender. Season to taste with salt and pepper, and serve immediately.

Note: The dish can be made up to 2 days in advance and refrigerated, tightly covered. Reheat it over low heat or in a 350°F oven for 30 minutes, or until hot.

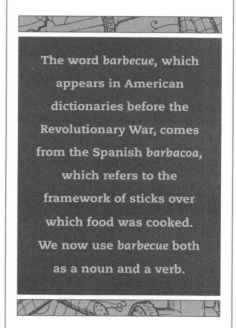

The word *barbecue*, which appears in American dictionaries before the Revolutionary War, comes from the Spanish *barbacoa*, which refers to the framework of sticks over which food was cooked. We now use *barbecue* both as a noun and a verb.

Chorizo in Chipotle-Beer Sauce

Makes 4 to 6 servings

Active time: 20 minutes

Start to finish: 40 minutes

VARIATIONS

Add 1 large sweet potato, peeled and cut into ¾-inch cubes, to the pan.

Add 1 (15-ounce) can kidney beans, drained and rinsed, to the pan.

Sausages and beer is as much a universal pairing as sausages and mustard. Flavorful chorizo is enhanced with chipotle chiles in a spicy sauce. Serve this over rice with some pico de gallo on the side.

1½ pounds Fresh Mexican Chorizo (page 66) links, Chaurice (page 64) links, or purchased chorizo
2 tablespoons olive oil
1 large onion, diced
3 garlic cloves, minced
2 tablespoons chili powder
2 teaspoons ground cumin
1 teaspoon dried oregano
1 (12-ounce) can or bottle beer
¼ cup Chicken Stock (page 296) or purchased low-sodium stock
2 chipotle chiles in adobo sauce, finely chopped
2 tablespoons adobo sauce
3 tablespoons chopped fresh cilantro
Salt and freshly ground black pepper to taste

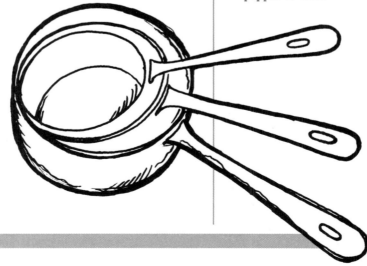

1. Separate sausage into links, if necessary, and prick sausages with the tip of paring knife or the tines of a sharp meat fork.

2. Heat oil in a large skillet over medium-high heat. Brown sausages on all sides, turning them gently with tongs. Set aside.

3. Add onion and garlic to the pan, and cook, stirring frequently, for 3 minutes, or until onion is translucent. Add chili powder, cumin, and oregano, and cook for 1 minute, stirring constantly. Add beer, stock, chiles, and adobo sauce, and stir well. Bring to a boil and simmer sauce, uncovered, for 10 minutes.

4. Return sausages to the pan, and cover the pan, and simmer for 20 to 25 minutes, or until sausages are very tender. Stir in cilantro, and season to taste with salt and pepper, and serve immediately.

Note: The dish can be made up to 2 days in advance and refrigerated, tightly covered. Reheat it over low heat or in a 350°F oven for 30 minutes, or until hot.

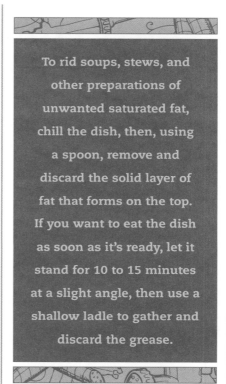

To rid soups, stews, and other preparations of unwanted saturated fat, chill the dish, then, using a spoon, remove and discard the solid layer of fat that forms on the top. If you want to eat the dish as soon as it's ready, let it stand for 10 to 15 minutes at a slight angle, then use a shallow ladle to gather and discard the grease.

Sausage Siciliana

Like many Sicilian dishes, this one is made with a combination of dried currants, salty capers, and toasted pine nuts. Serve the sausage on top of pasta with a colorful tossed side salad.

Makes 4 to 6 servings

Active time:
25 minutes

Start to finish:
50 minutes

VARIATION

Substitute chopped dried apricots, dried cranberries, or raisins for dried currants.

½ cup pine nuts

1½ pounds Sweet Italian Sausage (page 52) links, Luganega (page 58) links, or purchased sausage

3 tablespoons olive oil

1 medium onion, diced

2 garlic cloves, minced

1 small carrot, chopped

1 celery rib, chopped

1 (28-ounce) can crushed tomatoes in tomato puree

½ cup dry red wine

¼ cup dried currants

¼ cup chopped fresh parsley

2 tablespoon nonpareil capers, drained and rinsed

1 teaspoon dried thyme

Salt and freshly ground black pepper to taste

1. Place pine nuts in a dry large skillet, and toast over medium heat for 2 to 3 minutes, stirring frequently, or until browned. Remove nuts from the skillet, and set aside. Separate sausage into links, if necessary, and prick sausages with the tip of paring knife or the tines of a sharp meat fork.

2. Heat oil in the skillet over medium-high heat. Brown sausages on all sides, turning them gently with tongs. Remove sausages from the skillet, and set aside.

3. Add onion, garlic, carrot, and celery to the skillet. Cook, stirring frequently, for 3 minutes, or until onion is translucent. Add tomatoes, wine, currants, parsley, capers, and thyme to the skillet, and bring to a boil over medium-high heat. Reduce the heat to low, and simmer sauce, uncovered, stirring occasionally for 15 minutes.

4. Return sausages to the skillet, bring to a boil, and simmer sausages, covered, over low heat, turning occasionally with a slotted spoon, for 20 to 25 minutes, or until sausages are very tender. Season to taste with salt and pepper, and serve immediately.

Note: The dish can be made up to 2 days in advance and refrigerated, tightly covered. Reheat it over low heat or in a 350°F oven for 30 minutes, or until hot.

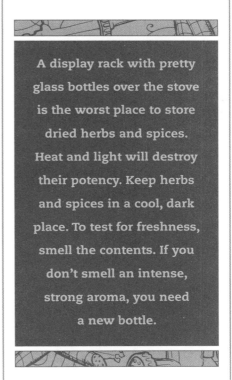

A display rack with pretty glass bottles over the stove is the worst place to store dried herbs and spices. Heat and light will destroy their potency. Keep herbs and spices in a cool, dark place. To test for freshness, smell the contents. If you don't smell an intense, strong aroma, you need a new bottle.

Italian Sausage Cacciatore

Makes 4 to 6 servings

Active time: 20 minutes

Start to finish: 50 minutes

VARIATIONS

Substitute chopped Genoa salami for prosciutto.

Substitute diced Portobello mushrooms for white mushrooms.

Wild mushrooms add a deep, woodsy flavor to the tomato sauce in which these sausages are cooked. Serve atop fusilli or rigatoni so the sauce gets into every nook and cranny of the pasta. A tossed salad completes the meal.

¾ cup Chicken Stock (page 296) or purchased low-sodium stock

½ cup dried porcini

1½ pounds Sweet Italian Sausage (page 52) links, Italian Chicken and Olive Sausage (page 158) links, or purchased sausage

¼ cup olive oil

2 ounces prosciutto, finely chopped

1 large onion, chopped

4 garlic cloves, minced

½ pound mushrooms, wiped with a damp paper towel, trimmed, and sliced

1 (28-ounce) can diced tomatoes, drained

3 tablespoons chopped fresh parsley

1 teaspoon Italian seasoning

1 bay leaf

Salt and freshly ground black pepper to taste

1. Place stock in a small saucepan, and bring to a boil over high heat. Add dried mushrooms, pushing them into stock with the back of a spoon. Soak for 15 minutes, then drain, reserving soaking liquid. Discard stems and finely chop mushrooms, and strain liquid through a sieve lined with a paper coffee filter or a paper towel. Reserve mushrooms and liquid.

2. Separate sausage into links, if necessary, and prick sausages with the tip of paring knife or the tines of a sharp meat fork.

3. Heat oil in a large skillet over medium-high heat. Brown sausages on all sides, turning them gently with tongs. Remove sausages from the skillet, and set aside. Add prosciutto, onion, and garlic to the pan, and cook, stirring frequently, for 3 minutes, or until onion is translucent. Add fresh mushrooms, and cook for 2 minutes, stirring frequently.

4. Add chopped porcini, stock, tomatoes, parsley, Italian seasoning, and bay leaf. Bring to a boil, and cook over low heat, uncovered, for 10 minutes. Return sausages to the pan, and cook over low heat, covered, for 20 to 25 minutes, or until sausages are very tender. Remove and discard bay leaf, season to taste with salt and pepper, and serve immediately.

Note: The dish can be made up to 2 days in advance and refrigerated, tightly covered. Reheat it over low heat or in a 350°F oven for 30 minutes, or until hot.

Cacciatore is Italian for "hunter's style." Whether it's chicken, beef, or game cacciatore, it means that the dish is cooked with tomatoes and mushrooms.

Chicken Sausage Piccata

Makes 4 to 6 servings

Active time:
20 minutes

Start to finish:
50 minutes

VARIATION

Substitute freshly squeezed lime juice for lemon juice.

Boil up some rice or small pasta like orzo so you can savor every drop of this lemony, caper-dotted sauce. A light, dry white wine and a frisée salad are all that should be added.

1½ pounds Garlicky Chicken and Rosemary Sausage (page 164) links, Provençal Chicken Sausage (page 162) links, or purchased raw poultry sausage links

2 tablespoons olive oil

½ small onion, chopped

2 garlic cloves, minced

2 tablespoons unsalted butter

3 tablespoons all-purpose flour

1½ cups Chicken Stock (page 296) or purchased low-sodium stock

⅓ cup freshly squeezed lemon juice

¼ cup chopped fresh parsley

¼ cup small capers, drained and rinsed

Salt and freshly ground black pepper to taste

1. Separate sausage into links, if necessary, and prick sausages with the tip of paring knife or the tines of a sharp meat fork.

2. Heat oil in a skillet over medium-high heat. Brown sausages on all sides, turning them gently with tongs. Remove sausages from the skillet, and set aside. Add onion and garlic to the pan, and cook, stirring frequently, for 3 minutes, or until onion is translucent.

3. Add butter to the skillet over medium-high heat. Reduce the heat to low, stir in flour and cook for 2 minutes, stirring constantly. Whisk in stock, and lemon juice, and bring to a boil over medium-high heat, whisking constantly. Stir in parsley and capers, and simmer 3 minutes, uncovered.

4. Return sausages to the skillet, bring to a boil, and simmer sausages, covered, over low heat, turning occasionally with a slotted spoon, for 20 to 25 minutes, or until sausages are very tender. Season to taste with salt and pepper, and serve immediately.

Note: The dish can be made up to 2 days in advance and refrigerated, tightly covered. Reheat it over low heat or in a 350°F oven for 30 minutes, or until hot.

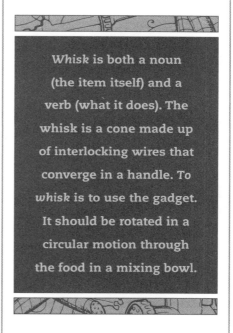

Whisk is both a noun (the item itself) and a verb (what it does). The whisk is a cone made up of interlocking wires that converge in a handle. *To whisk* is to use the gadget. It should be rotated in a circular motion through the food in a mixing bowl.

Chicken Sausage Tettrazini

Makes 4 to 6 servings

Active time: 20 minutes

Start to finish: 50 minutes

Mushrooms and turkey in a cream sauce laced with sherry and Parmesan over orzo can be doubled or tripled for buffet-style entertaining.

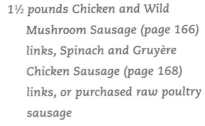

1½ pounds Chicken and Wild Mushroom Sausage (page 166) links, Spinach and Gruyère Chicken Sausage (page 168) links, or purchased raw poultry sausage

2 tablespoons olive oil

3 tablespoons unsalted butter

2 shallots, chopped

½ pound mushrooms, wiped with a damp paper towel, trimmed, and sliced

3 tablespoons all-purpose flour

½ cup medium dry sherry

1 cup half-and-half

1 cup Chicken Stock (page 296) or purchased low-sodium stock

¼ teaspoon freshly grated nutmeg

¾ cup freshly grated Parmesan

Salt and freshly ground black pepper to taste

VARIATION

Soak ½ cup dried porcini mushrooms in ½ cup boiling water for 10 minutes. Drain mushrooms, reserving soaking liquid. Chop mushrooms, and strain liquid through a paper coffee filter or paper towel. Add mushrooms to sauce, and use soaking liquid in place of ½ cup stock.

1. Separate sausage into links, if necessary, and prick sausages with the tip of paring knife or the tines of a sharp meat fork.

2. Heat oil in a skillet over medium-high heat. Brown sausages on all sides, turning them gently with tongs. Remove sausages from the skillet, and set aside. Add onion and garlic to the pan, and cook, stirring frequently, for 3 minutes, or until onion is translucent.

3. Add butter in the skillet over medium-high heat. Add shallots and mushrooms, and cook for 3 minutes, or until mushrooms begin to soften. Reduce the heat to low, stir in flour and cook for 2 minutes, stirring constantly. Whisk in sherry, and bring to a boil over medium-high heat, whisking constantly. Simmer 2 minutes, then add half-and-half, stock, nutmeg, and Parmesan, and simmer 3 minutes.

4. Return sausages to the skillet, bring to a boil, and simmer sausages, covered, over low heat, turning occasionally with a slotted spoon, for 20 to 25 minutes, or until sausages are very tender. Season to taste with salt and pepper, and serve immediately.

Note: The dish can be made up to 2 days in advance and refrigerated, tightly covered. Reheat it over low heat or in a 350°F oven for 30 minutes, or until hot.

Chicken Tetrazinni was named for Italian singer Luisa Tetrazzini, who was the toast of the American opera circuit in the early 1900s. Where the dish was created and by whom isn't known, but the diva said she was served it all across America.

Sausage Coq au Vin

Makes 4 to 6 servings

Active time: 20 minutes

Start to finish: 50 minutes

VARIATIONS

Cut red-skinned potatoes into ¾-inch cubes, and simmer them along with sausages.

Substitute white wine for red wine.

Chicken and red wine is a welcome change from the traditional white wine on a chilly night. Serve the sausages over buttered egg noodles or mashed potatoes with a good red wine.

1½ *pounds Garlicky Chicken and Rosemary Sausage (page 164) links, Provençal Chicken Sausage (page 162) links, or purchased raw poultry sausage*

2 *tablespoons olive oil*

3 *tablespoons unsalted butter*

1 *medium onion, chopped*

2 *garlic cloves, diced*

¼ *pound mushrooms, wiped with a damp paper towel, trimmed, and sliced*

3 *tablespoons all-purpose flour*

1¼ *cups dry red wine*

1 *cup Chicken Stock (page 296) or purchased low-sodium stock*

3 *tablespoons tomato paste*

3 *tablespoons chopped fresh parsley*

1 *tablespoon herbes de Provence*

1 *bay leaf*

Salt *and freshly ground black pepper to taste*

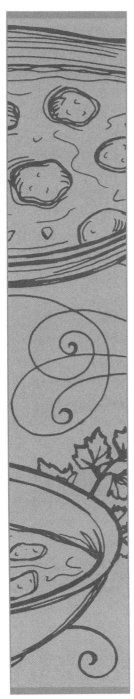

1. Separate sausage into links, if necessary, and prick sausages with the tip of paring knife or the tines of a sharp meat fork.

2. Heat oil in a large skillet over medium-high heat. Brown sausages on all sides, turning them gently with tongs. Remove sausages from the skillet, and set aside.

3. Add butter to the skillet, and then add onion, garlic, and mushrooms. Cook, stirring frequently, over medium-high heat for 3 minutes, or until onion is translucent. Reduce the heat to low, stir in flour and cook for 2 minutes, stirring constantly. Whisk in wine, and bring to a boil over medium-high heat, whisking constantly. Add stock, tomato paste, parsley, herbes de Provence, and bay leaf, and bring to a boil over medium heat, stirring frequently. Reduce the heat to low, and simmer sauce, uncovered, for 5 minutes.

4. Return sausages to the skillet, bring to a boil, and simmer sausages, covered, over low heat, turning occasionally with a slotted spoon, for 20 to 25 minutes, or until sausages are very tender. Remove and discard bay leaf, season to taste with salt and pepper, and serve immediately.

Note: The dish can be made up to 2 days in advance and refrigerated, tightly covered. Reheat it over low heat or in a 350°F oven for 30 minutes, or until hot.

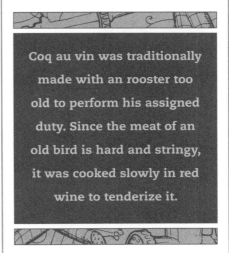

Coq au vin was traditionally made with an rooster too old to perform his assigned duty. Since the meat of an old bird is hard and stringy, it was cooked slowly in red wine to tenderize it.

Sausage with White Wine Mustard Sauce

Makes 4 to 6 servings

Active time: 20 minutes

Start to finish: 35 minutes

VARIATION

Substitute red wine for white wine and Beef Stock (page 299) for chicken stock.

Based on a classic dish *côtes de porc vigneronnes* from Burgundy, white wine, mustard, and sharp pickles create a light sauce. Since the sausages are fully cooked, this can be on the table in minutes.

1½ pounds French Garlic Sausage (page 72), Bockwurst (page 122), or purchased cooked sausage

2 tablespoons olive oil

3 tablespoons unsalted butter

1 large shallot, diced

2 garlic cloves, minced

3 tablespoons all-purpose flour

½ cup dry white wine

½ cup Chicken Stock (page 296) or purchased low-sodium stock

3 tablespoons chopped fresh parsley

3 tablespoons chopped cornichons, or other sweet pickle

2 tablespoons Dijon mustard

½ teaspoon dried thyme

Pinch freshly grated nutmeg

Salt and freshly ground black pepper to taste

1. Separate sausage into links, if necessary, and prick sausages with the tip of paring knife or the tines of a sharp meat fork.

2. Heat oil in a Dutch oven over medium-high heat. Brown sausages on all sides, turning them gently with tongs. Remove sausages from the skillet, and pour grease out of the skillet.

3. Add butter to the pan. When butter melts, add shallot and garlic, and cook, stirring frequently, for 3 minutes, or until onion is translucent. Stir in flour, reduce the heat to low, and cook for 2 minutes, stirring constantly. Whisk in wine and stock, and bring to a boil over medium-high heat. Add parsley, cornichons, mustard, thyme, and nutmeg to the skillet, and simmer for 5 minutes.

4. Return sausages to the skillet and bring to a boil. Reduce the heat to low, and simmer sausages, covered, for 15 minutes. Season sauce with salt and pepper, and serve immediately.

Note: The dish can be made up to 2 days in advance and refrigerated, tightly covered. Reheat it over low heat or in a 350°F oven for 30 minutes, or until hot.

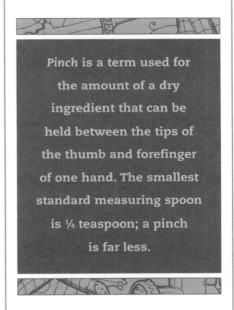

Pinch is a term used for the amount of a dry ingredient that can be held between the tips of the thumb and forefinger of one hand. The smallest standard measuring spoon is ¼ teaspoon; a pinch is far less.

Sausage Stroganoff

Makes 4 to 6 servings

Active time: 20 minutes

Start to finish: 50 minutes

VARIATION

Substitute Chicken and Wild Mushroom Sausage (page 166) or purchased raw poultry sausage for Fresh Kielbasa and substitute Chicken Stock (page 296) for beef stock.

Mushrooms and a rich tomato sauce finished with sour cream are the defining ingredients of a stroganoff sauce. You'll find that sausages benefit from being simmered in this sauce. Serve over buttered egg noodles with some steamed broccoli or green beans.

1½ pounds Fresh Kielbasa (page 70) links, or purchased mildly-spiced sausage

2 tablespoons olive oil

2 tablespoons unsalted butter

2 large onions, peeled and diced

2 garlic cloves, peeled and minced

½ pound mushrooms, wiped with a damp paper towel, trimmed, and sliced

2 tablespoons paprika

¼ cup all-purpose flour

1½ cups Beef Stock (page 299) or purchased low-sodium stock

3 tablespoons tomato paste

2 tablespoons chopped fresh parsley

1 tablespoon Dijon mustard

½ cup sour cream

Salt and freshly ground black pepper to taste

1. Separate sausage into links, if necessary, and prick sausages with the tip of paring knife or the tines of a sharp meat fork.

2. Heat oil in a large skillet over medium-high heat. Brown sausages on all sides, turning them gently with tongs. Remove sausages from the skillet, and set aside.

3. Add butter to the skillet. When butter melts, add onion and garlic, and cook, stirring frequently, for 3 minutes, or until onion is translucent. Add mushrooms, and cook for 2 minutes more. Add paprika to the pan, and cook for 1 minute, stirring constantly. Reduce the heat to low, and add flour. Cook for 2 minutes, stirring constantly.

4. Add stock, tomato paste, parsley, and mustard to the pan. Bring to a boil on top of the stove, stirring occasionally. Simmer sauce, uncovered for 5 minutes. Return sausages to the skillet, bring to a boil, and simmer sausages, covered, over low heat, turning occasionally with a slotted spoon, for 20 to 25 minutes, or until sausages are very tender.

5. Stir in sour cream, and season to taste with salt and pepper. Do not allow dish to boil. Season to taste with salt and pepper, and serve immediately.

Note: The dish can be made up to 2 days in advance and refrigerated, tightly covered. Reheat it over low heat or in a 350°F oven for 30 minutes, or until hot.

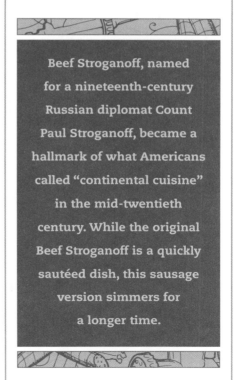

Beef Stroganoff, named for a nineteenth-century Russian diplomat Count Paul Stroganoff, became a hallmark of what Americans called "continental cuisine" in the mid-twentieth century. While the original Beef Stroganoff is a quickly sautéed dish, this sausage version simmers for a longer time.

Asian Sausage in Macadamia Coconut Sauce

Makes 4 to 6 servings

Active time: 25 minutes

Start to finish: 55 minutes

VARIATION

Add 1 tablespoon Chinese chile paste with garlic to sauce for a spicy dish.

This recipe is a variation on a number of dishes I enjoyed in Hawaii. The buttery richness of macadamia nuts with coconut milk and Asian seasonings make this a decadent treat.

1½ pounds Asian Duck and Shiitake Mushroom Sausage (page 176) links, Thai-Style Pork Sausage (page 76) links, or purchased raw Asian-flavored sausage

2 tablespoons vegetable oil

2 tablespoons Asian sesame oil

4 scallions, white parts and 3 inches of green tops, chopped

3 garlic cloves, minced

3 tablespoons grated fresh ginger

⅓ pound fresh shiitake mushrooms, stemmed and sliced

1 (14-ounce) can coconut milk

1 cup chopped salted macadamia nuts

2 tablespoons fish sauce (nam pla)

2 teaspoons cornstarch

¼ cup chopped fresh cilantro

Salt and freshly ground black pepper to taste

1. Separate sausage into links, if necessary, and prick sausages with the tip of paring knife or the tines of a sharp meat fork.

2. Heat vegetable oil and sesame oil in a large skillet over medium-high heat. Brown sausages on all sides, turning them gently with tongs. Remove sausages from the skillet, and set aside.

3. Add scallions, garlic, ginger, and mushrooms to the skillet, and cook, stirring frequently, for 3 minutes, or until scallions are translucent. Add coconut milk, macadamia nuts, and fish sauce, and bring to a boil over medium heat, stirring frequently. Reduce the heat to low, and simmer sauce, uncovered, for 5 minutes.

4. Return sausages to the skillet, bring to a boil, and simmer sausages, covered, over low heat, turning occasionally with a slotted spoon, for 20 to 25 minutes, or until sausages are very tender. Combine cornstarch and 1 tablespoon cold water in a small cup, and stir well. Add mixture to the skillet, and simmer for 2 minutes, or until slightly thickened. Stir in cilantro, season to taste with salt and pepper, and serve immediately.

Note: The dish can be made up to 2 days in advance and refrigerated, tightly covered. Reheat it over low heat or in a 350°F oven for 30 minutes, or until hot.

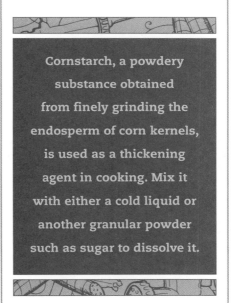

Cornstarch, a powdery substance obtained from finely grinding the endosperm of corn kernels, is used as a thickening agent in cooking. Mix it with either a cold liquid or another granular powder such as sugar to dissolve it.

Getting Saucy:

Sauces for Dipping and Topping Sausages

King Henry V of England is credited with saying "a war without arson is like sausage without mustard." While the monarch was correct—mustard is traditionally a great choice—there's no reason to limit sausages to one kind of condiment.

This chapter begins with some mustard variations on a theme and includes mayonnaise-based and tomato sauces as well.

Green Mustard Sauce

Makes 2 cups

Active time:
15 minutes

Start to finish:
15 minutes

VARIATIONS

Substitute arugula for watercress.

Substitute sour cream or plain nonfat yogurt for crème fraîche.

Add 1 to 2 tablespoons chopped fresh tarragon to sauce.

Bitter watercress and parsley add color as well as flavor to this creamy mustard sauce. Serve it with any delicate European sausage, such as Boudin Blanc (page 118) or Spinach and Gruyère Chicken Sausage (page 168).

2 tablespoons unsalted butter
1 large shallot, chopped
2 garlic cloves, minced
¼ cup dry white wine
1 cup crème fraîche
½ cup Dijon mustard
½ cup finely chopped fresh watercress leaves
¼ cup finely chopped fresh parsley
Salt and freshly ground black pepper to taste

1. Heat butter in a small skillet over medium heat. Add shallot and garlic, and cook, stirring frequently, for 5 to 7 minutes, or until vegetables soften. Add wine, and cook for 3 minutes, or until wine is almost evaporated.

2. Scrape mixture into a mixing bowl, and add crème fraîche, mustard, watercress, and parsley. Whisk well, and season to taste with salt and pepper. Serve at room temperature, refrigerating any leftover sauce.

Note: The sauce can be made up to 3 days in advance and refrigerated, tightly covered. Bring it to room temperature before serving.

Sweet and Hot Mustard Sauce

Makes 1 cup

Active time:
10 minutes

Start to finish:
10 minutes

Add 2 to 3 tablespoons ketchup.

Substitute 1 chipotle chile in adobo sauce, finely chopped, for hot red pepper sauce.

The combination of brown sugar, vinegar, and hot sauce creates a sauce that is perfect with all American sausages and sausages made with fruits, such as Thanksgiving Turkey Sausage (page 152) and Breakfast Sausage with Dried Fruit (page 50).

¼ cup firmly packed dark brown sugar

2 tablespoons cider vinegar

½ cup Dijon mustard

¼ cup grainy mustard

¼ to ½ teaspoon hot red pepper sauce

Salt and freshly ground black pepper to taste

Combine brown sugar, vinegar, Dijon mustard, grainy mustard, and hot red pepper sauce in a mixing bowl. Whisk well, and season to taste with salt and pepper. Refrigerate until ready to use.

Note: The sauce can be made up to 3 days in advance and refrigerated, tightly covered.

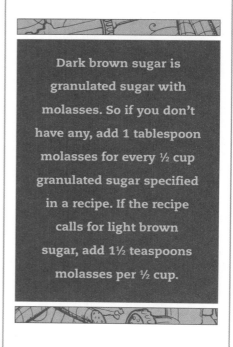

Dark brown sugar is granulated sugar with molasses. So if you don't have any, add 1 tablespoon molasses for every ½ cup granulated sugar specified in a recipe. If the recipe calls for light brown sugar, add 1½ teaspoons molasses per ½ cup.

Dilled Mustard Sauce

Makes 1½ cups

Active time:
10 minutes

Start to finish:
10 minutes

VARIATIONS

Substitute chopped watercress for dill.

Substitute smooth mustard for grainy mustard.

Aromatic fresh dill is frequently paired with sharp mustard, and this sauce goes nicely with many sausages such as Bockwurst (page 122) and Dilled Salmon Sausage (page 194).

½ cup whole grain mustard
½ cup heavy cream
2 tablespoons olive oil
1 tablespoon sugar
½ cup chopped fresh dill
Salt and freshly ground black
    pepper to taste

Combine mustard, cream, ¼ cup water, oil, and sugar in a mixing bowl. Whisk well, add dill, and season to taste with salt and pepper. Whisk well again. Refrigerate until ready to use.

Note: The sauce can be made up to 3 days in advance and refrigerated, tightly covered.

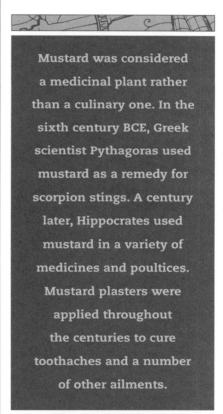

Mustard was considered a medicinal plant rather than a culinary one. In the sixth century BCE, Greek scientist Pythagoras used mustard as a remedy for scorpion stings. A century later, Hippocrates used mustard in a variety of medicines and poultices. Mustard plasters were applied throughout the centuries to cure toothaches and a number of other ailments.

Mustard Horseradish Sauce

Makes 1¼ cups

Active time:
10 minutes

Start to finish:
10 minutes

Add 2 tablespoons chopped fresh tarragon, oregano, or basil to sauce.

Substitute plain nonfat yogurt for the sour cream.

A hearty sauce to serve with full-flavored sausages such as Smoky Mettwurst (page 128) or Swedish Beef and Potato Sausage (page 84).

⅔ cup sour cream
¼ cup Dijon mustard
2 tablespoons prepared white
    horseradish
2 tablespoons olive oil
1 tablespoon sugar
Salt and freshly ground black
    pepper to taste

Combine sour cream, mustard, horseradish, oil, and sugar in a mixing bowl. Whisk well, and season to taste with salt and pepper. Refrigerate until ready to use.

Note: The sauce can be made up to 3 days in advance and refrigerated, tightly covered.

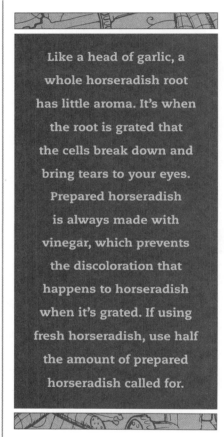

Like a head of garlic, a whole horseradish root has little aroma. It's when the root is grated that the cells break down and bring tears to your eyes. Prepared horseradish is always made with vinegar, which prevents the discoloration that happens to horseradish when it's grated. If using fresh horseradish, use half the amount of prepared horseradish called for.

Irish Mustard Sauce

Makes 1½ cups

Active time:
10 minutes

Start to finish:
10 minutes

VARIATIONS

Add 2 tablespoons finely chopped shallot to sauce.

Substitute Irish whisky for 2 tablespoons Guinness stout.

Stout is a dark, often bitter beer, originally produced by Guiness in Ireland, but now made by breweries all over the world. It adds distinctive character to this sauce. Serve with hot European sausages such as British Bangers (page 48) or German-Style Beef Sausage (page 90).

1 cup grainy mustard
¼ cup Dijon mustard
¼ cup stout or dark ale
2 tablespoons firmly packed dark
     brown sugar
¼ teaspoon freshly grated nutmeg
Salt and freshly ground black
     pepper to taste

Combine grainy mustard, Dijon mustard, beer, brown sugar, and nutmeg in a mixing bowl. Whisk well, and season to taste with salt and pepper. Refrigerate until ready to use.

Note: The sauce can be made up to 3 days in advance and refrigerated, tightly covered.

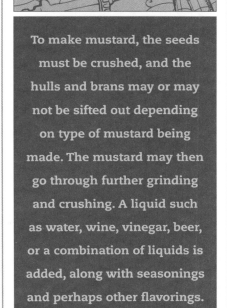

To make mustard, the seeds must be crushed, and the hulls and brans may or may not be sifted out depending on type of mustard being made. The mustard may then go through further grinding and crushing. A liquid such as water, wine, vinegar, beer, or a combination of liquids is added, along with seasonings and perhaps other flavorings.

Orange Mustard Sauce

Makes 1¼ cups

Active time:
10 minutes

Start to finish:
10 minutes

Try this mustard sauce with Asian sausages, such as Sweet Chinese Sausage (page 74) and Curried Chicken Sausage with Dried Fruit (page 172).

½ cup Dijon mustard
⅓ cup orange marmalade
¼ cup finely chopped crystallized ginger
1 tablespoon rice wine vinegar
Salt and freshly ground black pepper to taste

Combine mustard, marmalade, ginger, and vinegar in a mixing bowl. Whisk well, and season to taste with salt and pepper. Refrigerate until ready to use.

Note: The sauce can be made up to 3 days in advance and refrigerated, tightly covered.

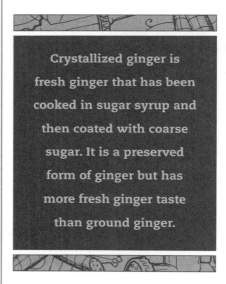

Crystallized ginger is fresh ginger that has been cooked in sugar syrup and then coated with coarse sugar. It is a preserved form of ginger but has more fresh ginger taste than ground ginger.

Asian Mustard Sauce

Makes 1½ cups

Active time:
10 minutes

Start to finish:
10 minutes

VARIATIONS

Add 1 to 2 tablespoons Chinese chile paste with garlic for a spicier sauce.

Substitute ketchup for hoisin sauce and add ½ teaspoon five-spice powder to the sauce.

Aromatic sesame oil and fresh cilantro perk up this mustard. Serve with any Asian-inspired sausage such as Sweet Chinese Sausage (page 74) or Thai-Style Pork Sausage (page 76).

¾ cup Dijon mustard
⅓ cup hoisin sauce
2 tablespoons Asian sesame oil
1 tablespoon soy sauce
½ cup finely chopped fresh cilantro
Freshly ground black pepper to taste

Combine mustard, hoisin sauce, sesame oil, and soy sauce in a mixing bowl. Whisk well, stir in cilantro, and season to taste with pepper. Refrigerate until ready to use.

Note: The sauce can be made up to 3 days in advance and refrigerated, tightly covered.

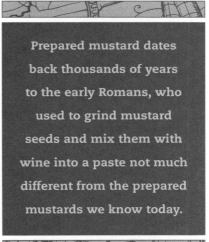

Prepared mustard dates back thousands of years to the early Romans, who used to grind mustard seeds and mix them with wine into a paste not much different from the prepared mustards we know today.

Herbed Marinara Sauce

Makes 2 cups

**Active time:
20 minutes**

**Start to finish:
1 hour**

VARIATIONS

Add basil, rosemary, or marjoram along with or instead of some of the herbs listed to vary the flavor.

Add crushed red pepper flakes to make the sauce spicier.

Use this basic tomato for simmering Mediterranean sausages—from Sweet Italian Sausage (page 52) to Veal Sausage with Prosciutto, Sage, and Cheese (page 104)—to accompany them.

¼ cup olive oil
1 medium onion, finely chopped
4 garlic cloves, minced
1 carrot, finely chopped
1 celery rib, finely chopped
1 (28-ounce) can crushed tomatoes, undrained
½ cup dry red wine
2 tablespoons chopped fresh parsley
2 tablespoons chopped fresh oregano or 2 teaspoons dried
1 tablespoon fresh thyme or 1 teaspoon dried
2 bay leaves
Salt and freshly ground black pepper to taste

1. Heat olive oil in 2-quart heavy saucepan over medium heat. Add onion and garlic and cook, stirring frequently, for 3 minutes, or until onion is translucent.

2. Add carrot, celery, tomatoes, wine, parsley, oregano, thyme, and bay leaves. Bring to a boil, reduce the heat to low, and simmer sauce, uncovered, stirring occasionally, for 40 minutes, or until lightly thickened. Season to taste with salt and pepper.

Note: The sauce can be refrigerated up to 4 days or frozen up to 3 months.

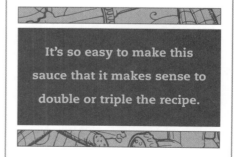

It's so easy to make this sauce that it makes sense to double or triple the recipe.

...n Tomato Sauce

A perfect accompaniment for sausages from Mexico, Latin America, and the Iberian Peninsula such as Fresh Mexican Chorizo (page 66) or Linguiça (page 68).

...ups

Active time:

15 minutes

Start to finish:

40 minutes

VARIATIONS

Substitute 2 finely chopped chipotle chiles in adobo sauce for mild green chiles for a spicier sauce.

Substitute red or white wine for stock.

3 tablespoons olive oil

1 small onion, finely chopped

3 garlic cloves, minced

3 tablespoons chili powder

1 tablespoon ground cumin

1 tablespoon dried oregano, preferably Mexican

¾ cup Chicken Stock (page 296) or purchased low-sodium stock

1 (15-ounce) can tomato sauce

1 (4-ounce) can chopped mild green chilies, drained

¼ cup chopped fresh cilantro

Salt and freshly ground black pepper to taste

1. Heat olive oil in a heavy saucepan over medium-high heat. Add onion and garlic and cook, stirring frequently, for 3 minutes, or until the onion is translucent. Reduce the heat to low, stir in the chili powder, cumin, and oregano, and cook, stirring constantly, for 1 minute.

2. Stir in stock, tomato sauce, and green chilies. Whisk well, bring to a boil, and simmer sauce, uncovered, for 15 minutes, stirring occasionally, or until the sauce is reduced by ¼.

3. Stir in cilantro, and season to taste with salt and pepper. Serve hot or at room temperature.

Note: The sauce can be refrigerated up to 4 days or frozen up to 3 months.

Sherried Tomato Sauce

Makes 2 cups

- - - - - - - - - - - - - - - - - - - -

Active time:

15 minutes

- - - - - - - - - - - - - - - - - - - -

Start to finish:

45 minutes

VARIATION

Substitute red wine for sherry.

With bits of ham as well as heady sherry, this sauce goes nicely with Mediterranean sausages like Loukanika (page 138) or Veal Sausage Marengo (page 106).

2 tablespoons olive oil

½ cup finely chopped smoked ham

1 medium onion, diced

½ green bell pepper, seeds and ribs removed, and diced

2 garlic cloves, minced

2 tablespoons chopped fresh parsley

1 tablespoon fresh thyme or 1 teaspoon dried

1 bay leaf

2 (14.5-ounce) cans diced tomatoes, undrained

2 tablespoons tomato paste

¼ cup dry sherry

Salt and freshly ground black pepper to taste

1. Heat oil in a saucepan over medium-high heat. Add ham, onion, green pepper, and garlic, and cook, stirring frequently, for 3 minutes or until onion is translucent. Add parsley, thyme, bay leaf, tomatoes, tomato paste, and sherry, and bring to a boil, stirring occasionally.

2. Reduce the heat to low and simmer sauce, uncovered, for 30 minutes, stirring occasionally. Remove and discard bay leaf, and season sauce to taste with salt and pepper. Serve hot.

Note: The sauce can be made up to 3 days in advance and refrigerated, tightly covered. Reheat it to a simmer over low heat, stirring occasionally.

Gingered Barbecue Sauce

Makes 2 cups

Active time:
10 minutes

Start to finish:
40 minutes

VARIATION

Substitute chili sauce for ketchup for chunky sauce.

Top American sausages cooked on the grill or in a skillet with this lemony-ginger barbecue sauce. It's great with American Breakfast Sausage (page 46) or Smoky Beef Summer Sausage (page 82).

1⅓ cups ketchup
½ cup cider vinegar
¼ cup firmly packed dark brown sugar
3 tablespoons Worcestershire sauce
3 tablespoons grated fresh ginger
2 tablespoons vegetable oil
1 tablespoon dry mustard powder
2 garlic cloves, minced
1 lemon, washed and thinly sliced
½ to 1 teaspoon hot red pepper
    sauce, or to taste

1. Combine ketchup, vinegar, brown sugar, Worcestershire sauce, ginger, vegetable oil, mustard, garlic, lemon, and red pepper sauce in a saucepan.

Bring to a boil over medium heat, stirring occasionally. Reduce the heat to low and simmer sauce, uncovered, for 30 minutes, or until thick, stirring occasionally.

2. Strain sauce, pressing with the back of a spoon to extract as much liquid as possible. Ladle sauce into containers. Refrigerate until ready to use.

Note: The sauce can be refrigerated up to 2 weeks or frozen up to 3 months.

Many producers apply a thin coating of wax on citrus fruits to keep them fresh. Instead of just rinsing the citrus fruits, I lightly scrub them with a mild soap and then rinse.

Southwestern Barbecue Sauce

Makes 3 cups

Active time:
15 minutes

Start to finish:
30 minutes

VARIATION

Substitute fresh jalapeño or serrano chiles for chipotle chiles.

This sauce gets some heat from chipotle chiles and some tang from lime juice. It's perfect with any Southwestern- or Mexican-inspired sausages like Fresh Mexican Chorizo (page 66).

2 tablespoons olive oil
1 large onion, chopped
2 garlic cloves, minced
2 canned chipotle chiles in adobo sauce, drained and finely chopped
2 cups crushed tomatoes in tomato puree
½ cup firmly packed dark brown sugar
¼ cup cider vinegar
3 tablespoons freshly squeezed lime juice
2 teaspoons dry mustard powder
Salt and hot red pepper sauce to taste

1. Heat oil in a saucepan over medium-high heat. Add onion, garlic, and chiles and cook, stirring frequently, for 5 minutes, or until onion softens. Stir in tomatoes, sugar, vinegar, lime juice, and mustard, and bring to a boil over medium heat, stirring frequently.

2. Reduce the heat to low and simmer sauce, uncovered, for 15 minutes. Keep warm.

Note: The sauce can be refrigerated up to 2 weeks or frozen up to 3 months.

When dealing with chipotles in adobo sauce, be sure to scrape off all the sauce from the chiles before chopping them, or they will be too hot.

Spicy Maple Barbecue Sauce

Makes 1½ cups

Active time:
15 minutes

Start to finish:
45 minutes

VARIATION

Substitute fresh jalapeño or serrano chiles for chipotle chiles.

Chipotle chilies impart heat to a thick barbecue sauce sweetened with maple syrup. Try it with Thanksgiving Turkey Sausage (page 152) or American Breakfast Sausage (page 46).

2 tablespoons vegetable oil
1 medium onion, chopped
2 garlic cloves, minced
2 to 3 canned chipotle chiles in adobo, drained and finely chopped
½ cup ketchup
½ cup pure maple syrup
1½ cups Chicken Stock (page 296) or purchased low-sodium stock
¼ teaspoon ground allspice
2 tablespoons freshly squeezed lemon juice
Salt and freshly ground black pepper to taste

1. Heat oil in a medium saucepan over medium heat. Add onion and garlic and cook, stirring frequently, for 3 minutes, or until onion is translucent.

2. Stir in peppers, ketchup, maple syrup, stock, and allspice, and bring to a boil over medium-high heat, stirring frequently. Reduce the heat to low, and simmer sauce, uncovered, for 30 minutes, or until reduced by half, stirring occasionally.

3. Stir in lemon juice, and season to taste with salt and pepper.

Note: The sauce can be refrigerated up to 2 weeks, tightly covered, or it can be frozen up to 6 months.

Homemade Ketchup

Makes 1½ cups

Active time:
20 minutes

Start to finish:
2 hours

Next to mustard, ketchup is the favored condiment for sausages. Once you've made your own you will never return to the squeeze bottle on your refrigerator door. Try this with Smoky Mettwurst (page 128) or Spicy Beef Sausage (page 88)—either by itself or with some mustard.

2 tablespoons vegetable oil
2 large onions, chopped
3 garlic cloves, minced
4 (28-ounce) cans diced tomatoes, drained
½ cup firmly packed dark brown sugar
⅔ cup cider vinegar
1 (3-inch) cinnamon stick
1 tablespoon dry mustard powder
1 tablespoon paprika
1 teaspoon celery seed
½ teaspoon ground allspice
¼ teaspoon ground cloves
Salt and cayenne to taste

1. Heat oil in a large saucepan over medium-high heat. Add onion and garlic, and cook, stirring frequently, for 3 minutes, or until onion is translucent. Add tomatoes, and bring to a boil. Reduce the heat to low, and simmer mixture, uncovered, for 45 minutes. Puree in a food processor fitted with the steel blade or in a blender.

2. Return puree to the saucepan, and add brown sugar, vinegar, cinnamon stick, mustard powder, paprika, celery seed, allspice, and cloves. Bring to a boil, and simmer over low heat, uncovered and stirring frequently, for 30 minutes, or until reduced by half. Season to taste with salt and cayenne, and ladle into jars. Refrigerate once cool.

Note: The ketchup can be prepared up to 1 week in advance, and refrigerated, tightly covered.

Easy Aïoli

Makes 2 cups

Active time:
10 minutes

Start to finish:
10 minutes

VARIATIONS

Add 2 tablespoons of chili powder.

Add ¼ cup pureed roasted red bell peppers.

Add 2 tablespoons grainy mustard.

Pair brightly flavored sausages like Provençal Chicken Sausage (page 162) or Porchetta-Style Sausage (page 56) with a south-of-France inspired garlicky mayonnaise.

1½ cups mayonnaise
6 garlic cloves, minced
3 tablespoons freshly squeezed
    lemon juice
2 tablespoons Dijon mustard
Salt and freshly ground black
    pepper to taste

Combine mayonnaise, garlic, lemon juice, and mustard in a mixing bowl. Whisk well, and season to taste with salt and pepper. Refrigerate until ready to use.

Note: The sauce can be refrigerated up to 4 days.

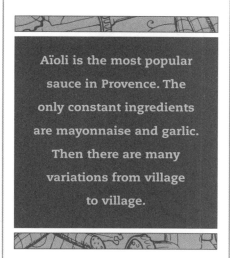

Aïoli is the most popular sauce in Provence. The only constant ingredients are mayonnaise and garlic. Then there are many variations from village to village.

Tartar Sauce

Makes 2 cups

Active time:
10 minutes

Start to finish:
10 minutes

While we think mayonnaise sauce with pickles and capers when it comes to fried seafood, it goes well with Southern sausages such as Andouille (page 62) or Cajun Boudin (page 132), too.

1½ cups mayonnaise

3 scallions, white parts only, chopped

¼ cup finely chopped cornichons

3 tablespoons small capers, drained and rinsed

2 tablespoons white wine vinegar

2 tablespoons chopped fresh parsley

1 tablespoon smooth Dijon mustard

1 tablespoon chopped fresh tarragon or 1 teaspoon dried

Salt and freshly ground black pepper to taste

Combine mayonnaise, scallions, cornichons, capers, vinegar, parsley, and tarragon in a mixing bowl. Whisk well, and season to taste with salt and pepper. Refrigerate until ready to use.

Note: The sauce can be refrigerated up to 4 days.

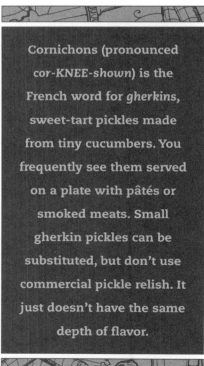

Cornichons (pronounced *cor-KNEE-shown*) is the French word for *gherkins*, sweet-tart pickles made from tiny cucumbers. You frequently see them served on a plate with pâtés or smoked meats. Small gherkin pickles can be substituted, but don't use commercial pickle relish. It just doesn't have the same depth of flavor.

Remoulade Sauce

Makes 2 cups

Active time:
10 minutes

Start to finish:
10 minutes

VARIATIONS

Add 1 or 2 grated hard-boiled eggs.

Add 2 tablespoons Worcestershire sauce.

This New Orleans classic belongs with any sausages from that region of the country, such as Cajun Shrimp Boudin (page 186) or Chaurice (page 64).

1⅓ cups mayonnaise
6 scallions, white parts and 3 inches of green tops, chopped
3 garlic cloves, minced
¼ cup freshly squeezed lemon juice
3 tablespoons whole grain mustard
3 tablespoons chopped fresh parsley
3 tablespoons prepared horseradish
2 tablespoons bottled chili sauce
Salt and freshly ground black pepper to taste

Combine mayonnaise, scallions, garlic, lemon juice, mustard, parsley, horseradish, and chili sauce in a mixing bowl. Whisk well, and season to taste with salt and pepper. Refrigerate until ready to use.

Note: The sauce can be refrigerated up to 4 days.

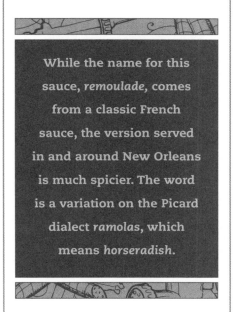

While the name for this sauce, *remoulade*, comes from a classic French sauce, the version served in and around New Orleans is much spicier. The word is a variation on the Picard dialect *ramolas*, which means *horseradish*.

Greek Feta Sauce

Makes 1½ cups

Active time:
10 minutes

Start to finish:
10 minutes

VARIATIONS

*Substitute
2 tablespoons
chopped fresh
parsley and
2 tablespoons
chopped fresh
oregano for dill.*

A feta, yogurt, and dill sauce can be served with many North African and Mediterranean sausages such as North African Lamb Sausage (page 100) or Loukanika (page 138).

½ pound mild feta cheese, diced
½ cup sour cream
¼ cup plain whole milk yogurt,
    preferably Greek
¼ cup olive oil
2 tablespoons freshly squeezed
    lemon juice
2 garlic cloves, peeled
¼ cup chopped fresh dill
Salt and freshly ground black
    pepper to taste

Combine feta, sour cream, yogurt, olive oil, lemon juice, and garlic in a food processor fitted with the steel blade or in a blender. Puree until smooth. Scrape mixture into a mixing bowl, and stir in dill. Season to taste with salt and pepper, and refrigerate sauce until ready to use.

Note: The sauce can be made up to 3 days in advance and refrigerated, tightly covered. Bring it back to room temperature before serving.

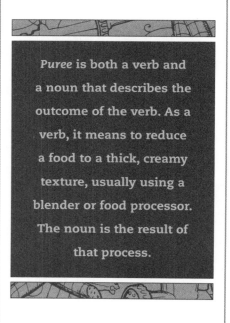

Puree is both a verb and a noun that describes the outcome of the verb. As a verb, it means to reduce a food to a thick, creamy texture, usually using a blender or food processor. The noun is the result of that process.

Cranberry Chutney

Makes 4 cups

Active time:
10 minutes

Start to finish:
35 minutes

VARIATION

Substitute chopped dried apricots for raisins.

Stir in ½ to ¾ cup Dijon mustard after chutney cools to room temperature.

This vivid chutney can accompany any grilled or smoked sausage such as Smoked Kielbasa (page 126), as well as any sausage made with fruit such as Turkey, Apple, and Sage Sausage (page 150).

1 *pound fresh cranberries*
1¾ *cups sugar*
1 *cup golden raisins*
¾ *cup red wine vinegar*
½ *cup red wine*
2 *tablespoons molasses*
2 *tablespoons grated fresh ginger*
1 *tablespoon curry powder*
1 *tablespoon Worcestershire sauce*
½ *to 1 teaspoon hot red pepper sauce, or to taste*

1. Rinse cranberries, picking out any shriveled ones or twigs. Combine cranberries with 1 cup water and sugar in a large saucepan and bring to a boil over medium heat, stirring occasionally. Boil for 10 minutes, or until cranberries pop.

2. Add raisins, vinegar, wine, molasses, ginger, curry, Worcestershire sauce, and red pepper sauce. Reduce the heat to low and simmer chutney, uncovered, for 20 minutes, or until thickened, stirring occasionally. Ladle the chutney into containers and refrigerate, tightly covered.

Note: The chutney keeps well up to 1 month, refrigerated tightly covered.

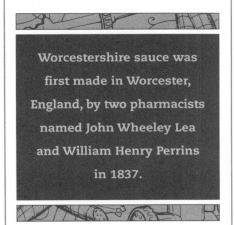

Worcestershire sauce was first made in Worcester, England, by two pharmacists named John Wheeley Lea and William Henry Perrins in 1837.

ACKNOWLEDGMENTS

While writing a book is a solitary task, it always takes a team to bring it to fruition. My thanks go:

To John Whalen of Cider Mill Press for deciding that sausage was worthy of such an encyclopedic treatment.

To Harriet Bell, editor extraordinaire and dear friend, for her guidance and help.

To designer Alicia Freile, illustrator Sherry Berger, and photo researcher Connie Hatzikalimnios for turning my words into this glorious-looking book.

To Ed Claflin, my agent, for his constant support, encouragement, and great humor.

To many dear friends who tasted innumerable sausages and sausage dishes including Fox Wetle, Richard Besdine, Constance Brown, Kenn Speiser, Vicki Veh, Joe Chazan, Steve Easton, Nick Brown, Bruce Tillinghast, Jan and Rob Mariani, Heidi Howard, Dan Potter, Karen Davidson, Beth and Ralph Kinder, Jim Reynolds, and Kim Montour.

And to Tigger-Cat Brown and Patches-Kitten Brown, who kept me company from their perches in the office each day, and personally approved all the fish and seafood sausages.

RESOURCES

Here is a list of companies specializing in sausage-making equipment and supplies such as casings. But for a good selection of all, also check out amazon.com in the House & Garden department; you'll find everything and at excellent prices. Also, a local butcher shop that makes its own sausages stocks casings, and most will sell you just a few at a time. My local Stop & Shop supermarket also carries casings, so start close to home before venturing onto the Internet.

Cabela's
www.cabelas.com
1-800-237-4444

The Sausage Maker
www.sausagemaker.com
1-888-490-8525

DeWied International
dewied.reachlocal.com
1-877-791-9172

The Sausage Source
www.sausagesource.com
1-800-LINK (5465)

Harvest Essentials
www.harvestessentials.com
1-877-759-3758

Metric Conversion Tables

The scientifically precise calculations needed for baking are not necessary when cooking conventionally. The tables in this appendix are designed for general cooking. If making conversions for baking, grab your calculator and compute the exact figure.

CONVERTING OUNCES TO GRAMS

The numbers in the following table are approximate. To reach the exact amount of grams, multiply the number of ounces by 28.35.

OUNCES	GRAMS	OUNCES	GRAMS
1 ounce	30 grams	9 ounces	250 grams
2 ounces	60 grams	10 ounces	285 grams
3 ounces	85 grams	11 ounces	300 grams
4 ounces	115 grams	12 ounces	340 grams
5 ounces	140 grams	13 ounces	370 grams
6 ounces	180 grams	14 ounces	400 grams
7 ounces	200 grams	15 ounces	425 grams
8 ounces	225 grams	16 ounces	450 grams

CONVERTING QUARTS TO LITERS

The numbers in the following table are approximate. To reach the exact amount of liters, multiply the number of quarts by 0.95.

QUARTS	LITER	QUARTS	LITER
1 cup (¼ quart)	¼ liter	4 quarts	3¾ liter
1 pint (½ quart)	½ liter	5 quarts	4¾ liter
1 quart	1 liter	6 quarts	5½ liter
2 quarts	2 liter	7 quarts	6½ liter
2½ quarts	2½ liter	8 quarts	7½ liter
3 quarts	2¾ liter		

CONVERTING POUNDS
TO GRAMS AND KILOGRAMS

The numbers in the following table are approximate. To reach the exact amount of grams, multiply the number of pounds by 453.6.

POUNDS	GRAMS; KILOGRAMS	POUNDS	GRAMS; KILOGRAMS
1 pound	450 grams	4½ pounds	2 kilograms
1½ pounds	675 grams	5 pounds	2¼ kilograms
2 pounds	900 grams	5½ pounds	2½ kilograms
2½ pounds	1,125 grams;	6 pounds	2¾ kilograms
	1¼ kilograms	6½ pounds	3 kilograms
3 pounds	1,350 grams	7 pounds	3¼ kilograms
3½ pounds	1,500 grams;	7½ pounds	3½ kilograms
	1½ kilograms	8 pounds	3¾ kilograms
4 pounds	1,800 grams		

CONVERTING FAHRENHEIT TO CELSIUS

The numbers in the following table are approximate. To reach the exact temperature, subtract 32 from the Fahrenheit reading, multiply the number by 5, and then divide by 9.

DEGREES FAHRENHEIT	DEGREES CELSIUS	DEGREES FAHRENHEIT	DEGREES CELSIUS
170°F	77°C	350°F	180°C
180°F	82°C	375°F	190°C
190°F	88°C	400°F	205°C
200°F	95°C	425°F	220°C
225°F	110°C	450°F	230°C
250°F	120°C	475°F	245°C
300°F	150°C	500°F	260°C
325°F	165°C		

CONVERTING INCHES TO CENTIMETERS

The numbers in the following table are approximate. To reach the exact number of centimeters, multiply the number of inches by 2.54.

INCHES	CENTIMETERS	INCHES	CENTIMETERS
½ inch	1.5 centimeters	7 inches	18 centimeters
1 inch	2.5 centimeters	8 inches	20 centimeters
2 inches	5 centimeters	9 inches	23 centimeters
3 inches	8 centimeters	10 inches	25 centimeters
4 inches	10 centimeters	11 inches	28 centimeters
5 inches	13 centimeters	12 inches	30 centimeters
6 inches	15 centimeters		

TABLE OF WEIGHTS AND MEASURES OF COMMON INGREDIENTS

FOOD	QUANTITY	YIELD
Apples	1 pound	2½ to 3 cups sliced
Avocado	1 pound	1 cup mashed fruit
Bananas	1 medium	1 cup, sliced
Bell Peppers	1 pound	3 to 4 cups sliced
Blueberries	1 pound	3⅓ cups
Butter	¼ pound (1 stick)	8 tablespoons
Cabbage	1 pound	4 cups packed shredded
Carrots	1 pound	3 cups diced or sliced
Chocolate, bulk	1 ounce	3 tablespoons grated
Chocolate, morsels	12 ounces	2 cups
Cocoa powder	1 ounce	¼ cup
Coconut, flaked	7 ounces	2½ cups
Cream	½ pt = 1 cup	2 cups whipped
Cream cheese	8 ounces	1 cup
Flour	1 pound	4 cups
Lemons	1 medium	3 tablespoons juice

FOOD	QUANTITY	YIELD
Lemons	1 medium	2 teaspoons zest
Milk	1 quart	4 cups
Molasses	12 ounces	1½ cups
Mushrooms	1 pound	5 cups sliced
Onions	1 medium	½ cup chopped
Peaches	1 pound	2 cups sliced
Peanuts	5 ounces	1 cup
Pecans	6 ounces	1½ cups
Pineapple	1 medium	3 cups diced fruit
Potatoes	1 pound	3 cups sliced
Raisins	1 pound	3 cups
Rice	1 pound	2 to 2½ cups raw
Spinach	1 pound	¾ cup cooked
Squash, summer	1 pound	3½ cups sliced
Strawberries	1 pint	1½ cups sliced
Sugar, brown	1 pound	2¼ cups, packed
Sugar, confectioner's	1 pound	4 cups
Sugar, granulated	1 pound	2¼ cups
Tomatoes	1 pound	1½ cups pulp
Walnuts	4 ounces	1 cup

TABLE OF LIQUID MEASUREMENTS

Dash	=	less than ⅛ teaspoon
3 teaspoons	=	1 tablespoon
2 tablespoons	=	1 ounce
8 tablespoons	=	½ cup
2 cups	=	1 pint
1 quart	=	2 pints
1 gallon	=	4 quarts

INDEX

ABOUT THE AUTHOR

Ellen Brown, the author of more than 20 cookbooks, gained the national limelight in 1982 as the founding food editor of *USA Today*. Her books include *Gourmet Gazelle Cookbook*, winner of the IACP Award, and *Cooking with the New American Chefs*, a Tastemaker Award finalist.

From 2003 to 2008 she was allied with Alpha Books as an author for its popular series on basic instruction, *The Complete Idiot's Guides*. Her nine books covered topics as diverse as slow cooker cooking and fondues to juicing and a dictionary of cooking substitutions. Just released by Lyons Press is a series of five regional American grilling books, and other topics she has written about range from sushi to smoothies.

Her writing has appeared in more than two dozen publications, including the *Washington Post*, *Los Angeles Times* syndicate, the Prodigy computer network, *Bon Appetit*, *Art Culinaire*, *Baltimore Sun*, *San Francisco Chronicle*, *Tables*, *Good Food*, *Showcase*, and *Diversion*.